To Frances Lipschitz,

With regards & best wishes.

Wm. D. Lindsey
March 2021

Fiat Flux

Fiat Flux

THE WRITINGS OF WILSON R. BACHELOR, NINETEENTH-CENTURY COUNTRY DOCTOR AND PHILOSOPHER

Edited and Introduced by William D. Lindsey

*With a Foreword by Thomas A. Bruce
and an Afterword by Jonathan Wolfe*

THE UNIVERSITY OF ARKANSAS PRESS
FAYETTEVILLE • 2013

ISBN-10: 1–55728–636–1
ISBN-13: 978–1–55728–636–9

17   16   15   14   13   5   4   3   2   1

Text design by Ellen Beeler

♾The paper used in this publication meets the minimum requirements of the
American National Standard for Permanence of Paper for Printed Library Materials
Z39.48–1984.

Library of Congress Control Number: 2013936905

Thanks to the University of Arkansas for Medical Sciences (UAMS), Mary Ryan, director of the UAMS Library, to the Dolores F. and Thomas A. Bruce Endowment Fund at
the Arkansas Community Foundation, and to the Ash Grove Charitable Foundation,
whose generous financial support to UAMS made this publication possible.

Time is change. It is as limitless as space. Cycles of time have wrought nature as we see it. Cycles will still make future changes.

Time is as deathless as eternity. It is eternity. It never had a beginning: it will never have an ending. Its silence is eloquent with colliding suns, grating worlds and hissing orbs.

Its pathway is strewn with wrecks. The Sphinx still gazes, while Balbec, Memphis and Thebes lie in ruins. The pyramids of the Toltecs are sinking in the sand, and Cholua is crumbling to dust. Where the priest offered sacrifice and chanted the weired [sic] rites of the Aztecs, the scorpion now rears her behind. Cortez has passed away, and the halls of the Montezumas are silent.

Human life is an electric sunbeam. Let us improve every moment. Good acts and kind words will never die. Let us not think of self, but for future humanity, and welcome 1893.

—Wilson R. Bachelor, "Midnight [1892]"

Contents

Acknowledgments

The biblical Wisdom-tradition writer Ecclesiastes says that of making books there is no end, and this is true in part because there's no end to the *number of people* through whose hands the text of a book passes before it's published, hands that help weave the strands that fashion the final text. *Text,* through its etymology, points to the metaphor of weaving on which I'm relying here to describe how a text, a book, is composed.

What's true in general of all books is true *a fortiori* of this particular book, which has been years in the making, and which draws on the concerted and patient research (and generous sharing) of individuals too numerous to mention, without whom the book would not ever have come to publication. The book publishes the work of an Arkansas country doctor-philosopher of the nineteenth century, after all, who labored for years to tend to the medical needs of his community in the upper Arkansas River Valley while farming. And then, as his diary published here for the first time notes, he spent many lonely nights in his study reading and writing, perhaps never dreaming that a day might come when his private thoughts in the diary would be published along with a collection of the occasional pieces he routinely sent to his local newspaper in his "retirement" years.

And in preparing Wilson Bachelor's diary, occasional pieces, and letters for publication in this volume in collaboration with Bill Russell, I'm painfully aware—and humbly and gratefully so—that my primary role in this book has been that of amanuensis. Literally so: throughout the composition of the text, I had the strong impression that in putting pen to paper, I was merely lending my hands to this impressive and wide-ranging nineteenth-century Arkansas thinker, whose work first came to my attention due to family connections that led to more family connections. And more documents, pictures, stories, artifacts: many hands, all of them acting as amanuenses for the man who is the primary author of this book, Wilson R. Bachelor.

That network of cousin-researchers includes a number of wonderful, thoughtful, intelligent, altruistic human beings who, unfortunately, didn't remain to see the book to completion, though several of these cousins envisioned this volume and worked toward its production. These include Bachelor's granddaughter Ruby Jefferson of Riverside, California, who safeguarded his diary, shared photocopies of it with interested relatives, and then handed it on to the safe-keeping of her daughter Paula, who has shared this valuable historical document with remarkable generosity and, as this book was being prepared for publication, donated the diary to the archives of the University of Arkansas for Medical Sciences (UAMS) Library.

Another granddaughter of Bachelor, Maude Russell Morris, compiled and shared with family members information and stories she heard as a girl growing up next door to her grandparents Wilson and Sarah Tankersley Bachelor. Her nephew Clayton Russell continued this process, as did Clayton's brother William Leon Russell, a multi-decorated army officer who received eight Purple Hearts for bravery during his years of military service, and who helped (along with a number of other cousins living and now dead) obtain a new tombstone marking the grave of his grandparents Wilson and Sarah Bachelor several years before his own death.

A step-grandson of Wilson Bachelor, Wendell Bumpers of Cecil, Arkansas, also shared generously with other relatives information and stories he heard as a child growing up in the household of Bachelor's son Victor H. Bachelor, who was the son who remained at home farming his father's land into Wilson and Sarah Bachelor's old age and following their deaths.

Most of the letters published in this book would not have been found and preserved without the diligence of Elsie McBurnett Hodges of Pine Bluff, Arkansas, whose mother, Janie Byrd McBurnett, was a great-niece of Bachelor and the recipient of one of the letters published in this book. Elsie also found and shared the letters of Bachelor to his niece Melissa Byrd Robinson published here, and Elsie's son Norman Hodges of Little Rock, who inherited these letters and the photograph of Janie's great-uncle of which his letter to Janie speaks, has generously made these materials available for publication.

Another cousin whose work on behalf of this book spanned many years and is also valuable beyond measure was Flora Rondeau, who for many years played a pivotal role in the historical society of Hot Spring County, Arkansas, where Bachelor's brother Moses and sister Delaney settled in the 1840s. Flora descended from a niece of Bachelor, Minerva Louisa Batchelor, to whose husband, Seaborn Walters, one of the letters of Bachelor published here was written. As with the other cousins named here, Flora did many years of research on her set of Batchelor family members, and shared that research freely in both private communications and published articles.

A number of the names I've just enumerated are those of cousins who no longer remain alive as this book appears in print, but without whose years of research, compiling information and recording stories, and sharing of materials the book would not have been written. Among cousins still living, several names are also absolutely indispensable to the writing of this book.

Bachelor's grandson William Leon Russell left a son of the same name, an indefatigable family historian, Bill Russell of Maumelle, Arkansas, who teaches communications at the University of Central Arkansas and who played an indispensable role in the writing of this book. Bill did the hard yeoman's work of deciphering the handwriting of the faded (and partially fragmented) old diary of his ancestor Wilson Bachelor. Bill also transcribed many of the occasional pieces of Bachelor published in this volume, and worked tirelessly to track down citations and find material needed to document various sections of the manuscripts. Without Bill and his hard work and perseverance, this book would never have come to pass. Bill has also provided an important and helpful manuscript on the history of the Russell family, which transcribes Russell family letters owned and shared by Sarah Lee Suttle, which are cited in this book on Wilson Bachelor's life and work.

The occasional pieces have been preserved in a scrapbook lovingly cherished and carefully preserved by two other descendants of Wilson Bachelor, Wanda Rentz Dailey of Fort Smith, Arkansas, and her daughter Susan Dailey Johnson of Pocola, Oklahoma, who are, as with Bill, descendants of Bachelor's daughter Alcie D. Bachelor Russell. Without the generosity of Wanda and Susan, the scrapbook with its treasure trove of documents would not have come to light. Wanda's mother, Elsie Golda Russell Rentz, and grandmother, Alcie D. Bachelor Russell, also deserve special mention for their role in the chain of transmission that led to the preservation of both the scrapbook and the diary. The diary was in their hands before it passed to Alcie's sister Pauline, and through her, to her daughter Ruby Jefferson and granddaughter Paula Jefferson. And the scrapbook was also preserved and added to lovingly by Elsie's brother Seaborn Bachelor Russell, who deserves special mention for his role in safeguarding this document, as well.

As with Bill, Susan has spent countless hours transcribing the material in the scrapbook and freely making it available to interested cousins. She and her mother have worked for years to piece together the family history and record family stories, and have been leading lights in the preparation of this book. Wanda and Wendell Bumpers, who has previously been mentioned, were part of the group that purchased a new stone to mark the grave of Wilson and Sarah Tankersley Bachelor several years back. Susan has also generously made available a number of the photographs of family members published in this book.

Also absolutely indispensable to the preparation of this book is Kay Brown Black of Antlers, Oklahoma, a descendant of Wilson Bachelor's daughter Lula G. Bachelor Harris. Kay has spent decades collecting information about the Bachelor family, and has made her family's treasure trove of priceless family pictures freely available for this book—as freely available as she has made her important research findings over many years.

Through Kay, the picture of the Bachelor family house at Pauline, Arkansas, published in this book came to light. That picture is now owned by Linda Anderson Silvey of Antlers, Oklahoma, another descendant of Bachelor's daughter Lula, who kindly allowed Kay to take the precious and fragile original and have it professionally scanned for this book.

The violin of which Bachelor speaks so fondly throughout much of his diary now belongs to Janelle Russell, the widow of Paul Russell, a brother of Clayton and William Leon mentioned previously. Janelle very helpfully allowed Bill Russell to photograph the violin for the purposes of this book, contributing a great deal to the work as she did so.

The group of family members collaborating on this project for some years now has also benefited tremendously—more than I can say—from the strong support and helpfulness of folks and institutions beyond the family circle. I owe a debt of profound gratitude to Dr. Tom Bruce, emeritus professor and dean of the College of Medicine at UAMS and associate dean at the Clinton School of Public Service, who recognized the importance of Bachelor's record of medical cases as soon as he began to hear about the diary and who highly encouraged us to publish the diary and brought it to the attention of the Arkansas Society for the History of Medicine and the Health Professions. Not only did Tom contribute a first-rate foreword to this book, but he also generously provided financial support for its production through his Bruce Family Foundation.

Deserving very special mention at UAMS is Dr. Jonathan Wolfe, professor of pharmacy, who contributed the wonderful afterword essay to this volume and who provided much valuable background information about the history of medicine in Arkansas in general and the Arkansas River Valley in particular in the period of Bachelor's residence there.

Mary L. Ryan, director of the UAMS Library, has supported this project from the outset in ways too numerous to list. As did Tom Bruce, Mary quickly saw the importance of Bachelor's medical cases as recorded in his diary, and committed the UAMS library to supporting the book, as she also offered archival assistance for the preservation of the valuable and fragile documents this book is publishing. To Tom, Jon, and Mary, I cannot say thanks loudly and long enough.

Also at UAMS: Amanda Saar, Historical Research Center librarian, has given hours of research work to the book, tracking obscure pieces of material, combing UAMS archival records for clues to help me with this and that question—

all with grace and an unfailing cheerfulness that made bringing yet another pesky research problem to Amanda a delight rather than a worry.

As with any book, I've relied on librarians in many places to help me fill in blanks as I cite material or to obtain material I couldn't find locally. These are too numerous to mention by name, but not a single one of these hard-working professionals is unimportant to the final product represented by this published work. Nor will I forget the helpfulness of a single one of these individuals.

Noted Shiloh historian Timothy Smith, who is on the faculty of the University of Tennessee at Martin, has answered a chain of questions I e-mailed to him about the early history of the Pittsburg Landing Cemetery that became the Shiloh National Cemetery, and for which Bachelor was made physician in charge when cemetery construction began in 1866. Without his guidance, I would have missed looking at a slew of archival holdings that I combed for possible pieces of information about that important period of Bachelor's life.

My friend Gary Toms, recently retired from the reference department of the Midwest Genealogy Center in Independence, Missouri, and an accomplished family historian, went out of his way to go to the Community of Christ archives in Independence and scroll through microfilm copies of old issues of the newspaper *Zion's Ensign* for me, as I looked for articles in that paper to which I knew Bachelor had written responses. In the process, he found significant new material written by Bachelor about which we hadn't known, opening whole new avenues of research for me.

Maps of the journey the Bachelor family made in 1870 from Tennessee to Arkansas, and of the 1891 journey that Wilson R. Bachelor and children Monroe and Nannie made to Hot Springs from their home in Pauline, were produced by Stan Kitchens of Maumelle, Arkansas, at Bill Russell's request. I am very grateful for these superb illustrations complementing the diary's narrative about both journeys, which form the template of the maps produced in this book.

Bill Russell and I owe a very large debt of gratitude to Bill's friend Robert Matchette and to Michael P. Musick, who helped us comb the archival holdings in the National Archives to see if any materials are extant regarding Bachelor's brief tenure as physician in charge when construction began on the Pittsburg Landing National Cemetery.

Deserving very special notice is the Reverend Dr. Richard Rosenbaum of Bloomfield Hills, Michigan, who, out of the kindness of his heart, offered to do the incredibly tedious work of proofreading the entire manuscript. No eyes are sharper than Richard's, and he has saved me from many a mistake and infelicity in the final work (those that remain being entirely mine).

And last but far from least, not any of this work would have moved along to the point of publication without the constant encouragement and behind-the-scenes footwork of someone particularly dear to me, Dr. Stephen J. Schafer, executive director of Development for Corporations and Foundations at UAMS. Steve is the glue that put together the UAMS team strongly supporting this project, and assisted in making valuable contacts with the family members who held the precious pieces of documentary material published here.

This book is dedicated, in particular, to all those descendants of Wilson and Alcie Odom Batchelor who laid the foundations for the book through many years of hard work and loving dedication, and who are not here to see its publication. I well remember the evening on which Bill Russell, Steve Schafer, and I descended on Paula Jefferson, Bill's and my distant cousin and the owner of Bachelor's diary, shortly before Christmas 2011, to talk about obtaining clear scanned copies of the diary. This was when Paula shocked Bill and me by placing the diary in Bill's hands and telling him to take it back to Arkansas and have UAMS scan it—a step along the way to her donation of the diary to UAMS.

As Bill and I talked to Paula that evening, she said at one point, "You know, you never could tell a member of that family anything at all." Paula was speaking of our Batchelor/Bachelor family. When Paula made that observation, I almost laughed out loud, as I thought to myself, "You've got that right, sister."

What came immediately to mind was hearing a first cousin of mine say, over and over for many years, "I have never in my life met any group of women, bar none, as stubborn as they are." The women whom my cousin is characterizing as excelling in stubbornness are Batchelor women; she's talking about our aunts (and my mother), the five daughters of Hattie Batchelor Simpson, our grandmother. And, since she and I strongly suspect that the cloth from which those five daughters were all cut is the same cloth from which our grandmother and her sisters were also cut, she means that observation to apply to the previous generation as well. I've certainly never disagreed with my cousin when I've heard her sum up the women in our family in this way, though I've also kept in mind, as I've heard her voice this characterization, that she is the next generation in the chain of transmission she's describing as singularly obstinate.

Stories about cantankerous single-mindedness run through our family history for generations. A story told about one of my grandmother's brothers who was addicted to wanting proof for any utterance that came out of the mouth of anyone at all is that his father, my great-grandfather George Richard

Batchelor, summed up his predicament by saying, "You'd argue with a signpost and throw rocks at it when it didn't answer back, wouldn't you?"

That's the Batchelor/Bachelor way. When coupled with high intelligence and wide reading, as in the case of Wilson R. Bachelor, it can be a well-nigh dangerous trait—dangerous, because one never knows what important signpost (the rock-thrower among my grandmother's siblings was hot after words he alone believed he knew how to spell correctly) one of our family members may choose to contest next, never counting the cost of the arguing and the rock-throwing. But the cantankerous stubbornness may also be a winning quality and a saving grace, when it prods people to imagine that where something like a book didn't previously exist, it *can* exist, and *ought* to exist, because they say so—and because they darned well intend to make the book exist.

To all those intellectually curious, mulish, and ornery doubting Thomases of the Batchelor/Bachelor family who pushed, prodded, cursed, and defied the odds to make this book happen and who are no longer with us: thank you. Since we know you don't ever give up, we're pretty sure you're just refractory enough to have remained around in spirit to see that this book is getting published, and to correct it and argue about it—even in heaven, where we like to imagine you have all landed, despite your obstinacy, even when you devoutly disputed the existence of any such outlandish place when you were walking the earth.

DALE BUMPERS
U.S. Senator (Ret.)
12723 Hunters Field Road
Little Rock, Arkansas 72211

July 4, 2012
Independence Day

Dear Reader,

We are pleased to recommend this fine study of the life and work of Wilson R. Bachelor, M.D., of Franklin County, Arkansas, the county where we were born and reared. In fact, in the 19th century the farm land of the extended Bumpers family adjoined the lands of Dr. Bachelor, with the two families sharing a history of many mutual interests. The county is located in the western part of our state, in the Arkansas River Valley, and is bisected by the river. It is also one of the ten counties in Arkansas to have two county seats. It has two courthouses, one in Ozark and one in Charleston.

We grew up on the south side of the river where Dr. Bachelor also settled and raised his family. We lived in Charleston among people whose lives were shaped by the adversities of rural life, such as the hardships of tough times and the need to work hard. We had the privilege of being influenced in our early years by many of these Franklin County citizens of intelligence and independent thinking. Dr. Bachelor was one of these independent spirits from an earlier generation in Franklin County.

The county continues to produce notable citizens like Denny Flynn of National Rodeo fame and W.L. "Bill" Russell, the only Arkansan with 8 Purple Hearts, for wartime service recently recognized by the Arkansas Military Veterans Hall of Fame. Moreover, in the difficult challenges of the civil rights movement in the latter half of the 20th century, Charleston, Arkansas, was the first town in the 11 states of the former Confederacy to fully integrate its public schools in 1954. The Supreme Court had directed that its order should be carried out "…with all deliberate speed." The citizens of Charleston assumed the court meant what it said! The citizens of Franklin County have been and are accustomed to living lives of courage and independence of thought.

This volume portrays the courage, independent action and determination that it took to live a life practicing medicine on the "wild frontier" of western Arkansas in the second half of the 19th century. In those post-Civil War times there were many threats to life and limb that Dr. Bachelor had to face in his daily medical practice caring for the citizens of Franklin County.

In celebration of the life of an independent spirit and thinker we wish to commend to you the writings of Wilson R. Bachelor, a "19th-Century Arkansas Country Doctor and Philosopher." We are grateful to William D. Lindsey, the University of Arkansas Press, and the University of Arkansas for Medical Sciences for bringing these writings to the light of day for us in the 21st century and for future generations that we might appreciate and understand more of our own Arkansas history.

Sincerely,

Senator Dale Bumpers   Mrs. Betty Bumpers

Foreword

"Bringing This Fine Man Back to Life": Life and Work of Wilson R. Bachelor

The range of serious health problems in southern communities during the decades just after the Civil War was enormous, probably larger than we see in the great medical centers today. For rural doctors the resources at hand were very limited, however. Such was the setting for the medical practice of Dr. Wilson R. Bachelor in west-central Arkansas. From his diary we get only a glimpse of the challenges he faced, but what is revealed makes a solid contribution to our understanding of medical practice at the time. What an incredible man emerges from the pages of his writings! He was a keen observer and lover of nature, camping in the great outdoors on frequent visits to other communities—always attentive to the sounds of birds and insects around him. He delighted in great literature and loved his time with learned friends. He played violin and guitar and taught his children to join in his love for making music. He treasured his family and the land on which he lived, but in his soul he was a physician, and in the quiet hours of reflection through the years he felt that his contribution through life was in that realm. In 1874, at age forty-seven, he wrote, "when I look back . . . I think I have not been the cause of pain to any person, but have sympathized with the Suffering, and endeavored to relieve corporeal pain and mental anguish . . . ." What more could any man desire?

Although the bulk of his writings are philosophical in nature, often with political leanings, Dr. Bachelor's thoughts repeatedly turned to personal and family affairs, and he wrote about them in poetic ways. His medical notes are rather limited, but they are of significant historic value. He documents several difficult obstetrical cases, and under the limited options of home delivery, few obstetricians today could have done better. Not all were successful in saving the life of the mother and child, but all denote heroic attempts to do so. What is so obvious in the light of today's knowledge is that with proper prenatal care and our current range of pharmaceutical options and surgical procedures, all would likely be managed successfully. Today's professionals can only admire Dr. Bachelor's equanimity and persistence in the face of adversity.

It seems likely that there was little financial reward for his medical attention, although the diary makes no mention of this. Most rural patients had no cash, particularly those with the most serious or longstanding health problems, so he might have been given a couple of chickens or a shank of ham for his labors. It has been said that the doctor ranked behind the blacksmith and dry goods store owner in getting paid, since the farmers were dependent on their products, whereas paying the doctor was elective. Dr. Bachelor paid great attention to his own land and crops, for they likely were the base of whatever material success he had, and the practice income was but an added component.

One note of special interest is the potential that he might have had incipient interest in germ theory. While most of his obstetrical manipulations apparently were done with bare hands, and he never made note that antisepsis was a special issue, he began treating one of his wounded patients in a new way. In August 1874, thus, the suppurating wound of his patient with a cranial fracture worried him a lot, and he began "detergent" washes and "chlorinated" washes. Although he later stuck his finger into the wound to assess the fracture size, these seem to have been approaches above and beyond routine debridement. We last are told of this patient in his tenth week of treatment, in which he is recovering slowly.

One is struck by how frequently Dr. Bachelor was asked to respond to knife and bullet injuries, and he commented pointedly on this in his journal. For instance, on 18 August 1874, he writes, "There is not a week, but the report of bloodshed and murder reaches us. . . . Since the first of January 1874 untill to day, the number of men who have died by violence equal(s) those, who have died of disease."

It's interesting to observe that Dr. Bachelor didn't appear to be very busy at times; two or three days might elapse before he was contacted for help. Of course that call usually came in the dark of night, often at some distance from his home, and he would be tied up on the case for two or more days. In his notes it seems obvious that rural practice in Arkansas during the post-reconstruction period had a different pace than today's family practice. He did ask for other professional help now and then from neighboring communities, so he was not as professionally isolated as one might think. This is more than of casual importance, since he records many occasions when he also was ill and likely unavailable.

His medical notes are essentially dropped from the diary after the autumn of 1874, although he appears to have continued his medical practice. At age seventy-one (15 April 1897) he notes parenthetically that he has walked one and a half miles to see a young lady who has had a nervous attack. The comment says more about the activity level of this elderly country doctor than about the medical problem, per se.

All in all, the discovery and publication of Dr. Bachelor's diary is an exciting event, and medical and other historians will be forever grateful to those who brought this fine man back to light.

Thomas A. Bruce

Fiat Flux

Wilson R. Bachelor, about 1890. *Courtesy Norman Hodges, Little Rock, AR.*

Introduction

WILSON R. BACHELOR, WHYS AND WHEREFORES

The nineteenth-century Arkansan on whose life and work this book focuses, Wilson Richard Bachelor (1827–1903), will hardly be a household name for most of those who read this collection of his writings. Even scholars who have a more than passing acquaintance with the state's history would probably be hard pressed to place him in its historical narrative. Bachelor did author a monograph of some sort, a work on freethought entitled *Fiat Flux*, which he published in 1884. Almost nothing is known of this work, however, and it appears not to be extant any longer.

As a result, we don't know whether *Fiat Flux* was a book, a pamphlet, or one of those brief compendia of information on selected subjects that social reformers and some academics of the latter half of the nineteenth century enjoyed writing for the education of popular audiences. The influential Chautauqua movement pioneered such adult education (as educators might now call it) for ordinary citizens whose schooling had not gone beyond elementary levels. At the time Bachelor published *Fiat Flux*, Chautauqua had also pioneered the widespread use of brief instructional monographs for such adult education.[1]

As his essays and occasional pieces published in this volume will indicate, Bachelor had a pronounced interest in such community-oriented educational initiatives, and a large percentage of his published articles that have survived were written to bring notions like women's rights, the need to abolish the death penalty, or the philosophy of freethought—his favorite subject—to a wide popular audience. Both the occasional pieces themselves and the fact that Bachelor evidently published them in local newspapers indicate such an educational interest on his part.

To be specific: the sparse bits of information about *Fiat Flux* that have survived suggest that Bachelor produced it with the intent of disseminating information about the freethought movement to readers in the area of northwest Arkansas in which he lived in the latter decades of his life. An autobiographical statement he wrote in 1889 for Goodspeed's history of northwest Arkansas states plainly that *Fiat Flux* was "a work of free thought" that he had published as "one of the leading Liberalists in Western Arkansas."[2]

As Susan Jacoby's recent overview of the American freethought movement notes, the term has had elastic significance over the course of American history and has been used to denote both those within various religious communities who have questioned orthodox tenets of their religious groups and those who reject religion altogether.[3] Jacoby notes that the movement reached its heyday in American culture in the period from 1875 to 1914, and that in this period, the disparate groups calling themselves freethinkers were bound together by a shared social progressivism and a belief that human affairs should be guided by reason and empirical evidence rather than reliance on the supernatural.[4]

This definition of freethought—a commitment to socially progressive ideas with an emphasis on science and reason that eschews appeals to the supernatural—certainly characterizes Bachelor's outlook throughout most of his written work that has survived. The commitment to freethinking also appears to have been sufficient to create problems for him in the community in which he lived. Whether book, pamphlet, or instructional manual, *Fiat Flux* elicited a negative response, for instance, from the Masonic chapter to which Bachelor belonged (and which he helped to found) in Franklin County, Arkansas, Lowe's Creek Lodge No. 346. After his death, the lodge issued a eulogy noting that he had published *Fiat Flux* in 1884, and that the work "disputed the divinity and authenticity of the Bible, the great light of Masonry and the world, for which he was tried by the lodge and expelled about the same year."[5]

It is very likely that Bachelor's 1884 monograph was in the vein of brief summaries and defenses of freethought produced in the same period by one of his heroes, the leading American freethinker Robert Green Ingersoll, whose picture, clipped from a magazine article and pasted into the inside cover of the scrapbook in which Bachelor preserved his published essays of the 1890s, is among the first items one encounters on opening the scrapbook.[6] From the 1870s through the 1890s, Ingersoll published one small monograph after another, pieces often originally delivered as lectures, about the predominant concerns of the freethought movement, including *The Gods and Other Lectures* (New York: D. M. Bennett, 1876), *Some Mistakes of Moses* (New York: C. P. Farrell, 1879), or *Why I Am an Agnostic* (New York: C. P. Farrell, 1897). The last-mentioned work was an 1896 lecture that was repeatedly republished in collections of Ingersoll's works for many years thereafter.[7]

Even a cursory glance at the occasional pieces he wrote in the 1890s and saved in his scrapbook suggests the predominant influence of Ingersoll's thinking on Bachelor the freethinker. The influence extends to the topics and the titles of works Bachelor himself published—for instance, the scrapbook contains a tripartite set of essays entitled "Reasons for Being an Agnostic"—and it seems highly likely that *Fiat Flux* was modeled on the numerous brief monographs Ingersoll published in the same period in which Bachelor wrote his work, all seeking to present to popular audiences the primary ideas of the freethought movement.

Given how little we know about the single (and now lost) monograph Wilson R. Bachelor produced, on what ground does one argue that the written work of his that *has* survived and is now being published in this book devoted to his life and legacy deserves attention? There is, first of all, the remarkable fact that a rather broad selection of his written work addressing a surprisingly wide range of topics *has* been preserved, largely due to the diligence of his descendants.

Among the written work of Bachelor safeguarded by his family members are a diary he kept from March 1870 to December 1902 and the scrapbook about which I've just spoken, which contains thirty-two essays or occasional pieces Bachelor published in the 1890s, apparently in local newspapers.[8] The scrapbook contains other valuable documents as well, including obituaries of family members, articles he appears to have saved from newspapers and journals, primarily about the freethought movement, pictures of freethinkers he admired, and material saved by his immediate family following Bachelor's death, including his Masonic eulogy.

And, finally, descendants of Bachelor's brother Moses and sister Delaney, both of whom moved with their families from Hardin County, Tennessee, to Hot Spring County, Arkansas, in the late 1840s, have saved six letters he wrote to their branches of the family from 1891 to 1899. With the exception of the thirty-two occasional pieces in the scrapbook, all of which appear to have been published in local newspapers (almost none of which has been identified), all of this material is being published here for the first time.

In this collection of such written work of Bachelor as has survived, there's a noteworthy breadth in both the topics the documents address and in the genres they employ. For instance, the diary has several subsidiary narratives embedded within it, including a selection of travelogues from a number of different periods of Bachelor's adult life, an important collection of detailed and carefully written medical cases from his medical practice in western Arkansas, several eulogies of family members, literary and scientific descriptions of natural scenes and events, notes about music various members of the family played (Bachelor says in his 11 August 1875 diary entry noting the death of his son Wils that his family had been tagged "the musical family"), and a recurring and highly stylized series of Christmas and New Year's reflections.

The thirty-two occasional pieces in the scrapbook are similarly diverse in both style and content. They run the gamut from letters to newspaper editors about political topics, to his three-part series of essays explaining Bachelor's momentous decision in the 1870s to become a freethinker, to eulogies, book reviews, essays defending the equality of women and men or denouncing the death penalty, to commentary on biblical books in light of modern science.

The work published here provides important documentation regarding the life and thought of an "ordinary" country doctor of the second half of the nineteenth century in northwestern Arkansas, who, while practicing medicine and farming, managed to read extensively a surprisingly wide range of academic and literary works, and to record impressions of what he was reading and of life in his area in prose that is uniformly engaging and sometimes touched with brilliance. Throughout his diary, Bachelor makes reference to authors whose work he happens to be reading ranging from Shakespeare, Milton, Dickens, Byron, and Shelley, to Tennyson, and others.

His diary and occasional pieces reveal his wide reading in scientific fields including medicine. They indicate that he kept abreast of the latest scientific theories and findings of his day by reading, among other sources, the popular journal *Harper's Monthly*. He indicates his familiarity with Thomas Henry Huxley's work on cerebration and James Croll on climate change.[9] Bachelor cites John William Draper's history of the conflict between religion and science.[10] It's clear he was reading Ingersoll on freethought, since a number of his documents cite Ingersoll, and Ingersoll's slogan about finding happiness in the present and making others happy becomes something of a mantra repeated at various points in his work.[11]

Bachelor's life-changing decision to become a freethinker, which seems to have occurred in the latter part of the 1870s, appears to have been preceded by wide reading in the field of the history of world religions. His essays on his reasons for having become an agnostic note, for instance, that he had read (or read about) Sanskrit mythic accounts of the origin of the world, and that he was acquainted with philological discussions about the relationship between the Jewish scriptures and the literature of other cultures of the ancient Near East including Egypt. He shows a more than passing familiarity with the significant research being done in the second half of the nineteenth century in biblical exegesis and the historical-critical method for analyzing biblical texts. At one point in his diary, he mentions that he's reading Simon Greenleaf, a classic writer on themes of American jurisprudence.[12]

Bachelor's occasional piece "Leaving the Old Ruts" indicates that he had read or read about the famous game-changing series of sermons Henry Ward Beecher and Frederic W. Farrar preached independently of each other in the late 1870s, questioning the existence of a literal hell. The same document suggests, in fact, that these sermons may have played a decisive role in his own decision to become a freethinker in this period.

Given the scope of his reading in such a variety of fields and the breadth of his scholarly interests, it is not surprising to find Bachelor's Masonic brethren commemorating him as "a scholarly man of great ability," though the brethren could not quite get around their objections to his freethinking, and concluded that "like many other bright men, he was not without his faults . . . [h]is one mistake in life being his attack on the Bible and the Christian Religion."[13] It is difficult to think of comparable collections of documents that provide such a comprehensive yet sharply incised picture of the multifaceted scholarly interests—and of the mind and heart—of a rural doctor of nineteenth-century Arkansas.

And then there are the medical cases. Bachelor's diary begins with a detailed account of his family's journey from Hardin County, Tennessee, to Franklin County, Arkansas, in March 1870. As the diary indicates, by October of the same year, he had begun his medical practice in Arkansas. A statement in one of the occasional pieces preserved in Bachelor's scrapbook, "Job and His Book as Viewed in the 19th Century by an Agnostic," indicates he had begun his practice of medicine in Hardin County in 1852, though his 1889 autobiographical statement says he began "active practice of the medical profession" in 1859.[14] It seems likely that the 1852 date refers to the date at which he began to "read medicine" with a local doctor, and 1859 to the year in which he began practicing medicine on his own. From 9 October 1870 through 19 October 1874, Bachelor records, formally and with considerable detail, a series of medical cases he treated in the formative period of his medical practice in his new Arkansas homeplace. Other medical notes are also scattered at various places in the diary, but with none of the detail of these initial case records from the 1870s.

The section of the diary focusing on the cases he was treating also records one case predating the move to Arkansas, one dating from 31 December 1869. As he enters notes on this case, "A Case of Dificult Labour," Bachelor states that he is transcribing the case from his diary of 1869—an indication that he had previously kept at least one other diary, and had used it, as well, to keep a record of cases he was treating.

Careful documentation of how a country doctor of the latter half of the nineteenth century practiced medicine on a day-by-day basis in Arkansas is relatively sparse, and the sections of Bachelor's diary capturing details of his medical practice are significant documentation of how at least one rural practitioner of medicine dealt with the diverse medical challenges of a particular community in this time frame. The cases Bachelor treats in the early 1870s range from ones involving an ox-goring of a farm boy, to ones dealing with men stabbed or shot by assailants, to one in which a young man is assaulted and has his skull broken by his brother.

Many of the cases in this portion of the diary have formal titles: "A Case of Puerperal Convulsion," "a case of obstetricks," "a case of abortion," and so on. As these titles suggest, not a few of the cases involve childbirth. One gathers from the documentation provided in Bachelor's diary that pregnancy and parturition were extraordinarily dangerous enterprises for many rural women in Arkansas prior to the twentieth century, and the morbidity rates for women giving birth and for the babies they bore were alarmingly high. The bulk of Bachelor's medical practice, in fact, appears to have had to do with childbirth issues.

And so Bachelor's written work is well worth studying for this additional reason: his medical diary—the subsection of his diary that deals with medical cases—is precious documentation of how a nineteenth-century physician in rural Arkansas practiced medicine. This portion of the diary provides invaluable documentation both of the kinds of medical challenges people living in rural communities in Arkansas at this period faced, and how local doctors may have sought to deal with those challenges. Nor is the medical diary entirely disconnected from the rest of his work: almost everything he writes and thinks about in all of his work circles back to the obligation—which he seems to have taken very seriously—to relieve suffering and avoid inflicting pain on his fellow human beings.

Wilson Richard Bachelor: A Biography

FAMILY ROOTS

Wilson Richard Bachelor was born 29 November 1827 in Lawrence County, Tennessee.[15] His parents, Wilson Richard Batchelor the elder (abt. 1775–1858) and Alcie Odom (1790–1848), were both North Carolinians of colonial Virginia stock, descendants of English families that had come to southeastern Virginia in the seventeenth century, whose progeny began moving into northeastern North Carolina prior to 1700 and who were with rare exceptions, generation after generation in Virginia and North Carolina, primarily planters or yeoman farmers of the "middling sort."[16]

Alcie Odom's parents have not been definitely established, but it seems very likely that her father was a Theophilus Odom who died shortly before 13 November 1811 in Nash County, North Carolina.[17] Court and land records of the northeastern North Carolina counties of Edgecombe, Granville, and Bute strongly suggest that Theophilus is a descendant of an Oldham (Odom, Odum) family of English background that came to Nansemond County, Virginia, prior to 1700, and had begun to appear in the records of Chowan and Northampton

Counties, North Carolina, by the early 1700s.[18] Tracking families with roots in colonial Nansemond County (which is now extinct) is severely hampered due to the loss of most of the county's records in a disastrous courthouse fire in 1866.

The Batchelor line descends from a seventeenth-century immigrant to Lower Norfolk County, Virginia, Richard Batchelor, who was born in or around 1645, according to a deposition he gave in the county court on 16 August 1671, giving his age as twenty-six.[19] Batchelor's birthplace was almost certainly England, since Manasses Porter of Lower Norfolk County received a headright grant on 15 August 1659 transferred to him by William Goldsmith for transporting Richard Batchelor and other immigrants to the colony—clearly from England.[20] There are two other Virginia records in roughly the same period showing a man named Richard Batchelor being imported to Virginia.[21] Though these are possibly separate importation records for the same person voyaging back and forth from the colonies to England, it seems far more likely they refer to other men of the same name who did not settle in Lower Norfolk County, Virginia.[22] No records appear to exist for any Richard Batchelor who remained in Virginia in this period other than the man in Lower Norfolk County, however.

The Richard Batchelor of Manasses Porter's 1659 headright grant in Lower Norfolk County is almost certainly the immigrant who settled in that same county and is the ancestor of Wilson R. Bachelor. As will be noted below, Richard married a daughter of John Biggs of Lower Norfolk County, and Biggs was a witness of the will of the brother of Manasses Porter, John Porter Sr. As will also be noted, the Porter and Biggs families seem to have had a number of close ties. Both had strong Quaker leanings after that religious movement arrived in Lower Norfolk County. Both John Biggs and John Porter Sr. suffered legal consequences for their religious dissent.

Like the Odom family, the Batchelors were among the earliest colonists of northeastern North Carolina, a region often regarded in the seventeenth century as part of Lower Norfolk County, Virginia, so indeterminate was the Carolina-Virginia boundary in this period.[23] It is worth noting here as well that Nansemond County, to which Alcie Odom's roots appear to run back, was established in 1637 as Upper Norfolk County. Nansemond was contiguous to Norfolk County on the west.

When Richard Batchelor died in Lower Norfolk County in 1682,[24] his widow, Ann (née Biggs),[25] married one James Fewox and moved with most of her Batchelor children[26] to the Scuppernong district of Chowan (later Tyrrell) County, North Carolina, where Fewox acquired a plantation to which he gave the name Heart's Delight, which was later to become the site of Tyrrell's county seat, Columbia.[27]

Not all of the children of Richard Batchelor followed their mother in her migration to North Carolina, however. Though Richard's will specifies that his eldest son John was to have the home plantation and manor house along with four hundred added acres at his father's death, John seems to have died soon after his father, the Batchelor plantation then passing to the next son Joseph, to whom his mother, Ann, and her subsequent husband, James Fewox, assigned their share of the land in 1696 as they prepared to move to North Carolina.[28]

It is from Joseph Batchelor (abt. 1668–February 1735) that Wilson Richard Bachelor descends. Having married Mary, daughter of William (1689–1763) and Mary Manning, Joseph's son Stephen (abt. 1723–bef. 23 November 1805) moved from Norfolk County, Virginia, to Edgecombe County, North Carolina, sometime between 1754 and 1757, settling on Sapony Creek in the portion of the county later to become Nash, east of the present community of Spring Hope in western Nash County. Stephen was father of a son Samuel (1748–July or August 1827), a Revolutionary soldier, who was the father of Wilson Richard Batchelor the elder.[29]

Wilson R. Batchelor the elder was born about 1775 in Nash County. By about 1805, he had married Alcie Odom, by whom he had children Moses B. (born 11 January 1808), William Skidmore (born 6 April 1816), Hannah Delaney (born about 1819), Sarah R. (born about 1824), and Wilson Richard. The first two children were born in Nash County, the last three in Tennessee.[30]

Having served in the First Regiment of North Carolina Detached Militia in the War of 1812 along with a brother, Wright Stephen Batchelor, Wilson the elder disappears from Nash County records after December 1815.[31] By 1820, he and Alcie had moved their family from North Carolina to Maury County in middle Tennessee, where Wilson is enumerated as head of their household on the federal census in the town of Columbia.

The family left North Carolina at a point at which there was a developing tide of emigration from North Carolina to Tennessee, where North Carolina had been awarding land for Revolutionary service, thereby spurring the movement of families from the mother state to its daughter. In his autobiography *Memories of an Old-Time Tar Heel*, Kemp Plummer Battle, who grew up in Louisburg in Franklin County, North Carolina, not far from where the Batchelors lived in Nash County, states that in his boyhood in the 1830s, there was a "fever for emigrating to Tennessee" from the counties of eastern North Carolina, where land had begun to wear out from prolonged production of tobacco, and where it had been parceled into ever-smaller units by large families for a number of generations: hence the interest in the virgin lands of the daughter state.[32]

THE HARDIN COUNTY, TENNESSEE, YEARS

The Batchelors may have chosen Maury County as their initial point of settlement because Alcie had relatives there.[33] Several Odoms who appear to have ties to her family are enumerated close to the Batchelors on the 1820 census. By 1830, however, the family had moved again, this time to its final point of settlement west of the Tennessee River in the southwestern corner of Hardin County in west Tennessee.[34]

The Batchelor family may initially have settled close to the McNairy County line west of the present-day community of Counce, since they appear on the federal census in 1830 and 1840 in McNairy County (the oldest son, Moses, is married and living in Hardin County by the 1840 census)—but carefully documenting the family's presence in either county is severely hampered by the fact that Hardin lost records in courthouse fires in 1859, 1864, and 1949, and McNairy in 1881. It also appears that at a later date, they lived or owned land near the Tennessee River close to what is now Counce, since they appear in several rare extant early land records of Hardin County in connection with transactions in that area of the county. These transactions show the Byrd, Monk, and Cherry families, all thickly connected to the Batchelors, also having land in the same area.[35]

It was in this recently settled portion of west Tennessee that Wilson the younger grew up—though note that his autobiography indicates that, while he grew up in Hardin County, he was born in 1827 in Lawrence County, which borders Maury on the south and was, in fact, formed in part from Maury County. And the Lawrence County birthplace is also given in his Masonic eulogy. Lawrence is two counties east of Hardin, and as is the latter, is on the southern border of Tennessee. It is possible that the Batchelor family was trekking through this county at the time of Wilson the younger's birth, or that it had settled there for a few years following its initial settlement in Maury County.

Wilson the younger's birth in Lawrence County occurred a scant five years after the legendary Davy Crockett had moved from the county, having represented Lawrence in the state legislature. In the American imagination, Crockett has come to typify the frontier of the old Southwest at its rawest.[36] Bachelor's birth in a Tennessee county known for its connection to Davy Crockett soon after Crockett left the county underscores the pioneer nature of his life experience from infancy through adulthood. As a child in middle and west Tennessee, where his parents were pioneer settlers, and then as an adult living on the cusp of western settlement in Arkansas in the troubled period following the Civil War, Bachelor was to spend his entire life on the frontier of the old South as that frontier moved westward.

At the time the Bachelor family arrived in Hardin County, the area was still virtual wilderness, though the rich farmland along the Tennessee River, which bisects the county north to south, had begun to attract settlers—many with roots in eastern North Carolina—as early as 1816.[37] As will be discussed below, not a few of these settlers had preexisting ties connecting them to one another in eastern North Carolina and southeastern Virginia, which continued to persist over a number of generations as they moved west and settled in Tennessee.

Not much is known of Bachelor's early life. The loss of almost all the county's records prior to 1864 makes documentation of *any* families living in Hardin County during this time frame difficult. Since his 1889 autobiographical statement notes that his father farmed in Hardin County, Tennessee, as he had done in Nash County, North Carolina, Bachelor's life as a boy growing up in west Tennessee would have been dominated by the routine of farm chores and the cycles of nature that remained of such significance to him to the end of his life, as evidenced by his diary. His diary does contain a number of tantalizing allusions to his boyhood, all suggesting that his formative years in Tennessee were happy ones. On 29 November 1874, he writes,

> When I look back to the innocent days of childhood I ruminate, and am sad, as I think of the friends of my boyhood and like the flowers of Summer they are gone, many lie in the Silent tomb while others are fare away, and their memory makes me Sad Indeed.[38]

Other references in the diary to his growing-up years in Tennessee are equally positive: indeed, the diary consistently plays Bachelor's glowing childhood memories of life in west Tennessee against the rough-and-tumble life he saw people leading on the frontier to which he moved in his manhood, that of western Arkansas in the tumultuous days after the Civil War.[39]

When the family settled in west Tennessee, in all likelihood, it built a log house for its initial homeplace. Benjamin G. Brazelton's 1885 history of Hardin County states that when his grandfather John Brazelton (1764–1816) arrived in 1816 with the first group of settlers from east Tennessee, he and his family erected a log cabin as the family's first dwelling place in the northern part of the county.[40] And a biography of William Harrell Cherry (1822–1885), who earned notoriety among some citizens of the county when General Grant was quartered at his Savannah house during the battle of Shiloh, notes that Cherry was born in a log cabin in the vicinity of what later became known as Lowryville in southeastern Hardin County in 1822.[41] The Cherry family has multiple connections to the Batchelors: Wilson Bachelor's brother Moses married Minerva, daughter of Strachan Monk and Talitha Cherry, and his sister Delaney married Lawrence Cherry Byrd, a son of William Edward Byrd and Lovey Cherry. Talitha and Lovey were sisters of William H. Cherry's grandfather Isham Cherry.

Bachelor's 1889 autobiography notes that he was reared and educated in Hardin County, but does not specify the manner or locale of his education. It seems likely that he would have been schooled in a common school in his area of the county. Within six years of its creation in 1819, the county began to create a school system.[42] During Bachelor's boyhood, a male academy had also been formed in Savannah, the county seat. William Harrell Cherry, who was roughly a contemporary of Bachelor, attended this academy, and it could have been the case that the academy in Savannah was the source of Bachelor's boyhood education, as well.[43]

On or shortly before 3 December 1847, Wilson R. Bachelor married Sarah H., daughter of Rowland Tankersley of Hardin County.[44] His autobiographical statement for Goodspeed indicates that he spent several years teaching in his early manhood, while he was studying medicine. The 1850 federal census shows that he was teaching in that year in the sixth district of the county, immediately south of Savannah and on the east side of the Tennessee River, with his aged father living next door to him (his mother having died two years earlier, according to the autobiography).[45] It's possible that the school in which Bachelor was teaching—evidently the district's common school—was maintained at this point by John Bowen and Robert Steele, both of whom the 1850 federal census for Hardin County lists as schoolmasters in the sixth district. Steele was the grandson of the county's founder Joseph Hardin through his daughter Rebecca, who married Ninian Steele.[46]

No records have been found regarding how or where Bachelor obtained his medical education, but if he received this training as he taught school as his 1889 autobiography suggests, then it is very likely that he "read medicine" with a local doctor, a practice common throughout the United States in the period prior to the establishment of medical schools in most areas of the country.[47] The 1850 census lists no physicians in the sixth district of Hardin County, but it shows four doctors living in Savannah—George Doherty Morrow, Robert B. Burwell, Joseph F. Moseley, and Thomas Seaman.[48] One or more of these local doctors may well have been the man who trained Bachelor in the field of medicine. The 1860 federal census, which lists him as a physician (again, in the sixth district of Hardin County), corroborates his 1889 autobiographical statement that he began the practice of medicine prior to 1860—in 1859, with the suggestion of his essay on the biblical book of Job that his reading medicine may have begun in 1852 as he taught school.

Soon after Bachelor began his medical practice, the Civil War began, creating serious turbulence in Hardin County and resulting in the temporary migration of the Bachelor family from Tennessee into the non-seceding state of Kentucky. Though, as a west Tennessee county bordering Mississippi and Alabama, Hardin was in a section of the state dominated by the slave system, a plantation economy had not firmly established itself in the county by the time the war broke out, and Hardin County voted against secession in both of Tennessee's plebiscites about the issue.[49] In 1860, the few planters found in the county were largely concentrated west of the Tennessee in the part of the county in which Confederate sentiment would run strongest when war broke out. Federal census statistics for 1860 show only five residents holding tracts exceeding five hundred acres, and only fourteen with more than 20 slaves. Of the county's total population of 11,214, there were only 1,623 slaves, with 37 free blacks.

Once war was declared, however, and particularly when the battle of Shiloh occurred in Hardin County, the sentiments of many of the county's residents began to shift. Because the county's vote against secession had been exceptionally strong, many of its citizens continued to hold Union sympathies well into the war. Civil War historian Bruce Catton indicates, in fact, that Lincoln and Grant chose Hardin County as the venue for a major military operation precisely because its pro-Union leanings were well known to them.[50] Just weeks in advance of the Shiloh battle on 19 March, the *Chicago Times* was reporting that it had received a dispatch from the *Savannah Times* dated 12 March which stated that Union sentiment remained strong in Hardin County.[51]

And then Shiloh happened—right on the doorstep of the Bachelor family's farm in southwestern Hardin County, with stories handed down among Wilson Bachelor's descendants that he watched the battle from a nearby hilltop—and with over 13,000 Union casualties and over 10,000 Confederate losses, the lines dividing Confederates and Unionists in the county hardened. So that in 1886, the Goodspeed history of the county would look back at the beginning of the war with what appears to be a revisionist twist on the county's initial Union loyalties, and would declare, "On the question of Union or Secession Hardin County was largely for the Union and on the vote of 'separation' or 'no separation' the latter was emphatically voted, 1,052 to 408 votes, but when the clash of arms came the county was in majority for the South."[52]

Whether Hardin County actually did shift largely to a Confederate-leaning position during the war seems open to debate. What is not in question, however, is that following Shiloh, the mood among some citizens shifted decisively against Grant and the Union side, following the Union-staged battle that had resulted in the loss of so many lives of young men from the county and from the families of their kinfolks in other areas of the South. And so things became increasingly heated for declared Unionists in Hardin County, Wilson Bachelor included, it seems (on this, more in a moment), and a number of these Unionist families left the county during the war to escape the heat.

In the very eye of the storm was the family of William Harrell Cherry of Savannah, who, as previously mentioned, had marriage ties to the Batchelor family through the spouses of Wilson Bachelor's siblings Moses and Delaney. Cherry was a leading Unionist in Hardin County, though Cherry's wife, Anna Maria Irwin (1830–1900)—whose mother, Nancy Conway Sevier, was a great-niece of Tennessee's first governor, John Sevier—was an ardent Rebel.[53] When the war broke out, the Cherrys owned forty slaves.[54]

Despite having extensive plantation interests and many slaves, Cherry was a well-known and influential Unionist. And so when Grant moved his army to Pittsburg Landing after the battle of Fort Donelson, he headquartered himself at the imposing Cherry mansion on the bluffs of the Tennessee River on the outskirts of Savannah. The house had been built about 1830 by David Robinson (1778–1847) and had passed to his daughter Elizabeth, who married Alexander McAlpin Hardin (1808–1850), a grandson of the county founder Joseph Hardin. Cherry's first wife, Sarah Scott Robinson, was Elizabeth's sister, and he acquired the house from Elizabeth Hardin.[55]

Because Grant chose Cherry's house as the nerve center of his military operation in Hardin County, and Cherry was permitted to run cotton through the Union lines blockading the Tennessee River and, after having sold it, to bring back embargoed commodities and sell them at a tidy profit, he and his family became the object of considerable local hostility during the war. Despite Cherry's wife's Confederate loyalties and the fact that several of her brothers were Confederate officers (and Cherry's son Edgar by his first wife, Sarah, was an officer in General Albert Sidney Johnston's intelligence unit), scurrilous rumors circulated about the family due to the connection with Grant.[56]

The upshot of the considerable hostility directed toward Cherry and his family as a result of the connection with Grant during the battle of Shiloh was that, after repeated acts of violence had been staged against them and other Unionists in the county following Shiloh, in 1863, Cherry took his family to New York and Minnesota until the war ended.[57] Reports in various newspapers corroborate that threats of violence precipitated this decision. For instance, on 25 March 1862, as St. Louis's *Daily Missouri Republican* reports that the federal steamer *The Empress* has landed at the Cherry plantation on the Tennessee

River, it notes that Cherry had nearly been hanged two or three times due to his Unionism, and that on the night of the twentieth, some forty bales of cotton in his warehouse had been set afire, evidently by Rebel sympathizers.[58]

Harassment of avowed Unionists seems to have increased steadily in Hardin County as the war continued.[59] Citing a special dispatch from Savannah to the *Cincinnati Gazetteer* dated 28 March, the 31 March 1862 issue of the *Chicago Times* reports that Rebel squads were raiding houses of Unionists in Hardin and McNairy Counties and seizing provisions from them.[60] Reading between the lines in the absence of many county documents from the period, one can deduce that these terrorist initiatives against Unionists in the region had everything to do with Wilson Bachelor's decision to do as Cherry also chose to do during the war: as his 1889 autobiography notes, in 1863, he moved his family out of Hardin County to Kentucky, returning to Tennessee only when the war had ended.

The autobiography notes that Bachelor was a leading Liberalist (that is, freethinker) and Republican in northwest Arkansas following the Civil War, and that on his return to Tennessee in 1866, the federal government appointed him physician in charge of the construction of the national cemetery at Pittsburg Landing (that is, what is now the Shiloh National Cemetery). Both pieces of information—not to mention the testimony of his diary and essays—strongly suggest that he would have been among the publicly known Unionists in Hardin County during the war, and that, as with the Cherry family, Bachelor and his family may very well have found things difficult in Hardin County as hostility mounted against the county's Union sympathizers following Shiloh.

About the appointment of Bachelor as physician in charge when the national cemetery began to be constructed in 1866, there is lamentably insufficient evidence beyond his own statement in 1889 that he received this appointment on his return to Hardin County. Exhaustive research has failed to find any documentation in materials held by the National Archives or the documentary holdings of the Shiloh National Cemetery that might explain precisely who made the appointment, with whom Bachelor worked, and, most important of all, why he made the fateful decision to leave the cemetery work in 1870 and move his family to Arkansas.

Here, too, however, it is possible to read between the lines in a few pieces of documentation that have survived from the inception of the cemetery project, and to deduce a plausible story of what may well have happened as Bachelor and others employed by the federal government to begin building the cemetery worked on the project—that is, it is possible to deduce what may have precipitated Bachelor's decision to leave this job and set out on a quest for a new homeplace. Timothy B. Smith's book *This Great Battlefield of Shiloh* contains important documentation of the strong tensions that continued to exist between Unionists and Confederates in Hardin County as the war ended, and, significantly, of how these tensions affected the Pittsburg Landing cemetery project as it got underway.[61]

According to Smith, the cemetery work began in March 1866 with marking of the sites at which Union soldiers were thought to be buried. Exhumation of the bodies started in the fall of that year.[62] The work was supervised by Brevet Lieutenant Colonel A.W. Wills, quartermaster department builder of the cemetery, who answered to General George H. Thomas, who had been involved in the Shiloh battle and who commanded the Department of the Cumberland in Kentucky and Tennessee following the war. Unfortunately, clear documentation of the first years of the cemetery work, including information about Wills himself, has not survived, if, indeed, such documentation was kept in these chaotic years immediately following the war. This makes piecing together a sharply focused picture of Bachelor's brief time as physician in charge of the work difficult.[63]

In 1867, the state of Tennessee ceded land to the federal government for the construction of the cemetery with a legislative enactment. And then this happened: the internecine tensions between Unionists and Confederates within the local community that had not abated following the war continued to assert themselves with rancor because those undertaking the cemetery work were focusing on reburial of *only* the Union dead and were ignoring the Confederate bodies.[64] And a sting operation was set up to ensnare Wills: Wills fell into the trap by selling three drinks of liquor one Sunday in April 1868 at the Shiloh site, an act prohibited by local law.[65]

Because the cemetery land had been ceded by the state to the federal government, Wills's understanding was that county blue laws did not apply to the cemetery. But the local circuit court considered otherwise, and in March 1869, it found Wills guilty of contravening Hardin County's Sabbath restrictions on the sale of liquor—a decision that the Tennessee Supreme Court reversed in April 1871.[66]

If one matches the chronology of the preceding events to the events of Bachelor's life from 1866 to 1870, the following narrative appears to emerge from the story of the cemetery's construction, which plausibly explains Bachelor's decision to move his family to Arkansas in March 1870: when he was made physician in charge of the construction of the Pittsburg Landing Cemetery in 1866, he (and his family) were placed back in the thick of the Unionist–Confederate tensions in Hardin County. The exhumation of bodies that began in the fall of that year exacerbated those tensions, and the tensions would have focused quite particularly on Bachelor as the physician overseeing the exhumation and reburial process under Wills's supervision.

If the local hostilities about this process became so pronounced that a sting operation was set up to ensnare Bachelor's supervisor, one can well imagine that those targeting Wills also found ways to make life difficult for Bachelor and his family.[67] Hence, as appears very likely, his decision to renounce a federal appointment of some consequence within four years after he had been awarded the government position and head to a new life on the western Arkansas frontier in 1870.

EXCURSUS: WILSON R. BACHELOR'S SIBLINGS AND THEIR FAMILIES

But before we leave the Tennessee period of Bachelor's life, some final notes about his parents and siblings and what had become of them by the time Bachelor chose to move his family to western Arkansas: as noted previously, Bachelor's mother, Alcie, had died in 1848. His father, Wilson the elder, who was living beside Bachelor and his wife, Sarah, in 1850, died in 1858, according to his son's autobiography. It seems reasonable to suppose that Wilson and Sarah were providing care for his father up to the point of the father's death, given the immediate proximity of the two households on the 1850 federal census.

By 1850 the only children of Wilson and Alcie Batchelor still living in Tennessee were, in fact, Wilson the younger and his sister Sarah, who was blind and who moved in 1870 with her brother to Arkansas, where she lived with his family until her death on 19 January 1892. On Christmas Eve 1891, Bachelor's diary will note that his sister "blind Sally" is with his family, and the following year on Christmas night, he will mention that she has died during the year. His scrapbook contains a copy of a eulogy he wrote at the time of Sarah's death, which says that she died of la grippe (i.e., influenza) and pneumonia, and gives her age at death as sixty-eight, placing her birth about 1824.

Both the 1850 and 1860 federal census list Sarah as blind, the latter saying she had been blind for seven years due to a nervous fever.[68] Bachelor's eulogy states that she had been blind for forty years when she died at age sixty-eight. The 1880 census reiterates that she is blind but does not indicate that she was also deaf, though the eulogy says that she had been deaf for fifteen years at the time of her death.

Bachelor's oldest brother Moses (who, along with his descendants, used the Batchelor spelling of the surname) had left Hardin County for Arkansas in the fall of 1848, after having married Minerva Monk about 1838.[69] As noted previously, Minerva was the daughter of Strachan Monk (abt. 1787–abt. 1858) and Talitha Cherry (abt. 1790–1860). As with Wilson Batchelor and Alcie Odom, Strachan and Talitha Monk were eastern North Carolinians who moved to middle Tennessee after 1810, and then to Hardin County after a short sojourn in Davidson County, Tennessee. The couple had married in Martin County, North Carolina, several counties east of Nash, from which the Batchelors hailed, about 1805.

Strachan Monk appears in P. M. Harbert's account of the early history of Hardin County as Strawhorn Monk, the chief of a "rather prosperous tribe of Indians" who had "large possessions of horses and other property."[70] Harbert may have reached the erroneous conclusion that Monk was a Native American living in the area prior to the settlement of the first white settlers because his given name, Strachan, appears in a number of records with phonetic spellings including "Strahon," "Strayhorn," or "Strawhorn."[71]

In fact, Monk is in Martin County, North Carolina, records up to about 1815, and thereafter in Davidson County, Tennessee, until his settling in Hardin County in 1822. The ancestry of his father, Nottingham Monk (abt. 1755–1818), can be confidently traced to seventeenth-century English immigrant ancestors to Northampton County, Virginia. Monk's mother, Rachel Strachan (abt. 1755–1816), was the daughter of a Scottish immigrant to Bertie County, North Carolina, George Strachan (bef. 1715–1760), who arrived in North Carolina before 1735 and who appears to have come to North Carolina as part of the migration of Scottish merchants to the Albemarle region in this period promoted by the Scottish-born governor Gabriel Johnston.[72] Nottingham Monk and Rachel Strachan married in Bertie County, North Carolina, in 1786.

When Moses Batchelor moved his family to Arkansas in 1848 (perhaps following the death of his mother in that year), he settled in eastern Hot Spring County several miles south of the present community of Poyen, which is now in Grant County (the latter county having been formed in 1870 out of Hot Spring and several other counties).[73] Two years prior to his move to this location, his sister Delaney and her husband, Lawrence Cherry Byrd (1822–abt. 1863), had moved to the same location. The couple had married 30 August 1842 in Hardin County.[74]

As already noted, the families of Moses and Delaney were connected not merely through their Batchelor blood, but also through Moses's and Delaney's spouses, who were first cousins. In settling together in Hot Spring County, Arkansas, these families were, in fact, continuing an intricate network of inter-marriage and kinship whose roots stretch back to eastern North Carolina in the 1700s, and, from there to southeast Virginia in the 1600s. When the Byrd, Cherry, and Batchelor families came from England to the colonies in the seventeenth-century families, they all settled close to one another in Lower Norfolk County, Virginia.

The following curious tidbit illustrates the thick intergenerational connections of these families: Lawrence Cherry Byrd was the son of William Edward Byrd (bef. 1790–1835) and Lovey Cherry (1784–1877), who married about 1800 in Martin County, North Carolina. Lovey's (and Talitha Cherry Monk's) parents were Jesse Cherry (1749–February 1808) and Elizabeth Gainer (1751–1836). When Jesse (who represented Martin County in the North Carolina House along with sons Lawrence and Darling)[75] died, his widow then married Edward Byrd (1737–1830), father of the William Edward Byrd who married Lovey Cherry.

By the time the elderly couple married in 1822, Edward's son William Edward and Elizabeth's daughter Lovey had, of course, already been married twenty years, and in recording the marriage of the aged Edward and Elizabeth, the *Raleigh Register* makes gentle fun at their expense by noting,

> The proverb is that, "Old Rats love Cheese," and by the information below it will be seen that, "Old Byrds love Cherrys," when fully ripe. On the 7th at the residence of Lawrence Cherry, Esq., by the Rev. Joseph Biggs, Mr. Edward Byrd, age 82, married Mrs. Elizabeth Cherry, late consort of Jesse Cherry, Esq., Dec'd., age 71. Both of the county of Martin.[76]

Reverend Joseph Biggs is, of course, a Batchelor relation, since the Batchelors of southeastern Virginia and northeastern North Carolina descend from the marriage of the immigrant Richard Batchelor to Ann Biggs.[77]

Wilson and Alcie Batchelor's son William Skidmore Batchelor (or, as he seems sometimes to have spelled his name, Batchelder) had also left Hardin County prior to the departure of his brother Wilson. But he followed a distinctly different migration path than that of his siblings Moses and Delaney, with their multiple ties of blood bringing them to central Arkansas on the heels of each other in the late 1840s.[78]

In 1839, William converted to Mormonism in Hardin County, and in 1841 or 1842, he followed the man who had converted him, Joseph Albert Andrews, to Nauvoo with other founding figures of the Latter Day Saints, where he married Huldah King on 21 February 1843. Following Joseph Smith's assassination and the scattering of the Latter Day Saints, William and his family lived for some years in Rock Island County, Illinois, and then settled in Independence, Missouri, where William and his wife, Huldah, were members of the group that became known as the Reorganized Church of Jesus Christ of Latter Day Saints and where both died and are buried.[79] Bachelor's scrapbook has an obituary—evidently from the newspaper *Zion's Ensign*—for his brother William clipped and pasted into it.[80]

According to a letter Wilson Bachelor sent to the *Zion's Ensign* paper early in 1893, which the paper published on 4 February, in the Mormon mission venture that resulted in the conversion of first Andrews and then Bachelor's brother William in 1839, Bachelor's father and mother and two sisters were also converted to Mormonism.[81] The letter notes that Bachelor was responding to an issue of the *Ensign* he had recently received from one of his nephews in Independence.[82] Reading the paper brought back memories dating from when he was a boy of ten or twelve years, at which time Mormon missionaries Clapp and Hunter had arrived in Hardin County, Tennessee, where his father lived, and had preached. Their preaching resulted in the conversion of Albert Andrews, a local minister (Bachelor spells the name Anderus, or the typesetter of the *Ensign* has—typically—read Bachelor's "w" as a "u"), who then converted several members of Bachelor's family to the Latter Day Saints.

A number of documents corroborate details provided in Bachelor's 1893 letter about the Mormon missions in west Tennessee in 1839. In the early Mormon newspaper *Times and Seasons*, Jesse D. Hunter reports from Jackson County, Illinois, on 26 December 1839 that he and Benjamin L. Clapp had recently gone on mission to McNairy County, Tennessee, where they had baptized fourteen persons, after which they had held five meetings in Tishomingo County, Mississippi, where they had baptized six more.[83] At the time Hunter sent this report, Clapp was still in Mississippi doing missionary work.[84]

A number of sources suggest that the early Mormon converts in west Tennessee and northeastern Mississippi were not well received by many of their neighbors—in addition to holding religious views considered heterodox, they were staunchly antislavery—and early in 1842 some eighty or ninety Mormons from these counties formed a wagon train and went to Nauvoo.[85] It is tempting to think that this is the point at which Bachelor's brother William and his mentor Andrews went to Nauvoo. William's obituary places their migration to Nauvoo in 1840, but the federal census of that year suggests that he was still living in his father's household as the census was taken. Andrews is also on the 1840 census living in McNairy County, Tennessee, and is a neighbor of the Batchelor family. Andrews would perform the marriage ceremony of William and Huldah King in Nauvoo in February 1843, and would die soon after that on 23 October as a young man of thirty-three, according to records kept by Nauvoo's sexton William D. Huntington.[86]

Because Wilson and Alcie Odom Batchelor and the rest of their children remained in Tennessee when William moved to Nauvoo, and because Bachelor's 1889 autobiography speaks of his mother as a member of the Methodist Episcopal Church and is silent about his father's religious background, it seems unlikely that the other family members who became Mormon in 1839 persisted in that faith. In fact, as will be noted in a moment, Bachelor's sister Delaney joined a Baptist church in Arkansas, and it seems his sister Sarah was a Baptist at the time of her death in 1892, since a Baptist minister officiated at her funeral.[87]

As the preceding narrative suggests, this was a family with noteworthy interfamilial religious diversity (and fluidity), and that diversity accounts, in part, for the very different migration paths that the children of Wilson R. and Alcie Batchelor followed. Wilson the younger stands apart, of course, as an avowed freethinker. His mother apparently had a Methodist background and would likely have raised the family's children in that faith—though she also seems to have transitioned to Mormonism for a period of time in the late 1830s.

His siblings Moses and Delaney both joined Baptist churches in Arkansas— Delaney is listed as a constituting member of Brush Creek Baptist Church in Hot Spring County on 1 April 1847, and Moses joined Francois Baptist Church in Hot Spring County in August 1870.[88] The Francois minutes recording Moses's acceptance as a church member note that he was joining "by experience" —that is, he had not previously been a Baptist, whereas his second wife, Louisa Waters Robertson (whom he married following the death of his wife, Minerva, in 1860), had joined the same church in September 1869 bringing a letter of membership from a previous Baptist church. Louisa's father John Waters was, in fact, a Baptist minister in contiguous Saline County.[89]

Moses's churchgoing career seems to have been brief. Francois church minutes report in December 1870, "Brother Moses Batchlor had bin to mutch to mutch," and note that brethren H. J. Clift and Lewis Collie had been sent to deal with him about some unspecified infraction. The infraction may well have had to with drinking alcohol or drinking to excess, since on the fourth Saturday of June 1872, Clift and Collie brought to the church a charge of "publick" drunkenness against Batchelor, and he was excluded from the church.

And so the children of Wilson and Alcie Batchelor ran the gamut from an avowed Mormon to a freethinker to several Baptists, two of whom had previously converted to Mormonism in Tennessee, and another of whom appears to have joined a Baptist church late in life (and after having married a Baptist minister's daughter) only to be excluded from membership within a short time after he joined the church. And, to repeat, these children were born to a Methodist mother, and a father who was perhaps unchurched, until both parents became Mormons for a brief period of their lives.

Wilson the younger's wife, Sarah Tankersley Bachelor, was also a member of a Baptist church both in Hardin County, Tennessee, and after the family moved to Franklin County, Arkansas. Minutes of Bethel Baptist Church in Hardin County show her on the membership roll in 1861. In Franklin County, Sarah belonged to Mill Creek Missionary Baptist Church.[90] According to stories handed down among the couple's descendants, Bachelor would drive his wife, Sarah, to church on Sundays in their buggy, but would sit outside in the buggy reading while she attended church. Significantly, his name does not appear in the membership roll of Bethel Church in Hardin County. And he would not, of course, have joined the Mill Creek church due to his commitment to freethinking after the family settled in Arkansas.

There may well be a strain of religious dissent running through branches of the Batchelor family from early in its settlement in the new world. Claims have been made that the immigrant ancestor Richard Batchelor came to Virginia as a Quaker, but I have seen no solid documentation to support that claim, nor does he appear as a Quaker in any records of Lower Norfolk County that document the persecution of that religious group in the county from the 1660s forward. He was, however, closely associated with a number of people in Lower Norfolk County who appear to have been influential members of the Quaker movement and who suffered legal reprisals as a result of their affiliation with the Friends. These include his father-in-law John Biggs.

There is fairly substantial evidence that John Biggs was a Friend by 16 April 1675, when a neighbor, John Edwards, reported Biggs to Lower Norfolk County court for not having had his children baptized.[91] Edwards and other county residents may already have had an animus against Biggs, who had been first the undersheriff of the county[92] and then surveyor of highways for the southern branch of Elizabeth River, and in both capacities, had elicited complaints that he abused his authority while in office. If he was already a religious nonconformist at this point, these complaints may, of course, have reflected religious animosity against him.[93]

In the court hearing provoked by Edwards's complaint, Biggs's kinsman, Francis Sayer, the county sheriff (with whom Richard Batchelor had witnessed a land transaction not long after the latter's appearance in the county),[94] testified against him, verifying Edwards's report about Biggs's failure to have his children baptized. And when the case was brought before Governor Berkeley later in the year, in June, the minister of Elizabeth River parish in Lower Norfolk County, Reverend Harne, confirmed that Biggs had not had his children baptized, and he was found guilty and fined.[95]

Both in this case and when he was summoned to the Lower Norfolk County court in February 1675 to prove the will of John Porter Sr., Biggs refused to swear an oath, which strongly suggests he was a Quaker. And he was obdurate, it appears: in June 1675, Reverend Harne reported that Biggs had still not had his children baptized in response to the court's order, and in August 1675, a fine of 3,500 pounds of tobacco was levied against him. He was, in fact, imprisoned for his refusal to swear an oath in the matter of John Porter Sr.'s will.[96]

As a number of historians including Philip A. Bruce, John Bennett Boddie, Jay Worrall Jr., Rufus M. Jones, James Horn, and April Lee Hatfield have noted, Puritans had an exceptionally strong presence in southeastern Virginia in the seventeenth century, and as the Quaker movement arrived in this area in the latter part of the 1650s, many of the colonists who had previously had Puritan views began to gravitate to Quakerism as a new way of expressing their dissent from the established church.[97] As Hatfield notes, the parish in which the Biggs and Batchelor families lived, Elizabeth River, was pastored from 1640 by an Anglican divine with decided Puritan leanings and close ties to the New England colonies, Reverend Thomas Harrison. Harrison was to be expelled from Virginia for his Puritan affiliations, provoking an exodus of settlers with similar views from Lower Norfolk, Nansemond, and Isle of Wight Counties to the more religiously tolerant colony of Maryland.

Harrison came to Lower Norfolk County in 1640 when a number of the county's inhabitants, including Thomas Sayer, a kinsman of John Biggs, Thomas Meares, who would help lead the exodus of Puritans expelled from southeastern Virginia, and John Gater/Gaither, who brought to Virginia William Goldsmith, Batchelor's sponsor, petitioned that he be appointed their pastor.[98] Both Sayer and Meares appear in close connection with John Biggs in county records—and this suggests that Biggs was very likely among the residents of Elizabeth River parish who may have had Puritan inclinations before he became a Quaker: for instance, on 19 June 1650 Sayer bought land from Meares with Biggs as a witness to the deed.[99]

The strong Puritan presence in Lower Norfolk and Nansemond Counties, and their close ties to the New England colonies, were already in evidence by the first half of the 1640s. As Hatfield has noted, when the Powhatans attacked a number of Virginia settlements in 1644 but did not attack settlers of the southeastern counties, both Governor John Winthrop and Captain Edward

Johnson of Massachusetts suggested that southeastern Virginia had been spared by divine providence because of the significant presence of Puritans in the region.[100]

According to Hatfield, Reverend Thomas Harrison had close connections to Winthrop, with whom he corresponded and to whom he reported late in 1646 that his flock in Elizabeth River parish was increasing.[101] By this point, however, Harrison had come under fire for his nonconformist views. In April 1645, the church wardens of Elizabeth River parish charged him with not using the Book of Common Prayer for worship, not catechizing on Sunday afternoons, and not baptizing correctly, and he was indicted.[102]

In 1648, Governor Berkeley, who was bitterly opposed to religious non-conformists of all stripes, began to move against those with Puritan sympathies in the colony, and in May of that year, the Lower Norfolk County court ordered that illegal Puritan gatherings in Elizabeth River parish cease—though the parishioners resisted the order. Reverend Harrison was then banished from the colony, and headed to Boston where he married a niece of Governor Winthrop.[103] He returned briefly to Virginia in the winter of 1649, as the vestry of Nansemond parish petitioned (ineffectually) that he be reinstated to his pastoral charge, and then left for England, where he became a chaplain for Oliver Cromwell in the latter's Irish campaign.[104]

It was at this point that Thomas Meares and others led a migration of settlers from the Puritan-leaning counties of southeastern Virginia to Maryland.[105] And then this interesting transition occurred in Meares's case: by 22 July 1658, he begins to appear in Maryland records as a Quaker refusing to swear oaths in court. And so, as Rufus Jones notes, Meares's transition from Puritanism to "full-fledged" Quakerism illustrates the movement of religious dissent among southeastern Virginians of the seventeenth century (and their offshoots in Maryland) from Puritanism to Quakerism by the latter part of the century.[106]

Because John Biggs had significant ties to Thomas Meares and would also be charged by the court of Lower Norfolk County with having Quaker inclinations, Meares's transition from Puritanism to Quakerism underscores the probability that Biggs (and perhaps Batchelor as well) arrived in Virginia with Puritan loyalties. And in the case of Biggs, the move to Quakerism may have been, as with Meares, a move to a new form of religious dissent as a novel way of expressing dissent from the established church came on the scene in the 1650s.[107]

The waves the Quaker movement made on its appearance in the colony can be measured by the fact that the Virginia legislature criminalized Friends' meetings in 1660 and in 1662 levied a fine of 2,000 pounds of tobacco for every refusal to have a child baptized, with half of the fine going to the informer.[108] Jones notes that there was a particular determination to stamp out Quakerism in such southeastern Virginia counties as Lower Norfolk and Nansemond because "there was a large convincement to Quakerism" in these counties.[109] And as Hatfield points out, "All of these relatively prominent Quakers [i.e., those punished for their Quaker ties by the Lower Norfolk County court] lived along or near the Elizabeth River, an area with strong Puritan traditions."[110]

Among the relatively prominent Quakers of Elizabeth River on whom Hatfield focuses are John Porter Sr. and Jr., who were brothers, distinguishing themselves from each other by using the "senior" and "junior" designations. As previously noted, these men are closely tied to both Richard Batchelor and his father-in-law John Biggs in Lower Norfolk County records. The Porters' brother Manasses received a 1659 headright grant for transporting Richard Batchelor to Virginia. And the will of John's elder brother, who appears in county records as John Porter Sr., was witnessed by John Biggs, who was imprisoned for refusing to swear an oath in court to prove the will. Because of their prominence in the county's governing structure, the Porters were specifically targeted by county and state authorities seeking to suppress the Quaker movement.

The crackdown on Quakers in Lower Norfolk County began in December 1662 when Colonel John Sidney, whose daughter Mary had married John Porter Jr. and who was at this point high sheriff of the county, began to move against the local Quaker community, including his daughter, whom he fined for attending a Friends' meeting.[111] Sidney was succeeded in the office of sheriff by John Hill, who had been part of the Puritan movement in the region and who turned his attention to Porter's older brother John Sr., who was representing the county in the House of Burgesses.[112] As Stephen B. Weeks notes, Hill's incentive for targeting Porter may well have had to do with rewards promised to those who reported suspected Quakers after Governor Berkeley appointed a commission in 1663 to eradicate the Quaker movement in Lower Norfolk County.[113]

The upshot of Hill's attack on John Porter Sr. was that after Hill reported Porter for being "loving to the Quakers," refusing to swear oaths in court, and holding Anabaptist views, the House of Burgesses expelled him from its membership in September 1663.[114] Hill then went on to report the younger Porter to the Lower Norfolk County court on 12 November 1663, charging him with having attended a Quaker meeting at the house of Richard Russell and with having preached at a Friends' meeting aboard the ship *Blessing* as it lay in harbor off the county's coastline.[115] Also in the list of those Hill reported on this occasion was William Goldsmith, from whom Manasses Porter obtained the grant he claimed in 1659 for the importation of Richard Batchelor, who would himself claim Batchelor as a headright in 1665.

William Goldsmith arrived in Lower Norfolk County by 26 July 1638, when John Gater or Gaither (both spellings of the surname occur in county records) claimed a headright for importing Goldsmith along with Gater's wife, Joane, and son John.[116] As noted previously, Gater was among the residents of the southern branch of the Elizabeth River who petitioned in 1640 for the appointment of the Puritan minister Reverend Thomas Harrison as pastor of Elizabeth River Parish. When the exodus of Puritans occurred from southeastern Virginia in the 1640s, John Gater and his family moved to Anne Arundel County, Maryland.[117]

As did John Biggs, John Porter Sr. remained obdurate in his religious dissent to the end of his life, since in 1672, within several years of Porter's death, George Fox noted in his journal that he stayed with Friend John Porter on a branch of the Elizabeth River as he traveled among the Quaker communities of the colony.[118] And Porter's nephew, whose name was also John and who was a son of John Jr., would go on to play a leading role in the Quaker communities of colonial North Carolina.[119]

With such decisive religious dissent encoded in its genetic DNA, as it were, from the colonial period forward (and, in all likelihood, the dissent was already configured in the family's roots in England prior to its migration to the new world), it is perhaps not surprising to find such lively religious diversity in the family of Wilson R. Batchelor and Alcie Odom. And, in particular, to note the obstinacy (and flair) with which their son Wilson clung to freethought once he affiliated himself with that movement on the western Arkansas frontier.

THE FRANKLIN COUNTY, ARKANSAS, YEARS

It will not be necessary to sketch the history of Wilson Bachelor and his family following their move to Arkansas in great detail, since the documents published here—in particular, his diary and occasional pieces from the 1890s—provide a fairly exhaustive account of the family's life once they moved to Arkansas. The diary itself suggests (see, e.g., the entry for 20 March 1870) that he had identified Franklin County as his new homeplace prior to the move to Tennessee, though none of the extant work specifies why or how the family selected that destination. For Tennesseans moving westward in the nineteenth century, the choice of Arkansas as a new home is not in itself surprising. From the 1840s onward, there had been continual migration of Tennessee families into Arkansas, many of them from west Tennessee, as the initial fertility of land subjected to exhaustive farming techniques in Tennessee began to wane.[120]

Many of these families had North Carolina roots and made the trek to Arkansas in the middle and later years of the nineteenth century just as they had made the trek early in the 1800s to Tennessee—in family units, settling among friends and neighbors with shared roots stretching back first to Tennessee and then to North Carolina.[121] The pattern of North Carolina-Tennessee-Arkansas migration prior to 1850 was so strong, in fact, that North Carolina was the state most commonly reported as the state of birth by Arkansans on the 1850 census.

Since Bachelor's siblings Moses and Delaney had preceded him to Arkansas, it would perhaps have made sense for him to choose Hot Spring or Grant County, where their families lived, as his new homeplace when he decided to move his family to Arkansas in 1870. It's possible that he avoided that part of the state, however, because it was in the part of the state that had somewhat stronger ties to the Confederacy during the Civil War, and his siblings' families definitely had Confederate connections during the war. Bachelor's nephew James, Moses's son, died as a Confederate soldier in 1861 at the Battle of Belmont near Columbus, Kentucky. On the same day that James enlisted in Company E of the Twelfth Arkansas Infantry, his cousins Pleasant, William, and Wilson Byrd, sons of Bachelor's sister Delaney, also enlisted in the same unit.

As a Republican who had taken the Union side in the war, Bachelor may have chosen Franklin rather than Grant or Hot Spring County as his new place of residence because it was in the area of Arkansas with the strongest Republican presence and situated, as well, in the area that had had the most pronounced resistance to secession.[122] There was also economic opportunity in Franklin County. Construction had begun on the railroad line from Little Rock to Fort Smith the year before Bachelor's move to Franklin County, and within five years of his settling in the county, the line would reach Ozark, his county seat.[123]

Part of the appeal of Franklin County, as well, may have been that after having been partly destroyed in the Civil War, Ozark was reincorporated in 1869 and as Bachelor moved to the area in 1870, the town was becoming a boom town.[124] In fact, it required rebuilding. Parties from both the Confederate and Union armies had passed through the town several times during the war, burning all the buildings except three houses to prevent the other side from using the buildings.[125]

In addition, the Bachelors may have chosen Franklin County as their new home because there was at least one other family there with Hardin County,

Tennessee, roots. Chesley Mack Gammill, a justice of the peace in Mill Creek Township in which the Bachelors would settle, also came to the county from Hardin County.[126] The Gammills are very likely the family hosting old friends from Tennessee whom Bachelor's diary mentions that he and his wife, Sarah, visited on 20 March 1873, when they exchanged news of their "Faderland," Tennessee. When Lowe's Creek Masonic Lodge was founded on 10 October 1876, both Wilson Bachelor and Chesley Gammill were charter members, signing the charter next to each other.[127]

As the diary will indicate, having acquired land in Franklin County, Bachelor launched a medical practice within months of settling there, as he built or remodeled a house and opened a farm on his new land. The diary will also suggest that he became disenchanted with the new place of residence he had chosen within several years of his relocation, and that by March 1873, he had begun to struggle with "vicissitudes, cares, toils, and pains" that may have had to do with "instances of a pecuniary nature" that had operated against him after his settling in the state.

As the nearest city of any size, Fort Smith did not particularly charm him, either. In October 1870, he'll indicate that he had visited the city in the spring, not long after the family arrived in Arkansas, and "found it rather a meagre place, or at least not according to my expectations." Repeatedly throughout the diary, Bachelor will note that he has not found in western Arkansas the sort of intellectual stimulation and companionship he had hoped to find, and that few of those he meets share his interests—his love of books and ideas. The diary will speak of many days spent alone in his study reading.

And then sometime in the 1870s, it appears, Bachelor made a fateful decision: as his diary entry for Christmas Day 1890 states, he had in the previous sixteen years (in which there is a hiatus in his diary) become a "confirmed Freethinker or agnostic." As his three-part series of essays explaining his reasons for the decision will suggest, the decision had much to do with his wide reading in the scriptures of the world religions, his comparison of those scriptures with one another, and his eventual conclusion that all of the scriptural narratives were mythological rather than scientific in their intent.

As a man of science convinced of the need to reason closely and observe the world carefully with empirical exactitude, he reaches the conclusion that science and reason rather than—as he puts it—superstition and the irrationality of religious ideas should govern human behavior. And so Bachelor's life will undergo a decisive turn sometime in the latter part of the 1870s: from the point of his conversion to freethought forward, he'll become something of an apostle for freethought in northwest Arkansas, writing at least one monograph, *Fiat Flux*, about the topic, and many essays and occasional pieces for his local newspaper to spread his new gospel of science and reason in the community in which he lives.

The diary, his essays of the 1890s, and his letters will sketch the life of his family from the establishment of his medical practice and his turn to free-thought in no little detail. As with other country doctors of his time and place, he will combine farming with the practice of medicine. Once settled in the small valley at the foot of Mill Creek Mountain on the south side of the Arkansas River and southwest of Ozark that he chooses for his new homeplace in March 1870, he will remain there with his family members who haven't left the area up to the point of his death in 1903.

By the time the family leaves Tennessee for Arkansas, Bachelor's wife, Sarah, will have borne him seven children. Two more will be born in Arkansas. The first son, Adam C., was born 24 September 1850, and died in infancy. Leander Monroe, the next, was born 26 October 1851 and would die in Fort Smith on 22 October 1897, having spent his adult life farming with his father, with occasional stints in Indian Territory.

The third child, James Hugo, was born 13 October 1853 and died 9 October 1934 in Fort Smith. "Dr. Jim," as a 5 September 1899 letter of Bachelor to his niece Melissa Byrd Robinson will call him, followed in his father's footsteps as a doctor. Jim was twice married—first to Augusta, daughter of George Eubanks and Elizabeth Birch, who died early in their marriage, after which Jim married Allie Vilola Rogers on 5 February 1888 in Franklin County.

On 19 October 1857, Wilson and Sarah's first daughter, Nancy Jane, was born. Nannie, as the diary and Bachelor's letters call her, died in May 1914 at Cecil in Franklin County. She married Frederick Eubanks, a brother of Jim's first wife, Augusta. After Frederick died early in the marriage leaving Nannie a young widow, she remained at home with her parents, raising their daughter Gertrude in her parents' home.

The next child, John Yeager Lynn, was born 24 November 1859 and died in 1940 in Denver, Colorado. As Bachelor's diary will indicate, Yeager spent some of his adult life moving back and forth between Arkansas, Oklahoma, and Texas before moving to Colorado. In 1904, he married Anna G. Sawyers (1883–1968), daughter of Alonzo L. Sawyers and Florence Elizabeth Stickler, who had moved from Washington County, Arkansas, to Las Animas County, Colorado. Yeager and his wife, Anna, lived at Plum Valley in Las Animas County, then at Gardner in Huerfano County, and for the final years of his life in Denver.

Wilson and Sarah's next child, Alcie Daisy, named for her Batchelor grand-mother, was born 29 October 1861 and died 6 August 1891 in Pauline. On 1

January 1880, Alcie married Dr. Seaborn Rentz Russell (1859–1928), son of Dr. William James Russell (1830–1892) and Avarilla Octavia Dunn Law (1830–1892). William was in turn the son of a doctor, William James Russell (1799–1872) and wife, Sophia A. Park (1800–1841).

After the marriage, Seaborn had moved his wife and family to various places as he sought to establish a medical practice. Letters of his mother document the moves in close detail. In August 1886, he bought land in Wills Point, Texas, hoping to set up a practice there, and in October his wife and children joined him. His parents were living with the family at this point, and Seaborn was studying surgery under his father, who had graduated from Philadelphia College of Medicine in 1850. A 14 September 1890 letter of Seaborn's mother says that Seaborn and his family were preparing to move into their new home at Wills Point, which was incomplete.

However, as Bachelor's diary will indicate, in the same month, Alcie returned to her parents with her five children and pregnant with her last child. A legal writ dissolving the marriage on 13 February 1904 says that she and Seaborn had bought land together in Texas in the 1880s, and that since that time, he had abandoned her. In 1900, Alcie is listed as head of the household in Franklin County on the federal census. From the point of the dissolution of her marriage up to her death, Alcie raised her children next to her parents at Pauline with a brief return to Texas to arrange business matters related to her marriage.

The next child of Wilson and Sarah Bachelor, another son, was named for his father, and appears throughout his father's diary as Wils. Wilson Richard was born 27 June 1864 while the family was sojourning in Kentucky during the war, and died of tuberculosis 7 August 1895 at his parents' home in Pauline. Both his father's diary and scrapbook contain eulogies of Wils, who was the first family member to die after the family had come to Arkansas.

Following Wils, Sarah gave birth to a daughter, Lula Georgeann, the last of the children born in Tennessee, on 12 November 1866. On 10 March 1884 in Franklin County, Lula married William David Harris and then moved with him to Atlas near Paris in Lamar County, Texas, where the couple raised stock. Lula died 1 December 1935 in Miller, Pushmataha County, Oklahoma.

The first of Wilson and Sarah's children born in Arkansas, a son Victor Hugo, was born 24 July 1870 and died at Cecil in Franklin County on 10 February 1946. Vick, as his father's diary calls him, remained near his parents throughout their lives and farmed with his father. He married Henrietta Dean, who was the widow of a Frank Rearden at the time of their marriage.

The last child of the family, Pauline Graham, was born 6 May 1874 and died in May 1954 in Checotah, McIntosh County, Oklahoma. As Bachelor's diary and letters will indicate, Pauline studied music in Franklin County under a Miss Carrie White, and then taught organ in the community. On 2 February 1903, she married William Clyde O'Bar, son of John O'Bar and Susan A. Wingfield of Sebastian County.

Notes about the Diary, the Scrapbook's Occasional Pieces, and the Letters

Finally, some brief observations about the work of Wilson R. Bachelor published in this volume: as noted in the opening section of this introductory essay, a diary Bachelor kept from March 1870 to December 1902 has been saved by his descendants, as has a scrapbook into which he pasted thirty-two essays or occasional pieces he published in the 1890s, apparently in local newspapers. Six letters that Bachelor wrote to members of the families of his siblings Moses and Delaney from 1891 to 1899 have also survived, and have been preserved by members of those two families, and are being presented to readers along with the diary and thirty-two occasional pieces.

Bachelor's diary passed to his daughter Pauline and from her to a daughter Ruby Jefferson and her daughter Paula Jefferson in Riverside, California. Paula Jefferson has kindly made the diary accessible for publication in this volume and, in conjunction with its publication here, has generously donated the diary to the medical history archives of the University of Arkansas Medical School. The diary notes that Bachelor had kept at least one previous diary from which he transcribed an 1869 medical case that appears in his surviving diary. That diary and any other diaries that he may have kept prior to 1870 are not extant.

Descendants of Bachelor in Fort Smith, Arkansas, whose ancestor is Bachelor's daughter Alcie, have preserved his scrapbook, and it currently belongs to Wanda Rentz Dailey and her daughter Susan Dailey Johnson of Fort Smith and Pocola, Oklahoma, who have also generously permitted the material in it to be transcribed and published.

A letter Bachelor wrote to Seaborn Walters, the husband of his niece Minerva Louisa Batchelor (a daughter of Moses) was in the possession of Flora Rondeau, a descendant of this couple in Malvern, Arkansas, up to her death in 2012, and she kindly allowed it to be published. A set of letters Bachelor wrote to his niece Melissa Ann Byrd Robinson, a daughter of his sister Delaney and her husband, Lawrence Cherry Byrd, along with a letter he wrote to Melissa's niece Janice Delaney Byrd McBurnett, daughter of Samuel Delaney Byrd and Polly Ann Thrower, passed on to Janie's daughter Elsie Delaney McBurnett Hodges of Pine Bluff, Arkansas, and are now owned by Elsie's son Norman Hodges in Little Rock, who has also generously allowed these materials to be published.

Of the three sets of documents, the diary is now in the most fragile condition. Bachelor wrote it in a postmaster's account book. The diary's front cover has a title reading, *Miller's Official Postmaster's Account & Record Book, Fourth Class*. Inside are ruled pages on which Bachelor has written his diary entries. The paper itself is extremely friable, and sections of the diary have been lost over the years.

Ruby and Paula Jefferson helpfully made a photocopy of the diary in the 1970s, and that copy preserves some passages of the diary that have now fallen away from the original due to its friability. Paula also permitted UAMS to produce a high-quality scan of the document in February 2012, and in transcribing the diary for publication, Bill Russell and I have worked from the photocopy and the scanned copy together, checking them carefully against one another.

At some point in the transmission of the diary from hand to hand following Bachelor's death, someone has kettle-stitched the left margins of both the diary and the scrapbook to preserve them. The most likely candidate for this preservation work is Bachelor's daughter Alcie, who raised her family next to her parents, and to whom both the diary and scrapbook initially passed, before the diary then went to her younger sister Pauline. Alcie supported her family as an expert seamstress, and this makes it even more likely that she stitched the margins of both precious documents—an action that very probably enabled both to be saved for posterity, since each is comprised of fragile paper that has yellowed considerably with age and is now falling apart.

As is the diary, the scrapbook is a postmaster's record book. The scrapbook shows signs of having been maintained by and having passed through a number of hands. Since it contains material that Bachelor himself could not have saved in it—for example, his Masonic eulogy, a handwritten note by his son Vick recording the date of Sarah Tankersley Bachelor's death on 9 May 1904, and so forth—it was obviously maintained and added to by some family member or members following the death of Bachelor himself.

The first section of the scrapbook, however, gives every appearance of having been preserved by Bachelor, and it consists largely of his own work clipped from some source or sources and pasted into the scrapbook. Since a number of these pieces state explicitly that they were written as letters to the editor of a newspaper, it seems reasonable to conclude that all of the pieces were published in a newspaper or newspapers—almost certainly one of the county newspapers in Bachelor's county seat of Ozark. This deduction is reinforced by the fact that all of these published pieces are set in the same typeface and appear to be on the same kind of newspaper stock. And so it seems likely that they were all published in the same newspaper.

Ozark had a newspaper as early as 1858, the *Southwestern*, but that paper was short-lived. As the Goodspeed history of northwest Arkansas notes, "The newspapers of Ozark have been more pungent and prolific than permanent, and few have ever been preserved."[128] Several papers succeeded the *Southwestern* in short-lived succession, among which the most long-lived were the *Democrat* and the *Enterprise*, which were to consolidate in 1909. Both the Webb and Bourland families had ties to the *Democrat*, which was appearing as a weekly during the period in which Bachelor seems to have published the occasional pieces saved in his scrapbook, and since he mentions having stayed with Perry F. Webb in Ozark on 10 May 1873, and the scrapbook contains a letter Bachelor wrote to Addison M. Bourland reviewing Bourland's book *Entolai*, it seems very likely most of the published articles preserved in the scrapbook originally appeared in the *Democrat*.

One of the pieces, the obituary of Bachelor's son Wils, which is dated 7 August 1895, ends with the line, "Fort Smith and Van Buren papers please copy." This is yet another indication that this and the other items that were his own written and published work and which Bachelor has kept in the scrapbook had appeared in his local newspaper.

As the notes accompanying the scrapbook pieces will explain, various clues internal to the published work of Bachelor collected in this scrapbook allow these pieces to be dated in the 1890s. The thirty-two published documents in the scrapbook comprise an assortment of occasional pieces ranging from letters to the editors of a newspaper or newspapers, to letters written to individuals and then published as articles, to obituaries and eulogies, to essays on topics such as freethought and agnosticism. Each of these occasional pieces has been clipped from the publication in which it appeared and pasted into the scrapbook without any indication of where the piece was published.

I am using the term "occasional piece" to describe most of Bachelor's published work saved in the scrapbook with due consideration. Most of the published items gathered in the scrapbook are akin to what might now be called op-ed pieces in newspapers. They fall somewhere between letters to the editor and essays proper. Even those pieces written *as* letters to a newspaper editor have the character of political, theological, or philosophical statements that go beyond anything that would today be considered appropriate for most letters sent to newspapers.

The scrapbook contains material in addition to Bachelor's published occasional pieces. Much of that additional material it appears likely he himself clipped and pasted into the scrapbook. There are, for instance, many newspaper clippings or clippings from magazines or journals about the freethought movement. As previously noted, there is also an ongoing series with snippets of Ingersoll's work, evidently drawing from the 1882 work *Ingersollia: Gems of Thought from the Lectures and Speeches of Col. Robert G. Ingersoll*, which some newspaper or journal appears to have been publishing bit by bit as a regular "Gems of Thought" column in the late 1880s and 1890s, and which Bachelor has clipped and saved.

A number of pages in the scrapbook contain pictures of freethinkers Bachelor admired. Several pages appear to have been clipped from a journal or newspaper that published a set of these engraved portraits under the heading "Four Hundred Years of Freethought." The pictures of freethinkers in this series and others Bachelor has collected in the scrapbook include Voltaire, Rousseau, Byron, Shelley, Hume, Goethe, George Elliot, John Stuart Mill, Robert Burns, and Mary Wollestonecraft.

Bachelor has also clipped and saved an engraved picture of Walt Whitman from some other source and has collected a number of Whitman's poems published in various places. The page that has Whitman's picture is artistically arranged with his poem "Come lovely and soothing death" beside it, with (among other items) a number of engravings on the theme of death and rest, a pansy clipped from a picture book, and a clipping from some source with the title "Pagan," followed by the statement, "The main object of the pagan philosophers was to dispel the terrors the imagination had cast around death, and by destroying this last cause of fear to secure the liberty of man." The citation is from William Edward Hartpole Lecky's *History of European Morals from Augustus to Charlemagne*.[129]

In all of the transcriptions of the work of Bachelor published here, I have faithfully preserved the original spelling, punctuation, and grammar, with the following exceptions. Where words or passages were not legible in the original (this is particularly the case with sections of the diary), I have noted the unclarities and *lacunae* by bracketing material that could not be read, and, when necessary, including explanatory notes about the original text. If the word or letters lost are fairly obvious from the context, I've placed in italicized text inside the brackets the word or portion of a word that appears to be missing. Bracketed words or portions of words that are not italicized represent additions to the text I have made (on very rare occasions) for the sake of clarity—for example, as when Bachelor writes in his 3 October 1870 diary entry that a place called Bee Bluff is eight miles from "whe" he lives, clearly meaning to write "where." Where Bachelor's orthography is unconventional, I have added non-italicized letters to emend the spelling only when it seemed clarity demanded the emendation.

There are two reasons that portions of words and whole words are missing from or unreadable in the diary. The first is that, as previously noted, the diary is now extremely fragile, and portions of the text have simply fallen away from the original and are no longer to be found. In several cases, pieces of pages have been torn away—notably in the Christmas Day 1890 diary entry in which Bachelor states that in the previous sixteen years (in which he has not written in the diary) he has become an avowed freethinker and explains the reason for his turn to freethought.

In other cases, portions of words or whole words cannot be read because the diary is tightly bound at its left margin, and some parts of the right margin of the diary have also fragmented over the years. The original is in such fragile condition that it would be very damaging to the document to unbind it and try to read the words obscured by the tight margins. So in transcribing the original, I have relied on both the scanned copy and the earlier photocopy, and have trusted my ability to piece together the whole word from the portion that is visible, using the context to make sense of the text.

The only substantial changes I've made as I've transcribed the original documents are the following. I have not preserved the uppercase format in which the titles of some of the occasional pieces appear in the original. These have been placed in capitals and lowercase letters, to conform to the usage of the other titles in the collection (and to contemporary usage). In texts (the diary, in particular) that fail to capitalize the word with which a sentence begins, I have also capitalized the word, noting the change from the lowercase of the original to the uppercase of the transcript by bracketing the first letter of the word. And where Bachelor ends a sentence with a comma instead of a period—a common habit of his, especially in the earlier portion of the diary— I have employed a period where it seems clearly warranted by the context.

And, finally, Bachelor tends to use the suffix "th" with *all* dates, where standard usage today would use "nd" and "st" with some dates: for example, the 10th, the 1st, and the 2nd. I have used the contemporary form when Bachelor writes 1th, 2th, and so on.

I have also not tried to reproduce the old form of medial or descending double "s" that Bachelor uses frequently throughout the diary, and which is often rendered in transcriptions as "fs" (e.g., "sucefs," "Tennefsee," etc.). Readers will also note that in other instances, he uses what is now considered British spelling of words—for example, "labour," "favour," or "centre." In the case of these usages, I have, of course, preserved the original spelling. In rare cases where Bachelor's spelling is seriously awry, especially in the occasional pieces, I have also added *sic* to note words I've faithfully transcribed, which might otherwise seem wrong to readers.

As observant readers will also note, there are a number of places at which the diary does not follow strict chronological order. Since Bachelor notes he had kept at least one previous diary, it appears he sometimes transcribed material from that previous document (and, in the case of some medical cases, from accounts he had written separately from the diary itself, per textual evidence embedded therein) into the diary. As he does so, he often inserts material out of chronological sequence. In other cases, it appears that he simply misrecorded certain dates.

In conclusion, my overriding objective in transcribing all of the original materials published here has been to be as faithful as possible to the original. Though the use of brackets and italicization of missing or partly missing text may appear cumbersome to some readers, my hope is that it will permit readers to approach these texts as closely as possible in the form in which they were originally composed and will allow them to appreciate the full flavor (Bachelor would undoubtedly say "flavour") of the original.

William D. Lindsey

1 March 1870 Diary Entry. *Courtesy Paula Jefferson, Riverside, CA.*

Diary of Wilson R. Bachelor (1870–1902)

A Voyage
March 1, 1870

I moved my family aboard [a] flat Boat[1] at Morris Landing[2] with another f[amily] and about 4 P.M. I bid adieu to my friends and the pine clad Hills of the Romantic Ten[nessee], unmoored and rowed out, and began to descend the stream; we stoped awhile in Bend Shoals to Receive[d] another family. [A]fter tarrying a sho[rt] time, and bidding adieu to some verry warm friends, we again Resumed our voy[age]. [A]fter Running about one hour, we again touched at Hamburg; to discharge some friends, again those painful farewells were Repeated, after which we committed ourselves, to the rather swollen waters [of] the Tennessee River. [T]he night passed rather gloomily: neither I, nor my wife, being ve[ry] well. [T]he night was clear ~~and~~ serene and beautiful. [A]nd we progressed Sple[ndidly]. [T]he wind which had been pretty high all day, had Subsided Shortly after dark [and] there was not a Ripple to disturb the tran[quil] waters. [A]nd the River Seemed to Sparkle between its banks like a vast cosmic repose.[3]

March 2nd [1870]

Morning came, brightening as the Sun rose directly out of the east before the Bow of our boat.[4] A pretty strong gale of wind came and continued to blow. [*Several?*] gentlemen took a canoe and out and went to the Chute, of <u>Beach Creek</u>[5] [*Is*]land, Expecting to find some wild geese [*and*] ducks, but saw none. [A]bout 5 P.M. we [*la*]nded just above old <u>Perryville,</u> and procured some firewood. [D]uring the evening of this day, two of the young men, went in a canoe gunning, and killed one duck and one Squirrel, I ate the Squirrel for Sup[*per*].[6] [I]t is now about 8 P.M.[,] the wind has nearly ceased, and we are being Rapidly bourn along on the buoyant bosom of old Tennessee. [A]bout 11th o'clock I was awoke by efforts being made to land, in which [*page torn*] <u>Britts Landing</u>,[7] here we remained until [*page torn: next?*] morning.

MARCH 3RD [1870]

This morning was quite gloomy, [*a*]nd drizzly. [H]owever we were Soon drifting downwards. Several little hunting [*exp*]editions along the Shore were indulged [*page torn: in?*], but were <u>attended</u> with no Success, [*page torn: in?*] one I participated, I visited the mouth [*of*] Duck River,[8] and shot the fatest and [*lar*]gest Squirrel, I have [*ever*] seen.[9] [*We arrived in?*] Johnsonville[10] about 1 P.M. [*page torn*] went up into Town, [*page torn*] for the purpose of buying [*page torn*] and also, to avail myself [*of the services?*] of a Barber. I found one but like Romeo's [*top right corner of page is missing*] Shop was destitute of everything that [*page torn*] a Barber. I entered cold and wet; [*there*] was no place to hang my hat and Shall,[11] [*so?*] I hung them on the door, which stood ajar. [T]he furniture of the Room, consisted in one half broken down chair, one disabled stool, two or three half grown negroes and white Boys came in a[nd] stood apparently amazed at the tragedy about to be enacted.

My colored professional friend,[12] Soon procured Some cold water, and commenced Operation; as soon as this unpleasant business was over, I Returned by the Depot back to the Boat. [T]his place was build up, during the war, and is a small dirty little place, with a few business houses and a depot. [I]t has a meagre and dilapidated appearance.

[T]hough to resume my narrative; we ag[*ain*] took in our cable, and moved out. [A]f[*ter*] running about 5 miles, the rain begin[*ning*] to fall in torrents, and night comming on, we thought best to land, which we did and procured fire-wood; the night, thus fare, has Rendered [*us?*] uncomfortable, for it has Rained [*bottom right corner of page is torn: incessantly?*], ever since before dark, and the boat, I find, leaks verry much. [*It is*] now midnight, I have taken a [*page torn: short?*] nap, but am now up now writing [*page torn: as rain?*] is Still falling; all besides me [*page torn: sleeping?*]. Some, are lying on Beadsteads [*page torn: some on?*] bunks, Some on pallets. [*The?*] fire on the hearth, is gradually dying [*away?*]. [A] couple of lazy pups, are lying before the fire on the hearth, while a [*s*]mall Spaniel, is dozing ~~with~~ with his head against the jam:[13] and I am getting tired of writing, So, good night.

MARCH 4TH [1870]

This morning the rain has ceased though, it is Still cloudy. [W]e turned loose about daybreak, and arrived at Danville[14] about 10 A.M., where we Stopped about 30 minutes, after which, we continued our course down the river; we have not progressed today So Splendidly, as we have had to contend with the waves and wind, the water being quite tumultuous. [N]othing occured to day of Interest. Some little hunting along the Shore, but without

Success. [T]he only thing killed was a Small waterfowl by myself. [T]o night we are tied [*up?*] to Some willows 20 yards from the Shore [*torn*] miles below Paris Landing,[15] on the west Side of the River. [I]t is now about 9 P.M. [A]ll have Retired, Excepting I, and my wife,[16] and while I am writing She is Sewing, and I feel [*like?*] retiring myself.

MARCH 5TH [1870]

[A]t 3 A.M. this morning we turned [*bottom left corner of page is torn: loose?*] and made a Splendid Days run, [*page torn*]. [W]e had much oaring to do in conse[*quence*] of a pretty Strong East wind, which [*page torn: blew?*] incessantly, on our Starboard, thus [*page torn*] us continually towards the Shore [*page torn*]. [W]e kept out and run about 40 m. [*page torn*] at Birmingham[17] at 3 P.M. [*page torn*] about one hour, hindren in cable, and were again gliding Rapidly. [W]e landed 6 miles below Birmingham at 27 mile Island, and again Supplied [*ourselves*] with firewood. As the sun went do[*wn*] it become cloudy, and we did not think it proper to run, So we have Remained to the present hour. [N]othing has occured [*to*]day worthy of note, Some of the crew have been hunting along Shore all day, [*but?*] killed nothing Excepting Some Squirrels. [*Sin*]ce I have commenced writing, distant thunders begin to mutter, and the pattering [*of*] drops of rain on the roof of the boat, announce, the approach of a heavy rain and perhaps wind. I have slept 4 hours to night and arose, and, am now writing, at 3 oclock in the morning, while all [*are*] buried in Slumber.

MARCH 6TH [1870]

[W]e unmoored early this morning, [*as?*] the rain was falling, and a pretty brisk gale blowing from the North; however, we Continued to run untill 2 P.M. and when within about 5 miles of Paducah,[18] we met wind in Such force, we were Compelled to land, which we did on the North [*Side of*] the River; and Spent the evening in [*bottom right corner of page torn: gathering?*] hickory nuts,[19] and getting firewood. [T]he hickory nut trees, a great many of them [*are*] Still full of nuts, altho so late in [*the*] Season; it is now, while I am writing, [*page torn*] oclock at night (an[d] Such a night) it [*bottom right corner torn: is?*] verry dark and the wind is Exceed[*ingly hi*]gh, the tumult of angry waters [*top left corner of page torn: tossed?*] in every direction; the Boat reels and trembles, the groanings of the forest [*m*]ay be heard, mingled with the mad roar [*o*]f the waves, as they lash the Shore. [T]he weather is Rapidly turning colder, and altho, the night is so gloomy, nature warns me to ~~take~~ take Repose; So I cease writing and retire.

MARCH 7TH [1870]

[T]his morning the thermometer was [*left margin of page torn: number is missing*] below zero, and the wind Still blowing from the north, and the waves running verry high.[20] [*At?*] about 8 A.M., the wind Stronger, and the waves exceedingly violent, So we could not leave the Shore with the Boat; however, I borrowed a good Skiff, and took 4 of the crew and went to Paducah; I returned late in the evening, Since dark, the wind has ceased, and all have retired excepting Myself, and now I retire.

MARCH 8TH [1870]

[T]his morning quite cold, Thermometer below zero, just at daybreak, we quietly untied our cable and, rowed out into the current. [T]he wind soon rose pretty high, however we kept on to Paducah. [W]e had Some cotton aboard which we had drayed up to the warehouse and [*bottom left corner of page torn: sold?*] at a verry low price.[21] [A]fter remaining in [*Pad*]ucah about 5 hours, and purchasing Such [*supplies*] as we needed, we departed, passed Metropolis[22] [*about*] dark and have landed on the South side [*of the*] River I Should Suppose about 25 miles [*west of?*] Paducah. I am alone writing, all have [*retired*] to their lodgins; this is a verry clear and still night and I anticipate a good day run tomorrow.

MARCH 9TH [1870]

[T]urned loose this morning, run about 10 miles, wind still blowing, changed [*to*] the west.[23] [W]e were compelled to land, which [*we*] did on the Kentucky Side. [T]he crew jinerally [*w*]ent hunting. [W]e lay here untill night, the wind ceasing a little, we unloosed, run down just below <u>Mound City</u>, and landed in Sight of Cairo.[24] [O]wing to so much windy weather, and other causes, Some of the crew become much dissatisfied, and after a general cons[*ulta*]tion it was decided to take a Steamboat at <u>Cairo</u>. [A]ctive preparations are now going on for our embarcation tomorrow.

MARCH 10TH [1870]

This morning, a violent gale, is blowing from the west; we dropped down erly to <u>Cairo</u>, two miles above the warf; I went down to the City, to sell our Boat, and ascertain when we could get a boat. I went to the news office, got a Cairo Paper, which reported, the <u>Steamer City of Cairo</u>, du[*e*] at 5 P.M. [A]fter a tiresome walk of 4 mi[*les*], I Returned, boxed up our effects, and prepared for our departure. [E]mployed Drays, and arrived at the warf at dark, the <u>City of [*Cairo; bottom right corner torn*]</u> did not arrive, but the <u>Saint Luke</u>,[25] w[*as*] ready to depart for <u>Memphis</u>, So we [*got*] aboard of her, She left about midnight [*and?*] we were Soon plowing the turbid waters of the majestic Mississippi.

MARCH 11TH [1870]

This morning, the wind is bl[*owing*] fearfully causing us to have to [*wait?*].

[*MAR*]CH 12TH [1870]

[T]his morning, we arrived in sight [*of*] Memphis, and was soon lying at the warf. [B]ut soon learned with no Small degree of Mortification, that no Arkansas Boat would leave untill Monday 5 P.M., this being Saturday.[26]

MARCH THE 13TH [1870]

During last night, I was violently attacted, with <u>Cholera Morbus</u>,[27] and confined to my room 24 hours; with great thirst and considerable Fever.

MARCH 14TH [1870]

[T]his morning, I took Some little nourishment, got up, and dressed and went up into the City;[28] visited the Barber, and am now writing at 2 P.M.

MARCH 15TH [1870]

[T]he <u>Thomas Allen</u>,[29] The <u>Memphis and Little Rock</u> Packet, on which we were aboard, did not depart at 5 P.M. but at 7 P.M. and Shortly after we left the warf, there came on a fearful Storm; and heavy rain. [T]he lightnings flashed, the thunders growled, [*th*]e rain fell in torrents, the old father of waters suddenly become frightfully angry. [T]he crested waves, fearfully menacing our frail Craft; the wind Seemed to increase [*in*] violence, and during the livelong night [*threa*]tened our destruction. [S]o terrible was [*bottom left corner of page torn: the?*] wind and waves during the night, that even the old and tried officers of the [*Bo*]at were alarmed and Spoke of doubts [*of the?*] issues.

MORNING OF THE 15TH OF MARCH [1870]

finally [*came?*], and there was quite a change in the atmosphere, a slight snow had fallen du[*ring*] the night, however, the Sun rose and Shin[*ed*] beautifully, though the wind and waves sti[*ll*] continued. [T]he Captain, considers it dangerous to run[.] [W]e landed at 12 oclock on the Arkansas Side about 40 miles from Napoleon,[30] and 150 miles from Memphis. I am sloly recuperating, I have remained up day untill this present hour, which is now 2 P.M. Nothing has transpired Since the last writing. [T]he wind and waves are yet violent, not having lost any of their fury; [w]e are still lying at the same landing, and will remain here the Captain says untill the wind somewhat Subsides. I am now sitting by the Stove, while the passengers are passing of the time in various ways, are Reading Newspapers, Some are playing Cards; Some in Social converse, my family are all in their room and I am now going to Join them.

MARCH 16TH [1870] 7 P.M.

[W]e are now under way as [*bottom right of page missing: we are*?] wending the Arkansas River. [B]ut I Return [*to*] my last writing; about 9 oclock last evening the wind Seemed to abate a little, we soon moved off, we arrived at the mouth o[*f the*] White River[31] about midnight and this m[*orning*] we are advancing towards our point of destination, wind continues high. [T]he Arkansas River, as Seen from the [*boat*?] is exceedingly crooked, with numerous Sandbars,[32] and, Snaggy bends. [W]e are [*now I*] suppose about 80 miles from Pine Bl[*uff and*] 160 miles from Little Rock.

MARCH 17TH [1870]

was fair and beautiful but pretty cold; morning found us, within 18 miles of Pine Bluff,[33] at which place, we arrived about 10 A.M. [A]fter discharging some freight,[34] we again proceeded, Soon afterwards took a Barge in tow, loaded with a Locomotive[35] and some Boxes, to be carried to Little Rock. [I]t is now 8 oclock at night, and the Pilot informs me, that we are 75 miles from Little Rock.

MARCH 18TH [1870]

[W]e arrived at the Rock,[36] yesterday at 2 P.M., here we found the Fort Gibson[37] destined for Fort Smith, we were Soon aboard of her, however, She did not Start till after dark, we are now under way; the first Tuesd[*ay*] [*word missing*] the first Rock seen on the River was at Little Rock. It is now midnight, and I am quite unwell, with derangement of the Bowels, just having took[38] a dose of Laudanum.[39]

SUNDAY MORNING, 9 A.M. MARCH 20TH [1870]

Yesterday we passed some Sublime Scenery; Some mountains, bounding the River, almost [*en*]tirely destitute of vegetation, the Rocks had a [*b*]lackish appearance, and dipted, towards [*left corner of page missing: the*] South.[40] Some of those rocks Seemed [*to*] be much disintegrated,[41] Some dwarfish [*ce*]dars, growing on their Summits.

[W]e run all night last night excepting [*a*] few hours early in the night, waiting on the moon to rise. [Th]is morning, while [*I*] am writing, we are under way, and [*to*]wing a Barge. [W]ith Reference to the [*top right corner of page torn: topic?*] of distances, I see we are 110 miles from <u>Little Rock</u>, and having left there 36 hours ago, we are Still 85 or 90 miles from <u>Ozark</u>, [*ou*]r point of distination.[42]

12 oclock, we have just left Dardanelle,[43] at which place we landed, and put off freight just below Dardanelle, the <u>Magazine Mountain</u>[44] rears its huge form in the distance, and just above Dardanelle a high and picturesque Rock[45] looks frowningly down on the River.

MONDAY, MARCH 21ST [1870] 2 P.M.

[W]e are now lying on a sandbar, we ran all night last night, and this morning we run run [*sic*] aground in Sight of a Landing called <u>Patterson Bluff</u>.[46]

TUESDAY MORNING, MARCH 22 [1870]

[W]e have arrived at Ozark at last,[47] we Succeeded in getting of[f] the Sandbar yesterday at 4 P.M. and run through the night[,] at North Ozark at 3 A.M. discharged Some freight, crossed over to South Ozark, where we got ashore at 4 A.M. We build a fire, it being pretty cold, had breakfast Soon, I

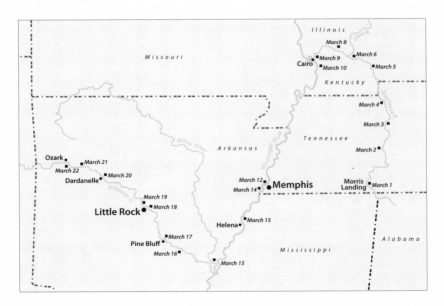

The route of the Bachelor family's migration from Tennessee to Arkansas. *Cartography by T. R. Paradise.*

borrowed a horse and rode out to procure Some Shelter, for a hut, one mile from Ozark.[48]

WEDNESDAY, MARCH 23RD [1870]

Moved out to [*bottom right corner of page missing: the*] place mentioned at last writing was quite Sick last night, I have taken cold from [*ex*]posure, and also have derangement of Stomach and Bowels, as soon as I am able to ride I shall go in search of a location.

[APRI]L THE 3RD [1870]

[A]fter riding for Several days [*I*] have at last Succeeded in procuring [*a*] Small cottage and 8 acres of land.[49]

OCT 3RD [1870]

[T]o day I Shot the first Deer I ever did,[50] killing it instantly; from the 3rd of April, untill to day I have made no record,[51] it is sufficient to Say, that I have killed time the best I could; I think I and my two Sons,[52] have killed 500 Squirrels; mostly the Fox Squirrel[53] variety; we have all had more or less Sickness,[54] my wife having been indisposed almost during the whole Six month; being confined during that time giving Birth to a Son.[55] I will briefly mention a few of the most important reminisicens.—

I visited Fort Smith in the Spring,[56] found it rather a meagre place, or at least not according to my expectations, however there Seemed to be a good deal of business and trade going on, judging from the number of Wagons, I Saw mooving in different directions.

Ozark, the County Cite of Franklin and my Postoffice, is Situated on the north [*side*] of the Arkansas River 40 miles below Fort Smith, and commands, quite an extensive [*bottom left corner of page torn*], and is being rapidly rebuild, as it [*was*] entirely devastated, during the war. It contains Several Stores, Saloons, and on[*e w*]eekly newspaper, is published there.[57] [B]ut to [*re*]turn from my digression,—I have Killed [*ti*]me, the best I could; Shooting Squirrels, untill [*I*] am fatigued, then return home, instruct my children[58] in writing and Arithmetic, rea[*ding*] Wood Practice of Medicine,[59] Bronson's System of elo-cution,[60] or some work on Geo[*graphy*], now try to Sketch a little, then practice the Guitar.[61] My professional Services not being called into requisition untill the latter part of Summer.[62] My associates have been my Books, as the people here don't Seem to be interested in what I do; so I can have no intellectual Recreation with them.[63] [T]here has been nothing to animate, amuse, or instruct; Sometimes I, and my Sons make an excursion to the Arkansas River;[64]

where from an elevated position of 400 feet, the Scenery is verry beautiful. [T]o the North across the River, rises fare in the distance, mountains piled on mountains, running back to the Boston ran[ge].[65] One Sabbath, we visited I believe on the 12th of June a place called the <u>Bee Bluff</u>.[66] [T]he place is about 8 miles of whe[re] I live and within 4 miles of Ozark, an elevated ridge approaches the South bank of the Arkansas River, I suppose its height, from the water to its Summit, to Some 700, or 800, feet, about 140 feet of [*its*] summit is precipatous, Craggy rocks pr[*ojecting*] fare over their base, like grimvasaged Sentinels looking down on the waters below.

The Scenery from the Summit of this mountain [*is*] grand, beautiful, and Sublime. [D]irectly across the River, as fare as the eye can reach, mountains rise on mountains untill the horizon closes the view.

[*To*] the east, which is here down the River, you again have another beautiful view, mountains rising majestically in the distance.

[T]he Little village of Ozark can almost be seen to the west, which is up the River, the Scene truly Sublime; a deep ravine fare below, [*with*] a luxuriant foliage; far beyond this, Some cornfields can be Seen with cottages; and you can here trace the River for Several mi[*les*] as it reposes between its verdant banks ~~like a vast serpent in repose~~ and its waters Seem to lave the base of the picturesque rocks of the Summit. [W]e decended [*and*] went round under those overhanging rocks, found about 80 feet of rock, next to the summit red Sandstone, next, a strata of grayish limestone, resting on grayish Shale, under which was a vain of coal; which I traced for 800 feet.[67] [B]eneath this coal, was a vast amount of blackish Shale, which probably Extends far towards the base of the mountain.

I procured Some of the coal, which has a fine glossy appearance, and looks as if [*it*] contained a large percentage of Carbon. [*How*]ever, I did not analyze it.[68]

I also found in the crevices of the Rocks [*an ab*]undance of Saltpetre, I procured one [*s*]ingle piece, weighing 4 oz.—

I shall now pass on to 1871, I have not kept [*a*] regular Diary, but have noted Some cases [*w*]hich I shall now put into this Diary; though I [*h*]ad one case in 1870 which I transfer,[69] a case of gun shot wounds.[70]

[Oc]t. 9 1870

[V]isited a man to day who had been waylaid, and Shot, with Buckshot, Several Shot grazing him, but only two. [O]ne Shot entered the Biceps muscle, of the right arm, and passing under a portion of that muscle, and then passing through the Triceps muscle, and resting against the skin. [T]he Humerus, was not fractured,

[T]he other Shot, entered his neck on the right Side, a little posterious to the Carotid, artery, and just behind its bifurcation; passing through the root of the tongue, and Phaynx, and lodging, in the left <u>Sternomastoid</u> muscle; and this Shot was deeply buried in the muscle, rendering its extraction dangerous. [T]here was verry little Bleeding attending either of the wounds.

Symptoms, deglutition verry difficult, ordered cold water dressings, gave an opiate.[71]

[O]CT. 10TH [1870]

[V]isited him to day, found his arm and neck, considerbly Swollen, deglutition Still difficult; but no worse, left a Saline Cathartic if he can Swallow it. [O]rdered cold water dressings continued, also orde[red] him to take Some gruel occasionally wh[en] he could Swallow, an[d] enjoined perfect quiet.

WEDNESDAY, OCT. 12TH [1870]

[V]isited him to day, find him doing well, wounds Suppurating free[ly], deglutition much improved, takes nourishment without much difficulty, though he has had no action on his bowels yet.[72]

[Ord]ered Epsome Salts in Solution to be given every 2 hours, untill his bowels act freely; ordered his diet to be a little more generous, but Still of a fluid nature.

OCT. 14TH [1870]

[V]isited him again to day, found him doing well; both wounds much better. [O]rdered wounds dressed with Simple Cerate;[73] consider him out of danger.

A CASE OF PUNCTURE & LACERATION
JANUARY 8TH 1871

Sent for to day in great ha[ste] to see a Boy, aged Some ten years who had be[en] hooked by an Oxen.— [T]he horn, entering the <u>Atrehens Auren</u>[74] muscle, passing down deep into the maseter[75] muscle, dividing and lacerating in its course the <u>temporal Artery</u>, and veins. [W]hen I arrived, I found him bleeding profusely, I immediately dr[ew] together the edges of the wound, it requiring five Stitches, then put on Some adhesive plaster, with a bandage, this arrested t[he] flow of Blood. Ordered cold water dres[sings] and enjoined quietude; a dose of <u>Morphine</u> to be taken at night.[76]

JANUARY 9TH [1871]

Visited my Patient [to] day, found him quiet, having Slept well [th]rough the night, though the wound bled Some little through the night. [H]ad an action on his bowels this morning, ordered Some nourishments, and the cold water applications to be continued, left an opiate, to be taken at night. Pulse 80 and quite compressable.

JANUARY 10TH [1871]

[F]ound my patient [*to*] day doing well, had rested well through [*the*] night, Bowels also having acted, wound doing well, cut, and took out the Stitches, dressed it with Simple cerate, it is Suppurating. [C]onsider him Safe.

CASE OF MIDWIFERY[77]
JANUARY 29TH 1871

[C]alled to day, to attend a Lady in childbirth, She is the mother of Several children, her age somewhere above 30 years, her health quite robust. She informed me She had been verry well, during the period of uterogestation. [L]abour advanced properly, altho the <u>Amniotic</u> fluid had escaped before I arrived. She was in due time delivered of a verry large healthy looking child. [T]he child however, had, two ulcers of the Size of ten cents each, on the top of its head, close together, these ulcers were verry red in the centre, with granular looking edges. [T]he mother knew of no cause that could have produced them Excepting, [*a*]s She expressed, that there was a child in the family, which had a verry sore head [*a*]t which she Said "I always Shuddered when I looked" —the child died in 8 days.[78] I think from Cerebral conjestion.[79]

MARCH 19TH 1871

To day I move to my homestead, the Chim[*ney*] is no higher than the mantlepiece; it is the Sabbath day, I find our house verry uncomf[*ortable*]. So, necessity Seems to justify us, using means to render ourselves more comfortable, by tightening our house, the wind is blowing quite chilly.[80]

MARCH 20TH [1871]

Still improving our house, and also gardening; to day I have been verry unwell, have taken cold.[81]

MARCH 21ST [1871]

I have just returned home, 11A.M., stupid, and drowsy, from a professional call I had last night.[82] [I]t being one of those kind of calls, where the professional capacities of the <u>Practitioner</u>, are immediately brought into requisition, for a limited time; case results favourbly, W. R. Bachelor

Wilson R. Bachelor Family House, Pauline, Arkansas. *Courtesy Linda Anderson Silvey, Antlers, OK.*

A Case of Puerperal Convulsions
May [i.e., March] the 22nd [1871][83]

Call to day, to visit Mrs. B, found her in the incipient pain of Parturition; She is a Primipera[84] about 17 years of age, and Sufficiently robust, and having enjoyed good health, up to her confinement. [U]pon examination, I found the Os uteri a little dilated, though I thought, the parts a little rigid, in three hours after I arrived, labour was getting verry strong, She about this time complained of blindness, and all her anxiety, Seemed to Subside, and in the intervals of rest partially comatose. [H]owever, labor continued properly, and in due time, she was delivered of a medium Sized healthy child, but now come the trouble; for just precisely at the instant the child was borned, She was fearfully convulsed. [A]s soon as the convultion left her, I delivered the Placenta without any trouble, and I observed, there was not a particle of Hemorrhage. [I]n about 15 minutes another severe [a]nd protracted convultion, she now had them every 15 or 20 minutes, there Recurrence, being almost uniformly regular. [T]he first remedial agent I resorted [to] was chloroform, which I used both internal[ly a]nd by inhalations, but without any apparent effect.

[Since?] there was no Hemorrhage, I resorted to venesection, [and] opened a vein in her left arm, it did not bleed well[.][85] I also opened a vein in her other a[*rm*], making a larger orifice. [A]bstracted about 18 oz. Of Blood. [T]he next Paroxysm, after bleeding, was fully one hour and I indulged a hope that the convulsions were arresti[*ng*], but they returned with just about the Same intervals [*of*] 15 or 20 minutes. [T]he only good I saw that resul[*ted*] from venesection was, the Paroxysm[s] wer[e] not so violent, and there was not so much <u>vascular turgescence</u> about the face. [T]hese convulsions were of a verry alarming character, they lasted five minutes, every voluntary muscle of body was ridgidly contracted, lips bluish[,] face turgid and flushed, carotids much distended, frothy mucus issuing from the mouth, in the intervals between the Paroxysms, She lay in profound <u>Coma</u>; breath Stertorous, rattling in the throat, pulse frequent and compressible, 130 to the minute. Convulsions continued till after dark, She have been delivered about 12 oclock in the day, I still used [*and*] administered <u>Anaesthetics</u>, but without Success[.] I again opened one of the orifices in one of the Arms, took 10 oz. More of Blood, Convulsions continued.— [A]bout 11 oclock in the night She had all the appearance, that She could not survive much longer. [A]t this time the face and neck were enormously emphysematous, prod[*uced*] I suppose by some Solution of Continuity of some of the air cells; deglutition had entirely [*word illegible due to margins*], respirations hurried, Pulse, exceedingly frequ[*ent*] and thready. [A] most distressing rattling in the throat and lungs, with bloody froth issuing from the mouth,—about midnight, the Convul[*sions*] ceased, and she lay in a perfect uncons[*cious*] stupor, apparently in the last struggle [*of n*]ature. I had her taken up and bathed [*in a ho*]gshead of tepid water, then wiped of[*f*] dry and put back to bead, I then Shaved the back of her head and applyed a blister.[86] I also used friction [*of*] the spine with a preparation, of Brandy Capsicum and Turpentine. [T]his was morning; I went home but visited her the same evening. I found her face, neck and chest w[h]ile emphysematous, She could Swallow a little water. [B]lister done well, Pulse verry frequent, and quite feeble Respiration[,] better but Still hurried. Verry restless and perfectly unconscious. [*I*] give her a dose of <u>Morphine</u>, ordered her kept quiet, visited her next day, fo[u]nd She had rested well during the night, found her on arriving quiet, though with some Fever, Pulse fuller and less frequent but tense abdomen, <u>Tympanitic</u>, still perfectly unconscious. [I] give her a mercurial Carthartic to be followed in 10 hours with oil & Turpentine, applied emolient poultices to the abdomen, also caused a tepid bland detergent preparation, to be thrown up the birthplace. [I] visited her next day, found her just Returning to consciousness, She had that morning, heard her child crying, and asked whose child it was, it was [*carried to?*] her, and She was told it was her child, She could not speak only in a whisper. She had not the Slightest remembrance, of anything that had passed after actual Strong labour commenced, She was greatly Surprised to find her hair cut off and her arms sore from venesection[.] [H]er Symptoms were all better, ordered nourishments, of which she had been jenerously allowed before.

A Case of Dificult Labour from My Diary of 1869
December 31st 1869

Sent for in great haste at [?] o'clock in the morning, to visit a lady, Mrs. L. who before I arrived had given birth to one Child, she being with twins. I was informed that She had been in labour about 10 hours, and had given birth to a child about 5 hours before I was called in. Upon examination I found the Os uteri Somewhat dilated and Soft, the Child occupying the Superior strait, and so firmly impacted that all my efforts at turning were unavailing.

Upon inquiry I found that after the birth of the first Child, the midwife had kept her on what they call the "lap" until I arrived, which was about five hours.

And what with this Sitting position, and the escaping of the amniotic fluid, and also a preternatural presentation, it was So firmly impacted I could not move it. At this time I was perfectly aware the child did not present properly but I could not [a]scertain precisely, what kind of presentation it was.

Her labour was Slow, and continued to get weaker. However, after Waiting awhile I gave her Some Ergot,[87] which had the effect of raising [he]r labour.

Believing it to be a difficult case of la[bour], I sent for a professional gentleman who lived nearby. The child continued to advance, though verry slowly, until it enga[ged] under the pubes.

About this time, I discovered, it was a Sho[ulder] presentation which was a disclosure that [we] were ill Prepared for: as neither I, nor my friend in consultation, had neither forceps nor crotchet;[88] and as for Spontaneous evolu[tion], it looked like A matter of impossability. However I prepared to do the best I could, under The Circumstances.

I had a strong fillet[89] ready, and wanting for a chance to do Something. Slowly, and w[ith] greate tediousness the child Seemed to Sink deeper under the Pubes, rise a little, then remain fixed. The child being dead, I made use of [my] right hand forefinger like a hook, and by laborious and painful efforts, finally detached the arm an[d s]capula. I then forced an opning into the ca[vity?] at the Same time by almost Superhuman effort, forced an opening on the other Side, with the forefinger of the left hand. Now, I attempted, to pass the fil[let] through this aperture, but I found this, the most diff[icult] job of all, though I untireingly persisted in my ef[forts]. [A]bout dark succeeded; my assistant now draw[ing] on the chord, while I with a knife divided the Sp[ine?] then introducing my hand, took out the thoracic and abdominal vicera, which caused the collapse of [*the*] body of the child, So I was enabled to take it away. The woman was greatly exhausted, though she had bourn this fearful ordeal with incredable fortit[*ude*]. I had Stimulated her through the day, but for the last three hours she appeared Stupid.

I delivered The placenta, give her an opiate, ordered Silence and rest, She died next day.

W. R. Bachelor

A CASE OF DIFACULT LABOUR
MARCH 25TH 1871

[C]alled last night, to visit a Lady Mrs. E. a Primipera, aged about 17 years, whom I found in incipient labour. [U]pon examination, I found the <u>uterus</u> Slightly dilated, I also found a very narrow pelvis.

Labour, came on rather sloly, but soon the membranes were ruptured, and I found a breech presentation.

I made some attemps turning, but on the account of the narrowness of the pelvis, I found I could not succeed. The breach had now, entered the inferior Strait; and her labour, which had been rather lingering all the while, now Seemed to Subside. I gave her a Scruple of ergot, and in a short time labour came on again, and for the Space of two hours the child had only yet engaged under the pubes.

Labour now, was not so Strong, and I conf[*ess*] I could not but feel a little anxious. Trusting as I was to a Spontaneous evolution of the child, I begin to fear exhaustion.

I concluded, to try the fillet, and after much effort, in consequence of the narrowness of the pelvis, and the breach being greatly impacted, I Succeeded in introducing through the groins of the child. I now encouraged the woman, giving her Some assistance each pain [*and*] in a short time, I had the Satisfaction of Seeing her delivered, of a living boy, and its Scrotum was enormously swollen, blackish and almost callous.

However, the organs of generation, Soon assumed their natural Size. The placenta easily came away, and the woman Soon was able to attend to her domestic concer[*ns*], but she Soon fell into an hysterical con[*dition*] which lasted three months.[90]

She fancied a great many things, and Especially, that She was going to die. Treated her for chronic inflammation of the uterus. Tonics, and a change of Scenes and associations restored her to health.[91]

ABORTION
APRIL 22ND 1871[92]

Called last night to attend a lady Mrs. H——. whom I had been attending [*for*] the last two weeks, I found her in the incipient pains of premature Parturition. I [*h*]ad succeeded in preventing this untill now. I had enjoined rest, administered Opiates, and bracing Tonics, but from weakness of the organs and a predisposition to abortion, nature now, seemed determined to Expell the uterine contents.

[F]or her labour continued to advance[,] notwithstanding, I gave her large doses of Opiates and in 6 hours She was delivered of a child. She was about five months advanced; the child lived about 10 minutes.

[A] generous diet, and a tonic treatment, soon restored her to health.

DIARY
EVENTS, AND A RETROSPECTIVE VIEW
MARCH 1ST 1873

It is now about 4 P.M. [O]n this day, an[*d*] about this hour, 3 years ago I bid adie[*u*] to Tennessee, my native State, and come to Arkansas.[93] [T]o day finds me on <u>Mill Creek</u> <u>Ark.</u>—where I have resided, ever since I have be[*en*] in the state.[94] [O]n taking a retrospective v[*iew*] of what has transpired in this brief la[*pse*] of time; I find vicissitude, car[*e*]s, anxie[*ties*], toils and pains; but time has been on [*the*] wing and is bearing us, Swiftly to th[*e*] bourn, from whence no traveller ret[*urns*].[95] [B]ut I pause, to ask myself the questi[*on*], what have I accomplished towards the improvement of myself and family, and amelioration of mankind, during the [*page torn: previous?*] three years. I hope, that I have [*f*]eebly contributed Something towards [*impr*]ovement of my own mind, and family. [H]owever, I have been Surrounded b[*y i*]nstances of a pecuniary,[96] which have ope[*rated a*]gainst me, in my aspirations and [*page torn: desires?*], which I trust have been praiseworthy.—I'm now in my office writing.—[97]

This morning I had a call; I visited a Lady [*page torn: who was?*] labouring under a catarrhal affect[*ion*]. Treatment, Expectant.[98] Stimulate the [*page torn: lungs?*] and trust to nature.

This evening a Gentleman came, for a [*page torn: case of?*] Intermittent Fever. Prescribed for him. [A]s it is, the third anniversary of our [*exo*]dus from our native and beloved State [*of Ten*]nessee, I think my wife is preparing a little different Supper from what we usually have, and now I am Summoned to Supper.[99]

MARCH 2ND [1873]
SUNDAY

I have remained at home [*to*] day with my honorable and Scientific friend [*and*] guest, <u>Professor Graham;</u>[100] we have Spent [*the*] day quite agreeably, reading Dickens and Harp[*er's Mon*]thly;[101] we also had so Splendid Guitar mu[*sic*].[102]

I have give several prescriptions to day for Catarrhal affections.[103] The people[104] call it [*e*]bizootie, but it is Catarrhal affection, with strong tendency to Eryesipelas,[105] and also, <u>Cerebro Spinal</u> <u>Meningitis</u>.

[*MA*]RCH 3RD [1873]

[I]t is now 9 P.M. I am alone in my [*page torn: office?*] writing. By reference, to my diary, I see [*that*] three years ago to night, at Midnight, I was [*on*] a moving boat decending the Tennessee [*Riv*]er. Well, to day I have been alone generally [*page torn: killing?*] time. Sometimes practicing on the Guitar. Prescribed, and issued medicine for one gentleman.[106]

[*MARC*]H 5TH [1873]

To day, I have had two calls, [*page torn, words missing*] a Lady, 8 months advanced in [*page torn: way to parturition?*], as she thinks. Found her with a lacinating[107] pain, in the left mam[*mary*]. [*Page torn, words missing*] pulse, Excited, Says she was taken [*page torn, words missing*] hill on yesterday. She has bronchial Expect[*oration*].

Treatment. I gave her a purgative to be followed in due time by an anodyne Diaphoretic.[108] There is a strong Epidemic predisposition to [*m*]alignant Erysipelas; I am fearful this is a case of <u>Erysipelatous Inflamation of the</u> <u>Pleura</u>.[109]

I shall visit her tomorrow.

[*MA*]RCH 6TH [1873]

[V]isited the sick Lady, I spoke of [*yes*]terday. She has give birth to a Small child. Her symptoms are more favour[*a*]ble, pain in the chest not so acute, but an obtuse pain [*be*]hind the right shoulder. Medicine acted well, [*has*] but little Fever this morning, and also perspiring. Pulse 100.—

Treatment. Anodyne Diaphoretics, and Stimulants.

MARCH 10TH [1873]

Went to Ozark to day. Circuit [*c*]ourt is in session.[110]

[*MA*]RCH 11TH [1873]

Still in Ozark. [W]as in consultation [*wi*]th Dr. Rutherford[111] in a case of a juror, [*w*]ho was taken violently Sick.
Prognosis, unfavourable. Severe pain, in the [*left?*] mamiary region, Pulse 135 beats, feeble [*and*] compressible. Respiration short, and Exp[*ectorating*] copiously, a bloody mucus, breath [*page torn, word missing*] fetid, tongue thickly coated, and [*page torn, words missing*] of the bowels.

MARCH 12TH [1873]

I left Ozark this [*page torn, words missing*].[112]

MARCH 13TH [1873]

To day, I visited the Same Sick Lady I Spoke of Some days ago.[113] I find her convalescent. Visited another Lady aged 18 years. She is quite a robust looking woman. She is the Mother of one child, and is at present between Six and Seven months Encient.[114] She has St. Vitus Dance.[115] All her right side is affected. Treatment. Gave her Iron by [*Hydrous*] and Bromide of Potassium.

I also to day visited a Gentleman, [*with*] Gonorrhea, he has a verry Sore Tumor in the Perinial region.[116]

MARCH 14TH [1873]

To day I visited a boy, who is [*sick*] with this catarrhal epidemic.[117]

MARCH 15TH [1873]

To day, I went to Ozark, 12 miles, and returned, a little before night. The gentlema[*n o*]n whose case I was in consultation died 5th day.[118] It is now about 9 P.M. I have just prescribed, and issued medicine, for a case of Intermittent Fever.[119] [F]eeling tired I retire.

SUNDAY, MARCH THE 16TH [1873]

I remained at home d[*uring*] the day; give out Some medicine, with Prescrip[*tions*]. Mrs. B. who has St. Vitus dance, is improving.[120]

[*MONDA*]Y, MARCH THE 17TH [1873]

I went to Ozark to day. [*page torn: Stayed at?*] Forest Hotel, practiced some on [*page torn, words missing*] the Drug store of Lotspeich & Rey[*nolds*] [*page torn, words missing*] night.[121]

[*T*]UESDAY, MARCH 18TH [1873]

[V]isited 2 patients to day [*word obscured*] Disease, abdominal Irritation, an enlarged [*visc*]era. Treatment. Deobstruents, and tonics. [*In the*] other Case, a Lady with <u>Chronic Intermittent</u> fever. Treatment. Antiperiodics and tonics.[122]

MARCH 20TH [1873]

I and my wife road out five miles [*to*] day, to See, some old acquaintances, who are just from Tennessee,[123] of course, we had a great many questions to ask, ~~in the Faderland~~ about our friends in the Faderland.[124] We passed [*qu*]ite an agreeable day, and returned home at [*n*]ight. I found two Gentlemen waiting for me, [*b*]oth wanting Medicine. Prescribed, and issued [*m*]edicine for both.

TUESDAY [*SIC*], MARCH 21ST [1873]

Visited a patient to day, a Lady, She is labouring, under an attact of [*hy*]steritis. I made an Examination with the <u>speculum</u>. [*I*] find Schirrous tumors around the <u>os uteri</u>, [*wi*]th chronic inflamation.[125]

This Evening, Professor Graham is my guest; again we passed quite an agreeable evening. The Profes[*sor*] elucidating some points, touching, the refraction [*of*] light.[126] He also, read, two Splendid Articles [*f*]rom Harpers Monthly, one, <u>Earth & Air</u>,[127] the other, <u>The New Magdalen</u>.[128] After which we had Guitar music, and Singing.

SATURDAY MARCH 22ND [1873]

This day three years ago, I [*la*]nded at South Ozark from Tennessee. [*To*] day, I have remained at home. Prescribed for one. Practiced on the Guitar, and read a portion, of <u>Child Harold</u>.[129]

MARCH THE 4TH 1873
A CASE OF APOPLEXY

Sent for last night, in great haste, to Visit a [*lady*] who the mesenger said had fallen down in [*a*] Fit. When I reach the place, She was dead. The Stroke must have been Severe, for she was a young Lady, in good health, the mother of [*two*] children. The attact, was almost instantly fatal. I could do nothing when I arrived [*but*] close her Eyes, and sympathize with her Hus[*band*] with his two little motherless children.

A CASE OF OBSTETRICKS
FEBRUARY THE 27TH 1873[130]

[*I vi*]sited last night about midnight, a Lady who I [*fo*]und in labour. This Lady Mrs. T—. is over [*number obscured by margins*] years of age, and is the mother of 12 children. [*He*]r health during uterogestation has been [*ra*]ther feeble, near her confinement, her feet and [*l*]egs, become quite edamatous. In about six [*ho*]urs after I saw her, She was delivered of a large [*he*]althy looking child. Hemorrhage came on rather [*pr*]ofuse; I immediately made an attempt to delive[*r the*] placenta, but found it Stubbornly retentive. A little further Examination, revealed, the fact, that I had a case of hourglass contraction of the uterus, to contend with.[131] I oiled well my hand and introduced it without much difficulty into [*the*] uterus, finding some little resistance at the [*os*] uteri, which however, was easily overcome. I found the placenta incarcerated, the uterus [*wa*]s entirely contracted, as if a ligature had been applied round its Centre. Following, the umbili[*cal*] with my index finger, and having reached the [*pa*]rt contracted, I made a persestent effort to dilate [*the*] contracted part, and did Succeed after Some time in introducing one finger. Hemorrhage [*n*]ow came on profusely, and She Seemed more exhausted and despondent, and I thought it [*p*]rudent, to let her rest a little, which I did [*a*]nd gave her toddy,[132] also an astringent with an [*a*]nodyne. Hemorrhage continued, Pulse become [*ve*]rry frequent and feeble, amounting to 140 [*page torn: beats*] the minute, and she evidenced a disposition to Faint, upon the least effort. After letting [*her*] rest awhile, I explained to her the necessity [*of*] delivering the placenta, giving her all the encouragement possible. She being a little inc[*lined*] to despondency rather backward in consenting [*word obscured*] finally, she yielded. I again as before, intro[*duced*] my hand, and following the cord, soon came [*to*] an aperture, through which the cord passed, [*but*] the contraction here was apparently as firm as [*and*] compressed by a ligature.

My hand was now fully introduced, and [*I*] made decided, and persistent efforts to introdu[*ce*] the forefinger of my right hand, which I at l[*ast*] accomplished. I then attempted the intro[*duction*] of one more finger, in which I Succeeded on[*ce*] after much manipulation and perseverance, but I could make no further progress. [*I*] could feel the placenta which seemed to be in part, or wholy detached.

Making use of my finger as a crotchet, I buried [*it*] into the placental mass, at the same time draw[*ing*] firmly, hoping the uterus would change [*its*] abnormal, and I may almost say its [*unusual*] contraction, but the only thing that I accomp[*lished*] was lacerating the placenta.

The patient now complained of great Exhaus[*tion*]. I gave her some toddy, and a dose of Morphine [*page torn: and?*] ordered quiet, and left her for the night. [*I*] visited her the next morning, found her a little [*word obscured: better?*], made an Examination per Vaginum, found the [*ut*]erus natural, placenta disengaged, and at [*the os u*]teri, which I took away without any trouble. [*Page torn: And a?*] fever comming on[133] in one or two days [*page torn, words missing*] the use of the female syringe, and the [*page torn, words missing*] with oil, She soon recovered her strength.

MAY THE 9TH 1873

[A]t Home this morning, went to Lowes Creek to [*word obscured: a?*] School Examination, and also an Exhibition [*to*] night.[134]

MAY 10TH [1873]

Went to Ozark to day, met with a [*f*]riend, and we have concluded to visit Clarksville[135] [*to*] morrow. I am Staying to night with P. F. Webb.[136]

MAY 11TH [1873]

[L]eft Ozark to day at 11A.M. proceeded [*ten?*] miles on the road towards Clarksville. Stayed [*a*]ll night with a gentleman by the name of [*Yarbaugh?*].

MAY 12TH [1873]

We arrived at Clarksville to day at [*word obscured*] A.M. [T]ook dinner at the Hotel, remained till [*word obscured*] P.M. come out three miles and are Staying to night with a gentleman by the name <u>Garrett</u>.

MAY 13TH [1873]

Left Garrett's this morning[.] [R]ode thre[*e m*]iles; and was compelled to stop on the account[*t of*] rain. Stoped with a Gentleman by the name [*of*] Brooks, took dinner with him; The rain [*c*]easing, after dinner, we resumed our journey [*an*]d arrived at 4 P.M. at a Mr. <u>Hamlins</u>, at [*wh*]ich place is a <u>stage stand</u>.

MAY 14TH [1873]

[R]esumed our journey this morning [*f*]ollowing the Railroad Survey two miles,[137] where I, and my friend, Oscar Jackson, sepa[*rated for o*]ur homes; being, on opposite Sides of the <u>Arkansas River</u>. I arrive[d] at Ozark at twelve oclock, remained there a couple [*of*] hours and reached home the same Evening.

MAY THE 18TH [1873]

[L]eft home to day, went to Ozark, attend[*ed*] the Sunday School at that place, and Singing, the pupils, led by W. W. Jennings; in the even[*ing*] rode out to Parson Rodgers, where I remain[*ed*] all night.[138]

MAY 19TH [1873]

I have, to day, been riding over a piece [*of*] land, lying adjacent to the railroad Survey [*and*] also, to the Spot Selected for a <u>Depot</u>, returning to Ozark, find upon an Examination of [the] Records that we are mistaken, in regard, to [*the*] locality of the land. So I again have rod[*e out*] of town, and am to night, Sharing, the [*house?*] of Judge Sutherland.[139]

MAY 20TH [1873]

To day, I again rode over the same tract of land[,] returned again, to Ozark, purc[*hased*] the above tract of land, arrived at Ozark at [*page torn*] P.M. crossed the River about 4 P.M. being much detained, on account of a Swollen Riv[*er*] and, an, impotent old horse <u>ferryboat</u>; I arrived home at 10 oclock in the night.[140]

JUNE THE 18TH 1873[141]
A CASE OF HYDROCEPHALUS

As, it is, my intention in this case, to record the progress of the disease, at various times, I shall [*on*]ly Record so much at a time, as may be consistent [*wi*]th such an arrangement.[142]

The case commences thus; about 3 months [*a*]go, I was sent for to visit a child, which was [*th*]en 3 or 4 weeks old. [W]hen I first Saw it, it [*wa*]s having Spasms, and had been having them about one week. [T[he convulsions were not [*un*]usually Severe, though, the usual phenomena [*of*] convulsion were present. [A]fter having them [*a*]lmost constantly for Several weeks, they ceased. [*I*] did not See the child for four weeks after the convulsions ceased. When I did, See it quite a change had taken place. Its head was [*ob*]viously much larger, the Expansion having ta[*ken p*]lace in all parts of the bony case of the bra[*in a*]nd most conspicuous, in the frontal parietal[*l a*]nd occipital regions. The enlargements contin[*ued f*]or some three months, during which time it w[*as u*]nder no treatment, at the end of that time, [*w*]hich was about Eight weeks ago, I put it o[*n a*] treatment of a Solution of the Iodi[*de of*] Potassium,[143] Since which, there has been [*no f*]urther enlargement of head, though [*the f*]ontanels are quite open, and fluctua[*page torn: words missing*]. The child is also beginning [*to*] [*page torn: words missing*] which has not before occurred. [*Page torn: words missing*] head. I should have mentioned, that shortly after the birth of the child, I saw at the time it begin having Spasms, but could See no organic nor abnormal physiological [*word obscured: cause?*] in the child.

W. R. Bachelor

APRIL 1ST 1874

[T]o day I called to see the Hydrocephalus case. The child has grown Some little, that is [*its*] limbs and trunk. [I]ts head has enlarge[*d*] considerably Since I last wrote about It. [I]t is now Sixteen months old, its head measures 24 inches in circumference, and is so heavy it cannot by any means r[*aise*] it from whatever position in which it was placed[.] [I]t is now labouring under an a[*ttack?*] of whooping cough, and has light sp[*asms*] ever time it has a paroxysm of coughing. It is now under no treatment.

The treatment I give it of Iodide of Potas[*sium*] did not seem to benefit it, and was discontinued. The child continues to gr[*ow*] little.

MAY THE 29TH 1873

Not being verry well to day, I have remained at home Excepting a stroll I took this morning [*th*]rough my farm, and some other adjacent [*o*]nes. This evening, I have read Romeo and Juliet. [N]otwithstanding, I have often read it [*be*]fore, I never get tired of Shak[*e*]speare.[144]

MAY 30 [1873]

[H]ealth improving, I have not [*ha*]d to visit any patients to day, however, I [*p*]rescribed and issued medicine for one patient [*to*] day. Being alone this evening I have again [*m*]ade Shak[*e*]speare, my companion. Have read Shak[*e*]speare's Dramatis Personae of King Richard III [*w*]hich I verry much appreciate, but not more than [*th*]e Play of Romeo and Juliet. Both Plays are [*f*]avourites of mine.[145] 6 P.M. in my Office alone.

W. R. Bachelor

JUNE THE 7TH 1873

Saturday night about 10 oclock after having Returned from hearing a Lec[*ture*] given by Professor Graham, on the "uses [*and*] abuses of the English Language" which, I ver[*ry*] much appreciated: I was Sent for in grea[*t*] haste to visit a gentleman, Mr. M., whom I fo[*und*] bleeding profusely. Mr. M. was returning [*ho*]me from Town, and on the road, unfortun[*ately*] encountered a drunken, and Exasperated m[*an*] by whom he was Stabbed.[146] When I arriv[*ed*] he was in a house on the roadside.

I found Seven rather ugly looking punct[ures] in his back and shoulder, five of them w[ere] about three inches deep. [T]hey all had an oblique direction, I suppose, caused by t[he] position the Patient was in when he received [the] Stabs. [T]wo, penetrated the Teres magor musc[le][147] of the left Scapula, three entered the latissim[us do]rsi muscle of the left side of the Back, those about [the S]capula, were the most painful, being also the [*words obscured and text missing*: "*most incised*"?][148] So much so, that, after Sponging [the w]ounds and making the necessary examinat[ion] I found it advisable, to take one stich, on [e]ach of those Stabs about the Scapula, I the[n a]pplied adhesive Strips over the wounds.

Finding my patient nearly pulseless, with tremitis cold, I gave him Some toddy, a[nd a d]ose of Morphine: ordered cold water dressings [and] quiet. [*In the*] morning I procured a spring wagon [in w]hich I placed a bed, and had him [carrie]d home, a distance of Six mile[s, a] thing I did not much like, however, [he has] arrived at home, without much inconvenience.[149] [C]old water dressings continued, left a dose [o]f Morphine to be taken to night.

June 9th [1873]

Visited my patient this morning, says [he] rested well through the night, pulse 102, and [st]ronger. [H]as Slight fever, complains of some [p]ain and Soreness in the left mammary region, [w]hich I think is Sympathy of the pectoralis magor muscle,[150] with the wounded muscles of the [S]capula.

Having had no action on his bowels, since [b]eing wounded, I gave him a large dose of [c]astor oil,[151] cold water dressings to be continued.

Saw him in the evening, his [b]owels having acted, pain in the mammary [reg]ion, gone, pulse about the Same. [Or]dered the cold water dressings to be continued [wi]th an occasional anodyne Diaphoretic. Regimen;—to be generous, but not Stimula[ting].[152]

June 11th [1873]

[V]isited my patient to day, found [hi]m doing well, wounds healing, no Fever. Extracted the Stitches, took off the adhesive Strips, ordered coldwater dressings 24 hours longe[r], then to [be] dressed, with Simple Cerate,[153] [an]d depur[ated] by a tepid lotion of lixivium[154] d[aily] un[til the] wounds, entirely heal.

W. R. Bachelor

June the 18th 1873

Called to day to visit a man Mr. W. who was attacked last Nov[ember] with Typhoid pneumonia fever. He was at[tended] by two physicians for twentyone days, when [*I had a?*] call to see him, he was under my treatm[*ent*] for a week perhaps, during which, altho h[*e was*] low, I thought the crisis had passed but, so happening that I could not visit him regu[*larly*], he called in another Physician.

[A]bout one month after he sent for me ag[*ain*] I found Him verry feeble, and much emac[*iated*]. [H]e also had several large tumors, which [*were?*] open, they discharged a considerable quanti[*ty of*] Saneous[155] fetid matter.

He also had a large Sloughing ulcer over [*the r*]egion of the Sacrum, produced of course, by [*word obscured by margin*] a Feeble capillary circulation, and diminish[*ed*] vitality of the surface.

I ordered Tonics, barks, Stimulants, and a g[*enerous d*]iet, also clenliness, and protection from [*pressure?*] on the Sloughed parts.[156]

About three months having elapsed he sent [*for*] me again, to day. I find him Still much emaciated, but not so bad as when I saw him last. He has had no more tumors, [*the*] Sloughing ulcer on the back [*has*] healed, b[*ut*] he is Still unable to raise him[*self*] on the [*bed*] without assistance, from great d[*isa*]bility [*of t*]he left hip, and distortion of the [*page torn, words missing*] it Being laterally drawn towards [*page torn, words missing: the right side?*] the ligaments rigid. I have [*page torn, words missing: found that?*] chylosis has taken place [*page torn, words missing*].

[JUNE 30TH 1873][157]
A CASE OF ABORTION[158]

I was Summoned June the 30th 1873 to [*se*]e a Lady, Mrs. C., who informed me, that She wa[*s ab*]out Eight months advanced in pregnancy. And, that during the last two months [*s*]he had felt no movement of the Foetus. And during which time, her health was [*f*]ully as good as Usual (her health habitually being delicate)[.] The only morbid sensation[*n s*]he Experienced, was, a rolling, or Swelling [*s*]ensation in the abdomen.

When I Saw her, She had slight hemorrhage [*an*]d complained of trivial pains about the [*gro*]ins and right iliac region.

Examination per vaginum, detected, a pres[*en*]ting mass, the os uteri being only a little [*di*]lated, I could ~~could~~ not with certainty [*d*]etermine what it was. [H]owever, in abo[*ut*] [*word obscured by margin*] hours she had a little labour and giv[*e b*]irth to a dead child. [I]t seemed to be ab[*out a*] 5 months child, and from its appearan[*ce d*]oubtless had been dead two months[.] The Lady done well, and soon regained her accostomed health.

W. R. Bachelor

[*Au*]GUST THE 27TH 1873

Last night about the hour of 9 " [*an*]d after I had retired, I was visited by thr[*ee*] Gentlemen, one of which, had been Shot, and he came to get me to Extract the bu[*llet*]. It had entered the Complexus muscle[159] a little to the left of the Spine, and about the fourth vertebra, then passing to the right, and lo[*dged*] in the <u>Splenius capitis</u> muscle.

I made a free incision with a bistaury[160] do[*wn*] to the ball, then introduced a crooked probe, and Extracted it, applied col[*d*] water dressings. Ordered rest.

This morning, his neck is pretty sore [*and*] Swollen, however, he departed for His ho[*me, a*] distance four miles.

I ordered him on leaving, to continue the cold water dressings, untill the heat and tension Subsided, and keep [*his b*]owels open, and keep quiet. I also g[*ave h*]im a couple of doses of Morphine to be taken if necessary, to procure Sleep [*and al*]lay pain.

August 28th 1873 9 A.M.

W. R. Bachelor

[MARCH 1ST 1874][161]

It is now about midnight, four years [*ago I*] left Tennessee and was at this hour [*f*]loating down The River. [O]ne year ago, [*I*] see from my diary, I was where [*I*] now am, on Mill Creek. I was then [*at*] 4 P.M. writing in my office writing.[162] [T]o [*ni*]ght March the 1st 1874 at midnight finds [*m*]e up writing. I have been asleep, but [*a*]m now up writing. [A]ll my family are [*s*]leeping while I have put on my Slippers [*an*]d cloak and am writing. [T]he Ple[*i*]ades[163] [*ar*]e getting low in the west, while pale Cynthia, Queen of the heavens, Sheds [*h*]er mild radiance, over the rocks and mountains.[164] [A]ll nature Seems lul[l]ed and silent and is to be heard but the roar of Mill Creek,[165] as it rushes [*t*]hrough the Craggy rocks at the foot of Mill Creek mountain.[166] [T]he last year that has passed has brought n[*o g*]reat change to me. [B]ut it has ha[d *i*]t[167] toils and care. I cannot say that [*I*] am either contented or happy. [Y]et I have been forced to remain here.[168] I am Still practicing medicine, have [*a*] few select friends only who like [*m*]yself love meditation, and Books[.] Sometimes I wish that I was like [*t*]hose of whom some rhymes Said "fixed [*li*]ke a plant, one peculiar Spot; to draw [*n*]utrition, propagate and rot[.]"[169] [*Bu*]t then again, I am glad, that natu[*re*] [*has so*] constituted my mind.

[*After*] midnight March the 2nd 1874

W. R. Bachelor

SUNDAY, MARCH 15TH 1874

To day has been verry rainy and di[*sagreeable?*]. [A]ltho the morning was gloomy I and two [*of*] my little Sons[170] went down the creek on[*e*] mile and ascended the mountain, the ra[*in*] increasing, we returned to the foot o[*f the*] mountain, entered a lonely hut, Stru[*ck*] up a fire, dryed ourselves and then [*went*] home. After which I took a nap [*and*] remained at home during the evening. I issued medicine and prescribed f[*or*] a man with op[h]thalmitis. [B]y reference to my Diary, I find that [*four*] years ago to night I was decending [*the*] Mississippi River Somewhere between M[*emphis*] and Helena. By further reference [*to the*] Diary I See that one year ago to day, being Saturday, I went to Ozark a[*nd*] returned before night, and issued and p[*rescribed*] medicine for a case of Intermittent fev[*er*] and was recording the Same at abou[*t*] this hour, which is now about 9 oc[*lock*] at night. [R]ainy days are generally ir[*ksome*] and to day has been quite so and time is on the wing, and we grow ol[*der and*] cares increase, and I cannot ~~better~~ descr[*ibe*] my feelings better than to quote Lord Byron, who says,

"Few are my years, and yet I feel
The world was ne'er designed for me:
Ah! why do dark'ning Shades conceal
The hour when man must cease to [*be?*]"
[*And*] again,   "Oh! that to me the wings were given
which bear the Turtle to he[*r nest!*]
Then would I cleave the [*vault of heaven,*]
to flee away, and be at [*rest.*"][171]
Sunday night 9 P.M. Mar[*ch 15th 1874*]

W. R. [*Bachelor*]

[*MAY*] THE 6TH 1874

[*Wedn*]esday night. [T]o day about 9 A.M. we had [*an*] addition to the family. [M]y wife give birth [*to*] a fine daughter. She at this hour, being [*ab*]out 8 oclock P.M.[,] is doing as well as could [*be*] Expected under the circumstances.[172]

[*I*] have been about home generally for the last [*word obscured: two?*] months, owing to the verry feeble condition [*of*] my wife. [D]uring which time I have obtained [*so*]me geological specimens from the mountains [*and*] also am turning rather to be an ornithologist[.] [*I*] have caught Several quadrupeds, an[d] fowls [*an*]d Stuffed their skins with Sawdust, and [*con*]template continuing the same through [*the s*]ummer.[173]

[B]y candlelight alone, all having [*re*]tired.
May 6th 1874
W. R. Bachelor

July the 1st 1874

Wednesday night. A co[*met*] to night is visible in the northwest al[*though*] here is very little vapourous emanation[,] yet I am sure it is a comet.[174]

July 5th [1874]

Sunday night. The most b[*eautiful*] rainbow I ever Saw, was be[*held*] this evening just before Sunset. It has been threatning to rain all da[*y,*] clouds dark and lowering. Suddenly [*a*] mist of rain began to fall, followe[*d*] immediately by a burst of light from [*the*] Setting Sun turning the raindrop[*s*] on the leaves to chrystals, and form[*ing*] the most lovely rainbow. To night the tail of the comet is qu[*ite*] perceptable, having increased rapid[*ly*] in length in four days.

[*Au*]gust the 7th, 1874

[C]alled last night, to see a man who had [*had*] a difficulty, received a severe blow on [*t*]he head, with a block of wood, making [*an*] ugly gash three inches in length.[175]

When I saw him, (which was near an hour [*af*]ter the difficulty) he Seemed conscious, though [*he*] was intoxicated, making it rather difficult [*to*] determine on his rationality.

[O]pportunities being unfavourable, to carefully [*ex*]amine his case owing to a want of light, [*I*] gave him a little mophia,[176] ordered cold water [*dr*]essing[,] leaving him till morning[.]

[*Saturda*]y Morning August 8th 1874

Visited him again, found him a little comatous, [*b*]ut rational when aroused, complains of [*he*]adache, also of numbness, and formication [*of*] the right arm. I examined the wound, [*f*]ound it Swollen and Slightly bleeding, and [*in*]troducing a probe I found the Skull [*f*]ractured.

The wound is near the vertex of the [*sk*]ull, on the left Side of the occipital, near the [*junc*]ture of the occipital and Parietal. There seems [*to*] be an indentation or removal of a porti[*on of*] the bone. [O]rdered cold water dressing to [*be*] continued also A dose of epsoms salts.[177] [*In*] this case, I fear there is Serious lesion of [*the*] meninges of the brain.[178]

Visited him again this evening[,] [*f*]ound him with Some fever, complains of his head, bowels acted twice through the day, ordered cold water [*dr*]essings continued.

[*Su*]nday August 9 [1874]

Visited my patient this morn[*ing*], found him clear of fever[,] rested well through the night. [W]ound lo[*oks*] like it is doing well. Ordered col[*d*] water dressing continued, left Som[*e*] purgative Pills for him to take to ni[*ght*], ordered an unstimulating, but gener[*ous*] diet; he complain[s] a little of his lef[*t*] Eye, his arm Still partially para[*lyzed*].[179]

MONDAY, AUGUST 10 [1874]

Visited my patient this evening, foun[*d him*] clear of fever, Sitting up a little, good appetite, bowels in good condition. [*The*] wound is not Suppurating, though Still discharges a little bloody Serum.

Paralysis of the arm continues. Order cold water dressings continu[*ed*], bowels kept open, nourishing diet.

WEDNESDAY, AUGUST 12 1874

Saw my patient again this morning, he [*is*] doing well, no fever[,] appetite good, wound s[*till*] offensive, order cold water dressings continue[*d*], with chlorinated washes,[180] bowels to be kept [*open*] and a generous diet.

FRIDAY AUGUST 14 [1874]

Visited my patient this morning[,] found him witho[*ut*] fever. Pulse About 80, appetite good, has rested through the night. I dressed his wound freely applying warm Soapsuds, introdu[*cing*] a mop into the wound, and removing [*a*] quantity of fetid Saneous pus. I exam[*ined*] the fracture by introducing my finger[.] I find a frightful chasm in the cran[*ium*]. [*Ed*]ges of the wound are granulating[.] [*Ord*]ered cold water continued, also detergent washes and also chlorinated washes, bowels [*ke*]pt open, and a generous diet.

SATURDAY AUGUST 15 [1874]

Saw my patient again this morning[.] [*H*]is general health is pretty good, dijestion and [*as*]similation good, also good appetite, no [*f*]ever, wound Supurating, but smells [*o*]ffensive[.] Ordered detergent washes, and [*a*] nutritious but unstimulating diet, [*wi*]th due attention to the bowels.

MONDAY [AUGUST] 17 [1874]

Sent for in the night to [*s*]ee my patient, found him with some [*f*]ever[.] [H]is wound had been bleeding [*f*]reely, but had ceased before I arrived[.] [*T*]his is the first time it has bled since [*I*] have been treating of him.

Ordered the same treatment as [*pr*]escribed on my last visit.

TUESDAY AUGUST 18 [1874]

[*Vi*]sited my patient this morning, found him nearly clear of fever. I dressed [*hi*]s wound, Edges curing, quite a deep [*pi*]t in the centre, the fractured skull [*p*]lainly visible. Ordered the Same treatment [*a*]s before.

WEDNESDAY, AUGUST 19 1874

[S]ent for this morning at 4 oclock to [*vi*]sit my wounded patient, found the wound [*b*]leeding profusely, or rather had bled [*word obscured*] freely, though it had ceased before [*I*] arrived[.] He is apparently no worse [*as*] To his jineral Symptoms, only th[*at*] he has lost a quantity of blood, as is [*word obscured*] from his pulse. Ordered cold water d[*ressings*] and gave him and astringent, an[*d a*] Powder.

SEPT. 2ND [1874]

It has now been twe[*lve*] day Since I have wrote.

[D]uring that time, I have occasion[*nally*] visited my patient. The wound jine[*rally*] bleeds once in 24 hours, and has re[*duced*] him Some, though his appetite is goo[*d*] and he rests well of nights.

The wound suppurates pretty free[*ly*] and has healed, Excepting a good s[*ized*] op[e]ning in the centre.

As to the fractured bone, there is no perceptible change.

The fracture is clearly of an alarm[*ing*] character, as there is quite a large piece [*of*] bone entirely depressed, and it is Strange that he evinces no cerebral dis[*tress*]. Mind active, intellect clear, and rema[*ins*] free from pain.

There is no evidences of compress[*ion*], only a partially Paralyzed limb, and [*it*] is improving.

OCT. THE 19 [1874]

It has now been about ten we[*eks*] Since my patient received his inj[*ury*] and Since my last writing (Sept. 2). [*He*] has been able to walk about and has been to my office twice, distan[*ce*] of ½ mile, he complains of pain and Soreness in his Shoulder an[*d c*]hest and Extremities, mostly the right s[*ide*]. [*T*]he wound has ceased bleeding, and [*s*]uppurates pretty freely.

To day a piece of bone was removed[.] It was about one inch long, and three quarters of an inch in width and [*w*]as the External Lamella of the cra-nium. [*H*]is arm improves sloly.[181]

JULY [14?, 1891]

After Staying in Hotsprings a week, we left there this morning about 8 A.M. [C]ome through the town of Malvern near sunset and are camped to night 2½ miles from Malvern. We have travelled about 25 miles to day. Hotsprings is a great watering place, and many go there to bathe in and drink the thermal waters. [T]here are Several magnificent Hotels, and many bathing rooms.

To night—as we are camped in the pines—the Negroes a[re] holding a revival in a Negro meeting hous[e] about 300 yards distant.[182]

MISCELLANEOUS
AUGUST THE 18TH 1874

Tuesday morning. I have just returned [f]rom visiting a patient, and as I [h]ave not been Keeping up my Diary [f]or Some times,[183] I thought I would [r]ecord Some circumstances that have occurred [d]uring the last 8 weeks.[184]

[9] or 10 weeks ago two young men hardly [g]rown had a little difficulty, drew their pistols, and commenced fireing on each other, and continued fire-ing, untill they both sunk, down and both expired almost Simultaneously, in a few minutes. This occurred at the little village of Charleston 10 miles from where I reside.

About three weeks ago, three men were arrested [n]ear Roseville, they were carried to Roseville [a]nd confined, but before they had any [tr]ial, a mob of men arrive on the spot and [to]ok them out and hung them dead. These men had been accused of robbing and [s]tealing.

[A]bout two weeks a young man went to [a] School house, or near one, meeting the pupils [g]oing home, he attacted a youth, a pupil, [s]lapping him and using him roughly, and [as] Soon as the youth resisted, he drew his [re]peater, and Shot him. The pupil lived [a] few days and died.

I am now treating a young man, whose [sk]ull is horribly fractured, this was don[e by] his brother a few days ago at his Fathers, [a]nd in the midst of the family.

[B]ut these are only a few isolated cases. [Th]ere is not a week, but the reports of bl[ood]shed and murder reaches us.

And the perpetrators of these acts, go unp[unished]. If any of these desper-ados are arrested, [they] almost invariably make their escape, [and] if they do not, they are Seldom punis[hed]. Since the first of January 1874 untill to [day], the number of men who have died by vio[lence] equal those, who have died of disease in my [practice]. I have been in Arkansas four years and six mo[nths], and I have heard of more men dieing by vio[lence] during that time, than in all my past lif[e].[185] It is nothing uncommon here, if Some o[f a] man[´s] neighbours become offended at hi[m,] to go in a crowd to his house and order him to leave in a given time, which [demand?] is implicitly obeyed.

Every person here are allowed to carry weapons. So every desperado, and hairbrained you[th] in the country has them Swung to his Sid[e.] [T]hey go to Church, with them, they go into [a] Gentleman[´s] house, with them, and think [it] an honor. And as to what they call [word obscured], they have them at least three or four a we[*ek*], go in with their pistol on, and a quart [*of*] Busthead not fare off, and if they See [*a*] genteel, and rather modest Gentleman destitute of [*we*]apons, who has obtained the consent of [*a la*]dy for a dance, when he and his dulcinea [*g*]oes to take their positions ~~where~~ he is sure to fin[*d o*]ne of those Semibarbarian vandals in h[*is*] place, and who will tell him he can't [*be*] there. The fair sex Seem to have become [*accustomed?*] to this and think nothing of it.[186]

MISCELLANEOUS
SEPTEMBER 2ND 1874

[*Si*]nce I last wrote, I have another [*tra*]dgedy to add, to my list.

About a week ago, a Gentleman living near Ozark, (ten miles from where I reside) [*we*]nt to town on Some business, left [*l*]ate in the evening in company with [*tw*]o Indians, who were living with a [G]entleman near by: he was found the [*n*]ext day on the road between Ozark [*a*]nd his home murdered.

He had been Shot once through the chest, [*a*]nd Stabbed thirteen times. [H]is horse was [*a*]lso taken, and his money and hat. The Indians left the same night. Men [*s*]oon afterwards Started in pursuit, but so [*f*]are, the Indians have not been arrested.[187]

SEPTEMBER 1ST 1874

To day I visited the Arkansas River, a[*nd*] am trapping for beaver.

I did not get a beaver, though I ca[*ught*] a duck. The River is Exceedingly l[*ow*] and is fordable in many places. [W]e hav[*e*] had the most Scorching Summer that I ha[*ve*] ever witnessed.[188]

There has been a hot pestilential win[*d*] blowing for Several Weeks, the blades [*of*] corn were instantly dried up, and fe[*ll*] from the stalks, and were carried ou[*t of the*] fields and into the woods by the win[*d*]. The growth of cotton was immedia[*tely*] check[ed], and the half grown bolls are opening rapidly. [T]housands of trees in [*the*] forest look like a heavy frost had fallen on them, leaves yellow, and perfectly dry. Nature has put on her melancholy livery, and premature autumn begin[*s*] her reign in midsummer.

This evening I prescribed, for a case of Syphilis, the first, since I have been in Arkansas.

AN EXCURSION
OCTOBER THE 28TH 1874

This morning, I an[*d*] a young friend [*s*]tarted to Fort Smith, arrangements had been made [*fo*]r four of us to go together, but the other two [*d*]id not arrive, So we started after waiting [*s*]ome time for them to arrive.[189]

We travelled untill 12 oclock, which found [*u*]s on the bank of the Arkansas River. [*W*]e took out our horses and fed them, also [*a*]te dinner ourselves, geared up again and [*w*]as Soon travelling (our mode of travelling [*w*]as in a wagon). [A]t Sunset we arrived [*a*]t a church house Eight miles from <u>Fort Smith</u> [*a*]nd twenty two miles from home, here we [*c*]amped, and Staid all night.[190]

We had Mark Twain's <u>Innocents abroad,</u> [*w*]hich my young friend read untill a late [*h*]our.[191] [W]e did look for our other two friends [*to*] overtake us to night but they have not [*c*]ome.

This morning Oct 24th we were up early and on [*t*]he road, we got to Fort Smith about 9 A.M. [*and*] spent the day there, about 2 P.M. this evening Professor Graham, and another ~~young~~ [*f*]riend arrived.

Sunday morning Oct. 25th[.] [W]e were camped [*l*]ast night under an old Shed in the Suburbs [*o*]f the Town, and saw the moon Eclipsed. I an[d] Professor Graham witnessed the Eclipse. [*I*]t began shortly after midnight and [*c*]ontinued for three hours. It was a total Eclipse, the Shadow begin[*ning*] on the East Side of the Moon and passing enti[*rely*] over her. It was a beautiful Starlight night, and while I and the Professor, were watching the Eclipse we saw several meteors Shooting westward.[192]

Night, we attended Service to day in t[*he*] Catholic Church, and also in the Episcop[*al*] Church and had some verry fine music and to night we are much amused at the incidence of <u>Mark Twain,</u> as the Pro[*fessor*] is a good reader and is Setting up late and interesting us verry much.[193]

We have left <u>Fort Smith</u> and come out [*8 miles?*] to the same Church house we stop[p]ed in as we went to ~~the~~ town.

Oct 26th. I arrived home to day about 2 P.M. [*and*] found my family all well, my comrades h[*ave*] gone home.

W. R. Bachelor

NOVEMBER THE 29 1874

It is now night and the Sabbath. I am in [*m*]y office writing. To day I have completed my forty Seventh year.

A retrospective view of my past life affords me both bitter & sweet reflection. When I look [*b*]ack to the innocent days of childhood I [*r*]uminate, and am sad; as I think of the friends of my boyhood and like the flowers ~~of~~ of Summer they are gone, many lie in the Silent tomb while others are fare away, and their memory makes me Sad Indeed. Then I think of the warm associations that I formed in manhood, which also have been disolved by the ruthless hand of dea[*th*]—many fond hopes crushed, and ardent [*a*]spirations abandoned.[194]

Again. [W]hen I think I have not [b]een the cause of pain to any person, but have Sympathized with the Suffering, and [e]ndeavoured to relieve corporeal pain, and mental anguish: the reflection is pleasant[.] A Gentleman has come after me to see to [a] Sick Lady.[195]

DEC. 24 1874

It is 20 minutes past 9 P.M. and Christmas E[ve] and I think the quietest Christmas Eve ~~I think~~ I ever saw.[196]

I am alone in my office writing. I and my student, J. D. Massey have performed Some pie[ces] of music, I playing on the Violin, he perform[ing] an accompaniment on the Guitar.[197]

And he is now reading medicine, while I am writing. Just now, the noise of Some revelle[rs] falls on my Ear, with the report of Some gun[fire], the first I have heard.[198] I think the crowd is dispersing from Hills, a neighbour of mine where there has been a dance.[199]

The night is cool and the Earth mostly covered with sn[ow], the moon is full, the night is clear and the Snowclad hills look beautiful in the moonlight.

W. R. Bachelor

[DECEMBER 25, 1890][200]

After a lapse of 16 years It is again Christmas. 1890.[201] It is rather a dull Christmas, I am in my room writing 9 P.M. [I]t rained yesterday and most of to day. I went up to Neighbor S. G. Teagues to day for dinner.[202] His youngest Son married yesterday. All of his children are now married excepting one son in Texas. My baby daughter went with a Lady friend across the river to spend Christmas.[203] I have missed her at the organ and her Singing.[204] My little granddaughter (<u>Gertrude</u>) thinks Santa Claus has been verry liberal with her, having filled her Stockings last night with candy and apples.[205] I have been reading Shell[ey], Edgar Poe, George Elliott, Tennyson, an[d] Browning—Give me Tennyson a[nd] Shelly.[206]

16 years have brought many changes. My family are all grown up—and I have become [a] confirmed Freethinker or Agnostic. [*From this point, the bottom right side of the page is torn off with many words missing.*] I do not believe in the inspira[tion] of the Bible. I have cut loose from [s]uperstition and take reason [*as my*] guide. My doctrine is [*words missing*] live for others and not [*words missing*] Contend for justice [*words missing*] Equality. Hell is a fan[tasy] [*words missing*] is unproven. Let us ma [*ke the most?*] of life, let us live res[ponsibly] Will Surely die right [*words missing*] [re]quire for any Sign to [*words missing*] are none put up by [*words missing*] before but by those [*words missing*].[207]

9 P.M. Christmas night

July the 2nd 1891

Left home this morning Myself, Monroe, and Nannie for Hotsprings. Travelling in a Wagon.[208] Nannie is sick and ha[s] been all day. Billious—and occasiona[lly] vomiting.[209] We are camped to night one mile South of Chisimville, having travelled about 24 miles today.[210] Our camping ground is well chosen. [W]e have taken Shelter in a large Church house or School house.[211] There is a beautifu[l] oak grove around the School house and while I am writing the Kadidids are busy piping their peculiar notes—and reminds one of Childhood day[s].[212]

9 P.M. W. R. Bachelor

P.S. I have just played on the violin the "[R]ose Wal[t]z"—and Monroe the "Lost [I]ndian" before retiring.[213] W. R. B.

July 3 [1891]

Started pretty early travelled [*page torn, words missing*] day over rocks and mountains [*page torn, words missing*], halted at 12 oclock to eat dinner [*page torn, words missing*] Small Stream emptying into [*page torn, words missing*]. We crossed Petit Jean [*page torn, words missing*] day, one time running east [*page torn, words missing*] time running west.[214] [W]e [*stop*]ped to night in 5 mile of [*page torn,*

The route taken by Bachelor, his son Monroe, and his daughter Nannie from Franklin County to Hot Springs. *Cartography by T. R. Paradise.*

words missing: Waldron?]—lacked that much of [*page torn, words missing*]. We crossed Poteau this [*page torn, words missing*] 6 P.M.[215] Nannie is verry [*page torn, words missing: sick and?*] has had to lie all day in [*page torn, words missing: the wagon, which?*] has caused me to [*page torn, words missing: sit on?*] the wagon seat all day.

She is taking medicine. The old house we are in to night has not been occupied this Summer.[216] [I]t is 75 yards from the road, old Garden partly torn down, dog fennel all over the yard.[217] While I am writing a Screech owl has perched near by and is issuing his plaintive cry as I Suppose he thinks we have intruded on his privacy.[218]

P.S. While I am writing Monroe has attended to everything, prepared Supper and is now playing the <u>Lost Indian</u> and Mollie Milligan.[219] Now I am going to play <u>Katy Hill</u> and then we will Seek Morpheus.[220]

JULY THE 4TH 1891

We are camped to night in a School house 5 miles South of Fourch[e] River.[221] [W]e have drove to day about 30 miles[.] The most of the road was verry rocky—and mountainous. Nannie is a little better but taking med. I got verry much fatigued to day, hot and giddy. Nannie took the wagon Seat and I lay down during part of the evening.

Well Monroe has got Supper[,] tied up and fed his mules, tied down his wagon Sheet—we have our bedding and everything in the house. It is thundering and may rain.

THIS MORNING SUNDAY JULY THE 5TH 1891

This morning we Started again on our journey—we passed through a place today Called the <u>Stretch</u>. There is only 2 houses in 13 miles—this is a desolate country.[222] We have not met a man—nor overtook one to day, we Stopped and eat dinner at a Small mountain Stre[a]m. I cannot describe this country as I wish.—Imagine yourself travelling all day over mountains, across rocky ravines, through tangled bushes, downhill—uphill, jolted untill you are Sick and Sore.[223] We have Struck a Settlement at last. We are camped tonight in an unoccupied house by the roadside. We have not heard a dog bark to day[,] a chicken crow, nor hardly a human voice[,] but at dark Since we have camped—I can hear out in the lonly pines human voices Singing and Shouting.[224] So is the world, the Ignorant and Superstitious always religious. We are to night within 5 miles of the Sulphur Springs.[225] I and Nannie are good shook up and almost Sick. I have Sy[m]ptoms of Flux.

Monroe is a busy man as he has everything to do, but if he cant do it Nobody could, for he knows how and is willing.

JULY THE 6TH 1891

We have just halted, Monroe and Nannie are getting supper.²²⁶ We have a good camping place to night. We found a verry good little house on the roadside and near by a branch, with three oldfashioned Tennessee Springs.²²⁷ One affords as much water as the Bluff Spring in Tennessee. I went to the Spring, the green fern grows all about it—and the <u>GreenSnake feeder fly</u> is flitting among them. We have travelled Something over 20 miles to day. The road was greatly improved. We crossed the north fork of the Washita twice today—and the Was[h]ita once.²²⁸ It rained on us from morning untill twelve oclock, when we Stopped for dinner. I bought a Squirril of a boy—and Monroe dressed and fried it for dinner. We are camped tonight 5 miles from <u>Bear Mountain,</u>²²⁹ and 21 miles from Hotsprings.

JULY THE 7TH [1891]

We arrived at Washita at 12 oclock: Eat dinner on the bank, then crossed over fording it with wagon and mules.
We passed a little mining village to day called (<u>Bear Mountain</u>) 15 miles from Hotsprings. [W]e got to Hotsprings at 4 P.M. travelling to day 21 miles.²³⁰ I have only passed through the City—and am with my Daughter Nannie Eubanks at Wm. Well's and [*sic*] old friend, he and his lady[,] of ours.²³¹ We a[re] tired of travelling Six days in a wagon over the roughest rockiest country I ever saw. The distance from home to this place Hotspring is 135 miles.

Left Hotsprings the morning, bidding adieu to the picturest city with its 60 thermal springs.²³²

AUGUST, TUESDAY THE 25TH 1891

To night we camped on <u>Walnut Fork</u> 22 miles from Hotsprings—it is the Same house we Stoped at as went to Hotspring.²³³ Supper being over—It was in order—for the <u>Arkansas Traveller</u> which I play, and now while I am writing, Monroe is playing the Lost Indian[.]²³⁴ We are returning home, and have had a pleasant visit.

WEDNESDAY, AUGUST THE 26TH [1891]

To night we are camped on a little creek on the Dallas road 47 miles from Hotsprings.²³⁵ To day we have tra[*velled*] about 30 miles—we could get [*no*] house to camp in to night, so we camped in the open air on the roadside, we are all tired to night. [M]usic is [in] order—but we have had none yet, though, Monroe may give the lost Indian before he goes to Sleep.

TO NIGHT THURSDAY NIGHT AUGUST THE 27TH 1891

[W]e are camped in a[n] unoccupied house ¾ of a mile South of <u>Fourch[e]</u> <u>La Fave</u> River[.][236] We have come through the Stretch of 18 miles known as the <u>Campbell's Back</u>,[237] then down Ceder Creek—rock mountains, mountains & Rock—I bought a chicken which Nannie & Monroe fried for Su[pper] and while I am writing 8 P.M. Monroe is playing <u>Mollie Milligan</u>.[238]

FRIDAY NIGHT AUGUST THE 28TH 1891

Tonight we are Camped at the Same house we camped at as we went to Hotsprings. It is 5 miles North of Waldron.[239] We are all verry much Shook up and fatigued travelling all day in a wagon on rock and mountains[.] As we passed through Waldron this evening we Stoped, and took a Shave.[240] It is now in order to have a little music, though we are So tired. I will now play <u>Katy Hill</u> and Monroe will follow with <u>Lost Indian</u>.

SATURDAY NIGHT AUGUST 29TH 1891

To night we are camped one mile south of Chisimville in a Schoolhouse. It is the Same place we camped the 2d night of July when we went to Hotsprings.[241] We have come 25 miles to day—Eat dinner on the Petit Jean River. Monroe bought a chicken which we had fried for Supper.[242] All are tired and will retire Soon.[243]

DECEMBER THE 24TH 1891

Christmas eve.[244] Time 9 P.M. I am in my Studio, all are gone to night except I and my wife, blind Sally, and my daughter <u>Alcie</u> (Dr Russell's wife) and her children,[245] and little Gertie my granddaughter[.][246] My family, gr. Childern, nine in all, Seven are at home,[247] one daughter in Texas.[248] And my oldest Son (Monroe) in the Indian territory.[249] To night is quite warm. Some have gone to a Christmas Tree,[250] and some to <u>neighbor Burcham's</u>.[251] The wind is beginning to blow, and the [sky] is overspread with clouds. Occasionally I hear the report of a gun—Some one [celebr]ating Christmas Eve.

W. R. Bachelor

DEC. THE 25TH 1892 AT NIGHT 9 P.M.

I am at home in my room writing. Most of my family are at home[.] [A] promiscuous crowd has been on hand all day. Neighbor Burcham was with me for dinner. Monroe is here to night, So is Yeager, Wils, and Vick, Alcie Russell and family, Pauline, and Nannie Eubanks, and my wife. Blind Sally, who was here last Christmas is not here to night—She has passed away. It is verry dark and cloudy, while the moanings of the wind can be heard. Christmas seems to come often. It is Sunday this time.

[H]aving entertained company to day, wrote two letters, played the violin.[252] I am going to retire, with a feeling of brotherhood for all humanity. I cheerfully can repeat what Thos. Pain[e] Said The world is my count[r]y[,] to do good my religion.[253]

W. R. Bachelor

[DECEMBER 25, 1893][254]

It is now 9 P.M., Christmas night, 1893 and Monday. We received visits from several friends to day. Some of which were friend Burcham[,] Fulks[255] and my isteemed and Solia freethought friend Joseph White and and his daughter Miss Carrie.[256] All my family are at home tonight excepting three J. H. Bachelor—J.Y. L. Bachelor and Lula Harris. To day has been pleasant and fair, and while I am writing to night the moon has just Risen over the eastern hills flooding the fields and vally with her mellow light.

It is a beautiful night, calm, and Still. Not even the report of any guns or distant noise of any revellers.

It is a quiet Christmas.

In view of the rapid flight [of] time, I feel but few regrets, believing "The time to be happy is now, The place to be happy is here, And the way to be happy is to make others happy."[257] Au-Revoir.

Dr. W. R. Bachelor

[DECEMBER 25, 1894][258]

It is Christmas night 8 P.M. 1894[.] I am alone in my room writing[.] Not many of the family at the old homestead tonight.

Monroe is in the Indian Territory. J. H. Bachelor at Central,[259] Yeager in Sebastian Co, Vick is gone to play for a ball, W. R. Bachelor Jr is at home in feeble health.[260] Lula is in Texas[,] Alcie at home, She lives near me.

Pauline is taking Christmas at Cecil[.] Nannie and two of my little granddaughters are here and my wife. It is a dark night no moon nor stars[.] [I]t is cloudy and rather cool. To day has been quiet for Christmas. Though, there has been much Shooting Some distance off. And while I am writing, the distant report of a gun is occasionally bourn on the night breeze.

The year just passing out has been a hard year. Bad crops—and low prices. It has been a year of drouths and So called revivals—and recently of marriages.[261] So the world rocks on—and the people evolute Slow. A great unrest pervades the people and there is great dissatisfaction among the people.[262] Yet

I am glad to see the tendency of the masses is towards better and grander manhood & womanhood. How long will it be before Superstition dies out—and manmade religions are things of the past. It is somoning—let [us] aid it.[263] Au-revoir.

W. R. Bachelor

COME AND GONE[264]
MID NIGHT—THE 31ST OF DECEMBER 189[4]

The old year of 1894 is just passing away—forever.—It, with its burdens pass[es] in review before us.[265] Wars,[266] drouths,[267] floo[ds],[268] fire,[269] railroad disasters,[270] suicides,[271] assassina[tions],[272] lynchings,[273] hangings, robberies, Strikes,[274] pov[erty], tramps, political differinces, new parties, coalitions, disintegrations of parties, and financial distresses.[275] The masses like the branches of the trees are swayed by eve[ry] political breese. Cranks, demagogues, a[nd] pseudo-reformers, and theoretical economist[s] augment the unrest.[276] The old year carries, as her burden tears, sorro[ws], sufferings, defered resolveds, broken promises, misplaced confidence, no[ble] impulses crushed, virtuous resolution[s] abandoned, reformations procrastinate[d], heartaches, farewells of loved ones, separa[tions] of friends. Also, the grand deeds of virtuous womanhood. And generous zeal of manhood, in their untiring efforts to help the poor and the fallen. So, passes like a meteor darklin 1894.[277] One more link in the endless chain of the eternal cycles.[278]

It is clear and frosty. The <u>Pleiades</u> look down with pity.[279] See, She comes. A magnificent Ship—mottoes and banners gleaming. It is the New Year. <u>Happy New Year</u>. All aboard. Now She Sweeps through infinite Space; and trembles in the undulations of ether. She curves to the great central orb and with the velocity of a thousand miles a minute Speeds her course.

Brothers, and Sisters, we cannot afford to be idle a minute. Don't you See how fast we are hurr[y]ing on? Don't you See time don't wait. Let us now resolved never again to procrastinate a good deed,—nor Strangle a noble impulse. Do good, do right, if we cannot relieve by charity the distressed, we can speak kindly and Sympathize—then a happy—and prosperous New Year.[280]

Pauline Ark W. R. Bachelor

[JANU]ARY 2ND 1895

[Y]esterday (New Years) we butchered Some hogs.[281] Snow began to fall about one P.M. this morning[.] Its depths is 8 inches, a good Sized Snow for Ark.[282] Snow reminds me of youth. When I So much delighted in Snowballing and hunting and trapping. How loth I was to See it melting away. And this morning how beautiful the fields and hills look covered with Snow.

Feb the 7th [1895]

Yesterday, the 6th[,] in the evening the Thermometer was 30 degrees above zero. Fer.[283] [T]his morning it was below. All last night the wind blew constantly. [I]t was a cold night—the howling—Shrieking and moaning of it could be heard[.] To night the wind is dying, but it is Still verry cold. 9 P.M. W. R. Bachelor

May the 11th 1895

9 oclock P.M. in my library room writing.[284] It is a quiet night. Pauline & Yeager are gone on a visit beyond the river. Nannie and Gertrude are also gone of[f] on a visit. Vick is also absent leaving at home only Monroe who has retired, and Wils who is in feeble health.[285] Myself—wife and Maud a granddaughter.[286] Years lengthen and time passes rapidly. My youngest daughter (Pauline) is 21 years of age. I have been in Arkansas 25 years. I am cultivating a garden this seson. I am much pleased to See the workings of nature—the growth of vegetables and plants. I am rather busy. Reading—writing—compareing, investigating. I am more then ever a FreeThinker.[287] I have attained to old age, and I have never saw anything above nature. "This life is what you make it." The destiny of men and women is in the hands of men and women. I neither See or know of any force—mental, moral or physical only the natural.

W.R. Bachelor

May the 31st 1895

Night—9 P.M. Well, with to day passes away lovely and beautiful May. We have just had a fine rain, and everything looks lovely. Prospects for good crops favourable[.] Pauline is absent this week Staying with her Music Teacher (Miss Carrie White).[288] W. R. Bachelor Jr is in quite feeble health.[289] He has not been able during this pretty month to go over the green fields and woods to enjoy Spring. Time is So fleeting—how Soon Seasons come and are gone.

W. R. Bachelor

June the 2nd [1895] 9 P.M.

This is Sunday night. It has been a beautiful day, Sunshiney, Singing birds and a pleasant breeze. Crops are growing and the fields are lovely. I have passed a part of the day at my garden where I have a little vine harbour. Have also been reading "Greenleaf, on evidence."[290] I See he is a Special pleader for his client, which is the church. [T]hat is all. Pauline came home last night with Victor at 11 P.M. It is a pretty moonshine night—as I write Stray moonbeams Struggle through the thick foliage of the Catalpas and Silver Poplars.[291] Chuck-

Wills–Widow is heard on the hill while Sometimes the Mockingbird cannot suppress his exuberance and Sing[s] a few notes.[292]

W. R. Bachelor

June the 12th 1895
Wednesday night

To day has been a growing day. We have had Some good rain, and the weather is warm. I have been destroying a kind of pumpkin bug that has infested my vines. I am also experimenting on Some vines and potatoes,—feeding the plants with fluid manures.[293] Prospects are Still good for a good crop. The political horison looks dubious. I think the democratic party is hopelessly divided on "free coinage" and "Sound money" and the Republican party not in harmony.[294]

Harvesting is near at hand.

Wils is quite feeble, can't be up but verry little.[295]

Dr. W. R. Bachelor

July the 2nd 1895

The beautiful month of June has passed, and Sultry July is upon us. It has been raining nearly every day for a week or more. Crops look well. Four years ago to day I and Monroe and Nannie Started to Hotsprings.[296] It dont Seem long ago. To night is still cloudy and the Katydids can be heard in the Silver Poplars, Sycamores, and catalpas in the yard. Wils is verry feeble. W. R. B.

August the 11th [1895]

The old homestead is Sad to night. W. R. Bachelor Jr has passed away.[297] He died on the 7th[.] A rent is made in a happy family. [F]or more than 20 years we have dwelt together and were called the musical family. Different members of the family played on different instruments[,] organ, violin, Banjo, and Guitar. He that passed away was a Banjoist. His Banjo and cheerful Songs will be missed. He was a Freethinker and died Such. His memory is enshrined in our hearts[.] He died in his manhood by that fell destroyer (consumption)[.] But his actions and deeds Still live, So he is Still with us. The Sound of music at the old homestead will always bring his memory fresh to our minds.[298]

Sept 17th [1895] night

It is excessively hot for the time of year. The thermometer has stood at 96. Fer. for weeks—one day 98 Fer. We are having some Sickness—chills & fevers. I intend next Sunday the 22nd to lecture on "The Bible" as I feel it my duty to oppose myths & Superstition.[299] The owls and bats Shrink from the light. Science—investigation and Freethought will finally reclaim the World from ignorance. But Freethinkers must be up and doing—Sowing the healthy Seed of naturalism.[300]

9 P.M. SEPT 21ST 1895

Farewell to the Summer of 1895—Altho we have passed through Sorrows and toils[,] yet in our lifes voyage we Kindly remmember 1895—its beautiful Sunshine, Singing birds, and lovely flowers, Green fields and meadows and forests yes its lovely nights[,] glittering Stars and mellow moonbeams. Its beautiful Sunsets and Sparkling dewy morns.[301]

Farewell to the Summer of 1895.

NIGHT—OCT THE 1ST 1895

First day of Oct. A beautiful day. [T]here was frost two days ago[.] It is cool to night. I am convalescent from a pretty Severe attact of malarial fever.[302] Much Sickness. Several of my family and Grand children have been Sick and relapsing. Cotton picking and corngathering have commenced[.] No excitement in the neighbourhood. No religious or political excitement.

W. R. Bachelor

NOVEMBER THE 29TH 1895

This is my birth day.[303] I have completed my 68th year. It is a pretty night[,] clear and frosty with a full moon[.] Winter has Set in rather early. We had one Snow. [C]otton is all gathered[,] a verry Short crop raised. Prices 8 cts—better than last year, which was only 5 cts per lb.[304] Health has improved.

Dr. W. R. Bachelor

Pauline Ark—8 P.M.

CHRISTMAS NIGHT 8 P.M. 1895

So the Christmas of 1895 has come[.] I have remained at home all day. Miss Carrie White and her brother Ben visited us; and was at dinner.[305] So also was Miss Barton.

At this hour while I am writing in my library they are having Music (Violen & Organ) in the parlor where Some ladies and gentlemen are. We have had several warm & rainy days. To day has been cloudy and to night it is getting cooler, looks like Snow.

W. R. Bachelor, Physician, Pauline, Ark.[306]

NEW YEAR'S NIGHT 1895 & 96
MIDNIGHT

As is my custom I am up and writing[.] It is full moon. [A]nd pale Cynthia is at her zenith. And pours her mellow light over the earth, while the Pleiades keep their course. It is clear, cold and frosty. Pauline and Vick went to a Social in the evening. Vick has just returned home, but Pauline remained to return tomorrow. The Year 1895 has gone with its laughter and tears carrying with it many bereavments. Taking one from the old homestead which we will not cease to think off.[307]

And now, for a new year—A happy New year to all.

Pauline, W. R. Bachelor

DIARY
JANY THE 23RD 1896

It has been cloudy two weeks, with Some rain. Snowed a little to day. To night it is Still cloudy and windy. My Nephew Elbert Bachelor and his wife Sylvia is with us. They arrive here on their way home to Grant co Ark. Having come all the way from California in a wagon. 2700 miles.[308]

JUNE THE 30TH (LAST DAY) [1896]

Summer is pretty here. Fields and forests are fully developed with Summer attire. Three of my Sons are making a crop—all at the old Homeste[a]d[.][309] It has been Sometime Since I have wrote any in my diary. But I could not let beautiful June pass without a notice. The Thrush to day has been Singing along the little branch, and the male quail mounted on the fence was calling to his mate "Bob White". To night the Katydids in the Silver poplars keep up their peculiar Song, while the whippoorwills back in the hills Sing their plaintive Song[.] While I write with the windows up hundreds of little moths attracted by the light of the lamp flit around, as I here Pauline playing on the organ while in another room I hear the violens[.] Such is life the last of June at the old Homestead.[310]

Night June the 30th 1896 W. R. Bachelor

DIARY, DEC. THE 25TH 1896

I See it has been Sometime Since I have written any. Well we have had the hottest Summer I ever Saw. It is now 9 PM Christmas night and as often before I am alone in my Studio. The family are mostly gone from home.

Pauline is up about Cecil. Monroe and Nannie and 4 of my granddaughters have gone to James Younger's to a dance. Vick is in Texas. It is a beautiful night, Starlight, clear and frosty. This Christmas passed as they usually do at the Old

Homestead. Several comers & goers, music. While I write I hear an occasional report of a gun, Some nocturnal reveller celebrating Christmas. There has been So little rain this Summer and Fall, the branches are yet dry, and for the first time we are hauling water. Years are fleeting to the Old. It Seems a Short time Since last Christmas. The year of 1896 is drawing to a close, with its great burden. We have passed through an exciting presidential election. Bryan and McKinly, for the presidency. McKinly was elected. Platforms—McKinly is for Sound money, Bryan for Free and unlimited coinage of Silver.[311]

W. R. Bachelor

April the 1st 1897

To day has been a beautiful day, Farmers are planting corn. [T]o night the frogs about the little branches are Swelling their throats—greeting Spring. The wood violets are comming out with their modest garb, and other little purple wild flowrs are peeping out—as March has disappeared. Peachtrees are in full bloom, and the little bees are busy Searching for nectar.[312]

8 P.M. Dr. W R Bachelor

April the 15th [1897]

I took quite a walk to day. Went to see a young lady who had a nervous attact.[313] I walked home 1½ miles. People are planting cotton. The forest is putting on its beautiful green attire. Birds are Singing—choosing mates— thousands of flowers have wakened from their frozen winter Sleep—wooed back to life by the Sun, and balmy winds from the tropics.

9 P.M. W. R. Bachelor

Sunday May the 9th [1897]

Spring has come, bringing Sunshine[,] Singing birds, and beautiful flowers. The forest is So green, and as distance lends enchantment[,] how beautiful the mountains look.

9 P.M. W R Bachelor

May the 20th 1897

Beautiful May, Singing birds, lovely flowers with all the rich perfume of Spring. The Catalpa trees with their green leaves and white blossoms are verry beautiful. The Humming bird has come back to revel among the flowers. The honey bee is busy extracting nectar from the flowers. The Honeysuckle vine on the verandah has filled the rooms with its delicious odor for weeks, but I never cloy with the odor of flowers.[314]

Night, 9 P.M. May the 20th W. R. B.

[JUNE 29, 1897][315]

Well the Summer of 1897 is fully here. [It] is June, forests and fields are at their best. Green leaves and green grass and flowers meet the vision in every direction. The old birds now Sing and are merry with their Young ones. And the honeybees are humming tonight after sending off Some colonies. The Catydids are vieing with each other with their lovecalls—While the distant tones of the <u>Chuck-Wills-Widow</u>, continually float in from the western window. Yes, grand glorious Summer is with us now. And O, let us appreciate it.[316]

Tuesday night, June the 29th 1897

W. R. Bachelor

[JULY 25, 1897][317]

Well, midsummer is here; and Sirius the dogstar is helping old Sol (Sun) to Scorch us.[318] The thermometer is 103.F° degrees at 4 P.M. to day July the 25th[.] Everything Seems to feel the lang[u]or of heat. The cattle in day Seek the Shade of the Spre[a]ding oak trees. The hogs lie Streach[ed] in Shades, Sometimes trotting off to wallow in the mud. The dog pants and Sleeps. Everything tries to avoid the heat of the Sun. But when he Sinks below the horizon in the west; then come forth thousands of insects, with their humming Sounds, while the Katydids begin their well-known song. Children go to Sleep quickly but grown-up people Sit up Sometimes for hours, or lie in the open air Seeking the night breeze. And then Sleep only to dream of Some phantasm. Even the lang[u]or is not dissipated in the morning for a want of energy is Still felt. But yet nature is forced, and we have picknics, protracted meeting, political conventions, while some are courting, Some trying to get religion, and Some electioneering for office.[319]

W. R. Bachelor

[SEPTEMBER 20, 1897][320]

The Summer of 1897 has passed away. It has been an exceedingly hot Summer and verry dry. Yet it had its beauties and usefulness, beautiful meadows, verdant forests, leafy bowers[,] luscious fruits, Sweet flowers and singing birds. We will cherish a happy remembrance as we pass on to Autumn which commences to day the 20th of September. To day has been a beautiful day, we have just had a rain. There is a change in the air. It is fair and pleasantly cool. The cotton pickers are busy gathering cotton. While we bid farewell to Summer with kindly regrets, we welcome Autumn.[321]

Monday night, Sept the 20th 1897

Dr. W. R. Bachelor

OCTOBER THE 29TH [1897]

First frost last night, But it has not rained yet.

The old Homestead is again made sad by the death of my Eldest Son L. M. Bachelor who passed away the 22nd.[322] He died at Fort Smith at the city Hospital. None of the family being present—as we thought him co[n]vales- cent. I had him brought home and burried beside my other son who died a little over two years ago. Thus Mother Nature is gathering back her children in her arms. All that live must die—for death feeds on life.[323] Night 9 P.M.

Dr. W. R. Bachelor

DECEMBER THE 3RD 1897

The golden wedding of I and my wife has just been celebrated at the old homestead, by our children and grandchildren.[324] I am threeScore and ten (70) years old, my wife 67. It is cold to night for the Season. Thermometer 5 degrees Fer below freesing. Two Elders of the latter-day Saints of the church of Christ (Mormons) Staid with me last night. They are from Utah, preaching and dis- tributing tracts.[325] W. R. Bachelor

[DECEMBER 25] CHRISTMAS OF 1897

Today I went over to friend James Nolen's and took dinner.[326] It is very quiet. I have not Saw an intoxicated man, nor noise of Guns. My daugh[t]er whom I have not saw in 8 years is with us, come from her Texas home to pay us a visit.[327] It Snowed Some days ago and it is not yet melted off. It is dark[,] damp & muddy to night. Yeager went across the river to take Christmas, Vick is gone out Somewhere[.] My oldest Son L. M. Bachelor who was with us last Christmas is not with us to night, but Sleeps beside his brother (W R Bachelor) having passed away from this life the 22nd of Oct 1897 in Fort Smith City hospital from whence I removed him home for burial.

So to night is Sad as well as Still. My wife, Nannie, Lula & Pauline and Some grand children are in the dwelling while I write in my library.[328]

Dec. the 25th 1897   W. R. Bachelor

DIARY OF 1898

MAY THE 31ST, 8 P.M. [1898]

It is the last day of beautiful May of 1898.[329] The moon is gibbous and gives a Mellow light. The odor of poppys and honeysuckles are bourn into the Studio. Chuck-wills-widow is heard on the hills mingled with the drowsy humming of bees. The tones of a guitar in an adjoining room can be heard. Ever an[d] anon the exuberance of the Mockingbird makes him heard from the orchard. The tired farmer Seeks rest. So, beautiful Sweet May too Soon leaves us. But grand, glorious June is our guest to night—So farewell lovely May with all your welth of flowers, Singing birds and rural Sweets. We Shall not forget your pleasant and mild Stay for your remembrance ~~is always~~ is always bright and desireable.[330]

Pauline Ark.

W. R. Bachelor

DIARY OF 1898
JUNE THE 17TH 1898—8 P.M.

We have had a rainy June so fare. Vegetation is exuberant.
May is Sometimes compared to a young Maiden—then Surely June Symbolizes glorious mature womanhood.[331] It is June that receives all the beauties of Spring untill She is almost Surfeited with plenary indulgence, and before She pays tribute to Autumn.[332] The rich green foliage of mountain and glen, the green fields of growing corn and cotton, growing fruits and gardens.

Dr. W. R. Bachelor

SEPTEMBER THE 1ST, 1898

We have all been Sick, but are getting well.[333] To day it begins to show Symptoms of Autumn. The Sky is verry blue, the breese a little cooler, while on the waving weeds in the fields the grasshopper can be heard chanting a prelude of his autumn Song. The Katydids to night Still call for their mates, but only a few are heard, as their merry Summer Season is nearly gone.[334]

W R Bachelor

DIARY OF 1898
[25 DECEMBER 1898]

Alone in my office 9 P.M.—Christmas night and Sunday night, 1898. It is a beautiful night. [N]ot a Single cloud to be Seen, The Moon is nearly full. Her mellow light dims the Stars. It has been a verry quiet day. Alcie Russell & Elsie & Bachelor Russell were with us at dinner and our own family, I, and my wife, Victor, Nannie, Pauline, and Gertrude. Yeager is in Texas & So is Lula. Dr. J. H. Bachelor lives near by, was here this evening. The Old Homestead is not just what it used to be.[335] But Still we had Some music to night—violen & Organ. And thus we have had for 28 years. To night the Sound of no revellers are heard. The god of Bacchus has few votaries, or satiety has Silenced them.[336] It

Seems Short since last Christmans: thus Speeds time, while the whirlling Sp[h]eres move and wheel in their circuits.[337]

With good will for all and malice for none au revoir.

Dr. W. R. Bachelor

DIARY OF 1899
FEB THE 11TH 1899

Saturday night 9 P.M. in my office[.] Thermometer at zero[;] at twelve oclock to day it was 22° above zero. Fer. It has fell 22°. Fer in 9 hours. It is snowing. Pauline returned home this evening from giving music lessons— Alcie Russell has moved to Texas—left Jany the 30th[.][338] To night while gusts of wind and Snow drive against the house making the windows rattle, the house Alcie moved out of Stand[s] empty and desolate. Hence Shipp is here tonight.

While I am trying to be comfortable by the Stove in my library—I think of the many with thin clothing and Scant bedding—with little to eat and coal scarce. May well freeze to night.[339]

[FEBRUARY 12, 1899][340]

This morning Feb the 12th Thermometer at 12. Fer. below zero. [C]oldest weather I have ever Saw in this State.[341]

DIARY OF 1899
SATURDAY NIGHT—JUNE THE 17TH 1899

Well, Summer is here.

May is a beautiful maiden fresh & fas[c]inating. But June makes me think of the glorious Female loveliness of perfect womanhood. Nothing lacking, Grand, Noble, full, complete, is June. So, is a well-sexed woman.[342]

There has been much rain this Spring, vegetation is verry rank. Vick and Girtie cultivating a crop.[343] Yeager in Texas. J H Bachelor at Central, Ark. Alcie & Lula in Texas, balance at home. We Still have music at the Old Homestead. To night Pauline is absent giving music lesson. Though, I and Vick have made some violen music.

Dr. W. R. Bachelor

TO NIGHT AUGUST THE 4TH 1899

Languid July has come and passed with her listless, dreamy, monotony. August come in with the Thermometer above 100°. F. The Catydids Still keep up their well-known music to night. While a Screech-owl occasionally quave[r]s his peculiar pla[i]ntive wail. Leo is barking, as there is a Brush-harbour preaching going on ¾ of a mile away; So all the canines within a radius of Some miles around answer each other.[344] Thinking perhaps, eternal vigilance is the price of liberty. The Old Homestead is lighted up, And while I write, Music on the Organ and violen by Pauline & Victor[.] And the lights Shine out against the dark foliage of the Locust and catalpas in the yard.

Friday night, August the 4th 1899

Dr. W. R. Bachelor

[25 DECEMBER] CHRISTMAS NIGHT, 1899

To day I drove down to Mrs. Burcham's, returned at noon.[345] Nannie Eubanks is on a visit to neighbours. Victor & Girtie have went to a dance. Pauline went yesterday to Cecil—has not returned. While I am writing my wife is in the Sitting room alone. A friend J. W. Smith is here.

So no music at the Old Homestead to night. Dr. J H Bachelor is at <u>Central</u>. Yeager Bachelor is in Texas. So is Lula. Alcie Russell has returned from Texas & lives near me. To night Millions of Stars Shine in their Splendor. [T]here is continuous firing of guns & anvils, with an occasional distant cheering. There is no moon, but visible in the Starlight, are the mountain Slopes, Silent & Slumbering.

Dr. W R Bachelor

Monday night Dec the 25th 1899

9 oclock—night—

DEC THE 31ST 1899

The Old year is passing away forever. The Earth is covered with Snow. No Stars appear—it is cloudy. A fitting emblem of the departure of a year that has witteness the Sanguinary Strife of Nations.[346] Farewell Old year. You made millions of hearts happy—but, Alas! millions wretched. The poets & optimists will sing your prases, while pessimist[s] will re[me]mber you with Sadness. You have saw friends & lovers part, tears & sighs, Joy and laughter. Welcome 1900. [L]et bygones go. But with willing hearts & bouyant hopes let us renew our energies to elevate humanity and the brotherhood of the race.

Studio

Sunday night. Dec the 31st 1899.

Dr. W. R. Bachelor

Studio. 9 P.M. Thursday, May the 10th 1900

It is beautiful May. [T]he Roses are in full bloom, and as I write the odor of honeysuckles fills the room. To day I have taken two long walks. Down the creek below Mrs. Burcham's, and afterwards went, a fishing in Mill creek. We have had frequent genial Showers of rain—crops look promising.

The moon is Shining beautifully to night. Tipping the dark foliage of the trees with a Silvery Sheen. The Chuck-will-widow on the mountain pours forth his Song—as he hovers near his mate. Venus Shines to night with great brilliancy—& grandeur.[347]

Dr. W R Bachelor

[December 25] Christmas—1900—night 9 P.M.

To night at home is verry quiet.[348] It is a beautiful & lovely night. Thousands of Stars twinkle in the ether, The cresent moon hangs above the western hills—her weiard beams outlining the mountains and valley. Only I, my wife, Nannie, and Pauline—who is playing upon the Organ are at home. Victor and Girtie are across the river at Alston. J. H. Bachelor at Central, Yeager & Lula in Texas. I drove out to Mrs. Burcham's this evening—returning late. Alcie Russell—Bach & Elsie were with us at Supper.

Just now, a distant boom of a gun Shows the festival is Still kept up by a few. But midnight approaches when the Christmas festival of 1900 will be a thing of the past forever. Thus, years come and go while throbbing humanity[349] on the ceaseless tide of universal life ebbs and flows.[350]

Dec the 25th 1900

Dr. W R Bachelor

Night Dec the 31st 1900

A few hours hence and 1900 w[*ill have*] passed and gone forever—while Old mother Earth Sweeps along her orbita[*l*] path in Silence. But she carries untold treasures. She never carried grander[,] nobler men and women than She does to night. Strong loving Souls who are not afraid to do and dare for the right. I am glad I am a[n] Optimist. I just went to the door and looked out. The air is crisp, thermomet[*er*] below freezing. How Still, the little [*page torn, word missing*] are asleep—and the noisy insects are silent. The Stars glitter as the [*page torn, words missing*] in their orbits. The denuded fores[*ts*] Shiver and look Sad. No music on the organ to night, Pauline's abse[*nt*] at a neighbours house, but Victor and James Russell played on their violens. Thus is the Old dear homestead to night. In a few hours the New year 1901 will be here. A happy new year—a glorio[*us br*]otherhood of humanity.[351]

Au revoir. Dr. W R Bachelor

JUNE THE 27TH 1901

Glorious Summer is here. Green forests and fields[,] millions of flowers. A tremendous energy is forcing cereals and luxurious vegetation towards maturity. The male of the feathered Songsters Songsters warble[s] his Sweetest music around about the nest [*of a*] loving mate in anticipation of the little Sweet birdlets that [*they*] will soon join in feeding. [*Hi*]s feelings are so jubilant[,] [*page torn, word missing: later?*] in the night between naps, he snatches Some pieces of his Song. It is a beautiful moonlight night. While Some ancient oak is Silouetted again[*st*] the background of the mountain tops.

Pauline Ark Dr. W. R. Bachelor

AUGUST THE 31ST 1901

The summer of 1901 is passin[*g*] away. It has been an excessive[*ly*] hot summer with droughts. A [*page torn, words missing: poor?*] crop of corn, and cotton is no[*thing*] to boast of. It is night. Vic[*tor*] and Pauline are visiting dow[*n abo*]ut Webb City[.] Nannie is sick. [*No*]body at the Old homestead to [*night only*] myself, wife, Nannie, Girtie, [*and*] Sophia. It is hazy—cloudy—f[*ull*] moon. It is a night for insect[*s*]—Katydids, Crickets and every insect that can make a n[*oise*]. [T]hey seem to be aware that the days are Shortning—

Dr. Bachelor

[NI]GHT 25TH OF DECEMBER 1901

Christmas again.

[*The*] Old Homestead is rather Still to [*nig*]ht. But I here the Soft Sweet notes [*of t*]he Guitar in the parlor.

[*It is*] a very beautiful night, fair and [*plea*]sant. The full moon rises over [*the we*]stern hills, and in the South [*page torn, words missing*] [*V*]enus was never more brilliant. [*Th*]ough the fields and forests ar[*e de*]nuded of their Summer verdure [*it is*] beautiful to night in the soft [*m*]oonlight. A quiet Christmas. Victor [*and*] Pauline are visiting. Only I and [*m*]y wife and Nannie, with one visito[*r at*] home. Members of the old [*ho*]mestead are Scattered, Some in [*Te*]xas—and other places. The Old Homestead not just what it used to be. Still, we live in the <u>now</u>.

[*Page torn, words missing: I hear?*] a distant explosion [*bottom of page fragmented*].

[*AUGU*]ST THE 7TH 1902

[*The*] languid listless dogdays [*are*] drawing to a close. The Katydi[*ds are*] still having their honeymoon. [*Page torn, words missing*] the grasshopper on the flexible [*page torn, words missing*] occasionally when shook by [*the*] wind gives a prelude of his [*au*]tumn Song. While the Screech Owl[*'s*] p[*lai*]ntive Schreech is become more frequent.

Yes, the glorious summer of 190[*2*] is on the wane. The birdlings are on the wing regaleing themselves with their happy parent birds. Bob White is heard at longer intervals. The noisy Jays ~~began~~ begin to visit the orchids[352] in flo[*cks*] while the perambulating crow [*is*] always an unwelcome visitor.

Dr. W. R. Bachelor

[DECEMBER 25] CHRISTMAS NIGHT 190[*2*]

[*T*]o day has been pleasan[*t. I*]t was a beautiful Sunset t[*his e*]vening. He sank in a floo[*d of g*]lory. Beautiful tints Stretch[*ing t*]owards the Zenith, awakening a [*page torn, words missing: chorus?*] of imperishable life. Grand Su[*nset*], Serene and Silent. Part of th[*e family*] Circle are at the Old Homestead to night. Some in Texas[,] Arkansas [*a*]nd Oklahoma. Such is life.

But we Still have music at the Homestead. All is Still to night, Touched by the icy finger of winter. The cricket is Silent, the Katydids [*are h*]ushed, the Mockingbird has sung [*his last*] song and gone away. Yet winter [*is*] not without its enjoyments. Then [*let*] us Think of the wise division of the f[*our*] Se[*a*]sons and love them all. An[*d let us*] not forget that "<u>As a man think[*eth, so*] he is.</u>"[353] Then let us think that [*page torn and fragmented at bottom*] and brotherhood [*words missing*] greed fear.[354]

Opening Page of Scrapbook and Second Page of Scrapbook.
Courtesy Wanda Rentz Dailey, Fort Smith, AR, and Susan Dailey Johnson, Pocola, OK.

Occasional Pieces from the Scrapbook of Wilson R. Bachelor (1890s)

I. Reasons for Being an Agnostic (No. 1)[1]

By W. R. Bachelor, Pauline, Ark.

Fifty years ago I read in the Bible, "And the Lord God formed man of the dust of the ground, and breathed into his nostrils the breath of life, and man became a living soul." Twelve years ago I read, "Brahma formed the man and the woman out of the purest of himself, and this done he rested etc." Taking reason as my compass and guiding star, I could not decide which of these declarations were facts.[2] Had I adhered to the teachings of my youth, exercised faith and ignored reason, I should have continued to believe the Biblical declaration. But taking reason for my light and truth for my guide, I could not decide that the Biblical account of the origin of the human race was more reasonable or trustworthy than the Brahimical account. This position was strengthened by the fact that it was not known who wrote the Biblical or Brahimical account of primeval man. A little more reading and reflection showed me, without a doubt that all ancient nation trace their origin to mystery and myth.[3] Then how could I decide who was right? The most reasonable conclusion that I could arrive at was, that the origin of all nations as given by some body was a myth, was false; so you see from whence sprang my doubt.[4] There are many other reasons which I shall hereafter give, why I am an agnostic. But what I have told is the origin and groundwork.[5] I have often had a friendly conversation with my Christian friends on these things but as you know the brain of every man is not alike. You find juries disagree after hearing the evidence; still all are supposed to be honest. This is a matter of evidence with me. I must have evidence of a fact before I will believe it.

(To be continued)

II. Reasons for Being an Agnostic (No. 2)

By W. R. Bachelor, Pauline, Ark.

Finding the origins of all ancient nations to be mythical; I attempted comparative chronology and hieroglyphics.[6] But the result was unsatisfactory. As I expected to find evidence of the Jews and their customs, but failed. The chronology of the Bible as given by Bishop Usher makes the Earth hard by 6000 years old.[7] While scientific geology shows that man antedates the last glacial period which is more than twenty million of years ago. So you see the 6000 years of patristic chronology will not do. Antedating all written books, the hieroglyphics, Inscriptions, monuments and tablets of Egypt, Assyria and Phinicia reveal the names of many kings that reigned, of their conquests and triumphal returns.

So Baal is found, but not God. Also in the Serapheion of Memphis is found the bull Apis. But not a word about Moses, Abraham, Joshua, Sampson or any other Hebrew. So you see an honest doubt arises here as to the antiquity authenticity of the Jewish scriptures.[8] On the monuments of Chaldea are found the names of sixteen kings who reigned, but nothing about any Hebrew.

The Bible says after God created Adam and Eve he put them in a garden. They afterwards disobeyed his orders and were drove out. A parallel myth of Hindoo says, Brahma created man and woman and placed them on the beautiful Island of Ceylon.

He gave them a command to love each other[,] to multiply and never leave the Island. But at last getting tired of their abode, they walked out on a narrow neck of land, and just as they turned to look back at their beautiful Island they saw it go down forever beneath the waters leaving them on a naked rock. Which of these myths shall I assent to—for to my mind, from honest investigation and reason I must regard them as parallel myths.[9] Here my mind turns to evolution as the only reasonable explanation of the human race. Let us see in what attitude the Jewish scriptures stand to philology. The fathers of the Church held for hundreds of years that Hebrew was the primitive language. But now it is known the Sanscrit is the oldest known language. And Bunsen says, "It took 20,000 years for rudimentary language to advance to the state in which it is found in the earliest records."[10] The Bible says all people were of one language, (of course Hebrew) until it was confounded at the Tower of Babel. But science has cleared away the cobwebs, and we find a language older than the Hebrew.[11] Now what must result? why, we see, "The world do moove."[12] The facts of science should be accepted.

III. Reasons for Being an Agnostic (No. 3)

By W. R. Bachelor, Pauline, Ark.

"And it repented the Lord that he had made man on the Earth." Gen. "I will destroy man whom I have created from the face of the Earth." Gen.[13]

Now reader, let us with impartiality and fairness investigate the deluge. Could an Omnipotent God do an act and repent of it afterwards? Did he know when he created man that man would sin and He would destroy all flesh with a flood of waters? "Shall not the judge of all the earth do right."[14] Was it right for the children to be drowned for the sins of their parents? To my mind it is not possible that an allwise and merciful God could repent, or destroy the innocent babes for the sins of their parents.[15]

Where did the water come from that deluged the Earth?[16] The Bible says "the foundations of the great deep were broken up, and the windows of Heaven were opened."[17] This solution to me is not satisfactory. It is demonstrated that for every 40 feet we desend into the earth, heat increases. Far. [W]hich shows at a depth of 30 miles all known substances would be disolved.[18] Ten miles below the surface water would become steam. "Windows of Heaven." Is Heaven a material structure? I take it the writer thought So. It is true a material structure will hold water. But I hardly think my christian friends will contend that a part of the waters of the deludge proceeded from the Windows of Heaven. Rain is caused by a fall of temperature. And is brought about by the meeting and mingling of air currents. Aqueous vapors becoming too heavy for suspension, decend in the form of small particles, uniting with others form raindrops and fall upon the Earth[.] So you see rain does not come from windows, nor from the home of earthquakes and lava rolling over earth's surface in disregard of the laws of gravity. The writers of the Bible record many miracles. There is Baalam's human talking donkey, Sampson drinking water out of a jawbone, a witch raising Samuel, and Jonah's gourd.

Subjected to human reason and common sense it smacks of thaumaturgy. I dont think the clergy preach about these things now. The experience of 10,00,000,000 [*sic*] of people today are against miracles. In my search after evidence of the inspiration of the Bible[19] I find three great manuscripts the Simaitic, the Vatican, and the Alexandrine.[20] These do not agree, besides they were tampered with by the christian fathers who were not overly scrupulous or impartial in their counsels. I have said nothing about the many cruelties and discrepancies of the Bible. My conceptions of a God according to the attributes attributed to him make me doubt the many petty human interferences recorded in the Bible. Why should everything bad be ascribed to God? He drowns the world, destroys 70,000 people because David numbered Israel.[21] If there is a God He is supremely happy in his own fullness and glory. But according to the writers of the Bible He is angry, vindictive, and revengeful. Can either God or man be happy and angry at the same time? When we examine into what we know, and what we don't know, we find we know but little. I certainly don't know the Bible is inspired—therefore I am an Agnostic. THE END.

IV. Untitled and Undated Letter to Editor about Prohibition Party

I always was in favor of gratitude. And surely the people should be grateful to the third party for their opportune discovery that the old parties have brought a once flourishing and contented and happy people to the very verge of ruin.

Now, as they are the only conservators of constitutional guarantees of the people's rights and liberties: they should be speedily put in power. How could Greece have lived without the Oracle of Delphi, or the Romans without Janus?

Then how can we expect to live and flourish without Seers and prognosticators? How welcome is the lighthouse to the tempest-tossed mariner. Or the casting of the steady anchor when the ship is in troubled waters.

The theocratic prohibition party abounds with a feeble wave but liberty loving educated people are getting tired of being told of what is right and what they should do. It is getting too late to try to revive puritanism. It is not pleasant to have so many advisors. One wants sometimes to think for themselves.[22]

Dr. W. R. Bachelor.

V. Come and Gone

The Old Year is passing away.[23] The moon that has shined beautifully for several nights is now (midnight) obscured with wintry clouds. Every thing looks sombre and sad. Perhaps it as it should be, a fitting representation of the death of the Old Year.

My reflections are in keeping with the scene. I see a vast concourse of people of all ages from the smiling babe to the bent form of old age. The millionaire, the beggar, the dainty queen of wealth and beauty, the factory girl with hands hardened with toil.[24] This procession, this Niagara of Humanity[25] is moving on to the Silent Ocean of the future.[26]

Brothers, sisters, we are not permitted to stand and gaze on this passing caravan. We are now already in the column. All going one way. We look behind us, still they come. We look before us, they disappear in the Ocean of Eternity. We will soon be there. The Buddhists say those who die are incarnated and live again in other bodies. The Christians say the good live in a celestial paradise, and the bad in darkness and despair. The Agnostic tells us he don't know. But there is one thing we do know, we know we are now living.

Then with the New Year let us commence anew. Let us be better men and women than ever before. Let us work for right—and join hands in charity with everyone that loves and suffers. If we don't all believe alike, let it not prevent us from doing our duty to our fellow man. Then with a determination to devote our lives to JUSTICE, KINDNESS, AND MERCY, we welcome the New Year 1890.[27]

W. R. Bachelor.

Pauline.

VI. Job and His Book as Viewed in the 19th Century by an Agnostic

Dr. Bachelor

J. E. J. gives a very interesting interview between Orthodox Job and Agnostic Bildad.[28] It was a friendly exchange of ideas and beliefs; good feelings prevailing. Well what about Job? All we know about him is from the Biblical account. "He lived in the land of W z."[29] No person pretends to know who Job was, or when he lived, or whether he ever lived. But the writer says he had seven sons and three daughters and owned much property. And says that the sons of God presented themselves and Satan came among them. These sons of God are mentioned in Gen. just before the deluge marrying the daughters of men. They seem to be the precursor of calamities. Perhaps they better have been kept at home. I thought God only had one only begotten Son. However the Lord and Satan were on speaking terms, and proposed to settle a mooted question of Job's loyalty to his master by a test, which the Lord admits is wrong. "And the Lord said unto satan hast thou considered my servant Job, that there is none like him in the Earth, a perfect and upright man, one that feareth God and escheweth evil! and still he holdeth fast his integrity, although thou movest me against him to destroy him without cause," Job 3–6.

Now as to Job's patience, I have been a practitioner of medicine for nearly 40 years.[30] During that time I have treated many patients of lingering and diversified diseases, but I have never treated a patient but what had more patience than Job. Hear him—"Let the day perish wherein I was bornd." ★ ★ ★ ★ "Let that day be darkness: let not God regard it from above." ★ ★ ★ ★ ★ "Let them curse it." ★ ★ ★ ★ ★ "Why did I not die."

And after it was all over Job still had seven sons and three daughters, and was rich. What sense is there in this book? Why should God wish to convince the devil that Job pleased God? Did he expect to convert him? Now let us take a reasonable and practical view of the matter. The writer of the book of Job was fully imbewed with the superstition of the childhood of the world. A Devil (Satan) is walking up and down the earth. Sabeans take his oxen and kill his servants. [It is the Lord]—The Chaldeans take his Camels and slay his servants[.] It is the Lord. A cyclone smote the house where his sons and daughters were eating and drinking wine. It is the Lord. Job has a bad case of the Itch or Smallpox or something worse. It is the Lord. After awhile he gets well and becomes prosperous.[31]

It is the Lord. Who believes in 1892 there is a devil walking about seeking whom he may devour? Who believes now, when the Mexicans make a raid into Texas and steal horses,—It is the Lord. Who believes when the Indians danced the war dance and killed a few of the whites, It was the Lord? Who believes now when a cyclone demolishes a building, It is the Lord. Who believes now when a man has a bad case of Itch or Smallpox, It is the Lord. And where is a man of intelligence today if disaster and sickness overtake him, will whine and curse the day he was bornd.

Why J. E. J. if he had Wrticarie and I were called in, I would say, my dear sir you will get well. If you don't rest well tonight take Anticamnia.[32] He would not like Job curse the day he was born. Job is evidently a failure so far as patience is concerned.

The superstition of Job has not yet eliminated from the human. It is so convenient for mankind to throw their sin on somebody. So between God's will and the devil's actions, they try to exculpate themselves. Why not be honest and say it was not God nor the devil, but I myself.

Job's ideas of Satan were no doubt of Persian origin. The dualism of Zoroaster.[33]

The devil had a great run through Norse Mythology and our superstitious Teutonic forefarthers. But in modern times the incarnation of devils has been destroyed by science, and reformed religious exegesis.

The book of Job is highly poetical and allegorical and I think a work of fiction.[34] No lesson can be drawn from it to benefit this age.

VII. Obituary [of Sarah Bachelor]

Died of la grippe and pneumonia January the 15th, 1892, Sarah R. Bachelor aged 68 years.[35]

Written by Dr. W. R. Bachelor and read by request, by Rev. J. T. Evans, at the grave.

My sister sleeps here. For forty years she saw neither sunshine nor flowers, or the faces of those she loved, for she was blind. For fifteen years she has not heard the singing of birds nor the happy laughter of children, for she was deaf. Yet how often I have heard her say when walking out into the sunshine, "Oh, the blessed sunshine." The greater part of her life being deprived of sight and hearing was shadow and gloom. But now, she is done with human life. We know she sleeps, and is at rest. What more can be said? Death makes all equal. There is neither rank nor distinction. Seeing and hearing with her now, is the same as with the countless dead who have gone before.[36] Yes, we shall miss Blind Sally.

May the sunshine which she loved but could not see, shine on her resting place, and soft winds murmur above her head. And now, to our loved and loving Sister, farewell, farewell.

Dr. W. R. Bachelor.

Pauline.

VIII. Obituary [of Rubie Bachelor]

Died, Dec. 4th, Rubie, the infant daughter of D. J. H. and Vilola Bachelor, aged nine weeks.[37]

Spoken at the grave by the writer.

The little babe Rubia, came like a sunbeam to brighten us a short time, and then passed on to the land of dreams.

A dewy rosebud soon wilted. What are we anyhow? Arrows shot from the darkness into darkness across a ray of light.

Strictly speaking there is no death—only a change of form.

Our ashes build new organizations; our lives pass out into the great universal life.[38]

So with the little babe that has passed away.

Its body we now consign to Mother Earth, its life is in the great universal life, and now; Farewell—a long Farewell.

Dr. W. R. Bachelor

Pauline.

IX. Unrest and Tendencies of Organization

To the Hon. Thos. Boles, Fort Smith[39]

Dear Sir:—Your very able and thoughtful letter of the 4th has been read and reread by me with much pleasure and profit.[40] Its tone is reasonable, manly, and optimistic. But the position I occupied before your letter is unchanged. With a little modification, the position or cause of unrest in the United States and in fact all the civilized world is the result of a higher civilization and more liberal ideas. In the medieval times during the feudal system of 400 years in Europe, was there any such dissatisfaction among the masses as is now in the civilized world? No[.] How did they live in medieval times? Let Dr. Draper answer, he says: "they had cabins of reed plastered with mud, houses of vaulted stakes, chimneyless peat fires from which there was scarcely any escape for smoke, dens of physical and moral pollution, swarming with vermin, wisps of straw twisted round the limbs to keep off the cold, the age-stricken peasant with no help except shrine cure."[41] Yet there was no unrest. None of them scarcely could and had nothing to read. Thus things continued with very little improvement until the year 1600 when Martin Luther boldly asserted the individalism of humanity. What was the result? A thirty years war. At the end of which the right of private interpretation of the Bible was conceded. So you see that war came with more freedom and enlightenment. Now we turn to the French revolution. The ideas of republicanism having been imbibed by the masses from the American war of freedom to which was added their burdensome taxes imposed by the nobles and clergy. Chamber's Encyclopedia says, "the clergy kept pace with the nobles in general depravity." Thus again individualism asserted itself precipitating a bloody revolution. Which was only a reaction of the people against depraved nobility and priestly rule. Englishmen[,] liberal ideas[,] and individualism has ended monarchy in France. Sixty years ago nothing much was said about slavery in the United States, but some fifteen years afterwards Loyd Garrison and Wendell Phillips started a crusade against slavery which never ceased until the last slave was set free. Was there any unrest among the people north and south on the subject of slavery? Surely there was and it culminated in a war, the effects of which are still felt. Now I ask, was it not a higher civilization and more liberal ideas that freed the slave? Of course it was. For there is not a highly civilized nation on the earth today that enslaved a race.[42] This leads us down to the present times. Again we are face to face with the greatest dissatisfaction and unrest with which we have ever been confronted. We have seen what it foreboded at the reformation. We have seen what it foreboded in the revolution of France. We have seen it as a precurser of the great rebellion in the United States, but who can lift the veil and tell us what is now coming. What means that clamor of multitude? That losing of confidence in the old political parties? That envy and dissatisfaction towards the aristocracy? Why is it the churches are asking "how can we reach the masses?" Why is it when the church bell tolls at a chapel of a manufacturing town now on a Sabbath morning but few respond? When thirty years ago the seats were all filled, then when the preacher came if any of the laborers were sick he visited them, and told them to be reconciled to their lot, that for their hardsdips [*sic*] here, if they were faithful they would receive a reward in heaven and they believed it[.] But now it is not so. They no longer propose to be fed on future promises, they want something now. And why? Because freethought literature is read by the thousands in every town and hamlet, and a leavel[43] of socalled infidelity or liberal ideas such as was never known before is passing over the world. What means all the talk about the criticisms of the bible and the remodeling of creeds. [I]t shows this is a transitional age, that a crisis is at hand. What is the remedy? Ah! There is none. Who offers one? The republican party, the democratic party, the alliance, the prohibition, and the churches. They cannot give it. It is the result of evolution to a higher integration. The outcome of advancing civilization and liberal ideas.[44] This great restless multitude, when once politically cemented together will sweep away all opposing forces. It behooves every man to keep cool and be vigilant. And help to bridge over the chasm without darkness and bloodshed. The culmination of humanity and the crowning of manhood and individuality must come. It is the work of evolution.[45]

Yours truly,

W. R. B.

X. Untitled (Commentary on Petition for Sabbath Closing, World's Fair)

Petitions continue to pour into the Senate asking that the World's Fair be closed on Sunday.[46] Some of the christian papers I see, are urging its closing. Why is this? Is it possible they think a secular government should be run by ecclesiasticism.[47] Did Christ or his disciples even interfere in secular matters? Christ said "render unto Caesar things that be of Caesar[.]" "My kingdom is not of this world[.]" The clergy claim their mission is to preach repentance and faith, yet I see many of them are sending in their petitions through congressmen to have the Fair closed on Sunday, they call it a national sin and crime for it to be opened on Sunday. Is it a national sin and crime to let the hundreds of thousands of poor people see the Fair on Sunday, the only day they can loose for they cannot afford to loose a single days pay during the working days? At the Centennial Exposition, in Philadelphia in 1876, 70,000 laborers and mechanics pleaded for admission on Sunday, but were refused, through the influence of the clergy. At the coming World's Fair ten times that number will be turned away if it is closed on Sunday. Will this be treating the poor people right? The wealthy can go in their fine carriages through the week, and rest, or go to church on Sunday, but not so with poor laboring men. This incessant talk about Sunday laws and christian government is enough to make one tired. This is not a christian government. George Washington said: "The government of the United States is not in any sense founded on the Christian religion."

Nor is it true that christianity is the common law of our country. The name of God is not in the constitution neither is it used when a President of the United States takes the oath of office.[48]

Chief Justice Story of the supreme court, speaking of the bill of rights says[,] "It must have been intended to extend equally to all sects, whether they believe in christianity or not, and whether they are Jews or infidels." It would seem that ecclesiasticism has forgotten the history of church and state. Talk about religious government—don't they all claim to be? Don't Russia? When our fathers came to this country and established a republican form of government did they still expect christianity to rule? If so, why rebel against their mother authorities? No, our government is secular. Let us have none of this national religion. Such has caused the butchery of 100,000,000 people. Let religion keep within its own province, the spiritual and emotional, and not arrogate to itself the seculary governing power. Every person who is a friend to the poor and is in favor of liberty should work for the opening of the Fair on Sunday.[49]

W. R. Bachelor.

XI. Mob Law

All newspaper readers must have observed the great increase of mob law.[50] Is it not about time to call a halt, and for every honest law-abiding citizen to denounce it and put himself in opposition to it? It is time this silly twaddle about threatened justice in courts should be sit down upon. How do these Solomons know that justice is not done?[51] It is unpardonable effrontery for a man to say after a case has been tried by a lawful tribunal that a mob could try cases better, is a crowd of angry men competent to decide the guilt or innocence of a prisoner? Did a mob ever declare the innocence of a prisoner? Has there ever been an appeal from a mob's decision? Are they always right (?) where courts are sometimes wrong. What is the leading spirit of a mob? Echo answers, "revenge." Every good citizen should say down with mob law, let the courts and juries do their duty fearlessly and people should be satisfied. Appeal to mob law is to enthrone a Robespierre and inaugurated a reign of terror.[52] It is a relief of barbarism, a twin sister of mediaevil [*sic*] cruelty, a stigma on the intelligence of the nineteenth century.[53]

W. R. B.

Pauline, Arkansas.

XII. A Dream[54]

After a democratic meeting in Alabama, at which Kolb and Jones factions rubbed their fists in each other's faces and finally, with the help of wildcat whiskey, pounded each other and shouted themselves hoarse, John Enos[55] returning home got benighted, and having imbibed a little too freely besides coming out second best in a fight with a Kolbite, lay down in the pine straw. He dreamed he went to heaven.[56] He was met by St. Peter, who, pushing the gate ajar, asked him for his credentials. His reply was, "I am a democrat." Peter, after surveying him a little, critically said, "We wish to know your creed and belief." Enos promptly responded, a little louder, "I am a democrat," surprised that that magic word did not obtain for him a welcome entrance. But Peter, looking at him suspiciously, said, "We tolerate no foolishness here; tell me your business." "Well," said Enos, "this is heaven, ain't it." "It is," said Peter. "Well," said Enos, "I want to go to the democratic headquarters, for I tell you Jones' letter yields the governorship up to Kolb than for Harrison to carry the State with his robber tariff and force bill."[57]

"See here, young man," said Peter, slowly elevating his keys, "I deprived a better man than you of an ear. Beware how you come here talking about politics and persons we have never heard of before."

"Please your saintship," said Enos in subdued tones, "have you never heard of democrats?"

"No; what are they distinguished for?"

"If your holy reverence will allow me to proceed, I will respectfully inform you."

"Speak," said Peter; "but if you utter untruth you are lost."

Enos was seized with great trepidation and trembling. His knees smote together and his tongue clove to the roof of his mouth. In his great fright he spoke thusly:

"The democrats are a political party that wants to rule a portion of the earth called the United States. It is a rich nation and the offices pay well. They believe the end justifies the means. That lying, fraud, misrepresentation, intimidation and shot-guns should be used if necessary to put them in power, or keep them there."

"Stop," said Peter, "that will do. And you came here expecting to find such men?"

Enos saw that in his great fear he had told the truth, and stood convicted and dumbfounded before the saint. He was speechless with fear.

Peter, pointing to a terrible chasm that looked like a sunken continent said, "Go! Join your friends!"

The gate shut; Enos felt in the darkness he was falling, falling, into the yawning depths. A shocking thrill, as if a thousand needles pierced him, and with a terrible effort he jumped to his feet. The gallinippers, disturbed in their picnic, sung about his ears.[58] He slowly wended his way home.

Pauline, Ark. W. R. B.

XIII. A Freethinker's View of Franklin, on the Presidential Election

(W. R. Bachelor)

Mr. Editor: In three weeks somebody has to eat crow.[59] Cleveland knows how it eats as he has tried it once. Harrison, I would think, could eat it pretty well; but could he return thanks?—as I suppose is his usual custom. This is an apathetic campaign. If it were Blaine and Reed against Hill and Boies, we would have lively times, with probably a democratic victory.[60] But as it stands now—the pensioner's vote, federal patronage, a disinclination for any change among capitalists, renders Harrison's election possible if not probable. I see the signs of the times point to the future when politics will determine everything. When a man proposes now to run for an office in some places he is asked if he is for or against license, or alliance. In others, is he of a labor organization. The time is coming when he will be asked if he is a Catholic, a Methodist, a Baptist, or Agnostic; and according to the answer he will be boycotted or supported. This tends to make politics more corrupt, for candidates will be and act the hypocrites for votes. While I deprecate this tendency, I accept the situation and hold liberty of thought above all political organizations.[61]

XIV. A Democratic Wall[62]

Tell it not in Gath, publish it not in the streets of Askelon[63] let the force bill and robber tariff men rejoice.[64] Where, Oh, where is Hill?[65] Gray Buzzards is silent.[66] Ominous sea gulls pass by. That great Democratic meeting in New York. Why, Oh, why did Hill go on the 10 o'clock train to Alabama? "He is a democrat," what can he be thinking about? Tammany is all right, so the democratic Papers.[67] I wonder if he don't know it. Somebody ought to tell him. "Tell it not in Gath."

This hippodroming of the occupant of Gray Buzzards at New York, to try and conciliate Tammany.[68] Nobody is fooled now. But has the American people, or a part of them, lost their individualism? When Grover Cleveland started to New York it was: "Now is the winter of our discontent made glorious summer by this (Dave Hill) and clouds which lowered upon our (party), in the deep bosom of the ocean buried."[69] But when he stood upon the platform there was Hill! "Mr. Cochran how is your throat?"[70] How humiliating! Does anyone know how Mr. Cochran's throat is? Thirty speeches to make in three weeks! Who is scared about New York now? Yes, Tammany is all right; everything is harmonious. Hill and Cochran are going to speak. "They are democrats." Is truth at discount while there is a premium on lying?

W. R. B.

Pauline, Ark.

XV. Don't Let the Senate See God's Denuded Arm

Pauline, Ark., Jan. 22, 1894

Mr. Editor: Talmage's wail: "Arm of the Lord Awake!"[71] "God has never half tried!" "There is such a reserve force." After contemplating the inroads of Mohammedanism he yells: "We are looking for the stretched-down, bared arm of the God of Nations."[72] This is news. We thought the distinguished person (Talmage's God) had "half tried" when he worked once six days and got so tired he had to rest, and for sometime afterwards could only walk in the garden in the cool of the day; when he drowned the world in the cause of morality; stopped the sun to murder; when he wrestled all night with Jacob. But now we know what was the matter—he didn't roll up his sleeve to the shoulder and "bare his right arm." Still we suggest a better way would be to go into training for three months and then strip bare to the belt and try Corbett.[73]

Since I come to think of it, Talmage's prize-fighter has killed but three or four himself. Let us see—there was Er, and Onan, and Nabal, and perhaps one or two more.[74] It was his followers who did the killing, but said he told them to do it. We hope to hear from Heston on that comet's-tail arm.

Dr. W. R. Bachelor.

XVI. Christmas

A festival celebrated in christian countries to commemorate the birth of Christ.[75]

Every month of the year has held claim to this honor. But they have finally settled down to the 25th, of Dec. But that is hardly correct, as shepherds would not likely be watching their flocks in winter in Syria.

As a matter of fact hundred of years before the birth of Christ the Scandinavians held the festival of the Winter Solstice, and later the Germans the "Yule Feast." It was a Pagan festival adopted by the christians a few centuries after Christ.[76]

The announcement by an angel of the birth of Christ as given in Luke gives rise to reflections. We read Angels eat calf bread and butter with Abraham;[77] unleavened bread with Lot.[78] The one that visited old Manoah's wife wouldn't eat.[79] The one that visited Mary, I believe, was not asked to eat.[80] The last one we read of was standing with his right foot upon the sea and his left foot upon the earth swearing there should be time no longer.[81] That has been nearly 2,000 years ago. It seems in this age when the steam engine rushes through the glens and crashes through the bowels of the everlasting hills; when on the wings of the lightning, we speed our messages over the nations of the continents and under the billows of the oceans: and when the press lays at the feet of the humblest the mind wealth of the world we don't need angels any longer.[82] That is to say the business world. Though I believe our christian friends say that they are guarded by angels of nights—but not of the Abraham variety. Superstition is surely departing before science as mist before the morning sun. The ideal must give way to the practical while manhood and womanhood rises in the scale of humanity.[83]

Dr. Bachelor.

Pauline, Ark.

XVII. Midnight

1892 is gone![84]

Gone, with its clamor of multitudes and the unrest of millions.—Gone with its statesmen, poets, millionares and paupers.

Gone. High throbbing hopes and abject despair. All gone into the great maelstrom of nature's laboratory.[85] The sinking ship,[86] the devastating cyclone,[87] the cholera pestilence.[88]

Time. What can I say of time? Turning toward the vision of the past, what do I see? Millions of solar systems. Before the nebular coheared to an orb, time was.[89]

The primeval beds of oceans—the sunken Atlantis, are the trophies of time. The extinct mastodon, the cave bear and the maker of flint arrows. The Incas of Peru, and the Negritos of India, swallowed up in time.[90]

Time is change. It is as limitless as space. Cycles of time have wrought nature as we see it. Cycles will still make future changes.[91]

Time is as deathless as eternity. It is eternity. It never had a beginning: it will never have an ending. Its silence is eloquent with colliding suns, grating worlds and hissing orbs.

Its pathway is strewn with wrecks. The Sphinx still gazes, while Balbec, Memphis and Thebes lie in ruins.[92] The pyramids of the Toltecs are sinking in the sand, and Cholua is crumbling to dust.[93] Where the priest offered sacrifice and chanted the weired [*sic*] rites of the Aztecs, the scorpion now rears her behind. Cortez has passed away, and the halls of the Montezumas are silent.[94]

Human life is an electric sunbeam.[95] Let us improve every moment. Good acts and kind words will never die. Let us not think of self, but for future humanity, and welcome 1893.

Pauline. Dr. W. R. Bachelor.

XVIII. Leaving the Old Ruts[96]

Some 15 years ago Cannon Farrar[97] and Henry Ward Beecher[98] publicly announced from their pulpits their disbelief in a literal burning hell. The religious world was startled and shocked at such heresy. Now, the orthodox of the orthodoxy don't believe in such a hell: A Few years ago a question was sprung at a Missionary Board, some one asserting that he did not believe that heathens would be damned who had never heard of Christ.[99] Heresy again. Since that the Westminster confession of faith has been revised.[100] The latest, Dr. Briggs who affirmed and stuck to it—that a man could be saved by reason.[101] That Moses did not write the pentateuch. That the Bible contained errors—and errors were in the original text. The smell of heresy was again rank in the air. Well might the old grayhaired professors view the proceedings with alarm when Dr. Briggs was sustained after these utterences.

Considering the puritanical and conservative position of the Presbyterian church, those strides towards liberalism indicate investigation[,] Scholarship and deep research coupled with manhood and individuality. Is not Dr. Briggs a freethinker? We commend the good Dr. and extend to him the right hand of fellowship.

The Dr. need not be afraid of heresy in rationalism. The air is pure—the intellect untrammeled.

Pauline. Dr. Bachelor.

XIX. The Old and the New

Will we be Burned or Will we be Drowned?

Time—Midnight, 1893–1894[102]

According to Professor Croll every 10,000 years, owing to the eccentricity of the earth's orbit, and the procession of the equinoxes, accumulations of ice take place at one of the poles, causing the earth to change its centre of gravity, thus inundating the heavy parts and raising submerged continents.[103] These cataclysms send boulder drift over the earth's surface, while islands sink beneath the waters. Our planet has been subjected to many such changes, which are always attended with destruction of organic life. Accordingly in about 4,000 years hence the center of gravity will again be changed, burying most of the civilized world and upheaving mountains from the bottom of the ocean. Men and animals—in fact, everything that breatheth will become extinct. The earth, in one of two ways, is certainly doomed to destruction, so far as animal life is concerned, either by being submerged beneath the waters, or by explosion (fire). When the centre of gravity changes and the earth careens in its orbit the cavities caused by the abstraction of petroleum being filled by the heated, melted matter of the interior of the earth, will likely produce an explosion promiscuously throwing together soil, rocks and water. Geology teaches us that the earth has passed through many cataclysms and a future one is certain.

Then to the old year we say, farewell with your burden. You belong with the past. We hail the incoming new year with joy, though it is another step towards our extinction. Happy New Year! Let us love humanity—we are brothers and sisters. My Motto is: The time to be happy is now, the place to be happy is here; the way to be happy is to make others happy.[104]

Dr. W. R. Bachelor.

Pauline, Ark.

XX. Untitled Letter to Editor

Editor News: In a recent article penned by J. R. Dunn M. D. he says:—if one party be true (that is the Adventist or materialist) "we can only use ourselves during this life." "This life is only a shadow:['] Again he says "I am aware that Adventists or Materialists will say I am misrepresenting them.["][105]

I presume the Adventists can take care of themselves. But as he seems not to understand the Materialists I would say to him, he need not fear that he will be accused of misrepresenting them, by intimating that a man cannot "use himself only during this life."

Now, as a matter of fact, Materialists don't believe in immaterial entities. Such metaphysical, hypothesis don't enter into their reasonings. They hold that every function of the living organism—will, observation, reflection and memory, are the results of molecular change in the cerebrum. They would ask you to demonstrate that man possessed that individual entity (soul)[,] When it entered the organism, and where it was before it entered. The writer also says if materialism be true, "we can only use ourselves in this life." Well, can he prove we will "use ourselves in another life?['] What is ourselves? Is it the ego? When a man dies is the ego buried?[106]

"We use ourselves" what is we—what is ourselves? Is we the soul, and we the ego? Suppose we say we voted ourselves for Cleveland, or we did not get for ourselves religion and will be lost—which will be lost—we or ourselves? A materialist believes in a soul the concensus of all the faculties of the human organism. The writer should study cerebration and read Huxley.[107]

Dr. Bachelor.

Pauline.

XXI. Correspondence[108]

"The very hairs of your head are numbered."[109]

O! vain man. To think, you can penetrate the wisdom of God.[110]

Presumptions mortal! To dare, to think to know what is for your own good. When cyclones wreck houses, and deal death and destruction to families. Floods rushing over the earth, destroying life and leaving destruction, sorrow, and suffering, in their wake. Of course all come from the hand of Him who tempers the wind to the shorn lamb.[111]

Yes, as death rides on earthquakes, floods and tornadoes, and the wails and shrieks of the dying rise above the din of elemental strife, it is consoling to know that we have a kind and merciful Father who doeth all things for the best.

I see the husband as he rushes wildly through the wrecks hunting for his wife and child. Ah! God, here they are. She holds her jewel in he[r] arms—but it is dead. Her white breast is purple where the cruel beam has done i[t]s deathly work. The husband with a wild cry falls on his knees beside his dead darlings and clasp[s] them to his breast, and for the moment forgets God is merciful and good.

A woman with five helpless children finds her husband mangled and lying beneath heavy timbers. Yes, there are the hands hardened by toil that cheerfully worked for his loved ones, now still forever. She will never again send little Bertie to papa in the field with a cool drink of water. The baby never more will climb on his knees and put its arms around his neck. No, the fond lips that kissed his darling babe are now stilled forever. But it ought to be a consolation to the mother to know, that God is merciful. And that God's ways are not as man's ways—that while man is sometimes cruel, God is always merciful and pities his children.

A valuable lesson could be drawn from the man whose wife and three children were burned in a conflagration. He was reduced to a contorted skeleton by rheumatism. Next received into the poor-house. There helpless and fed by the nurse, thanked God for his mercies and fatherly care. He was one of the [man]y men who appreciates the bless[ings] of divine providence. Why cannot the human race value the great blessings that are continually showered on them in disguise. Some men are simple enough to think that force is uncreated, and not directed by intelligent design.[112] But how are such, to account for that Fatherly care and protection exercised over us?[113]

Some are so wicked as to build storm houses to protect themselves—relying on their own strength. Is not that flying in the face of providence? For who can resist His will?[114] When Oh when will vain man learn to trust with humility?[115]

Dr. Bachelor.[116]

Pauline.

XXII. Providence

I wonder if President Harrison still believes in providence.[117] If he does he must feel badly, to think providence is against him, a good man, and in favor of a man that sometimes says such emphatic words as are not supposed to come from those of "true inwardness."

It does seem that this belief in providence ought to give rest. But does it? Just now, as the powers of government are passing from the hands of the republican party to the democratic party, the republicans, if they believe in a Supreme Ruler and providence, should cheerfully accept defeat and gladly make the transfer.[118] "He doeth according to his will in the army of Heaven, and among the inhabitants of the earth." Daniel 4, 35. So that settles it. If the democrats had thought of this, they need not have sung the force bill. Of course this is a christian government—with either party in power. So are all nations governed by this power. ★ ★ ★ ★ "For there is no power but of God: the powers that be are ordained of God." Rom. 13, 1. Thus are all nations governed. England, France, Germany, China and Russia govern their subjects by the same power. So you see this boast about our government being Christian is nothing to brag about. When the Czar of Russia sends his subjects to the mines of Siberia, they should be thankful and accept the dispensation of providence cheerfully, knowing all governing powers are from God. And, by the way, is it not presumption and sinful audacity for the people's party to try to wrest the administration of the government from the old parties? Somebody ought to show[119] them Romans 13, 2. "For this cause pay ye tribute also." So as the inscrutable ways of providence are the ministrations of the divine will for the ruling of nations, no person ought to kick, for if they do, ★ ★ ★ ★ "They that resist shall receive to themselves damnation." Romans 13, 2. So never interfere with providence.

Dr. Bachelor.

Pauline.

XXIII. The Death Penalty

That the shadows of the gallows[120] should still fall upon the salt of civilization[121] is one of the enigmas of the present age.[122] The auto-da-fe, the wheel, the rack had their victims of torture and death, but the gallows-tree still remains a relic of barbarism.

The object of punishment it is said is two-fold—the reformation of the criminal, and to deter others from committing crime. Does it do it? That is the question. The advocates of capital punishment say so—let us see. So far from preventing crime it seems often to stimulate it, by obtunding the sensibilities, hardening the heart and strangely fascinating the animal propensities. A man witnessed a hanging at Alexandria, Va., and murdered a man as he returned home. He was executed. The man who saw it murdered his wife that night. Murdering and suicides are much increased by the presence of danger. It gives rise to a sensation akin to a feeling some people experience when standing on the edge of a precipice that they must jump off.

What is the effect of capital punishment on the officers of the law? The judge on pronouncing the first sentence his voice is husky with emotion but soon passes away upon a repetition. It is said Nero was once tender hearted and that Robespiere in his youth resigned his judgeship rather than sign a death warrant.

"Deter others from committing crime." Why an English Chaplain tells us out of 167 prisoners he prepared for execution 161 had witnessed executions.

Why don't the executions, torturing and burnings in the South deter rapists? Why are men casting about trying to find some way to destroy life without pain? Certainly because they have become more civilized and refined. When a stream of decapitated heads rolled from the guillotine in France did it deter anybody? Constant contact with criminals and executions blunt the sensibilities even of an enlightened conscience. Sometimes innocent people are executed. In England during 200 years 200 innocent people were butchered. How do we know but what crime is a disease as same as insanity? The presumption is strange—in fact, I think it can be demonstrated that parents transmit to their children a propensity to crime, which in some constitutions is irresistible. If consumption and scrofula[123] are transmitted, why not theft and homicide? If nervousness from prenatal impressions why not dipsomania?[124] We need light here. I am glad to see more talented men and women are beginning to pay attention to this subject.

Again, why should counsel for prosecution and judges nearly always be in favor of conviction? Some years ago in New York when a jury brought in a verdict of not guilty the judge said: "You are discharged from this term—leave the room. You are not fit to sit as jurors in my court." It is no uncommon thing now in case a jury don't convict to be told by the judge "they have erred." A jury must be guarded—not allowed to read the morning papers. While the judge converses with whom he pleases and reads the morning papers that have prejudged the case—like this: "John Smith will be convicted for Judge ———- is trying the case and he will see that justice is done." Who is most likely to be biased by public sentiment.

The death penalty was abolished in Holland, Switzerland, Portugal, Belgium and Roumania, also Michigan, Rhode Island, Wisconsin and Maine in the United States. Crime did not increase.[125] But I am asked, "What makes so many lynchings?"[126] My answer is, because this is an age for suicide and mobomania.[127] A period of moral and criminal epidemics. The world has witnessed in the past such epidemics as Demonomania, Theomania, Flagellants and Witches.[128]

This is a transitional age.[129] Men are losing faith in the theology and rulership of the world, while many are not yet prepared for the new. But I am asked again what about the reforming influences of punishment?" A man under sentence of death for mu[r]der, he has killed his man thus sealing his fate. Now he is told to seek forgiveness of his judge before whom he must soon appear. Is it right that one man should be so fortunate to kill a man and be hung for it to go to Heaven, while the murdered man goes to hell? This sheet-iron thunder[130] of future punishment can't reform—nobody is frightened now. We must look to pre-natal conditions—rightly borned.[131] The rule of life should be for the sentiment of honor instead of fear.[132]

Dr. Bachelor.

Pauline, August 1, 1893.

XXIV. Sub Rosa Items (Eulogy for Henderson Rice)

Departed this life on Friday, Sept. [page torn], 1888, Hencerson Rice,[133] in his seventieth year, after an illness of several weeks. His grieved friends have our sympathy.

The following address was rendered at his grave by Dr. W. R. Bachelor of Pauline:

Friends: It being the request of our departed brother that I should make some remarks at his grave, in discharging this painful duty we but return to nature what her laws have given forth. For him life's fitful fever is over. The duties of earth he has nobly filled by generous deeds ane [*sic*] free invertigation. His religion was the religion of kindness and humanity. He was an independent thinker and worked for truth, justice and morality. He was not afraid to die because he had lived life aright. He was not afraid of Hell (t[*he*] Heathen myth), believing in that shin[*ing*] universe, there was no room for such a black spot.

Our departed brother was a free think[*er*] because he had bursted the shackles [*of*] hide-bound creeds and dared to think [*for*] himself. His liberality, courage, calm and fortitude, let us endeavor to emu[*late*].

Our brother, although now at rest, [*his*] words we still hear, urging us on to d[*eeds*] of right and usefulness.

To him death had no terror, but c[*ame*] as a soothing friend to release him f[*rom*] the toils and sufferings of humanity. In the sear and yellow lief [*sic*] of his life, he pa[*ss*]ed to that undiscovered country; that bo[*urne*] from which no traveler returns.

Brethren, Death is that kind friend wh[*o*] takes us by the hand when we are sick [*and*] weary, and leads us to the cool and sil[*ent*] shade. In the repose of the tomb, [*our*] friend has found that eternal rest, wh[*ich*] is the heritage of the weary. When h[*is*] end drew near he said: "I die a free-thin[*k*]er and am not ashamed of it. No ar[*gu*]ment can change me; no prayers can ma[*ke*] me more resigned to death, I have liv[*ed*] long enough and am ready and willing [*to*] go." These were his words, So to you his bereaved friends, I can only say, all is well.

Our brother feared no angry or vind[*ic*]tive Being beyond the grave; for he believed in no superstition, nor eternal punishment. And now as the grave closes over his once beloved form, may the earth l[*ie*] lightly on him. May the flowers eve[*r*] bloom over his silent remains, while evening zephyrs softly sigh, as they herald the coming night. Peace and rest to his ashes; his memory we will always love and cherish. "Farewell; a long farewell."[134]

Observer.

XXV. A Letter

Editor Ensign:[135]—I very much admired some articles appearing in your most excellent Paper on "Societal Purity."[136] It is a question fast coming to the front and all reformers and humanitarians would do well to dig to the bed rock. The previous constructions put on such passages as: "Thy desire shall be unto thy husband and he shall rule over thee."[137] "Wives be in subjection to your own husbands."[138] etc., has caused untold cruelties and suffering to wives and mothers. Women for thousands of years were looked upon as only property, servants and beasts of burden.[139]

The fathers of the church, or Christian fathers as they are called, regarded women as the next thing to the devil. Chrysostrum said "Women is a necessary evil."[140] Gregory Thaumaturgus said, "One man among a thousand may be pure, a woman, never."[141] Hear the great Milton:[142]

"Oh, Why did God
Creator wise, that peopled highest heaven
With spirits masculine, create at last
This novelty on earth, this fair defect
Of nature, and not fill the world at once
With man as angels, without feminine?"

I contend the emancipation and elevation of women to be the first step in "Social Purity". So long as she remains a slave, subject to master, having no rights of her own "Social Purity" is hampered. Give her all the rights of womanhood. Surround her ante-natal conditions with favorable influences. Let her study physiology and her responsibilities as a mother, and the foundation of "Social Purity" is laid.[143]

Dr. Bachelor.

Pauline, Ark.

XXVI. Correspondence[144]

"What bloody man is that? He can report as seemeth his plight."—Macbeth. Sam Jones[145] preached in Memphis for the purpose of improving morals and saving souls—and thanked God for mob law.[146] I had just been reading of Harrison's selection of Jackson for the supreme bench.[147] And Cleveland's choice of Judge Gresham for Secretary of State.[148] So I was beginning to think that I could see streaks of the early dawn of the millennium.[149] Then imagine my surprise when I saw Sam Jones's treasonable gush. Now, if Sam had talked about "the lamb and the lion lying down together" "resist no evil." Probably I would have thought erelong Gabriel might send us a blast.[150] But alas! Sam says "Your eyes drop millstones when fool's fall tears." King Richard III.[151] As to mob law there is food for reflection. Why should we have more in the United States than any other country? Is it because the rights of minorities are less respected here than in any other country? The French went from a convention to a constitution; and we are now fast going from a constitution to a convention.

What is the difference between the "sovereignty of a king and the sovereignty of the people"? Mob law is the ebullition of the worst passions of a lawless majority—the sovereignty of an element destructive to law and order. It is the brute force of majorities over minorities.[152]

It will soon be found out that mob law instead of restraining viciousness and crime—only stimulates the worst passions of human nature.[153]

"Whither are we d[r]ifting?" What is the remedy? Christianity, law, and the "sovereignty of the people" have failed.[154] Is it not about time to try individualism backed by reason[,] freedom and intelligence?[155]

Pauline. Dr. Bachelor.

XXVII. "Entolai"[156]

Dr. A. M. Bourland's new book, "Entolai" is being well received.[157] The following extracts from two letters written by an aged and well known physician, show in what estimation the work is held by reading, thinking people:[158]

Pauline, Ark., March 28, 1894

A.M. Bourland, M. D.

My Dear Friend—Your book, "Entolai," has been received and read; many thanks for it. The index is very convenient. I must say that I prize your book very highly. It is philosophic and scientific—written in that happy style which must strike a chord of unison in every lover of nature. It is anti–superstitious, and contains truths that will not only live, but are bound to progress. What a grand character is Nena. What a world we would have if there were a million of Nenas. There is a grand possibility for the world when women are awakened and emancipated.[159] Yes, my friend, your book has not been written in vain— its truths are founded on nature and fact. I'm truly glad to have it. I am a child of nature—I love nature. I have a responsive throb for my brothers and sisters who feel the same. Yes, I too have passed to where the shadows lengthen, on in the sunset of life, when the pensive evening sky warns us of approaching night.

Your book will be read—and I am glad I am one of those to be included in your dedication, "To those I love."

Amidst the jarring discords of rival creeds, the dying faiths of fanatics in man-made religions, how pleasant to withdraw from the surface and dwell with nature and infinity. Your book invites us to the grand, glorious fountain from which flows intelligence, purity and love. I am glad, brother, to tell you that I am not sorry that the friction and conflicts in the great arena of human life, to me, have become insipid. I would rest. I have passed out and beyond the bars that have been set about me. I see the battleground receding; I still hear its clash and din; but I can rest only in the contemplation of nature.[160]

I know really there is no death—the organism vanishes, but the atoms are there: the universal whole is eternal. The great universal life gives us, and receives us. Yes, brother, I and you will pass on forever through its universal life. We have nothing to fear when we glide into the great unknown. We are of that essence that never had a beginning, and will never have an ending. Then we are all brothers and sisters. Yes, we are one with every object on earth, and with the dear old earth itself. Life is an electric sunbeam! It is an arrow shot across a ray of life! Rut[161] it is eternal—uncaused and uncreated. Yes, as Nena says: "We must all pass from the scenes of this life into the great Infinite—the unfathomably [sic] destiny." Then we are the ones who should and do sometimes feel an inspiration, which is the true inspiration from grand, glorious and sublime Nature.[162]

Hoping and believing your book will instruct and console many, I am Sincerely Yours,

W. R. Bachelor, M. D.

XXVIII. Obituary (of W. R. Bachelor Jr.)

Pauline, Ark., Aug. 7th 1895

On the 7th inst in the 31st year of his age, after a lingering illness of many months (consumption), W. R. Bachelor, a son of Dr. W. R. Bachelor, passed away.[163]

Some words spoken at the grave by the father: Friends, I undertake the painful task of speaking a few words at the final resting place of my son. What shall I say of death? It is birth, it is life.[164] Every moment a man is borned, every moment one dies. A few years ago we were not; a few years hence and all now living will be gone. Death is the inexorable law of nature. Do you ask me what becomes of the intelligence, love, hopes, fears of the dead? My answer is where is motion when the wheel stops, or light gone when the candle goes out? All in nature—all in the Universe. The tearful eyes of thousands follow loved ones daily to that curtain that has never been lifted. Then we all have to die; for nature's laws are unchangeable. She seems to "create man without purpose and destroy him without regret." Thus I fail to see any special providence—or the execution of any divine will. Prayers and supprications [sic] cannot effect the laws of fate.

He that is before you; the fell hand of a wasting disease (consumption) was laid upon him in the days of his manhood. He lingered many months with the certainty of death before him. He belonged to no church—he was a Freethinker. He never murmured in his long illness, but met death with calmness and without fear. He was conscious to the last. A short time before he passed away, he called me and told me he was dying. And thus passed away and now rests.

He was a filial son, a loving brother, a true friend. He stood for truth and right. We leave him in the arms of mother earth. Among the birds and flowers, greenfields, babbling brooks and the golden sunshine. Farewell—a long farewell.

Fort Smith and Van Buren papers please copy.

XXIX. L. M. Bachelor (Obituary)

Departed this life Oct. 22, 1897, after a painful illness of several weeks, L. M. Bachelor, Pauline, Ark., aged 45 years.[165]

SPOKEN AT THE GRAVE BY HIS FATHER, DR. W. R. BACHELOR

Friends: A little over two years ago, I followed one of my sons to his last resting place. To-day I follow another to take a long farewell.[166] He that lies here is my eldest son. A better-hearted man never lived—always ready to help his fellow-man in sickness and distress; never guilty of an unkind act.[167] But now his voyage through human life is ended. For him trouble and sorrow have ceased. He has joined that innumerable caravan—has passed from our view back to the great universal life.[168] He was a Freethinker. He belonged to no church. Believing in one world at a time, he did not believe in the dogma of eternal pain. He was willing to trust great Nature. And Mother Nature stands ready to take back to her arms her children that sprang from the blank chaos of the past. Friends, we should not fear death. It is only Nature taking back what she gave. For the fountain of life is fed by death.

Live evermore is fed by death
In earth and sea and sky,
And that a rose may breathe its breath
Something must die.[169]

Then we consign him back to Mother Nature to sleep—to rest. We leave him with flowers, singing birds, silvery streams, setting sun, jeweled night, and rosy dawn.[170]

XXX. From Pauline

It is customary to diagnose a case and then afterwards to prescribe a remedy. But in this case I shall not prescribe a remedy. I will leave that to others. The turbulent and dissatisfied condition of the masses—and the public mind generally, is, I think, caused by blindly seeking unattainable ideals.[171] Too much theory, and too much liberty. When one man like Debs by simply sending a few telegraph dispatches can bring all trains on the large trunks to a stand still, causing great suffering and destruction of property.[172] Somebody is following a wrong theory—and somebody is exercising dangerous liberty. The trend of all nations is toward anarchy. And if anarchy should succeed, the weakest governments will succumb first. Monarchical governments rest on a strong foundation; a republican government on sand.

The dynasty of China continued 2000 years. And the Emperor today, his power is absolute. While our government, the age of a century, and still on trial, is almost at the mercy of anarchists at times. Urged on by cheap orators of school house notoriety. The greed for money and office make men pour their Phillipics and vituperations upon the government and law-making power, as all are wanting government pap.[173]

Now let us see what we are confronted with. The greatest menace to our republic. I think it is anarchy. If the republicans had remained in power with the McKinley bill intact, yet the democratic had carried out their platform, it would not have removed or quieted the unrest. And let no man lay the flattering unction to his soul that any of the theoretical and ephemeral isms of the day can give peace and prosperity to the people after the two old parties have failed.

As an indication of future coalitions see the meeting and convention at Springfield, Ill., July the 3rd. There we find trying to effect an organization the federation of labor, people's party, socialists and single tax clubs, with Gov. Altgeld's pets just pardoned out of the penitentiary—Neebe and Schuab— who were given a welcome.[174]

Reader, what does this mean? Think for a moment what this portends. Who can say that the integrity of our government is not menaced? And who by? Who was at that Springfield love-feast? Any democrats or republicans? No. The tail end of every organization outside the two old parties, is anarchy, socialism. I am proud that I am an independent thinker—I have no axe to grind. I propose to be true to myself. These are troublesome times, let no man hereafter be a camp follower of any party—but stand for the integrity of the best government in the world.

Dr. W. R. Bachelor

XXXI. Come and Gone[175]

The old year is just passing away forever. In review it passes with its burden before us. Wars, drough[t]s, floods, fire, railroad disaster, suicides, assassinations, lynchings, hangings, robberies, strikes, poverty, tramps, political differences, new Parties, coalitions, disintegration of parties, financial distresses. The masses like branches of the trees are swayed by every political breeze. Cranks, demagogues, pseudo reformers and theoretical economists[176] augment the unrest. The old year carries as her burden, tears, sorrows, sufferings, deferred resolves, broken promises, misplaced confidence, noble impulses crushed, virtuous resolutions abandoned, reformations procrastinated, heartaches, farwells of loved ones, separation of friends. Also, the noble efforts of grand men and women in behalf of suffering and fallen humanity. So passes like a meteor dark in 1894.[177] One more link in the endless chain of the eternal cycles.

It is clear and frosty. The Pleiades look down with pity. See she comes—a magnificent ship—her mottoes and banners gleaming. Aboard. It is the New Year. HAPPY NEW YEAR. Now she sweeps through infinite space—and trembles in the undulation of Ether. She curves towards the great central Orb—and speeds on her way at the rate of a thousand miles a minute.

Brothers, sisters—we can't afford to be idle a minute. Don't you see time don't wait. Don't you see how we are hurrying on. Let us now resolve never again to procrastinate a good deed, nor strangle a noble impulse. Do good. Do right. If we cannot relieve by charity the distressed we can sympathize and speak kindly. A happy and prosperous New Year—to all.

Dr. W. R. Bachelor

Pauline, Ark.

XXXII. Letter from Dr. W. R. Batchelor[178]

Sovereign of the knights of labor before the committee said:

"The discharged laborer without just cause should have the right to go into court and establish a claim for damages." "Our rights are overridden," said McBride, president of the United Mine Workers, when issuing a call for a convention of all labor organizations to form a political party.[179]

Now the time fixed for this convention was the day previous to the populist's meeting to nominate a State ticket. Was that a coincidence? It is not a cut and dried program to make a common cause with the populist sympathizers to form a party in opposition to the existing government.

Why do I say this? The facts in this matter are these: Because Pullman could not afford to pay his employees higher wages without loss, Debs orders a strike, which results in loss of millions of dollars worth of property. And when the arm of the law is extended for the protection of life and property, they cry out "O, the government is in league with the capital against labor, you are overriding our rights." Is putting down lawlessness and rebellion overriding anybody's rights? Suppose an incendiary is applying the torch to your barnes [*sic*], and you restrain him by law, are you overriding his rights? Now reader, don't think strikes are over, or anarchy quelled. There will be a lull, but it is only the lull that precedes the storm. It is only a flank movement of the enemies of law and order. Suppose that when Chicago was at the mercy of a howling mob that Peffer or Atgeld had been president, instead of Grover Cleveland, think what would have been the result. How can any patriotic citizen of the United States encourage anarchy? Is anyone doing it? Yes. And I fear some are doing it without knowing it. It is so easy to say, the government is on the side of the rich against the poor. And every man who says it is either an anarchist or a sympathizer. My friends, I warn you not to be led astray by the wild theories of economists.[180] It is not the force bill, nor the tariff, nor democratic ascendancy that imperil the country to day but anarchy. So called *liberty—rights.*

Let us take the facts. Farmer Jones hires four men at fourteen dollars per month to make a crop. In the midst of the work they strike for fifteen dollars. He can't afford to give it. He pays them off and hires four other men at fourteen dollars. The paid off men remain, and by intimidation and assault prevent the men from working[.] And when Mr. Jones takes legal steps to remove them, they cry out "you are overriding our rights." That is rank anarchy. And if not properly checked will destroy this government. Let every man, it matters not to what party he belongs, support the government, law and order.[181]

Dr. Batchelor.

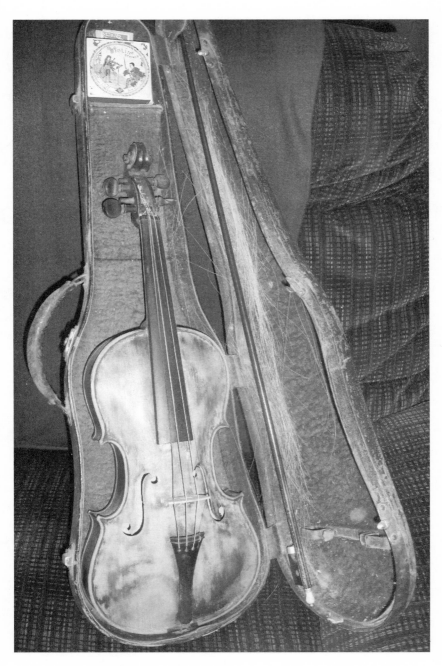

Wilson R. Bachelor's Violin. *Courtesy Janelle Russell, Fort Smith, AR.*

Wilson R. Bachelor, about 1870. *Courtesy Wanda Rentz Dailey, Fort Smith, AR, and Susan Dailey Johnson, Pocola, OK.*

Wilson R. Bachelor, 1880s. *Courtesy Wanda Rentz Dailey, Fort Smith, AR, and Susan Dailey Johnson, Pocola, OK.*

Wilson R. Bachelor, 1890s. *Courtesy Wanda Rentz Dailey, Fort Smith, AR, and Susan Dailey Johnson, Pocola, OK.*

Sarah Tankersley
Bachelor, abt. 1870.
*Courtesy Wanda Rentz
Dailey, Fort Smith, AR,
and Susan Dailey
Johnson, Pocola, OK.*

Sarah Tankersley
Bachelor, 1890s.
*Courtesy Linda
Anderson Silvey,
Antlers, OK.*

James Hugo Bachelor, 1870s. *Courtesy Kay Brown Black, Antlers, OK.*

James Hugo and Augusta Eubanks Bachelor, about 1880. *Courtesy Kay Brown Black, Antlers, OK.*

125

Pauline Graham Bachelor, Gertrude Eubanks, Nancy Jane Bachelor Eubanks, about 1895. *Courtesy Kay Brown Black, Antlers, OK.*

John Yeager Lynn and Anna Bachelor, 1900. *Courtesy Kay Brown Black, Antlers, OK.*

Alcie Daisy Bachelor Russell, 1890s. *Courtesy Bill Russell, Maumelle, AR.*

Alcie Daisy
Bachelor and
Husband
Seaborn Rentz
Russell, 1880.
*Courtesy Kay
Brown Black,
Antlers, OK.*

Lula Georgeann
Bachelor (left), 1884.
*Courtesy Kay Brown
Black, Antlers, OK.*

Lula Georgeann Bachelor
and Husband William
David Harris, 1890s.
*Courtesy Linda Anderson
Silvey, Antlers, OK.*

James Hugo Bachelor and Victor Hugo Bachelor, 1930s. *Courtesy Wanda Rentz Dailey, Fort Smith, AR.*

Pauline Graham Bachelor, about 1890. *Courtesy Wanda Rentz Dailey, Fort Smith, AR, and Susan Dailey Johnson, Pocola, OK.*

A Son of Wilson R. and Sarah Bachelor, Perhaps Leander Monroe, 1890s. *Courtesy Kay Brown Black, Antlers, OK.*

Office of
DR. W. R. BACHELOR,
DEALER IN

Drugs, Paints and Oils

Pauline, Ark., *Sept. 21* 189_1_

Melissa Roberson
Ops Ark

My Dear Niece,

I am at home again. We stopped 2 days
in Holsprings — then turned our faces toward
home, & 6 days travel over rocks and
Mountains brought us home. Found all
well. My daughter from Texas arrived
last night, to stay a year. I stood the
trip home pretty well — we had fair cool
a pretty weather. Well Melissa I will not write
much this time as I have to write back to
so many but next time I will write a long
letter. But I wish to express My appreciation
of your kindness and goodness to me while
at your house I shall always recollect my
stay with you all, with pleasure. I will
write more next time. All send their love
to you and family. Your Uncle W R Bachelor

21 September 1891 Letter, Wilson R. Bachelor to Melissa Robinson. *Courtesy Norman Hodges, Little Rock, AR.*

Letters of Wilson R. Bachelor (1890s)

I. 21 September 1891 Letter to Melissa Byrd Robertson, Ops, Arkansas[1]

PAULINE, ARK.
SEPT. 21 1891
MELISSA ROBERTSON[2]
OPS ARK.[3]

My Dear Niece,

I am at home again.[4] We Stopped 2 days in Hotsprings then turned our faces towards home, and 6 days travel over rocks and mountains brought us home. [F]ound all well. My daughter from Texas arrived last night to Stay a year.[5] I Stood the trip home pretty well we had[,] fair cool a[nd] pretty weather. Well Melissa I will not write much this time as I have to write back to so many but next time I will write a long letter. But I wish to express my appreciation of your kindness and Joshua's to me while at your house. I Shall always recollect my Stay with you all, with pleasure. I will write more next time[.] All Send their love to you and family.

Your Uncle W R Bachelor

II. 14 October 1891 Letter to Melissa Byrd Robinson, Ops, Arkansas[6]

PAULINE, ARK.
OCT 14TH 1891
MRS MELISSA ROBINSON
OP ARK.

My Dear Niece,

I have not answered your letter yet.[7] We are all well—hoping this may find you the Same. We have had much dry weather[.] It has not rained Since I returned home intill last night a small Shower. Well Melissa, they are not all So punctual to write as you, Several of them in your country have never answered the letters I wrote them.[8] Melissa I often think of you and your family, and particularly of you—as you favour your Mother and often remind me of her.[9] Corn crops is good in this country, but cotton—it will take 3 acres to the bale[.][10] I think I will come down in your country again next Summer.[11] I begin to want to see you all worse than I did, before I visited you. Nannie sends her love, so do all. Write your uncle,

W R Batchelor[12]

III. 20 December 1898 Letter to Seaborn Walters, Gifford, Arkansas[13]

PAULINE, ARK.
DEC THE 20TH 1898
SAMUEL WALTERS—ESQR[14]
GIFFORD ARK.

My dear Friend & family.

It looks like its a mighty long time Since we have wrote to each others. I think I wrote last; However, it dont matter. <u>Well how do you all do?</u> I can Say we are all up now—but we have had more Sickness in my family this year than ever before. "Malarial Fever[.]"[15] We have had So far a bad winter[,] two snows, the last one just melted off been lying on the ground two weeks. We are not done picking cotton yet.[16] [L]ack some two bales on my farm. Well <u>Uncle Sam</u> and Spain had a war, I recon you have no notion of moving to Cuba.[17] None of my boys at home now but Vick. Yeager in Texas. Dr. Jim lives near me[.][18] The crop this year was reasonably good, though I have not maid much. I did not have the force. Some 40 or 50 acres laid out. Times hard here, this 4½ cent Cotton is getting away with us. Some have commenced raising Potatoes[,] Some Strawberries. Well I wish I could See you all. I would like to see you, Minerva & the children. I recon your oldest boys are grown & that fat girl[19] how much does She weigh now, and that other wild boy, what have you done with him?[20] And Minerva how is She? Still <u>as plump as a partridge</u>? Well, write me about all of them down there. I never get any letters from any of them. What is John Byrd a doing? Is he as religious as ever? Is he preaching or practicing medicine?[21] Hoping you are all well I am

As ever your
Sincere friend,
Give my love to all
Dr W. R. Bachelor

IV. 6 February 1899 Letter to Melissa Byrd Robertson, Ops, Arkansas[22]

PAULINE, ARK.
FEB THE 6TH 1899
MELISSA ROBERTSON—OPS ARK
My Dear Niece,

I write you again to let you know I have not forgotten you. I love you because you have done much in the world, rearing your brothers and keeping house when you were a girl. Then, the mother of a large family doing your work with a will.[23] And then to me you are the image of my loving Sister (your mother) whom I parted with among the romantic hills of Tennessee— never to See again, but who in the wilds of Arkansas Succombed to disease and mental hallucination.[24]

I would like so much to See you again, and your quiet good husband and children. Write me a letter, tell me all about your family[,] how many is married, do you live at the same place? Who lives at the old Elliott Place? Where does the widow Elliott live?[25]

Does Mr Warrenton live where he did when I was there.[26] Who lives at the old John W Bachelor place?[27] My dear niece, I do hope you[r] latter days will be quiet and happy restful, for I know you have worked enoughf. Tell your husband I have not forgotten him—nor the children give them my Sincere love.[28]

This leaves us all on foot. And I hope it may find you all well. I have not forgotten the kindness of you all: but appreciate your kindness and considerations for my comfort during my visit, among you all. Tell my friends and connection I would like to get a letter from each one[.] This from Dr W.R. Bachelor to his Niece Melissa Robertson. Give my love to all—reserve a portion for yourself[.]

Dr W R Bachelor

V. 21 February 1899 Letter to Jane Byrd, Ops, Arkansas[29]

PAULINE ARK.
FEB THE 21ST 1899
MISS JANIE BYRD[30]
OPS ARK.
My dear Niece,

Your welcome letter with Melissa's at hand[.] I was verry glad to rcve a letter from you both[.] I remember you, and thought you would make a Sensible and lovely woman. It is greatly to your credit that you have remained with you[r] uncle so long keeping house for him.[31] [A]nd I am sure he appreciates it[.] Well, you are not married yet—another Sensible thing—as a woman Should be 20 or more years old before she marries. And if She was not to marry at all she would Save much labour and worry. However, if you marry dont marry a drunkard, a liar, nor a hypocrite nor any man unless he can love you always, support and protect[32] you.

Women are never treated as they Should be. They are petted and caressed by the man who marries them till the honeymoon is over[.] When too often they need love and protection they hardly get a kind word when in fact their husbands ought to share in their hardships and give them all the gallantry & love they did when first married.[33]

Pauline is at home, She is teaching music (organ) visits her pupils once a week. Nannie is with me, and her granddaughter <u>Gertrude</u>.

Yes my dear niece—I will with pleasure Send you my photograph[.] [H]ave it framed and keep it—and always—when tempted to do [w]rong, look at it, and remember you[r] uncle wishes you to be good, kind, generous, cheerful, lovely & womanly.[34] Don't forget to write me occasionally. From your affectionate uncle

Dr. W Bachelor

VI. 5 September 1899 Letter to Melissa Byrd Robertson, Malvern, Arkansas[35]

PAULINE ARK.
SEPT THE 5TH 1899
MELISSA ROBERTSON
MALVERN ARK.
My dear niece,

I have not forgotten you, can never forget my Sister's only daughter. I often think of the cares that has always been on your hands. You have never had the easy, free, time of other women. You are not old, Still you have raised two families, you commenced when a child.[36] Your brothers ought to love you, for you were the little mother that cared for them when left alone.

Well we have had a dry and hot Summer.[37] Of corn we will make enoughf to do. Cotton is ruined by the drouth, it will take 6 acres of land to make one bale. Fall crop of Potatoes also an entire failure.

There is much Sickness, a mild type of malarial Fever, not many deaths. I have had Sickness in my family, Nannie was Sick 7 or 8 weeks—verry Sick—

you know She has feeble health anyhow.[38] My wife is just getting up after Several weeks of Sickness. I, have had two or three attacks of indigestion—complicated with my old chronic Rheumatism & Neuralgia.[39] I wish we lived nearer, so we could see each other oftner. But we can't have everything we want.

My family is not So large as it used to be. Yeager is in Texas—So also is Alcie and Lula. Dr Jim Bachelor lives near Fort Smit[h].[40] Still the Old Homestead is lighted up of nights, and the Sound of the violen & Organ is Still heard. Pauline is teaching music in the neighbourhood. There are 10 organs in 4 miles Square[.] I am the first Started it up.[41] Give my love to you[r] good husband, & family.

W. R. Bachelor

Afterword

MEDICINE IN THE WESTERN ARKANSAS RIVER VALLEY, 1865–1890

Foundations of the Healing Arts in Arkansas

When Dr. Wilson R. Bachelor came to the Arkansas River Valley shortly after the Civil War, he would have found himself truly on the frontier of both society and medical practice. The years of Civil War and Reconstruction witnessed a descent into near-anarchy in the counties lying east of the Indian Territory border and south of the Arkansas River. Indeed, farther south near the Red River, United States troops had fought a war against Ku Klux Klan forces and rebel militias that lasted for years after Lee's surrender at Appomattox.

Arkansans in the river valley understood that prosperity would return only after the rule of law had been guaranteed and property had become again secure. To this end they welcomed the coming of economic and social institutions previously unknown in western Arkansas. The first of these was the railroad. Before the Civil War there had been no single direct road between Little Rock and Fort Smith. The Arkansas River offered a tenuous connection for commerce and personal travel. However, the river itself remained in its wild state. The channel shifted constantly within the river's floodplain. Snags offered to hold up steamboats, and perhaps to wreck their paddle wheels or gash open their hulls. In summer, low water frequently meant that no steamer could proceed beyond Dardanelle.

The population of the Arkansas River Valley at this period was not particularly diverse. The bulk of settlers were products of immigration from southeastern states, with Tennessee and North Carolina prominent in that list. Chattel slavery had certainly existed in the area, but the pattern had never developed of large holdings worked by large numbers of African Americans in servitude. The percentage of African Americans in the region was far lower than in the eastern portion of the state. The Native American population had been almost entirely removed. The presence of French settlers in the colonial years was a faint memory, preserved in some place-names and a few scattered families in the lower reaches of the valley from Petit Jean Mountain and eastward.

The culture was little changed since early territorial times in Arkansas. Few European immigrants were to be found at the time the Bachelor family arrived in the region. Most persons who claimed religious affiliation would have called themselves Protestants, principally of Baptist, Methodist, and Presbyterian denominations. Public schools were only established around 1870 by action of the Republican-dominated Reconstruction state legislature. Many people remained illiterate. There were few towns of more consequence than to have a courthouse, a cadre of basic commercial buildings, and a scattering of small homes whose dependencies included stables and outhouses.

The 1870s brought change. That change came in the guise of commerce, education, and novel populations. Dr. Bachelor was both part of that change and an observer of it.

The healing arts in Arkansas were little changed from the condition before the Civil War. The larger cities such as Little Rock, Pine Bluff, Camden, and Fort Smith were served to a limited extent by physicians who had achieved some formal medical education, as well as clinical instruction. Many others who called themselves physicians had no formal medical education. They had instead "read medicine" with a local practitioner, or in some cases simply apprenticed themselves to an established local physician whom they had assisted on his rounds. The state did not as yet have a medical school. That would not be established until 1879.

There was no popular prejudice against physicians who were not formally schooled. The presence of vernacular practitioners was common and accepted. Indeed, Arkansas demonstrates well the continuing tension among various healing practices. For some, healing derived from folk practices embedded in family memory and transmitted verbally from one generation to another. This "folk" tradition of healing was the only sort of medicine available to many poor persons living in isolation on the frontier. Indeed, the frontier could be in a trackless forest, in a slum on the edge of a town, or in the sparsely settled flatness of delta cropland. The memories of family medicine that had crossed the Appalachians, and in some cases crossed the Atlantic, still provided comfort and some degree of relief in nineteenth-century Arkansas. It did not matter if a cabin sheltered descendants of settlers from Scotland, England, or Africa, folk practices persisted. The use of Arkansas native plants for healing and for disease prevention continued uninterrupted. One challenge to the physician was to adapt care to what these beliefs included.

The Native American school of healing still possessed strength. The concept of the "Noble Savage" that had entranced eighteenth-century thinkers may have passed, but white and black citizens alike still tended to ascribe particular power to the use of Native American remedies. This grew in part from the recognition that shamans and other native healers possessed a familiarity with the identity and preparation of native plants as drugs that far outstripped any knowledge that later settlers may have acquired. The perceived dignity and self-reliance of the native peoples also lent credence to their status as the principal interpreters of the use of local resources for healing.

The last healing tradition to arrive in the state was related to college-educated physicians; and it was not necessarily always positive. Since the earliest days of colonial America, formally educated physicians had seldom been a part of frontier life. Only in the longest-settled cities could one find the division of labor and the economic resources to support a recognized cadre of persons professionally educated and licensed as physicians. Even more rare would be a professionally prepared dentist, veterinarian, or pharmacist. On the agricultural frontier of the late-nineteenth-century Arkansas River Valley, medical institutions were little changed from those of the southeastern backcountry of a century earlier.

In many cases, and particularly among the poorest and least educated, the prejudice tended toward distrust of elites. This included any elite of physicians. People viewed medicine not as we do today—maintenance of health and adherence to wholesome practices. Rather, medicine was viewed as a true last resort. Formal medicine could no more offer superior outcomes in the nineteenth century than it could in the fifteenth century. Why so? The physician such as Dr. Bachelor had essentially the same drugs at his command as any of his predecessors. The few exceptions would have been considered true miracles. The new offerings of the nineteenth century would have included anesthesia, a small number of plant-derived standardized drugs, and such radical instrumentation as the stethoscope. Civil War medicine had brought remarkable advances in the treatment of wounds. However, the introduction of reliable commercially available drugs, of vaccines, of x-ray, and acceptance of the germ theory of infectious disease were medical interventions of which a country doctor in a remote state like Arkansas could only dream until the nineteenth century neared its end.

Dr. Bachelor would live to see "Listerian" surgical disinfectant techniques. He would not himself ever see blood transfusion, intravenous fluid therapy, antibiotics, or insulin. The practical x-ray would not be available to rural physicians for many more years. Indeed, hospitals where patients could have diagnostic procedures and where surgery could be performed in specially prepared rooms were mostly in the future. A hospital in rural Arkansas at that time would typically have been some rooms in the physician's own house, or in an ordinary house that was designated for use as a hospital.

Medicine was, by necessity, a series of crisis interventions. It was also intervention by invitation, for the site of care was almost always the patient's home. The physician came when summoned by the patient or the family. Most families feared the expense of a physician's services. The amounts may seem small to us today, but the cost of a house call and a prescription could easily be a week's wages. In most cases the doctor was called only after all other resources had been tried with the patient, and found insufficient. The physician arriving to see a patient with "the dropsy" might well find a person whose ankles and feet were swollen to elephantine proportions due to long-untreated congestive heart failure. A physician summoned to attend a "difficult birth" (as we can see from Dr. Bachelor's diary, often the case in his practice) might well find a patient who had already labored for two days, who was exhausted and dehydrated, and whose child was already dead. Folk remedies and uneducated midwifery might have sufficed in many cases, but their use delayed treatment disastrously in others.

Infancy of Formal Medical Education in Arkansas

As previously noted, the state of Arkansas offered no formal education in medicine in the period when Dr. Bachelor arrived in the state. Indeed, the state had almost no standards for the designation, let alone exclusive licensure, of properly prepared physicians to provide patient care. As was common outside the nation's few urban centers, physicians did not enjoy today's high social and economic status. Physicians, just like attorneys, were widely derided for making their living from persons in difficulty who had no choice but to pay the fees that professional persons demanded. At the same time, slow payment of bills was a common feature of commercial life. In a society based upon agriculture, most farmers had cash to settle debts only after harvest. The necessity to "carry" customers on credit through most of a year affected every enterprise from banking to merchandising to professional practice. It was also quite common for physicians in all parts of Arkansas to engage in other work full-time, practicing medicine only when summoned to provide emergency care. Many physicians also served their communities as pharmacists, often owning drugstore buildings in which their medical offices were situated. The drugstore lines of goods other than medications offered a source of supplementary income. Physicians also often farmed and pursued other nonprofessional employment.

Medical licensure did not exist because it was not politically possible. In the nineteenth century there was no proper consensus about what constituted proper medical theory and practice. We in America are pretty well agreed that regular (allopathic) medicine as taught in accredited colleges of medicine and supported by internship and residency education is the proper foundation for health care. The claims of osteopathic physicians are well accepted; and they are admitted to the regular practice of medicine. In Dr. Bachelor's Arkansas there were many more competitors to the doctor of medicine than osteopathy. These included different "schools" of medicine that taught competing systems to account for the causes and treatments of disease. Among them were homeopathy and also Thomsonian medicine, which relied on herbalist treatments.

The adherents of all the varying schools of medicine competed freely and loudly. Each sought advantage in practice by trying to influence potential licensure laws. The idea was to have other schools branded as unscientific and banned in one's state. This would then confer a monopoly of practice on the variety of medicine accepted legally as orthodox. Arkansans and those they elected to public office were profoundly skeptical of monopolies. Indeed, some proved downright hostile to the concept. Many in the postwar South, and certainly in Arkansas, looked upon monopolies in transportation, banking, and manufacturing as alien (or at least northern) combinations that held down the prices for southern crops while also raising the prices of goods and reducing the wages paid to workers. For Dr. Bachelor, practice in rural Franklin County would have been, as for other country doctors throughout the state, a continuing engagement with critics, each of whom had decided ideas about the only possible way to bring a patient to health.

Medical education itself had not reached its modern consensus before 1900. When Abraham Flexner published his *Report* (1909), his survey of most medical colleges in the United States contained scathing criticisms. Flexner, himself an educator and not a physician, clearly considered the emerging model of medical education according to the European (chiefly German) paradigm as the proper course. When formal medical education did arrive, in Arkansas as in most of the rest of the country, medical school would consist of three years' instruction.

In the first year, students purchased tickets admitting them to lectures by the faculty, most of whom were practitioners in the community where the school was located. The lectures were given over two semesters. Students were instructed in ethics, the laws governing practice, and *materia medica* (the drugs approved for medical treatment). The medical curriculum would involve performance of some basic laboratory work, focusing on processes necessary to analyze blood and urine. Dissection formed the core of anatomic study. Students also performed practical exercises in suturing and other operative skills.

The second year of the curriculum was a repetition of the first. Students, now sophomores, would again purchase lecture tickets (their tuition) and attend for a second time the lectures and laboratories that had made up the freshman curriculum. Students did not then usually move directly into the third year of study, in which they accompanied physicians on clinic and hospital rounds, assuming progressive degrees of responsibility for patient care. The more common course was for the student to apprentice with an established physician and perform the work of a doctor in private practice. A student might remain in this status for a single year or continue in it for several years. Finally, when the preceptor considered the student ready, and when the student had tuition money in hand, the learner would register for the final year of medical school.

It is worth noting that physicians in private practice jealously guarded their patient population. For a patient to seek the advice of a different doctor was a serious matter. Physicians considered it scandalous and unethical for another to provide care to a patient, except in grave circumstances and when one was unavailable. The third-year clinical experiences did not ordinarily include caring for private patients. Rather, the populations of public hospitals and teaching clinics tended to be the marginalized persons in a community. This meant in Arkansas the poor, and particularly the African American poor.

Today's College of Medicine was initially the Medical Department of the Arkansas Industrial University. The main university campus was in Fayetteville. The Medical Department was in Little Rock, in a converted hotel purchased by its founding faculty. It would move by the early twentieth century to a building on Sherman Street in downtown Little Rock, adjacent to the public hospital. Students there found their own living arrangements, usually in rented rooms. They purchased their textbooks and laboratory supplies from a downtown drugstore. Life for them was Spartan; and career hopes in Arkansas were limited throughout much of the early part of the century.

A Time of Radical Change in Medical Care

Though formal medical training and professional doctors were still regarded with suspicion by those relying on traditional folk medicine when Dr. Bachelor arrived in Arkansas, at a wider level, all of medical practice was immersed at this period in a complex of changes that would eventually produce a standard of care unknown to humankind in any previous time. The innovations then borning were extensive and dramatic. The revolution in anatomy associated with Vesalius and the Renaissance had overthrown Galenic medicine. Practical application of that knowledge had gained sophistication in response to surgical treatment of wounds and the ravages of disease.

What was still lacking, however, was a strong connection of anatomic sophistication to the diagnosis and progression of diseases. From the time of the Greeks, medicine had shone in its descriptive powers. But physicians lacked a method to link description to an understanding of disease processes. Once that link emerged, practitioners and teachers of medicine found themselves needing a revolution in teaching in order to remain current with transforming discoveries.

One foundation of that link was the germ theory of disease. Despite the rejection of Ignaz Semmelweiss's ideas about transmission of disease and the need for such basic practices as effective hand washing, evidence continued to demand investigation of how infection occurred. By the 1880s so-called Listerian surgery, employing carbolic acid solutions for sterilization of instruments and carbolic acid sprays to sanitize the operative wound site, had become the standard for modern physicians. More advances in managing the operative theater would quickly follow. Louis Pasteur broke through the resistance of his medical establishment to demonstrate that microorganisms produced infectious disease. He also provided the hopeful proof that use of vaccines and serum preparations could combat infections once thought untreatable.

The application of autopsy to medical practice and to teaching also revolutionized diagnosis of disease. Although not so common today as in the past, the autopsy offered a window into disease during an age with no access to x-ray or other sorts of body imaging. The work of the Curies and Wilhelm Roentgen would bring early x-ray and fluoroscopy to medical practice, but unfortunately not in time for Dr. Bachelor to avail himself of these technologies. The autopsy, however, allowed a look after death at the status of a patient's unseen anatomy. Coupled with careful clinical records of symptoms and signs of disease, changes in structure from the normal to the abnormal showed the mechanisms by which diseases originated and proceeded.

Finally, medications themselves were changing rapidly. Prior to the Civil War, many diseases could be treated in limited fashion by the use of chemical substances. Mercury had provided the basis for treating syphilis since ancient times. Its toxicity was well known, but there was no alternative treatment. Mercury also provided for other medical needs. In the form of Blue Mass and other pill forms, mercury produced profound evacuation of colonic contents. In the form of mercuric chloride poison tablets, mercury provided a solution that sterilized items to be used in patient care. An application of mercurochrome provided painless local treatment of small cuts. Iron and strychnine, in various combinations, were used to alleviate anemia.

Vegetable drugs were also being revolutionized. Opium had been well characterized and ably used since antiquity in the treatment of pain and of diarrhea. Chemists of the nineteenth century, many of them also pharmacists, began systematically applying processes of dissolution, filtering, and crystallization to separate vegetable drugs into definable constituents. The separation of morphine from opium, for instance, allowed patients access to a pain reliever whose strength was known, and that could be dosed in relation to a patient's weight and height. That same separation allowed other chemicals (alkaloids) found in opium to be applied as separate remedies, while reducing the side effects associated with the mixture that was opium. In America an industry was emerging, based in Philadelphia, Indianapolis, Chicago, and Detroit that would scour the world to discover medicinal plants, and then prepare single elements from those plants into effective medicines. The effect of Merck, Lilly, Parke and Davis, Dohme, and others would soon enough reach the western frontier counties of Arkansas.

Dr. Bachelor, educated in medicine in keeping with older models, practiced medicine as he had been apprenticed, without resort to many of the technologies and medications just described. The instruments and the drugs available to him were relatively simple, and yet they met the standard for practice in most American communities. The changes in his profession would have powerfully challenged both his store of learning and his skeptical penchant to challenge the accepted.

The Social Matrix of the Arkansas River Valley

It must also be kept in mind that the medical treatment Dr. Bachelor provided his patients in the Arkansas River Valley in the latter part of the nineteenth century occurred in a certain distinctive cultural and social context. Disorder had been the chief legacy of the Civil War in this region. The river valley region emerged from Reconstruction with its morale at a low point and its economy unformed.

That status would not long persist, however. Soon after the war, the building of the Little Rock and Fort Smith (LR & FS) Railroad opened a decade of change. Prior to completion of that line, now part of the Union Pacific, there was no contiguous land connection between Little Rock and Van Buren, except the old Butterfield Stagecoach line that looped north almost to Missouri before dropping south from the Boston Mountains to the river opposite Fort Smith. The coming of the railroad offered convenient and low-cost facilities to distribute goods and to transport people. It would do more.

The financing of the railroad brought new things to Arkansas that were not typical of the antebellum South. The first was education. The LR & FS was a land-grant railroad. The Morrill Land Grant Act was conceived as a Civil War measure. Intended to increase the economic leverage of the Union against those attempting to secede, the act brought unexpected peacetime effects. One of these was to provide Arkansas with sections of land in the railroad grant that were mandated for sale to support a university. This public university was to offer collegiate instruction, and pay particular attention to the commercial and mechanical arts. This, the act's authors felt, would diminish the differences among sections of the United States and make a future civil war less likely. The university would also provide mandatory military officer training for its male students. This would benefit the nation in any emergency by providing a cadre of men able swiftly to lead military formations, allowing rapid expansion of the army in the face of any threat. A nationally focused corps of soldiers with compatible training would also lead to a lessened sectionalism.

When one considers that before 1865 Arkansas had no public schools, it is easier to appreciate the profound changes that these factors initiated up to 1900. When Dr. Bachelor ended his career, every county in Arkansas was obliged to provide standardized elementary school instruction. The state also had by this point a university and a band of fledgling church-affiliated colleges, where it had had no institution of higher education before the war.

The railroad also brought new people to the valley. The railroads, strapped for ready cash, cast a wide net to attract farmers to come and purchase land-grant acreage. Some were found among manumitted slaves, such as those who fled South Carolina and the racist Wade Hampton, settling near Morrilton. However, the majority of people living in this region of the state and their leaders preferred not to increase the numbers of African Americans living among them. Thus motivated, they looked overseas. Among the notable successes of railroad land agents in Europe was the attraction of significant numbers of immigrants from the Rhineland, Switzerland, and as far east as Poland. These immigrants were for the most part Roman Catholics, motivated powerfully to escape the statist and anticlerical policies epitomized by the *Kulturkampf* associated with the Prussian chancellor Otto von Bismarck. With them came new congregations of priests and other religious, including monks and nuns. The stamp of the Holy Ghost Fathers and of the Benedictines was quickly fastened upon the valley and found powerful support among the ethnic Europeans suddenly planted there.

Arkansans certainly had memories of Germans before the Civil War, but mainly as the rural hunters visited by Friedrich Gerstäcker in the late 1840s, and as early urban settlers on the east side of Little Rock. Roman Catholics had formerly been small groups associated with three establishments: colonial French settlers near Pine Bluff, Irish settlers near the military post in Fort Smith, and the Sisters of Mercy, who established a convent and a school near the cathedral in downtown Little Rock. There had been little dilution of the old American stock that formed the prewar free population of the state. The railroad brought permanent diversity to many areas of the state, and notably to the upper Arkansas River Valley in which Dr. Bachelor chose to relocate his family in 1870.

Summary

In fine, Dr. Bachelor chose to migrate to the Arkansas River Valley at a time of fundamental change. It was perhaps to his advantage that he had lived his early life elsewhere, and along a river important to interstate commerce. He came into a place without large cities, but one beginning to undergo rapid cultural and economic change just as he arrived in the area. He came to a place in great need of health care. He also came to a place where his role and the expectations that his fellow Arkansans harbored of all physicians would challenge him profoundly. The record he left us of his medical practice as these cultural and economic shifts were occurring is a precious one, since we have few other records from this time and place of how a country doctor did his work in Arkansas.

Jonathan Wolfe

Bibliography

Baird, W. David. *Medical Education in Arkansas, 1879–1978*. Memphis: Memphis State UP, 1979.

Barnes, Kenneth C. *Journey of Hope: The Back-to-Africa Movement in Arkansas in the Late 1800s*. Chapel Hill: Univ. of North Carolina Press, 2004.

Blair, Diane D., and Jay Barth. *Arkansas Politics and Government*. 2nd ed. Lincoln: Univ. of Nebraska Press, 2005.

Blevins, Brooks. *Hill Folks: A History of Arkansas Ozarkers & Their Image*. Chapel Hill: Univ. of North Carolina Press, 2002.

Bolton, S. Charles. *Arkansas, 1800–1860: Remote and Restless*. Fayetteville: Univ. of Arkansas Press, 1998.

Clayton, Powell. *The Aftermath of the Civil War, in Arkansas*. New York: Neale, 1915.

Dougan, Michael B. *Arkansas Odyssey: The Saga of Arkansas from Prehistoric Times to Present*. Little Rock: Rose, 1995.

Johnson, Ben F. III. *Arkansas in Modern America*. Fayetteville: Univ. of Arkansas Press, 2000.

Moneyhon, Carl H. *The Impact of the Civil War and Reconstruction on Arkansas: Persistence in the Midst of Ruin*. Fayetteville: Univ. of Arkansas Press, 2002.

Monks, William. *A History of Southern Missouri and Northern Arkansas: Being an Account of the Early Settlements, the Civil War, the Ku-Klux, and Times of Peace*. West Plains, MO: West Plains Journal Co., 1907.

Thompson, George H. *Arkansas and Reconstruction: The Influence of Geography, Economics, and Personality*. Port Washington, NY: Kennikat Press, 1976.

Tucker, David M. *Arkansas: A People and Their Reputation*. Memphis: Memphis State UP, 1985.

Whayne, Jeannie M. *A New Plantation South: Land, Labor, and Federal Favor in Twentieth-Century Arkansas*. Charlottesville: Univ. of Virginia Press, 1996.

White, Lonnie J. *Politics on the Southwestern Frontier: Arkansas Territory, 1819–1836*. Memphis: Memphis State UP, 1964.

Appendix I

GOODSPEED AUTOBIOGRAPHY OF WILSON R. BACHELOR
(1889)

The following biography of Wilson R. Bachelor (which appears to
be his own autobiographical statement) appeared in *History of Benton,
Washington, Carroll, Madison, Crawford, Franklin, and Sebastian Counties,
Arkansas* (Chicago: Goodspeed, 1889), 1223.

Dr. W. R. Bachelor, of Franklin County, was born November 29, 1827, in
Lawrence County, Tenn., and is a son of W. R. and Alcie (Odom) Bachelor,
natives of North Carolina. The father was a farmer by occupation, and located
upon a farm in Nash County, after his marriage, whence he removed to
Tennessee in an early day, where he continued farming until his death, which
occurred in Hardin County in 1858. He was the father of six children, four
sons and two daughters, three of whom are living, viz.: Dr. W. R., William S.
and Sarah, the latter now living with our subject. The mother died in 1848,
having been a member of the Methodist Episcopal Church. Dr. W. R. Bachelor
was reared and educated in Hardin County, Tenn., and for several years in his
early manhood engaged in teaching, during which time he was studying medicine. He began active practice of the medical profession in Hardin County in
1859, where he remained until 1863, and then went to Kentucky. In 1866 he
returned to Hardin County, Tenn., and was employed by the Government as
physician in charge of the men engaged in building the National Cemetery at
Pittsburg Landing. In 1870 he purchased and moved to his present fine farm
of 250 acres in Franklin County, Ark., which is well improved and stocked. In
1848 Dr. Bachelor married Sarah Tankersly, daughter of Roling Tankersly, of
Hardin County, Tenn. To this union have been born nine children, viz.:
Leander M., Dr. James H., of Central City; John Y. L., Wilson R., Jr., Victor H.,
Nancy J., Alcie D., wife of Dr. S. R. Russell; Lulu, now Mrs. William Harris,
and Pauline G. Dr. Bachelor is one of the leading Liberalists in Western
Arkansas, and is the author of a work on free thought, called "Fiat-Flux." As a
doctor he is well and favorably known, and has a good practice. Politically he
is a Republican. Mrs. Bachelor is a member of the Baptist Church.

Appendix II

MASONIC EULOGY OF WILSON R. BACHELOR (1903)

The following eulogy of Wilson R. Bachelor was published by his local
Masonic lodge, Lowe's Creek Lodge No. 346, in Franklin County,
Arkansas, in May 1903. A copy of the eulogy,[1] which appears to have
been published in either a local newspaper or a Masonic publication, is
in the scrapbook he began maintaining in the 1890s, and which
members of his family continued to maintain following his death.

Resolutions of Respect to the Memory of Dr. W. R. Bachelor

We, your committee appointed to draft resolutions of respect suitable to the
memory of Dr. W. R. Bachelor, beg leave to report as follows:

Whereas, on the 5th inst., the Great God of heaven and earth saw fit to
remove from our midst Bro. W. R. Bachelor, "to that undiscovered country
from whose bourne no travelor ever returns," we can but bow in humble sub-
mission to His will. Dr. Bachelor was born in Lawrence County, Tenn., Nov.
29th, 1827, came to Arkansas in 1870 and settled in Mill Creek T'p. Franklin
County, where he continued to reside 'till his death. He was made a mason
about the year '73 in Ozark Lodge No. 79, F. A. M. Was a charter member of
Lowe's Creek Lodge No. 346.

In 1884 he wrote a book entitled "Fiat Lux" in which he disputed the
divinity and authenticity of the Bible, the great light of Masonry and the
world, for which he was tried by the lodge and expelled about the same year
and remained thus 'till about two months ago, when he petitioned the lodge
for restoration, setting forth the necessary declaration in said petition, and was
restored to membership April 11th, 1903. Ten years ago he wrote the following
lines to a friend: "I freely adopt what two of the pioneers of freethought have
said, 'the world is my country, to do good, my religion.' 'The place to be
happy is here, the time to be happy is now, the way to be happy, is to make
others happy.'" We are very sorry he was unable to attend lodge meeting after
restoration. He had expressed a desire to make a public declaration regarding
his belief prior to this time. His record as a citizen was such as endeared him
to all who knew him. He was noted for the gentleness of his manners and
kindliness of disposition. He possessed pleasing and winning manners, and in

153

all his social relations, he bore the character of an estimable, generous, kindly and true man. Like many other bright men he was not without faults and with a resourceful mind wielded a strong influence over the community in which he lived an honored and respected citizen. His one mistake in life being his attack on the Bible and the Christian religion, which he himself fully realized but too late in life to counteract the influences set in motion by his teaching. His theory during this period of life was: "Be just and kind to all men, do right because it is right, without the recognition of or the intervention of a higher power and without the fear of future punishment, or the hope of a blissful immortality beyond the grave, but that life ends in physical death." Let us thus throw the mantle of charity over his mistakes and remember that he was but a frail mortal and strive to emulate those virtues that characterized his life. Therefore be it

Resolved. First. That in his death our lodge has lost one of her most intelligent and respected members; our country a just, patriotic and upright citizen, and the family, an indulgent and affectionate husband and father.

Second. That this lodge extend its sympathy to the grief-stricken wife and aged mother and family and pray God's grace to sustain and comfort them in this their sad bereavement, and commend them to Him who has promised to be "a husband to the widow and a father to the [*fatherless*]."[2]

Appendix III

REPORT OF WILSON R. AND SARAH BACHELOR'S GOLDEN WEDDING ANNIVERSARY (1897)

The following article reporting on the golden wedding anniversary of Wilson R. Bachelor and his wife, Sarah Tankersley Bachelor, is preserved in his scrapbook, and appears to have been clipped from the Fort Smith newspaper *The Elevator*.

Golden Wedding

Editors Elevator:

Doctor Bachelor's golden wedding was celebrated last Monday by his children and grand-children assembling at the old homestead. The Doctor had up some mottoes—"this World is What You Make it;" "The Way to be Happy is to Make Others Happy," etc. There was music and festivity through the day. In the evening the Doctor played the violin while his children and grand-children danced. He is just three score and ten, but is not cloyed with life nor afflicted with senility.

Attendant.

Pauline, Ark., December 4, 1897

Appendix IV

LETTER OF WILSON R. BACHELOR TO ZION'S ENSIGN (4 FEBRUARY 1893)

The following letter of Wilson R. Bachelor appeared in *Zion's Ensign*, a newspaper of the Reorganized Church of Jesus Christ of Latter Day Saints, on 4 February 1893 (*Ensign* 4, no. 6 [4 February 1893], 3).

LETTER FROM PAULINE, ARK.

Editor *Zion's Ensign:*—

Through the kindness of my nephew living in your city, I am the recipient of a copy of your paper. After reading it my mind was carried back to reminiscences of some fifty-four years ago when I was a boy some ten or twelve years old. At that time two Latter Day Saints (Clapp and Hunter) passed through Hardin County, Tenn., where my father lived. They stopped in the neighborhood and preached. A few joined and were baptized. One of them had a debate with a Christian Minister (Albert Anderus) Anderus coming out second best. He afterwards joined the church and went to Nauvoo. He preached some time before he left, and many united with the church; among them my father and mother two sisters and one brother. I remember reading the Book of Mormon, Parley P. Pratt's works, and others. A diversified practice of medicine of thirty-eight years has not obliterated these recollections. I have always been a great reader, and as I have now about retired from the practice of medicine, I devote my time to reading. Were I rationally convinced of the inspiration of the Bible, I should join the church of the Latter Day Saints, for it seems to me that they are the only church that follows the teachings of the Bible. I believe that the Book of Mormon is as well authenticated as the Bible. I believe that Joseph Smith was the founder of a religion like Gautama, Confucius, and Moses. But I look upon them all as evolutional developments to a higher integration. Please find twenty five cents for *Zion's Ensign*.

Sincerely,
W. R. Bachelor

Appendix V

DESCENT OF WILSON RICHARD BACHELOR FROM RICHARD BACHELOR, THE IMMIGRANT

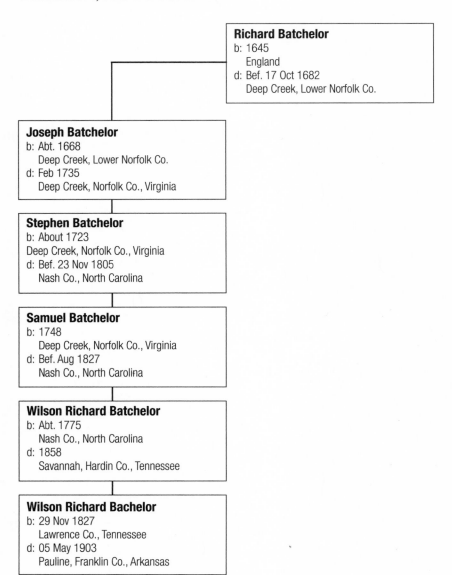

Richard Batchelor
b: 1645
    England
d: Bef. 17 Oct 1682
    Deep Creek, Lower Norfolk Co.

Joseph Batchelor
b: Abt. 1668
    Deep Creek, Lower Norfolk Co.
d: Feb 1735
    Deep Creek, Norfolk Co., Virginia

Stephen Batchelor
b: About 1723
Deep Creek, Norfolk Co., Virginia
d: Bef. 23 Nov 1805
    Nash Co., North Carolina

Samuel Batchelor
b: 1748
    Deep Creek, Norfolk Co., Virginia
d: Bef. Aug 1827
    Nash Co., North Carolina

Wilson Richard Batchelor
b: Abt. 1775
    Nash Co., North Carolina
d: 1858
    Savannah, Hardin Co., Tennessee

Wilson Richard Bachelor
b: 29 Nov 1827
    Lawrence Co., Tennessee
d: 05 May 1903
    Pauline, Franklin Co., Arkansas

WILSON RICHARD BATCHELOR DESCENDANTS CHART

Wilson Richard Batchelor
Wilson Richard Batchelor b: Abt. 1775 in Nash Co., North Carolina, d: 1858 in Savannah, Hardin Co., Tennessee

Alice Odom
Alcie Odom b: 1790 in Nash Co.?, North Carolina, m: Abt. 1805 in Nash Co.?, North Carolina, d: 1848 in Hardin Co.?, Tennessee

Moses B. Batchelor
b: 11 Jan 1808 in Nash Co., North Carolina, d: 09 Apr 1883 in Fenter, Hot Spring Co., Arkansas

William Skidmore Batchelor
b: 06 Apr 1816 in Nash Co., North Carolina, d: 16 Jun 1896 in Independence, Jackson Co., Missouri

Minerva Monk
b: Abt. 1812 in Davidson Co., Tennessee, m: Abt. 1838 in Hardin Co., Tennessee, d: Aft. 14 Aug 1860 in Clear Creek, Hot Spring Co., Arkansas

Huldah King
b: 24 Jun 1822 in Sunderland, Bennington Co., Vermont, m: 21 Feb 1843 in Nauvoo, Hancock Co., Illinois, d: 17 Mar 1897 in Independence, Jackson Co., Missouri

John Wilson Batchelor
m. Talitha Emeline Robinson

Wiley Batchelor

James Decalvin Batchelor

George Richard Batchelor
m. Catherine Ryan

Daniel Tucker Batchelor

Edward Eli Batchelor
m. Mary
m. Mary Paralee Bagley

William W. Batchelor
m. Emma

George Wllis Batchelor
m. Phebe J. McIntire
m. Mary Ellen Horham

Mary Louisa Batchelor
m. Benjamin F. Beever
m. Worrell

John H. Batchelor

Enoch Robert Batchelor

Pemillia Batchelor
m. Charles Pius Thompson

Permillous W. Batchelor
m. Emma L. Sullivan

Nancy Ellen Batchelor
m. Thomas J. Williams

James F. Batchelor

Sarah Batchelor

Etta Ann Batchelor
m.. James Alexander Henderson

Queen Victoria Batchelor
m. George Spellman Henderson

Louisa Waters (Robertson)
b: 03 Aug 1821 in North Carolina, m: Abt. Oct. 1860 in Hot Spring Co., Arkansas, d: 21 Aug 1887 in Fenter, Hot Spring Co., Arkansas

Minerva Louisa Batchelor
m. Seaborn Walters
m. John G. Hames

Hannah Delaney Batchelor
b: Abt. 1819 in Maury Co.,
Tennessee, d: Bef. 1863 in Big
Creek Twp., Hot Spring Co.,
Arkansas

Sarah R. Batchelor
b: 1824 in Maury
Co.?, Tennessee,
d: 19 Jan 1892 in
Pauline, Franklin Co.,
Arkansas

Wilson Richard Bachelor
b: 29 Nov 1827 in Lawrence Co.,
Tennessee, d: 05 May 1903 in
Pauline, Franklin Co., Arkansas

Lawrence Cherry Byrd
b: 02 Jul 1822 in Lawrence
Co., Tennessee, m: 30 Aug
1842 in Hardin Co., Tennessee,
d: Bef. 1863 in Hot Spring Co.,
Arkansas?

Sarah H. Tankersley
b: 29 Nov 1830 in Hardin
Co.?, Tennessee, m: 03 Dec
1847 in Savannah, Hardin
Co., Tennessee, d: 09 May
1904 in Pauline, Franklin
Co., Arkansas

Pleasant A. Byrd
  m. Elizabeth M. Rucker

Wilson Batchelor Byrd

William Edward Byrd
  m. Matilda Bailey

Melissa Ann Byrd
  m. Joshua Marion Robinson

Samuel Delaney Byrd
  m. Polly Ann Thrower
  m. Laura Warlick

John Lawrence Byrd
  m. Susan Catherine Elliott
  m. Ruth Bule

Henry C. Byrd
  m. Sarah Lutitia Collie

Adam C. Bachelor

Leander Monroe Bachelor

James Hugo Bachelor
  m. Augusta Eubanks
  m. Allie Viola Rogers

Wilson Richard Bachelor

Nancy Jane Bachelor
  m. Frederick Eubanks

John Yeager Lynn Bachelor
  m. Melissa or Margaret Valentine
  m. Anna G. Sawyers

Alcie Daisy Bachelor
  m. William Seaborn Rentz Russell

Wilson Richard Bachelor

Lula Georgeann Bachelor
  m. William David Harris

Victor Hugo Bachelor
  m. Henrietta Dean

Pauline Graham Bachelor
  m. William Clyde O'Bar

Notes

Introduction: Wilson R. Bachelor, Whys and Wherefores

1. See Andrew Rieser, *The Chautauqua Moment: Protestants, Progressives, and the Culture of Modern Liberalism* (New York: Columbia UP, 2003).

2. *History of Benton, Washington, Carroll, Madison, Crawford, Franklin, and Sebastian Counties, Arkansas* (Chicago: Goodspeed, 1889), 1223. For this auto-biographical statement, see Appendix I.

3. Susan Jacoby, *Freethinkers: A History of American Secularism* (New York: Henry Holt, 2004), 2. On the rapid spread of the freethought movement in western states including Kansas and Texas in the latter half of the nineteenth century, see Fred Whitehead and Verle Muhrer, "Introduction," in *Freethought on the American Frontier*, ed. Whitehead and Muhrer (Buffalo, NY: Prometheus, 1992), 22–23; and Aaron K. Ketchell, "Contesting Tradition and Combating Intolerance: A History of Freethought in Kansas," *Great Plains Quarterly* 20, no. 4 (2000): 281–95.

4. *Freethinkers*, 2, 151–53. See also Ketchell, "Contesting Tradition," who emphasizes that the freethought movement in Kansas in the latter half of the nineteenth century was heavily invested in the progressivist movement and endorsed progressivist ideas including support for women's rights, workers' rights, and the need for separation of church and state and the application of reason and scientific knowledge in the political sphere.

5. A copy of the eulogy, which appears to have been published in either a local newspaper or a Masonic publication and which indicates it was published in May 1903 (since it notes that Bachelor died on the "5th inst."), is in a scrapbook kept by Bachelor in the 1890s, and by members of his family following his death. The eulogy erroneously gives the title of Bachelor's work as *Fiat Lux*, whereas his autobiographical statement for Goodspeed shows the title as *Fiat Flux*, a play on the Vulgate translation of Genesis 1:3, which has God making the world and then commanding, *Fiat lux!* As a freethinker, Bachelor would have chosen his title to ring a freethinker's change on the divine command, and to stress that the world remains in constant flux and is not under the immediate control of a divine being who manipulates nature and events in the world in a direct or providential fashion. For a transcript of the eulogy, see Appendix II.

6. The picture of Ingersoll appears to be pasted into the scrapbook's front cover with pictures of other freethinkers that have been obscured by a picture of a seamstress at work and a woman wearing a fashionable dress. The scrapbook

passed to Bachelor's daughter Alcie, who supported her family as an accomplished seamstress following the dissolution of her marriage to Dr. Seaborn Rentz Russell and who apparently affixed these illustrations to the inside of the scrapbook. Throughout the scrapbook, Bachelor has cut and pasted quotations of Ingersoll from what seems to have been a regularly published column in some newspaper or journal. Each such column is entitled "Gems of Thought." The columns provide snippets of Ingersoll's work and evidently draw on the 1882 work *Ingersollia: Gems of Thought from the Lectures and Speeches of Col. Robert G. Ingersoll* (Chicago: Belford Clarke & Co., 1882). On Ingersoll and the freethought movement, see Jacoby, *Freethinkers*, 157–73; and Sidney Warren, *American Freethought 1860–1914* (New York: Columbia UP, 1943), 84.

7. See, for example, Ingersoll and Herman E. Kittredge, *The Works of Robert G. Ingersoll*, vol. 4: *Lectures* (New York: Dresden, C. P. Farrell, 1909), 4–67.

8. In a number of cases, the occasional pieces contain internal evidence that strongly suggests they were published in a Franklin County newspaper—most likely, a paper in Ozark. The eulogy of Henderson Rice, for instance, has a heading indicating it was published as part of a regular column that a Franklin County paper carried to publish news about the small community of Sub Rosa. The piece called "A Freethinker's View of Franklin, on the Presidential Election," responding to the 1892 elections, is obviously a county-specific item. The obituary of Bachelor's son Wils asks Van Buren and Fort Smith papers to pick up the item, again suggesting that the original was published in his own county paper. Finally, many of the pieces note that he was writing from Pauline—a reference that would not have made much sense outside Franklin and nearby counties, without explanation.

9. See his untitled letter to a newspaper editor addressing the work of a Dr. J. R. Dunn on the survival of consciousness or of the soul following death, and "Will we be Burned or Will we be Drowned?"

10. *History of the Conflict between Religion and Science* (New York: Appleton, 1874): see "Unrest and Tendencies of Organization."

11. See, for example, his Christmas Day 1893 diary entry.

12. See the diary entry for 2 June 1895.

13. See the Masonic Lodge eulogy, Appendix II.

14. Note that Bachelor's 4 February 1893 letter to the *Zion's Ensign* newspaper (see Appendix IV) will imply yet another date for when he began practicing medicine: it speaks of his "diversified practice of medicine" for thirty-eight years, implying that he began his medical practice in 1855.

15. Bachelor provides his date and place of birth and the names of his parents in his autobiography in *History of . . . Franklin and Sebastian Counties, Arkansas*. The date and place of birth also appear in his Masonic eulogy. The autobiography gives his father's name as "W. R. Bachelor." It's apparent from a number of sources that the full name of Bachelor's father, for whom he was named, was Wilson Richard Batchelor. In the generation following Wilson the

elder, the spelling of the surname shifted to Bachelor in the family of Wilson the younger, and his brother William Skidmore Batchelor seems sometimes to have spelled the name Batchelder, though his children reverted to the Batchelor spelling that had long been used in Virginia and North Carolina.

16. Among descendants of Richard Batchelor who stand out in North Carolina history as exceptions to this rule are Edward Batchelor and Joseph John Branch Batchelor. Edward Batchelor, who appears to have been either a son or grandson of Richard Batchelor's son Edward (d. 1706, Tyrrell County, North Carolina), died in New Bern 22 November 1777 owning considerable property in North Carolina and the middle colonies, including a number of ships. Much of his wealth came from trading in slaves (see *inter alia* H. T. Lefler and A. R. Newsome, *The History of a Southern State: North Carolina*, 3rd ed. [Chapel Hill: Univ. of North Carolina Press, 1973], 100; and L. Michael Kay and Lorin Lee Cary, *Slavery in North Carolina* [Chapel Hill: Univ. of North Carolina Press, 1995], 129). Joseph John Branch Batchelor (1825–1903) was the state's attorney general in 1855 and 1856: see Edward McCrady and Samuel A. Ashe, *Cyclopedia of Eminent and Representative Men of the Carolinas of the Nineteenth Century*, vol. 2 (Madison, WI: Brant & Fuller, 1892), 628–29.

17. See Odom's original estate papers on file at the North Carolina state archives, and Nash County Court Minutes 1804–15, 280, noting that William Lindsey had appealed to administer Theophilus Odom's estate on 13 November 1811. At the sale of Theophilus Odom's estate on 9 December 1811, Wilson R. Batchelor was a buyer.

18. See Rebecca L. Dozier, *Twelve Northampton County, North Carolina, Families* (Baltimore: Gateway Press, 2004), 269–92.

19. See Lower Norfolk County Record Book E, 99; for an abstract, see Charles F. McIntosh, "Ages of Lower Norfolk County People, Abstracted from Depositions in Book E, 1666–1675, Norfolk County Clerk's Office," *William and Mary Quarterly* 25, no. 2, series 1 (October 1916): 135.

20. The headright grant to Porter is recorded in Lower Norfolk County Record Book D, 213, and was filed at the county's court on 15 August 1659. Headright grants were often traded as scrip in Virginia in this period, and were not always filed by the person who had actually paid for an immigrant's transportation to the colonies. In the case of this claim, however, it is clear that Manasses Porter is claiming a headright for Batchelor after William Goldsmith had brought him from England. All three men lived in Lower Norfolk County and are connected in various ways in the county records. Like Porter and like Batchelor's father-in-law, Goldsmith would become a Quaker when that movement reached Lower Norfolk County.

21. A Richard Batchelor who had indentured himself as a servant to William Donning sailed from Bristol to Virginia on 23 August 1661—see Peter Wilson Coldham, *The Bristol Registers of Servants Sent to Foreign Plantations, 1654–1686* (Baltimore: Genealogical Publishing Co., 1988), 159. Coldham is

transcribing a register held by Bristol's city council kept from 1645 to 1686. And on 15 September 1658, Henry Forrest received a headright grant in Gloucester County, Virginia, for transporting a list of colonists including Richard Batchelor (Virginia Patent Book 4, 217; see Nell Marion Nugent, *Cavaliers and Pioneers: Abstracts of Virginia Land Patents and Grants, 1623–1666*, vol. 1 [Baltimore: Genealogical Publishing Co., 1963], 377).

22. The possibility that Richard Batchelor made at least one voyage from Lower Norfolk County back to England, then returned to Virginia, is suggested, as well, by a 17 April 1665 record showing William Goldsmith receiving a headright grant on that date from the county court for transporting a number of persons to Virginia, including Richard Batchelor (Lower Norfolk County Record Book D, 422a). Batchelor himself claimed 700 acres in headright grants on Deep Creek of the southern branch of the Elizabeth River on 15 March 1675/6, for transporting eight persons to the colonies (Virginia Patent Book O, 600).

23. See Elizabeth Gregory McPherson, "Nathaniel Batts, Landholder on Pasquotank River, 1660," *North Carolina Historical Review* 43 (1966): 73–74. McPherson notes that early eastern North Carolina records are filed in Norfolk County, Virginia, court books. The family of Richard Batchelor touches tangentially on that of Nathaniel Batts: Albemarle County, North Carolina, court records indicate that James Fewox, who married Richard Batchelor's widow, Ann (Biggs) Batchelor, and was stepfather of Richard's children, was grazing hogs in 1694 on Batts Island at the mouth of the Yeoppim River; Nathaniel Batts is said to have lived and been buried on the island.

24. Richard Batchelor died in Lower Norfolk County between 12 March 1680/1, when he wrote his will, and 17 October 1682, when the will was probated (Lower Norfolk County Record Book 4, f. 128; for an abstract, see Charles F. McIntosh, *Abstracts of Norfolk County Wills* [Richmond: Colonial Dames of America in the State of Virginia, 1914], 84).

25. Ann was the daughter of an English immigrant to Lower Norfolk County, John Biggs (also Bigg and Bigge), who appears to have been born about 1620 and who died testate (with wife, Joan or Joanna) in Lower Norfolk County before 15 March 1697. He appears to be the John Bigge who witnessed the will of John Putnam of Chesham, Buckinghamshire, England, aboard the ship *Increase* on 29 December 1647, as the *Increase* was bound for Virginia (see Lothrop Withington, "Virginia Gleanings in England," *Virginia Magazine of History and Biography* 14, no. 3 [January 1907], 305–6, transcribing the original will from Principal Probate Registry, Register Bks. 197 [Ruthen], Index of Wills PCC, vol. 8, 490). Biggs was in Lower Norfolk County by 15 February 1648/9, when he gave notice at the court door of his intended voyage back to England at the present shipping (see Lower Norfolk County Record Book B, 107). Ann Biggs (Batchelor, Fewox) appears to have been

born about 1650 and to have died after October 1712 in Tyrrell County, North Carolina.

26. Ann's children by Richard Batchelor were John (abt. 1665–bef. 19 November 1712), Alice (b. 1665–1670), Edith (abt. 1668–aft. 29 September 1717, married William, son of John Hardy and Charity Odier), Joseph (abt. 1668–February 1735, married Mary), Edward (abt. 1671–aft. 21 September 1706, married Pathelia), and Richard (abt. 1674–aft. 30 December 1726, married Katherine, widow of John Spellman).

27. See Mary Weeks Lambeth, *Memories and Records of Eastern North Carolina* (Nashville: Curley, 1957), 179; and J. R. B. Hathaway, "Abstract of Conveyances [From Register's Office of Chowan County, Book C, No. 1]," *North Carolina Historical and Genealogical Register* 2, no. 2 (April 1901): 291. As Lambeth notes, Heart's Delight had passed to the Hassell family (descendants of John Biggs's daughter Johannah, who married Edward Hassell). James Fewox's son Robert deeded the plantation to his cousin John Hassell on 24 March 1717 (Chowan County Deed Book B-1, 541). According to David E. Davis, *History of Tyrrell County, North Carolina* (Norfolk, VA: Joseph Christopher, 1963), when Thomas Miller and Joshua Tarkington explored the region that became Tyrrell County, they called the region Heart's Delight (179).

28. See Norfolk County Deed Book 6, 113.

29. Stephen is named as a son in Joseph's will, Norfolk County Will Book 12, 79 (19 January 1733/4, before 21 February 1734/5). Stephen disappears from Norfolk County tax lists after 1754, and on 30 November 1757, buys land in Edgecombe County, North Carolina, on the north side of Sapony Swamp (Edgecombe County Deed Book 6, 265). Stephen's will names son Samuel (Nash County Will Book 1, 347; 26 February 1796, probate 10 February 1806), and Samuel's will names son Wilson (Nash County Will Book 1, 165; 19 January 1818, probate August 1827). The original wills are on file at the North Carolina state archives. Samuel is listed in North Carolina Revolutionary Army Accounts, vol. 8, 54, folio 4.

30. The elder Wilson's date of birth is implied by the federal 1850 census, Hardin County, Tennessee, which lists him as seventy-five years old and born in North Carolina. The Goodspeed autobiography of his son indicates that Wilson and Alcie Odom Batchelor had four sons and two daughters, of whom three were living in 1889. These are named as Wilson R., William S., and Sarah Bachelor. The letters of Wilson Bachelor to his niece Melissa identify her mother, Delaney, as his sister. A number of family documents identify Moses as a brother of Wilson the younger, and on 23 January 1896, Bachelor records in his diary that his nephew Elbert Batchelor of Grant County, Arkansas, was visiting him. It can easily be demonstrated that Elbert was the son of Moses's eldest son John Wilson Batchelor, so the diary entry proves that Moses was one of the two unnamed brothers of whom Wilson R. Bachelor's autobiography speaks. The name of the fourth son of Wilson the elder has not been found.

He appears in his father's household on the 1830 federal census, aged ten to
fifteen years, but not in 1840, so it seems likely that he died in that decade. On
both the 1830 and 1840 census, the Batchelors are enumerated in McNairy
County, though, as will be noted below, they appear in Hardin County records
in this time frame as well—and so they apparently lived near the line separat-
ing the two counties.

31. On the 1812 service, see *Muster Rolls of the Soldiers of the War of 1812:
Detached from the Militia of North Carolina, in 1812 and 1814* (Raleigh: Charles
C. Raboteau, 1851), 81; and Ruth Smith Williams and Margaret Glenn Griffin,
Bible Records of Early Edgecombe (Rocky Mount, NC: Dixie Letter Service,
1958), 334. Nash court minutes for 16 August 1815 indicate that Batchelor
may have been making preparations to leave the county at that time, since they
indicate that he had been replaced as overseer of a portion of county road: see
Court Minutes, 1804–15, 493. The last reference to Wilson Batchelor found in
Nash County records is his appearance in the 2 December 1815 estate sale of
his brother Barnaby.

32. *Memories of an Old-Time Tar Heel*, ed. William James Battle (Chapel Hill:
Univ. of North Carolina Press, 1945), 3. Battle's family was actually connected
to the Batchelors by marriage: his first cousin Mary Carey Plummer married
Joseph John Branch Batchelor, a cousin of Wilson R. Batchelor. Speculation
in Revolutionary land grants given by North Carolina in Tennessee further
spurred the movement of North Carolina families into Tennessee in this
period. Numerous records in various middle and west Tennessee counties suggest, for example, that the sons of Jesse Cherry of Martin County, North
Carolina, a family to which the Batchelor family would connect by marriage
in Hardin County, Tennessee, bought up many tracts of land from grantees and
resold these at profit to themselves. All of Jesse Cherry's sons except two
moved to Tennessee in the second decade of the nineteenth century. According
to stories handed down among the Cherry descendants, when the brothers
remaining in Martin County, Lawrence and Darling Cherry, heard of grantees
wishing to sell their grants, they would get word about this to their brothers in
Tennessee, enabling them to make the first offer on the land. One brother,
Isham Cherry, settled in Hardin County, Tennessee, about 1819, serving as the
first justice in Hardin County's Court of Common Pleas (see Mary Elizabeth
Stricklin, *History of Cherry's Chapel United Methodist Church* [Savannah:
Savannah Publ. Co., 1983], 1–2). On the attraction of new virgin land on the
western frontier for Carolinians in this period, see Malcolm J. Rohrbough, *The
Trans-Appalachian Frontier* (New York: Oxford UP, 1978), 192–96. Rohrbough
notes that from 1810 to 1820, the population of Tennessee increased from
261,727 to 422,823 (204).

33. On the pattern of families from the old Southeast moving onto the
frontier of the old Southwest in the early 1800s to resettle as interconnected
kinship units, see Carolyn Earle Billingsley, *Communities of Kinship: Antebellum*

Families and the Settlement of the Cotton Frontier (Athens: Univ. of Georgia Press, 2004). See also William Oates Ragsdale's close and illuminating study of the migration of Presbyterian families with Ulster Scots roots from Gaston and Lincoln Counties, North Carolina, to Pope County, Arkansas, in the mid-nineteenth century: *They Sought a Land: A Settlement in the Arkansas River Valley* (Fayetteville: Univ. of Arkansas Press, 1997). Ragsdale notes that these settlers in the Arkansas River Valley moved as interrelated networks of kinfolks and neighbors, many with shared church ties (1–5, 13–22). As he notes, "Studies have indicated that kinship and previous community ties determined settlement patterns in Arkansas in the nineteenth century" (57). Ragsdale also notes the predominant influence of settlers from the Carolinas (some with previous ties to Tennessee) in the nineteenth-century migration to Pope County.

34. As John R. Finger notes, migration from middle to west Tennessee increased dramatically in the period after 1825, in part, because those who had claimed large tracts in the western district wanted to sell parcels of land following the depression that began in 1819, and actively encouraged this migration (*Tennessee Frontiers: Three Regions in Transition* [Bloomington: Indiana UP, 2001], 255–56).

35. As an example: on 24 February 1847, Wilson Batchelor witnessed a deed of Strachan and Talitha Cherry Monk to their son Eli Cherry Monk of land that had been deeded to Talitha by her brother Daniel on Sulphur Creek on 25 September 1837 (Deed Book H, 13–15). The deed notes that the land lay on the Tennessee River, evidently near what is now Pickwick Landing. The other witness to the deed was Rufus W. Byrd, a son of Talitha's sister Lovey Cherry Byrd and William Edward Byrd. Strachan and Talitha Cherry Monk were the parents of Minerva Monk, who married Moses Batchelor. Members of the Byrd family have been buried for successive generations in the White Sulphur and Old White Sulphur cemeteries in this area of the county, and traditions handed down among the Byrd descendants in Hot Spring and Grant Counties, Arkansas, indicate that both the Bachelor and Byrd families lived near what is now Counce, Tennessee, before moving to Arkansas.

Another interesting feature of this chain of deeds is that they state that the land Daniel was deeding his sister Talitha Monk for love and affection adjoined a tract belonging to their brother Lawrence, who had never moved to Tennessee. This indicates that residents of North Carolina (and other states) may have held tracts of land in Hardin County, perhaps to speculate in land or raise crops on it while they resided elsewhere. Another Cherry sibling, Isham, also seems to have owned land in the same vicinity along the Tennessee River, which he had deeded at some point to his sister Lovey and her husband, William Edward Byrd, since William's heirs deeded this land on 3 February 1845 to David Kennedy Reed, husband of William and Lovey's daughter Mary Cherry Byrd, with Moses B. Batchelor witnessing the transaction. Interestingly, this deed states that part of the land had also previously belonged to John Job Williams, who was a distant cousin of both the Cherrys and the Batchelors through his maternal grandparents, James Biggs and Jemima Cherry. As with the Monk, Byrd, and Cherry family, Williams came to Hardin County from Martin County, North Carolina.

36. See Finger, *Tennessee Frontiers*, 267–74.

37. On the settlement of the area in 1816 by settlers from east Tennessee (with North Carolina background), see P. M. Harbert, "Early History of Hardin County," *West Tennessee Historical Society Papers* 1 (1947): 45; and B. G. [Benjamin G.] Brazelton, *History of Hardin County, Tennessee* (Nashville: Cumberland Presbyterian, 1885), 16. Brazelton's grandfather John Brazelton was a member of the first party of white settlers to come to the area in 1816. The Brazelton family had come to Jefferson County, Tennessee, from Guilford County, North Carolina, after the Revolution. Colonel Joseph Hardin, for whom the county is named and who spearheaded the 1816 settlement, had entered a warrant for 3,000 acres in west Tennessee on 5 April 1784 ("Early History of Hardin County," 43, citing North Carolina Land Entries in Tennessee, #1619). In addition to the Harbert and Brazelton accounts, histories of the early settlement of the county by white settlers are found in A. A. Watson, "Bits of Hardin County History," *Courier* [Savannah] 48, no. 30 (29 July 1932): 3, col. 1; and *History of Tennessee, from the Earliest Time to the Present, Together with an Historical and a Biographical Sketch of Henderson, Chester, McNairy, Decatur, and Hardin Counties* (Chicago: Goodspeed, 1886), 830. For a comparative study of the various histories of Hardin County's foundation, see Monty Watson, "Early History of Hardin County, Tennessee," *Hardin County Historical Quarterly* 10, no. 4 (1993): 1–10.

38. Bachelor's spelling of the word "far" as "fare" is consistent throughout his written work, and seems to have been common among many southerners of his generation, perhaps reflecting how the word was commonly pronounced. As the concluding section of this introduction will note, I have faithfully preserved the spelling of the original of all the documents of Bachelor I'm publishing here.

39. See, for example, the entries for 1 and 20 March 1873, 1 March and 4 August 1874, and 2 July 1891. On 1 March 1873, Bachelor notes that his wife was preparing a special supper for the family's commemoration of its "exodus from our native and beloved State Tennessee." The twentieth finds Bachelor and his wife driving into the countryside to visit old friends from Tennessee, so that they could ask about their "friends in the Faderland." On 4 August 1874, Bachelor remarks that in his four years and six months in Arkansas, he had heard of more men dying by violence than in all his growing-up years in Tennessee.

40. *History of Hardin County, Tennessee*, 16–18. See also the excerpt of the Brazelton history in *Hardin County Historical Quarterly* 10, no. 4 (1993): 4. John Brazelton died within his first year in the area.

41. Andrew P. Hitt, *Short Life Sketches of Some Prominent Hardin Countians* (Savannah: Fundco, 1980), 78–79.

42. *History of Tennessee* states that the first act to create a public school system in the county was 23 June 1825, at which point school commissioners were appointed. This source also states that the county's first schoolhouse had been built the year before near Clifton Ford on Indian Creek, and that similar schools were found "in various neighborhoods" of the county after this. After the new state constitution of 1834–1835, a standardized system of public schools was established, and an act of the General Assembly of 1839–1840 required each district to hold school three months of the year. According to this source, the academy in Savannah began in 1832 near the house of Dr. Barlow. According to Rohrbough, *Trans-Appalachian Frontier*, the county common schools were usually operated in this period on a subscription basis: families of scholars paid the schoolmaster for schooling their children (215–16).

43. On the academy and its history, see, in addition to *History of Tennessee* (cited in the previous note), Tony Hays, "Savannah Male Academy," *Courier* 102, no. 23 [Savannah] (5 June 1986): 17, col. 1–4.

44. Hardin County's marriage records through 1863 have been lost in courthouse fires. The diary entry for 3 December 1897 states that the couple had just celebrated its golden wedding anniversary. Note, however, that *History of . . . Franklin and Sebastian Counties, Arkansas* gives the date of marriage as 1848. This source identifies Sarah as the daughter of Rowling Tankersly of Hardin County, Tennessee. An account of the golden wedding celebration from the *Fort Smith Elevator* dated 4 December 1897 is clipped and saved in Bachelor's scrapbook—see Appendix III. This states that the family held the golden wedding celebration the previous Monday, which would have been 29 November. If the celebration was held on the actual date of the wedding, then it appears the couple married 29 November 1847.

45. The interest in education continued into Bachelor's adult life: a 9 May 1873 entry in his diary notes that he was hearing recitals of pupils in a local school in Franklin County, Arkansas; and other entries note that he taught his children at home (e.g., 3 October 1870).

46. According to Brazelton, *History of Hardin County* (11), Ninian Steele married Joseph Hardin's daughter Margaret, but the marriage records of Greene County, Tennessee (Book 1, 24), show Ninian Steele marrying *Rebecca* Hardin on 8 June 1792, and this is borne out by the minutes of the Chancery Court of the Sixth Circuit of Tennessee in the case of John Ervin versus the heirs of Joseph Hardin, 8 September 1825 (38). The school of which Robert Steele was a schoolmaster in 1850 could possibly have been a school attached to a Presbyterian church built in 1822 at what became Hardinsville: Monty Watson notes that a Mrs. Steele, née Hardin, was the teacher in this school at the time it began, and that it later became the town school ("Early History of Hardin County," 2). According to Watson, the county schools

operated only sporadically in the early period and were not well funded. The preceding article of Watson publishes material compiled by his father, A. A. Watson, about the county's early history, which the elder Watson intended to publish in his lifetime, but did not publish. This material is now collected in a monograph entitled *A History of Hardin County, Tennessee: "Bits of Hardin County History,"* ed. Ronney Brewington (Savannah: Hardin County Hist. Soc., 2004). Watson notes that the early settlers of the county resisted school taxes, and built four courthouses before they built a schoolhouse (151). Watson also notes that the school taught by Mrs. Steele was at Campground Spring (159–60), and that the school was the town school for Hardinsville, and eventually became connected with a Methodist church. Tony Hays says that many of the early settlers of the county were well-educated men, and these included Ninean Steele, who was an outstanding mathematician, and Robert A. Hardin, Steele's brother-in-law, who was a Princeton-educated Presbyterian minister (*On the Banks of the River: A History of Hardin County, Tennessee* [Savannah: Tennessee River Museum, 1996], 48).

47. Bachelor's diary for 24 December 1874 indicates that a student, J. D. Massey, was reading medicine with him on that date.

48. Morrow is a particularly interesting character. His brother William I. I. Morrow, who was also a doctor, accompanied the Cherokees removed to western Arkansas and Indian Territory from Georgia under Chief John Ross in 1838–1839. Morrow kept a diary documenting the removal that is now held by the Western Historical Manuscript Collection of the University of Missouri at Columbia in its W. I. I. Morrow Collection (box 36, vol. 75). In 1850, William Morrow's brother George Doherty Morrow was living beside William Harrell Cherry in Savannah.

49. See James B. Phillips, "Hardin County," *The Tennessee Encyclopedia of History and Culture* (online at http://tennesseeencyclopedia.net/ entry.php?rec=599 [accessed March 2012]).

50. *Grant Moves South* (Boston: Little, Brown, 1960), 222–23, 298–99. Larry J. Daniel also notes the exceptionally strong Union sympathy in Hardin County as war approached, which was, as he notes, "well known": *Shiloh: The Battle That Changed the Civil War* (New York: Simon & Schuster, 1997), 77–78. Daniel notes that the locals in Savannah welcomed the Unionists when troops arrived in town, and many local residents joined Union army units.

51. "From the Tennessee River: A Steamboat Trip from Fort Henry to Savannah," *Chicago Times* 8, no. 182 (19 March 1862), 1, col. 8.

52. *History of Tennessee*, 835. As Noel Franklin Cherry wrote his parents, Eli and Cynthia Ward Cherry, in Hardin County from Nashville on 25 April 1861, secession and the war were precipitated by a powerful minority throughout the South, resulting in an internecine war in which brother was fighting brother: see Hays, *On the Banks of the River*, 91, citing the original letter in possession of John J. Ross Jr. of Savannah. Noel was a brother of William Harrell Cherry.

53. See Cora Bales Sevier and Nancy S. Madden, *Sevier Family History* (Washington, DC: Kaufmann, 1961), 379–84.

54. Alex Haley and David Stevens's novel *Queen* (New York: Avon, 1994), a work of historical fiction based on Haley's family history, has his grandmother Queen Haley working for the Cherry family in their Savannah mansion, and his grandfather Alex Sr. operating the family's ferry on the Tennessee River.

55. See Harbert, "Early History," 50; *Sevier Family History*, 381; and Garden Study Club of Nashville, "History of Homes and Gardens of Tennessee," ms. collection, Tennessee State Library and Archives (95–602, box 2, file 4). There appear to have been business connections between David Robinson and members of the Cherry family prior to William Harrell Cherry's acquisition of the house: on 9 April 1824, Daniel Cherry, a brother of William's grandfather Isham Cherry, deeded eleven acres in Hardin County to David Robinson (Hardin County Court Minutes, Book A, 210).

56. See Wade Pruitt, *Bugger Saga* (Columbia, TN: P-Vine Press, 1977), 54–56; and Tony Hays, *No Man's Land: The Civil War and Reconstruction in Hardin County, Tennessee* (Savannah: Tennessee River Press, 2001), 23.

57. *Sevier Family History*, 379–84; and "Death of W.H. Cherry," *Courier* [Savannah] 1, no. 1 (15 September 1885), 2.

58. "From the Tennessee River: Steamer *Empress* off for the Wars," *Daily Missouri Republican* 40, no. 71 (25 March 1862), 1, col. 7.

59. Among the other Unionists in Hardin County who suffered much from hostile actions within the county during the war was a distant cousin of both William Harrell Cherry and Wilson Bachelor, John Job Williams, a Savannah merchant whose mother, Martha Biggs, was a daughter of James Biggs and Jemima Cherry of Norfolk County, Virginia, and Martin County, North Carolina—see Hays, *On the Banks of the River*, 92. See also the "Family of John J. Williams of Savannah, Hardin County, Tennessee, Brother of C. B. Hassell of Williamston, North Carolina," in Cushing Biggs Hassell Papers, Southern Historical Collection, Univ. of North Carolina (#810). The article is an 1874 piece written by Hassell, who was a half-brother of John Job Williams; it details Williams's losses during the war. Williams shifted to sympathies for the South after war was declared, and in 1863, Federal troops burned his house in Savannah and seized his blacksmith shop. See also Martha Ann Williams Lackey and Mary Lou Clayton Williams, *The Descendants of John Williams and Martha Biggs of Williamston, Martin County, North Carolina* (Savannah, 1997).

60. "From the Tennessee River: A Battle Impending between the Forces under Generals Grant and Beauregard," *Chicago Times* 7, no. 191 (31 March 1862), 2, col. 8.

61. Timothy B. Smith, *This Great Battlefield of Shiloh: History, Memory, and the Establishment of a Civil War National Military Park* (Knoxville: Univ. of Tennessee Press, 2004), especially 11–15. See also Smith, *The Untold Story of Shiloh: The Battle and the Battlefield* (Knoxville: Univ. of Tennessee Press, 2006).

62. *This Great Battlefield*, 10–11. Smith cites NARA Office of Quarter-master General, General Correspondence file, box 2116, folder 601.1; NARA RG 92, E 576, Box 53; and *Annual Report of the Secretary of War 1866*.

63. See Smith (*This Great Battlefield of Shiloh*, 135), who notes how little we know about Wills.

64. As Smith notes (ibid., 10), this was in conformity to General Orders 33, issued by Quartermaster General Montgomery Meigs in 1866, which man-dated the location and reburial of Union soldiers.

65. As Smith indicates (ibid., 10–11), though the state legislative act ceding the land was on 9 March 1867, the heirs of Thomas Stubbs would not cede the land until 6 January 1869, when the case of *United States v. Mary A. Harmon* finally cleared the title to the land for the government.

66. See Joseph Brown Heiskell, *Reports of Cases Argued and Determined in the Supreme Court of Tennessee*, vol. 3 (Nashville: Jones, Purvis, 1872), 141–48 (*Wills v. State of Tennessee*).

67. Hays notes the volatility and confusion that followed the war years in Hardin County (*No Man's Land*, 55). As he notes, immediately following the war, the county was represented in the state legislature by Republican Unionists Thomas Maxwell and Alfred Pitts, but in 1869, William Fields Hinkle, a Conservative, took the county's legislative seat, and in the 1870s, Democrat Daniel William Herring was elected (56–57).

68. In 1850, Sarah is living in the household of a Susannah Franks several houses away from her father and brother Wilson. In 1860, she is in the house-hold of a William Pyburn, again near her brother. On the 1880 federal census, she is living with her brother Wilson and his family. The 1850 census gives her age as thirty, the 1860 as thirty-seven, and the 1880 as fifty-six.

69. Moses and Minerva Monk Batchelor were the parents of six sons—John Wilson (1840–1894, married Talitha Emeline Robinson), Wiley (abt. 1842–aft. 1860), James Decalvin (abt. 1844–1861), George Richard (1845–1907, married Catherine Ryan), Daniel Tucker (abt. 1848–aft. 1880), and Edward (1849–1920, married 1] Mary, 2] Mary Paralee Bagley).

70. Harbert, "Early History," 40.

71. For instance, on 17 June 1825, the *Raleigh Register* printed a notice that Strahon Monk was a defendant in the suit of Amos Raynor v. the administrators of the estate of Monk's father, Nottingham Monk, and that notice was being given to Strahon Monk to appear at the September term of court in Bertie County, North Carolina (*Register* 24, no. 1324 [17 June 1825], 4, col. 4). A receipt in the estate file of his father (held by the North Carolina Archives) shows that Strahon Monk was summoned from 20 May 1825 to 9 September 1825 to appear and give testimony in the case. The receipt indicates that he traveled back from Tennessee to North Carolina for the court appearances.

72. See James P. Whittenburg, "Scotch Merchants," in *Encyclopedia of North Carolina*, ed. William S. Powell (Chapel Hill: Univ. of North Carolina Press,

2006), 1012; David Dobson, *Scottish Emigration to Colonial America* (Athens: Univ. of Georgia Press, 1994), 109; Samuel A. Ashe, *History of North Carolina* (Greensboro: Charles L. Van Noppen, 1908), 252–53; and Arthur Herman, *How the Scots Invented the Modern World* (New York: Three Rivers Press, 2001), 161–62.

73. See Elwin L. Goolsby, *Our Timberland Home: A History of Grant County, Arkansas* (Little Rock: Rose, 1984), which states that the Batchelor settlement was about two miles south of what is now Poyen (139).

74. The date of marriage is recorded in the Bible of Lawrence's niece Lovey Jane Reed. Lawrence Cherry Byrd and Hannah Delaney Batchelor had the following children: Pleasant A. (1843–1880/1890, married Elizabeth M. Rucker), Wilson Batchelor (1844–1850), William Edward (1846–1926, married Matilda Bailey), Melissa Ann (1849–1936, married Joshua Marion Robinson), Samuel Delaney (1852–1890, married 1] Polly Ann Thrower, 2] Laura Warlick), John Lawrence (1859–1946, married Susan Catherine Elliott), and Henry C. (1860–1927, married Sarah Letitia Collie).

75. See Francis M. Manning and W. H. Booker, *Martin County History*, vol. 1 (Williamston, NC: Enterprise, 1977), 233.

76. *Raleigh Register* 23, no. 1170 (22 February 1822), 3, col. 5.

77. As noted previously, John Job Williams, a leading merchant of Savannah who came to Hardin County from Martin County, North Carolina, as the Monk and Cherry families also did, was both a Biggs and Cherry descendant. A second cousin of Williams, Jesse Biggs (1801–1875), also came to Hardin County (see Rayma Biggs and Mary Louise Biggs, *The Jesse Tree: History of Biggs-Dexter Families in America* [Iuka, MS, 1980]).

78. The 1850 federal census shows Moses living beside Delaney's brother-in-law Samuel Daniel Byrd, who is living next to his brother Lawrence Cherry Byrd with wife, Delaney.

79. Biographical information is in Susan Easton Black, *Early Members of the Reorganized Church of Jesus Christ of Latter Day Saints*, vol. 1 (Salt Lake City: Brigham Young Univ., 1993), 326–27; Pearl Wilcox, *Saints of the Reorganization in Missouri* (Independence, 1974), 267–69; *The Saints' Herald* 43, no. 29 (15 July 1896), 480; and *Zion's Ensign* 7, no. 26 (1896), 8. The latter two are obituaries for William. William Skidmore Batchelor and Huldah King had the following children: William W. (1844–bef. 1920, married Emma), George Willis (1845–aft. 1920, married 1] Phebe J. McEntire, 2] Mary Ellen Horan), Mary Louisa (1847–1925, married Benjamin F. Beever), John H. (1849–1850/1860), Enoch Robert (1850–1930), Permilla (1853–1930, married Charles Pius Thompson), Permillous W. (1853–1914, married Emma L. Sullivan), Nancy Ellen (1856–1935, married Thomas J. Williams), James F. (1856–?), Sarah (1858–1860/1870), Etta Ann (1860–1943, married James Alexander Henderson), and Queen Victoria (1862–1932, married George Spellman Henderson).

80. Someone, perhaps Bachelor himself, has written corrections to the published text at several points. For instance, the obituary says that William moved

to Iowa in childhood, and "Iowa" has been crossed out and replaced with "Tennessee." And it says he converted to Mormonism in "Murray Co. [*sic*]," Tennessee, in 1839, and the county name has been changed to "Hardin."

81. *Zion's Ensign* 4, no. 6 (4 February 1893), 3—see Appendix IV.

82. The issue of the *Ensign* that Bachelor had received was evidently its 28 January 1893 issue, since his scrapbook contains a copy of another letter he sent the *Ensign* for publication responding to an article by an author whose name is given only as Eleanor, entitled "Social Purity," which appeared on page 6 of the 4, no. 5 (28 January 1893) edition of the *Ensign*.

83. *Times and Seasons* 1, no. 4 (February 1840), 59. *Times and Seasons* 2, no. 9 (1 March 1841), 338–39, also contains a report of the conference of elders and members of the Church of Jesus Christ of the Latter Day Saints prepared on 7 November 1840 in Lincoln, Vermont, which states that Elder Norvel M. Head reported that he had taken a mission to the south with Elder Saunders in the past season, and at a conference in McNairy County, Tennessee, they had baptized eight people and organized a branch of twenty-eight members. Head also reported that there was a small branch of Latter Day Saints in Tishomingo County, Mississippi, with six members in good standing, and he had added seven more to the numbers. Note that on 3 December 1897, Bachelor's diary says Mormon missionaries were staying with his family in Franklin County, Arkansas, as they delivered pamphlets in the area.

84. Documents in the manuscript collection of the Church History Library of the LDS Church in Salt Lake City contain further information about the missions in west Tennessee in the late 1830s and early 1840s: both Hunter and Clapp filed missionary reports in the early 1840s showing that they continued to return from Nauvoo to Tennessee to carry on further missions and to col-lect tithes from those they had previously converted—see "Missionary Reports [Tennessee], 1831–1900" (MS-6104, folder 10). Neither Clapp's 17 November 1845 report recounting his Tennessee missions beginning on 12 August 1843 and 7 June 1844 nor Hunter's 2 April 1845 report recounting his mission beginning 27 January 1845 specifically mentions Hardin or McNairy County, Tennessee. The diary of the early LDS leader Wilford Woodruff indicates that the mission in Tennessee began on 13 January 1835 with Warren Parrish and A. O. Smoot and continued from 27 March to 12 April that year with Woodruff himself. On 18 July, Woodruff mentions ordaining Benjamin Clapp at the house of his brother Lewis in Kentucky, and he notes on 11–12 September that Benjamin Clapp was then living in Calloway County, Kentucky: see *Wilford Woodruff's Journal, 1833–1898: Typescript*, ed. Scott G. Kenney, vol. 1: *29 Dec. 1833–1893* (Midvale, UT: Signature, 1983): 25, 27, 36–38, and 43.

85. See, for example, Hal Pierce, "A History of the Rise of the Church of Jesus Christ of Latter-Day Saints in Mississippi" (2008), which states that Hunter and Clapp began their missions in Tishomingo County in 1839, and

that in April 1842, some forty wagons with eighty to ninety Mormons arrived in Nauvoo as the Mississippi converts escaped persecution (online at http://www.ldshistoryblog.com/Mississippi.pdf [accessed April 2012]).

86. See Fred E. Woods, "The Cemetery Records of William T. Huntington, Nauvoo Sexton," *Mormon Historical Studies* 3, no. 1 (March 2002): 143.

87. Sarah's eulogy notes that the Reverend J. T. Evans read the eulogy at her funeral, though her brother Wilson wrote the eulogy. Evans was a Baptist minister in Franklin County at the time, so it seems very likely that Sarah belonged to a local Baptist church.

88. The original minutes of both churches have been microfilmed and copies are held by the Arkansas History Commission. I am citing the original minutes. The Brush Creek minutes for 1 November 1847 show Delaney being dismissed by letter on that date. The same minutes show her husband, Lawrence C. Byrd, being dismissed by letter on the same date. It seems likely a church closer to their residence had been formed by this point, and they were "moving their letters" to that church.

89. The 1860 federal census for Saline County, Arkansas, shows John Waters as a Baptist minister living in Marble Township. On 13 February 1861, the newspaper *Arkansas Baptist* published a list of all Missionary Baptist ministers in Arkansas, in which John Waters is listed as pastor of Belfast Baptist Church in Saline County.

90. Sarah Bachelor appears on a list of founding members of Mill Creek Baptist Church in August 1878—see *History of . . . Franklin and Sebastian Counties*, 669.

91. An account of the case from Lower Norfolk County court records is in Philip A. Bruce, *Institutional History of Virginia in the Seventeenth* Century, vol. 1 (New York: G. P. Putnam's Sons, 1910), 221. William P. Palmer, ed., *Calendar of Virginia State Papers*, vol. 1 (Richmond: R. F. Walker, 1875), 9, transcribes Edwards's complaint.

92. See Lower Norfolk County court minutes for 15 May and 15 June 1657, showing John Biggs sworn in as undersheriff of the county at this court session (Record Book D, 72).

93. On 15 June 1658, John Lownes petitioned against Biggs as undersheriff, claiming abuses by Biggs: ibid.,148. In the same court session, Christopher Bustian was fined for making abusive statements about Biggs as undersheriff: ibid., 150. At this court session, Bustian, Lownes, and several others filed a petition claiming abuse by Biggs and asking for his removal as undersheriff: ibid., 156. By 17 October 1659, county records note that Biggs is "late undersheriff" (ibid., 228). Biggs appears in county records as surveyor of roads on the southern branch of the Elizabeth River by 16 August 1669 (see Order Book 1665–1675, 38a, as cited, Marilu Burch Smallwood, *Some Colonial and Revolutionary Families of North Carolina*, vol. 3 [Gainesville, FL: Storter, 1976], 12). Edwards complained to Governor Berkeley in 1670 that Biggs was abusing his authority

as surveyor of highways. Transcripts of the complaint are in "Some Colonial Virginia Records," *Virginia Magazine of History and Biography* 10, no. 4 (1903), 376, and *Calendar of Virginia State Papers*, vol. 1, 2.

94. The deed of land was from Thomas Nash to Richard Taylor, on 4 November 1664 (Record Book D, 430).

95. See *Calendar of Virginia State Papers*, vol. 9, 9; and Edward W. James, "The Church in Lower Norfolk County, Virginia," *Lower Norfolk County, Virginia, Antiquary* 5, no. 1 (1906): 122–23.

96. See Bruce, *Institutional History*, 221; and *Calendar of Virginia State Papers*, vol. 1, 9.

97. See Bruce, *Institutional History*, 221; Boddie, *Seventeenth-Century Isle of Wight County, Virginia* (Chicago: Chicago Law Printing Co., 1938), 55–56); Worrall, *The Friendly Virginians* (Athens, GA: Iberian, 1994), 6, 20; Jones, *The Quakers in the American Colonies* (New York: Russell & Russell, 1962), 274–77; Horn, *Adapting to a New World: English Society in the Seventeenth-Century Chesapeake* (Chapel Hill: Univ. of North Carolina Press, 1994), 56–58; and Hatfield, *Atlantic Virginia: Intercolonial Relations in the Seventeenth Century* (Philadelphia: Univ. of Pennsylvania Press, 2004), 118–36. Both Worrall and Hatfield note that Puritanism predominated in Elizabeth River Parish, the parish of the Batchelor and Biggs families (and the Cherry and Byrd families with whom they were to be so interconnected by marriage over the generations).

98. Boddie, *Seventeenth-Century Isle of Wight*, 58.

99. See Lower Norfolk County Record Book B, 150A.

100. Hatfield, *Atlantic Virginia*, 118, citing Winthrop's journals and Johnson's *Wonder-Working Providence of Sion's Saviour in New England* (London: Nathaniel Brooke, 1653).

101. Hatfield, *Atlantic Virginia*, 119.

102. Ibid. As Bruce notes (*Institutional History*, 221), the charges instance Harrison's Puritanism.

103. Hatfield, *Atlantic Virginia*, 120–21.

104. Ibid.

105. Boddie, *Seventeenth-Century Isle of Wight,* 59, 79; and Horn, *Adapting to the New World*, 388–94. On the strong Puritan stamp on Anglicanism throughout Virginia prior to Berkeley, and Berkeley's determination to extirpate nonconformity, especially in southeast Virginia, see Carl Bridenbaugh, *Jamestown, 1544–1699* (New York: Oxford UP, 1980), 61–66.

106. See Jones, *Quakers in the American Colonies*, 277, citing the minutes of the Council of Maryland for 22 July 1658; and Edward James, "The Church in Lower Norfolk County," *Lower Norfolk County, Virginia, Antiquary* 2, no. 3 (1897): 83–88, transcribing Lower Norfolk County court records naming Meares a "seditious sectarie." Meares was accused in court on 15 August 1649 of not attending church and ordered to conform. On 1 October 1649, he was ordered to give bond for his irreligious behavior.

107. On the arrival of the Quaker movement in Virginia, see Bridenbaugh, *Jamestown*, 67. On the appearance of Quakers in Lower Norfolk County by 1660, see Douglas Summers Brown, "Virginia Yearly Meeting," in William Wade Hinshaw and Thomas Worth Marshall, *Encyclopedia of American Quaker Genealogy*, vol. 6: *Virginia* (Ann Arbor: Edwards Bros., 1950), 5–13. Brown notes the determination of the Virginia government to extirpate the Quaker presence in Lower Norfolk and Nansemond Counties, in particular (7, 11–12). John W. H. Porter summarizes the early history of Quakerism in Norfolk County in an article entitled "Norfolk Quakers," *Richmond Dispatch* 13, no. 211 (3 December 1892), 7, col. 1–2. Porter notes the significance of the story of John Biggs as an illustration of both the emergence of the Quaker movement in the county and the hostile reaction it elicited from governing authorities.

108. Jones, *Quakers in American Colonies*, 270–71.

109. Ibid. See also Horn, *Adapting to the New World*, 394–99.

110. Hatfield, *Atlantic Virginia*, 126.

111. Stephen B. Weeks, *Southern Quakers and Slavery* (New York: Bergman, 1968), 22; and Boddie, *Seventeenth-Century Isle of Wight*, 113. See also Hatfield, *Atlantic Virginia*, 126f; Samuel A. Ashe, "John Porter," in *Biographical History of North Carolina from Colonial Times to the Present*, ed. Ashe et al. (Greensboro, NC: Charles L. Van Noppen, 1905), 369–73; and Claiborne Smith, "Porters of Lower Norfolk County, Virginia, and North Carolina," in *Historical Southern Families*, vol. 8, ed. John Bennett Boddie (1964; repr. Baltimore: Geneal. Publ. Co., 1970), 138–44.

112. Weeks, *Southern Quakers*, 22–23; John W. H. Porter, "Norfolk Quakers"; Jones, *Quakers in the American Colonies*, 335.

113. *Southern Quakers*, 22–23. On Berkeley's appointment of a commission, see Horn, *Adapting to a New World*, 274, 290.

114. Weeks, *Southern Quakers*, 22–23; John W. H. Porter, "Norfolk Quakers"; Ashe, "John Porter," 369.

115. Weeks, *Southern Quakers*, 23–24; "Church in Lower Norfolk County," 110; and Boddie, *Seventeenth-Century Isle of Wight*, 113–14. The reference to the ship *Blessing* is interesting for the following reason: the ship was co-owned not long before these events by a John Bigge. Peter Wilson Coldham's *English Adventurers and Emigrants, 1609–1660: Abstracts of Examinations in the High Court of Admiralty With Reference to Colonial America* (Baltimore: Geneal. Publ. Co., 1984) abstracts testimony given in a 1637–1638 [English] High Court of Admiralty case involving the *Blessing*, *Roger Phillips v. William White* and *Cobham and Cobham v. John Bigge and Thomas Besbech*. Testimony in the case given by John Jobson of Rochester, Kent, states that he was master of the *Blessing*, which was or had been owned by Bigge and Besbech and which made voyages to New England. Coldham is abstracting cases from High Court of Admiralty Examinations in Equity Causes (HCA 13/39–73). The John Bigge who owned

the *Blessing* was, it seems, a descendant of a John Bigge (abt. 1561–1605) of Cranbrook, Kent, a number of whose descendants went to Massachusetts as part of the Kentish migration of Puritans to the colonies: see John Brooks Threlfall, *Fifty Great Migration Colonists to New England and Their Origins* (Madison, WI, 1990), 37–62, 556; Elizabeth French, "Bigge Wills and Records," *New England Historical and Genealogical Register* 56 (1912): 54–61; and W. H. Whitmore, "Will of John Bigg," *New England Historical and Genealogical Register* 29 (1875): 253–60. This Puritan Kentish Bigge family was intermarried with a Batchelor family, which also came to New England. It is tempting to wonder if the Bigge family of Kent who emigrated from there to New England and owned a ship that appears in both the records of the Puritan colonies of New England and in Lower Norfolk County, Virginia, records is somehow connected to the Biggs/Bigg/Bigge family of Lower Norfolk County, Virginia.

116. Virginia Patent Book 5, 381; Nugent, *Cavaliers,* vol. 1, 518.

117. Robert W. Barnes, *Colonial Families of Anne Arundel County, Maryland* (Westminster, MD: Family Line Publications, 1996), 152.

118. As cited, Smith, "Porter of Lower Norfolk County," 139.

119. Ibid., 140; and Ashe, "John Porter," 369–73.

120. See Margaret Jones Bolsterli's introduction to the 1849–1872 diary of Harriet Bailey Bullock published as *A Remembrance of Eden: Harriet Bailey Bullock Daniel's Memories of a Frontier Plantation in Arkansas, 1849–1872,* ed. and introduced by Bolsterli (Fayetteville: Univ. of Arkansas Press, 1993), 1–23. As Bolsterli notes, Charles Lewis Bullock, Harriet's father, moved his family from Warren County, North Carolina, to Fayette County in west Tennessee and then, in 1848, to Dallas County, Arkansas—following closely the migration path pursued by Wilson Bachelor's parents and then his siblings Moses and Delaney, and in the same time frame that these siblings moved to Arkansas (11–15).

121. See S. Charles Bolton, *Arkansas, 1800–1860: Remote and Restless* (Fayetteville: Univ. of Arkansas Press, 1999), 18, which says that the historian Robert Walz estimates a third of Arkansas settlers by 1850 had Tennessee roots (citing Robert B. Walz, "Migration into Arkansas, 1820–1880: Incentives and Means of Travel," *Arkansas Historical Quarterly* 17 [1958]: 309–24). According to Gerald T. Hanson and Carl H. Moneyhon, *Historical Atlas of Arkansas* (Norman: Univ. of Oklahoma Press, 1989), Tennesseans dominated among migrants to Arkansas up to 1850, accounting for 36 percent of settlers in the period to 1850 (37). Hanson and Moneyhon are, of course, referring here to the place from which these settlers migrated and not necessarily to the place in which these settlers were born. A high proportion of the Tennesseans coming to Arkansas in this period were North Carolina-born.

122. As *History of . . . Franklin and Sebastian Counties, Arkansas* notes, the county sent W. W. Mansfield to the Constitutional Convention in Little Rock in March 1861 to vote against secession—though this source also suggests that

once other states seceded and war began, Franklin Countians favored succession (637–38).

123. See Michael Hodge, "Railroads," *Encyclopedia of Arkansas History and Culture*, online at http://encyclopediaofarkansas.net/encyclopedia/entry-detail. aspx?search=1&entryID=1185 (accessed February 2012). On the importance of the development of the railroad line from Little Rock to Fort Smith in spurring the settlement of the Arkansas River Valley area in which Bachelor settled in the final decades of the nineteenth century, see Orville W. Taylor, "Arkansas," in *Religion in the Southern States: A Historical Study*, ed. Samuel S. Hill (Macon: Mercer UP, 1983), 41. Taylor notes in particular the promotion of German Catholic immigration to northwest Arkansas as the railroads reached there. As Ragsdale notes (*They Sought a Land*, 14–15), the Arkansas River Valley region also appealed to nineteenth-century immigrants to Arkansas because Fort Smith had already been a major center for forming wagon trains to the west prior to the advent of the railroad, and this produced economic opportunity down the valley in the regions close to Fort Smith.

124. See Vernon McDaniel, "Ozark (Franklin County)," *Encyclopedia of Arkansas History and Culture*, online at http://encyclopediaofarkansas.net/encyclopedia/entry-detail.aspx?search=1&entryID=884 (accessed February 2012). Bachelor will mention the town's burning in his 3 October 1870 diary entry.

125. George M. Henry, "The History of Franklin County, Arkansas" (unpubl. M.A. thesis, Univ. of Wyoming, Laramie, 1940). As Matthew M. Stith notes, with the constant back-and-forth guerilla fighting in northwest Arkansas and southwest Missouri during the war, citizens of some towns in the area abandoned their towns altogether to escape from the guerilla warfare: "Social War: People, Nature, and Irregular Warfare on the Trans-Mississippi Frontier, 1861–1865" (unpubl. Ph.D. thesis, Univ. of Arkansas, 2010), 102. On the "brutal guerilla struggle that involved all levels of Arkansas society" during the Civil War, see Robert B. Mackey, "Bushwhackers, Provosts, and Tories: The Guerilla War in Arkansas," in *Guerillas, Unionists, and Violence on the Confederate Home Front*, ed. Daniel E. Sutherland (Fayetteville: Univ. of Arkansas Press, 1999), 171–85.

126. *History of . . . Franklin, and Sebastian Counties, Arkansas*, 1237–38.

127. Mayme Vest, *Remembering the Small Communities of South Franklin County* (Branch, AR, 1993), 115, reproduces the charter.

128. *History of . . . Franklin, and Sebastian Counties, Arkansas*, 649.

129. Lecky, *History of European Morals from Augustus to Charlemagne*, vol. 1 (London: Longman, Greens, 1869), 221.

Diary of Wilson R. Bachelor (1870–1902)

1. Note that the Bachelor family's journey from Tennessee to Arkansas begins aboard a flatboat, though on 9 March, the flatboat crew will suggest that

182 Notes to Page 39

the increasingly inclement weather makes a steamboat safer, and the migrating families will take a steamboat down the Mississippi from Cairo, switching on 15 March to another steamer to head up the Arkansas. They'll then switch to yet another steamboat at Little Rock on 18 March. Though flatboats had generally been superseded by steamboats at this period, the initial choice of a flatboat was probably dictated by the fact that, as this diary entry suggests, several families were making the move together. Traditions handed down among Bachelors descendants indicate that at least one of his wife Sarah's brothers and his family accompanied the Bachelors to Arkansas. It's not clear what items in addition to their personal effects the families are bringing with them. The 8 March entry will indicate they are also carrying cotton that they will sell in Paducah, and descendants of Bachelor state that he brought along saplings of the silver poplars that he will mention later in his diary, which were planted about his Arkansas homeplace (see, e.g., the 2 June 1895 diary entry). The 10 March entry indicates that the families traveling to Arkansas owned the flatboat, which they will sell in Cairo when they decide to shift to a steamboat. On the dominance of the steamboat on the Tennessee and its subsidiaries after this newer mode of travel was introduced, see Donald Davidson, *The Tennessee*, vol. 1: *The Old River: Frontier to Secession* (Nashville: J. S. Sanders, 1946), 230–54. On flatboats as the preferred mode of relocation when pioneer families moved to Arkansas from the states of the old Southeast, see Donald P. McNeilly, *The Old South Frontier: Cotton Plantations and the Formation of Arkansas Society, 1819–1861* (Fayetteville: Univ. of Arkansas Press, 2000), 39. McNeilly notes that though steamboats were also used for the relocation process, they were more expensive, and this is another reason flatboats were more commonly used (ibid.).

2. Morris Landing appears to be Boyd's Landing, thirteen miles south of Savannah at what is now Pickwick Dam. According to *History of Tennessee*, 841, a W. E. Morris & Co. had a business at Boyd's Landing in the latter half of the nineteenth century. The site is under Pickwick Lake today. Bend Shoals and Hamburg, mentioned next as stopping points in the narrative, are between this area and Savannah.

3. Several lines are illegible in the original, which has a tear and a portion of which has also fallen from the page due to the fragility of the paper. The photocopy of the diary made in the 1970s preserves some of the text that is now missing, including the phrase "like a vast cosmic repose." In the portion missing, the words "measured" and "the bark of some Sleepless" can be made out.

The phrase "like a vast cosmic repose" may reflect Bachelor's interest in Sanskrit mythological literature, if he had begun reading in that field by this date. His occasional piece entitled "Reasons for Being an Agnostic, No. 1" will mention his interest in Sanskrit literature by the latter part of the 1870s. In his occasional piece entitled "Come and Gone," he will speak of the "silent

Ocean of the future" and "Ocean of eternity," and in his eulogy of his son
Monroe, he will speak of the "great universal life" that his son joins in death.
All of these phrases reflect themes that fascinated him as he moved toward
freethought, and his belief, articulated in his occasional piece responding to Dr.
Addison M. Bourland's novel *Entolai*, that death represents the dissolution of
our individual atoms by which we join the universal whole. See also the 31
December 1894 diary entry speaking of the "endless chain of eternal cycles,"
which draws on a similar concept.

4. As with the previous entry, here, too, significant portions of the text are
now missing, though some of these are clear in the photocopy of the diary
made before further deterioration had occurred.

5. Beech Creek is in Wayne County on the east side of the Tennessee.

6. Squirrel was long a staple of the southern table, for all classes. As John
Egerton notes, squirrel was long eaten by the Native Americans in the pre-
colonial period, and the colonists followed suit (*Southern Food* [New York:
Alfred A. Knopf, 1987], 248). According to Egerton, Jefferson considered
squirrel an essential ingredient of Brunswick stew. See also Waverly Root,
Eating in America (New York: William Morrow, 1976), 73; and Joe Gray Taylor,
Eating, Drinking, and Visiting in the South (Baton Rouge: Louisiana State UP,
1982), 8, which maintains that "squirrels were the most plentiful meat in the
stewpot [of frontier southerners], which almost constantly hung over the coals
of the frontier fireplace" (8). As Katharine E. Harbury notes, William Byrd is
perhaps one of the most reliable sources we have concerning the everyday cui-
sine of Virginians of higher social status in the eighteenth century, and he
speaks casually of the cooking of squirrel by Virginians of his class: *Colonial
Virginia's Cooking Dynasty* (Columbia: Univ. of South Carolina Press, 2004), 78.
Mary Randolph's *Virginia House-Wife* (1824), contains a sophisticated recipe
for hare soup made with a red wine base seasoned with thyme, parsley, and
pounded cloves, with a note that the soup is equally good made with squirrel:
see Karen Hess's facsimile edition of this work (Columbia: Univ. of South
Carolina Press, 1984), 35. Marion Cabell Tyree's *Housekeeping in Old Virginia*
(Louisville: John P. Morton, 1879) has a recipe for barbecued squirrel (108),
and Lettice Bryan's *The Kentucky Housewife* (1839) has recipes for stewed, fried,
and broiled squirrel (see Bill Neal's facsimile edition [Columbia: Univ. of
South Carolina Press, 1991], 136–37). In his 6 July 1891 diary entry, Bachelor
will mention that he and his son Monroe and daughter Nannie eat fried squirrel for supper as they journey from Franklin County, Arkansas, to Hot Springs.
The consumption of squirrel has not by any means been confined to the
southern part of the United States: Imogene Wolcott's *The New England Yankee
Cookbook* (New York: Coward-McCann, 1939) has recipes for squirrel pie
(from New Hampshire: 98) and squirrel soup (with the provenance of this
recipe attributed to the Seminoles: 279).

7. Britt's Landing is on the east side of the Tennessee in Perry County.

History of Tennessee says that a community was established there in 1839 which was of considerable commercial importance by the 1840s (785).

8. The mouth of Duck River is in Humphrey County, Tennessee, where the Duck connects to the Tennessee.

9. Here, there are tears in the middle of the text, and a portion of the text on the left-hand margin is lost for eight lines. Fragments of text that can be made out include "Soon passed," "channel," and "and round rocky bars."

10. In Benton County, Tennessee. A Civil War battle occurred there on 4–5 November 1864.

11. "Shall" = "shawl." The *Oxford English Dictionary* shows the word entering English as early as 1662, from Persian. In its original usage, it referred primarily to an article of clothing worn by men in the Middle East. By the mid-eighteenth century, as shawls became fashionable among English and French women, the word began to refer commonly to a wrap worn by women, though its use to denote a male garment is not unheard of in the nineteenth century according to the *OED*.

12. Bachelor's reference to the barber, his "colored professional friend," and the reference to Negroes are worth noting. In anything he writes touching on racial matters, there is never a hint of the racial prejudice all too common in the American South in the period in which he wrote. To the contrary, here and in other places in which he deals with the topic of race (e.g., in his occasional piece "Unrest and Tendencies of Organization," in which he deplores slavery), he displays a sensitivity to racial matters and an avoidance of racially stigmatizing terms remarkable for his time and place. The 14 July 1891 diary entry will find him and his children camping on their trip to Hot Springs near a Negro church holding a revival. Compare the terminology Bachelor uses to speak of African Americans with the everyday speech of many people of his region as suggested by Mark Twain in novels like *Huck Finn* and *Tom Sawyer*, and his racial sensitivity stands out all the more. It's also worth noting here that barbershops would later be strictly segregated throughout most of the South in the period from Jim Crow up to the civil rights breakthroughs of the 1950s and 1960s.

13. "Jam" = "jamb," of course. The pattern of writing diary entries at night when everyone around him has retired for the night will recur throughout the diary.

14. Danville is on the east side of the Tennessee in Benton County, Tennessee, and was once a steamboat landing. The town itself is now defunct.

15. In Henry County, Tennessee, near the Kentucky border.

16. In none of Bachelor's extant writings does he ever refer to his wife, Sarah Tankersley, by name. She is always "my wife"—even when he's reporting on her having given birth to a child, as he does on 6 May 1874 when he speaks of the birth of their daughter Pauline.

17. Birmingham was a community in Marshall County, Kentucky, on the Tennessee River that was flooded by the formation of Kentucky Lake in the 1940s. 27 Mile Island is also now under the lake.

18. Paducah, the county seat of McCracken County, Kentucky, is at the confluence of the Tennessee and Ohio, and because of its location, was a major hub for steamboat and flatboat travel in the region in the nineteenth century.

19. Several varieties of hickories, a tree in the genus *Carya* of the walnut family, bear edible nuts that have long been prized as a foodstuff in the southern part of North America. As Alan Davidson notes, the early colonists learned of the culinary use of hickory nuts from the native peoples of the continent: *The Oxford Companion to Food* (Oxford: Oxford UP, 1999), 380. Thomas Harriot, *Briefe and True Report of the New Found Land of Virginia* (London, 1588), reports the native peoples crushing hickory nuts and then mixing them with water to produce a milk with which they seasoned various foods (on this, see Root, *Eating in America*, 33–34). In his *Travels* (Philadelphia: James & Johnson, 1791), William Bartram notes a similar use of hickory nuts by Creeks west of Augusta, Georgia (57; see the reproduction of Bartram's *Travels,* edited by Mark Van Doren [New York: Dover, 1928]). On the widespread culinary use of the hickory nut in the southern Appalachian region (and the native American roots of its use), see Joseph E. Dabney, *Smokehouse Ham, Spoon Bread, & Scuppernong Wine* (Nashville: Cumberland House, 1989), 385–86. In the postcolonial southern kitchen, the primary use for the nuts was in sweets including cakes, pies, cookies, candy, and ice cream. The reason Bachelor mentions that the traveling families were gathering the nuts "so late in the Season" is that they ripen and fall from trees in the autumn months and are usually gathered then.

20. At later points in the diary when Bachelor refers to temperatures, particularly ones related to weather, he often notes he's using a Fahrenheit measurement. Since a temperature below zero F would be rather surprisingly cold for this season in the region around Kentucky—and might freeze the river along its banks—it's tempting to think he's using a Celsius measurement here and on the subsequent day when he also speaks of it being below zero.

21. The cotton the families sell at Paducah has evidently been brought along to help them finance their trip. According to J. B. Killebrew, *Introduction to the Resources of Tennessee*, vol. 2 (Nashville: Tavel, Eastman & Harrell, 1874), Hardin County produced 2,026 bales of cotton in 1870 (1090). U.S. Department of Agriculture statistics show cotton selling for about 15 cents per pound in that year. This is in sharp contrast to the situation during the years of the Civil War, when its price skyrocketed to as high as $1 per pound: see James L. Watkins, *Production and Price of Cotton for One Hundred Years* (Washington, D.C.: Government Printing Office, 1895), 11. As McNeilly notes (*Old South Frontier*, 112), the good cotton market of the 1860s had enticed yeoman

farmers in places like Arkansas into growing cotton, whereas cotton growing had previously been an activity primarily restricted to planters. The group purchases supplies at Paducah because it is the first community of any real size they have reached at this point on their trip.

22. Metropolis is on the Ohio in Massac County, Illinois, and is now part of the greater Paducah metropolitan area.

23. At Paducah, the travelers have entered the Ohio and are proceeding down that river to Cairo, which is at the confluence of the Ohio and the Mississippi. They'll then take the Mississippi to the mouth of the Arkansas, heading up the Arkansas to their final destination in northwest Arkansas.

24. Cairo is the county seat of Alexander County, Illinois, and is at the confluence of the Ohio and the Mississippi. Because of its location it was and remains a major hub for traffic on the two rivers. Hence the decision to look for a steamboat here when the flatboat crew hesitates to travel further under weather conditions the crew regard as dangerous.

25. The *St. Luke* will sink not too many years after the traveling families take it from Cairo to Memphis: on 4 May 1875, the *New York Times* reported that the boat had sunk on the third, bound from Leavenworth, Kansas, to St. Louis. It sank when it hit a pier of the St. Charles bridge, and eleven people lost their lives ("Disaster on the Missouri: Sinking of the Steamboat *St. Luke*— Ten or Eleven Lives Believed to Have Been Lost," *Times* 24, no. 7373 [4 May 1875], 1, col. 4). The ship was carrying about one hundred people. The boat belonged to Joseph Kinney, a noted steamboat mogul in this region: see Thomas J. Scharf, *History of Saint Louis City and County, From the Earliest Periods to the Present Day: Including Biographical Sketches of Representative Men*, vol. 2 (Philadelphia: Louis H. Everts & Co., 1883), 1122. Steamboat travel at this period could be notoriously dangerous: on the night of 26 April 1865, the steamboat *Sultana*, bound from Vicksburg to Cairo, sank at Memphis, with some 1,800 soldiers losing their lives—more than the number who died when the *Titanic* sank (see Nancy Hendricks, "*Sultana* [Steamboat]," in *Encyclopedia of Arkansas History and Culture*, online at http://encyclopediaofarkansas.net/encyclopedia/entry-detail.aspx?search=1&entryID=2269 [accessed February 2012]).

26. "This being Saturday" may indicate that no steamboat was available until Monday because some boats didn't operate on Sunday; but if that was the reason for the hiatus in boat operation, then the Sabbath restriction doesn't apply everywhere, since the diary has the group traveling a week later on Sunday, 20 March, up the Arkansas. Memphis is, of course, another significant river city at which the group charters a new steamboat to carry them to the mouth of the Arkansas and then upriver.

27. *Cholera morbus* was a term used in the nineteenth and early twentieth centuries to describe both nonepidemic forms of cholera and other cholera-like gastrointestinal disturbances. The term is no longer in use. Since Bachelor

is up and visiting a barber in the city on the fourteenth, also taking nourishment, it seems doubtful he has anything akin to cholera proper. The problem
persists, however, since he mentions it again on the eighteenth, when he takes
laudanum for it. He mentions being sick again on the twenty-third when they
reach their destination of Ozark, as he suffers from exposure to the cold while
he builds a hut, adding to the derangement of his stomach and bowels. Gastric
problems may have been persistent in his life: in a 5 September 1899 letter to
his niece Melissa Byrd Robinson, he will speak of being troubled by chronic
indigestion. Bachelor sometimes spells Melissa's surname as Robertson.

28. That is, Memphis.

29. The full name of the steamer appears to be the *Thomas H. Allen*, named
for the president of the Cairo and Fulton Railroad, who also owned the first
telegraph company in Memphis. The *Thomas H. Allen* will sink at the end of
1872 about five miles above De Valls Bluff, Arkansas, a Captain Ashford then
piloting it: see Duane Huddleston, Sammie Rose, and Pat Wood, *Steamboats and
Ferries on the White River: A Heritage Revisited* (Fayetteville: Univ. of Arkansas
Press, 1999), 79–80. As Leslie C. Stewart-Abernathy notes, in the pre-railroad
era in which travel by roads in Arkansas was notoriously difficult because of the
rudimentary nature of roads and frequent flooding in the eastern part of the
state at various times of the year, the development of steamboat travel opened
the state to many new settlers in the first part of the nineteenth century, including both yeoman farmers and planters (see "Steamboats," *Encyclopedia of
Arkansas History and Culture*, online at http://encyclopediaofarkansas.net/
encyclopedia/entry-detail.aspx?search=1&entryID=4466 [accessed February
2012]). See also Rohrbough, *Trans-Appalachian Frontier*, 282–83; and Works
Project Administration, *Arkansas: A Guide to the State* (1941; repr. as *WPA
Guide to 1930s Arkansas* [Lawrence: Univ. Press of Kansas, 1987], 51–52). The
alarm of the crew of the *Thomas H. Allen* is understandable, given the sinking
of the *Sultana* at Memphis five years previous, with tremendous loss of life.

30. Napoleon, once a thriving port town at the confluence of the
Mississippi and Arkansas Rivers, is now a ghost town after it was repeatedly
flooded. Its marine hospital had already fallen into the Mississippi in 1868, and
the town was to be submerged completely in 1874 (see Steven Teske,
"Napoleon," *Encyclopedia of Arkansas History and Culture*, online at
http://encyclopediaofarkansas.net/encyclopedia/entry-detail.aspx?search=
1&entryID=356 [accessed February 2012]). Mark Twain wrote about
Napoleon and its reputed propensity for violence in *Life on the Mississippi*
(Boston: James R. Osgood, 1883). Bachelor's description of how people pass
time aboard the boat prefigures passages Twain was to write in the 1883 work.

31. The White flows into the Mississippi in Desha County, Arkansas.

32. Bachelor will mention sandbars in the Arkansas again on 21 March,
when he notes a large sandbar at Patterson's Bluff on which their boat runs
aground.

33. Pine Bluff is about forty-five miles downstream from Little Rock, and was an important river port in the nineteenth century, with strong ties to Little Rock upriver and to New Orleans downriver. It was the site of an early French settlement, Mont Marie, mentioned by Thomas Nuttall in his *Journal of Travels into the Arkansas Territory* (Philadelphia: Palmer, 1821), recording his 1819 travels in Arkansas Territory: see John Gould Fletcher, *Arkansas* (Chapel Hill: Univ. of North Carolina Press, 1947; repr. Fayetteville: Univ. of Arkansas Press, 1989), 40. Thomas James's 1846 book *Three Years among the Indians and Mexicans* (Waterloo, IL: War Eagle, 1846), recounts his experiences traveling up the Arkansas in May 1821. James notes (99) that he and his party spent time with a French settler of considerable wealth, a Mr. "Veaugean" (i.e., Vaugine). François Vaugine lived in the vicinity of Mont Marie (later Pine Bluff), and the city of Pine Bluff is now in Vaugine Township. Though the diary makes no mention of it, this is the point on his journey at which Bachelor passes closest to the families of his siblings who moved to Arkansas in the late 1840s, Moses and Delaney, who settled with their families near what later became the community of Poyen in Grant County about forty miles due west of Pine Bluff.

34. Bachelor will mention freight being discharged again on 20 March at Dardanelle and on 22 March when the group finally reaches Ozark.

35. The reference to a locomotive is interesting, since very little railroad track has yet been laid in Arkansas by this date—notably, a portion of the Memphis-to-Little Rock railroad. Since construction has begun on the Little Rock-to-Fort Smith railroad in 1869, it's tempting to think the locomotive being hauled by the *Thomas H. Allen* is for that project. Pine Bluff would become a major center of the Cotton Belt line at a slightly later date.

36. Little Rock takes its name from an outcropping of schist and sandstone on the south bank of the Arkansas marking the transition from the alluvial plains of the southern and eastern part of the state to the highlands of the northwest section of Arkansas: see Fletcher, *Arkansas*, 30, who maintains that in 1719, the French explorer, Bernard de la Harpe, first identified what became the city with this rock outcropping. As Bachelor notes in this entry, the first rock he and his fellow travelers spot as they travel upriver is at Little Rock, since they have been traveling through the flat, rich alluvial land of the Delta and then through a section of the Coastal Plains, neither of which is characterized by significant rock formations. The location that became the city of Little Rock had already long had significance as a crossing point of an ancient trail used by the native peoples of the area that later became known as the Southwest Trail, which bisects the state roughly from its northeast to its southwest corner. The path simultaneously skirts the swampiest parts of the lowlands and the highest parts of the highlands, facilitating movement by foot, horse, or wagon through what became the state of Arkansas: see Bolton, *Arkansas, 1800– 1860*, 4–5; McNeilly, *Old South Frontier*, 19–22; WPA, *Arkansas: A Guide*, 203; and Hanson and Moneyhon, *Historical Atlas of Arkansas*, 33.

37. The traveling party shifts yet again to a new steamboat, the *Fort Gibson*. According to Frederick Way, *Way's Packet Directory: Passenger Steamboats of the Mississippi River System Since the Advent of Photography in Mid-Continent America* (Athens: Ohio UP, 1999), the boat was a sternwheel packet that was to sink 1 January 1876 near Bayou Meto in Arkansas County, en route to St. Louis (169, entry #2098).

38. Here and throughout the diary (and in his published work, as well), Bachelor often uses verb forms and other grammatical constructions now regarded as nonstandard English, but which had long been accepted in the folk speech of the American South, which had been imported from the British Isles, and which were commonly used by southerners of all classes—as had been the case in Britain when their ancestors came to the colonies.

39. Laudanum was an opiate widely used in the period to treat a variety of ailments ranging from sleeplessness to diarrhea. The opium was in a tincture of alcohol flavored with herbs or spices to mask its bitter taste. The medication was available without a prescription until the early twentieth century, when the addictive properties of opium-based medicines caused many governments to proscribe their use except under physicians' supervision. Bachelor is evidently still suffering from the attack of *cholera morbus* he has mentioned on the thirteenth.

40. Bachelor's fascination with the geology (and flora and fauna) of his new home state will be apparent throughout the diary—for example, in the 3 October 1870 diary entry in which he will recount an excursion with two of his younger sons to a promontory called Bee Bluff near his new home.

41. The observation that the rocks along the river are "much disintegrated" is very accurate. The Ozark region is characterized by a layer of friable, easily eroded shale atop a more durable sandstone base—and this is the typical geological feature of the region he appears to be referring to as he notes the disintegration of the rocks.

42. As this entry indicates, at some point prior to their removal from Tennessee to Arkansas, Bachelor and the other new settlers have already identified Franklin County and Ozark (the county seat of Franklin) as their destination and new place of settlement.

43. Dardanelle is in Yell County. According to *Arkansas: A Guide*, the source of the name is debated, with some accounts indicating the name may have derived from early French settlers of the region, and others claiming that the community was named by early explorers for the Dardanelles in Turkey, of which the local geography reminded them (285). The latter explanation was accepted as early as 1821 when Nuttall gave credit to it in his *Journal of Travels into the Arkansas Territory* (126). As Earnie Deane notes (*Arkansas Place Names* [Republic, MO: Western Printing, 1988]), Dardanelle has the distinction of being one of the earliest places in Arkansas Territory to be recorded on maps and mentioned in reports (85). See also Mildred Diane Gleason, "Dardanelle

(Yell County)," in *Encyclopedia of Arkansas History and Culture*, which speaks of the town's "boomtown" reputation by the 1860s, when it was an important steamboat landing attracting settlers from North Carolina and Tennessee (the article is online at http://encyclopediaofarkansas.net/encyclopedia/entry-detail.aspx?search=1&entryID=1020 [accessed February 2012]).

44. It seems likely that the promontory Bachelor mistakes for Mount Magazine, which is quite a distance inland from the river, is Mount Nebo, which is at Dardanelle.

45. It is this rock face, some three hundred feet in height and on the river, that those who think the town is named after the Turkish Dardanelles cite as the reason for the town's name.

46. Patterson's Bluff is in Logan County. Ella Molloy Langford, *Johnson County, Arkansas, the First Hundred Years* (Clarksville, AR: Sallis, Threadgill & Sallis, 1921), notes that it was a stopping place for steamboats traveling up and down the river (147), and that a Winningham family from Hardin County, Tennessee, lived near this area in Lamar (49).

47. They have arrived at their destination after a twenty-one-day journey. The distance between Savannah, Tennessee, and Ozark, Arkansas, is about 350 miles over land.

48. The hut is presumably for his own temporary shelter as he rides around the countryside (something he mentions in this and his next two diary entries) looking for land and a place for the family to live. It's difficult to imagine that his wife, Sarah, and their eight children live in a hut along with Bachelor while he looks for a place for them to live. Sarah is heavily pregnant with their son who will be born in July, Vick. As Bachelor will note in his 3 October entry, she has been "indisposed" during the previous six months, "being confined during that time giving Birth to a son." Sarah and the children very likely stay with friends in Ozark, or rent lodgings there, as Bachelor identifies land and a new house for the family. The next entry on 23 March will further imply that he has built the hut for his own temporary lodging as he rides around the area, and it notes that he has taken cold from exposure in building it and continues to suffer from the "derangement of Stomach and Bowels" that began early in their journey. As these diary entries suggest, living conditions are somewhat primitive in this area of Arkansas, which is still, in some respects, the edge of the western frontier at the point the Bachelors settle there. The entire state remained to some extent in a frontier condition when the Civil War arrived, and the disruption the war caused did not help the state move easily out of its frontier conditions in subsequent years.

49. It's not clear that the family moves immediately into the "small cottage," since the 19 March 1871 entry will state that he (i.e., the entire family) moves on that date into the house on the land they have purchased, and they find the house "verry uncomfortable." It's probable he means to write "80 acres" instead of "8 acres" in this 3 April entry, since his homestead application

case file shows him making application for 80 acres in Franklin County on 9 November 1870 at the Dardanelle land office (homestead application #5566, certificate #1727). The land was in section 29 of township 9 north, range 28 west south of the Arkansas River, with Mill Creek running to the south of the tract. Documents in the file show that he filed an affidavit 26 February 1877 stating that he settled on the 80 acres when he entered the homestead entry on 9 November 1870, building a house there when he settled on the land. The affidavit also notes that he had cultivated 20 acres of land since he filed the application, and had built another dwelling house to add to the first, along with two cribs and stables and a smokehouse. The document also says he had planted peach and apple orchards. The land warrant was finally approved on 9 September 1882, with a patent issued 20 October that year. The 1877 affidavit in the homestead application file suggests that the family either rebuilt or added onto the original cottage, or built two separate new dwelling places on the 80 acres between 1870 and 1877. As the rest of the diary will make plain in many repeated entries, Bachelor maintained a working farm on which he grew a variety of crops with the assistance of his sons at the same time that he practiced medicine. This combination of farming with medical practice was the norm for most country doctors in the American South at this period. By the point of his death, Bachelor had acquired 250 acres in Franklin County.

50. This statement might refer to the first deer he has shot in *Arkansas*, but it appears it's a statement that he has not shot a deer at any point up to this date. This is rather surprising, since Bachelor clearly hunts, as almost all southern males of any age did at the period: he says on 3 March 1870 that he has shot a squirrel as the families are en route to Arkansas (and the entry goes on to note that he and his sons have shot five hundred squirrels [!] in the past few months). Deer would no doubt have been more abundant on the Arkansas frontier than they would have been in the more settled area of west Tennessee in which he grew up—especially the town of Savannah near which he and his family lived for some years before their removal to Arkansas. In fact, Brazelton's *History of Hardin County* does specifically note (79) in its commentary on the situation in the county following the Civil War that deer had become rare in Hardin County by the time of the war.

51. As the entry notes, one reason for the hiatus in writing is Sarah's confinement and then delivery of their son Vick on 24 July. He and sons Monroe, who is twenty, and perhaps Jim and Wils, nineteen and fifteen, would also have been occupied building on their land, perhaps clearing portions of and beginning to till and plant it. Finally, as the series of medical entries that begin on 9 October indicate, he would also have been busy during the period between the 3 April and 3 October entries establishing his new medical practice in Arkansas.

52. The two sons are probably Monroe and Jim.

53. *Sciurus niger*, the largest species of tree squirrels in North America. They range through much of the eastern United States (with the exception of New England) west to the Dakotas, Colorado, and Texas and now as far west as California, where they are not native. Bachelor's reference to the large number of fox squirrels he and his sons have shot brings to mind reports of the casual way in which passenger pigeons were shot in such large numbers in the nineteenth century that the species became extinct, as well as accounts of the similar casual shooting of bison, when railroad cars traveling through the western states would stop so that passengers could kill the animals by shooting them from train windows. Audubon notes the practice of shooting passenger pigeons (which became extinct in his lifetime) in huge numbers in *Birds of America* (1840)—see volume 5 of the 1861 edition of the original work that Audubon's son J. W. Audubon issued (New York: Roe Lockwood & Son, 1861), 28. It's possible Bachelor and his son are shooting squirrels in such large numbers because they have begun cultivating and planting their land, and in the spring months, when squirrels have exhausted their winter supply of nuts, they often eat tender seedlings and seeds sown for crops. The family would also no doubt have welcomed the squirrels as food as they opened a new farm.

54.   There will be recurring reports throughout the diary that family members are sick during the summer months, when malarial afflictions were common in the southern states, especially among those living near waterways: see, for example, the 4 July 1891 entry reporting that he and daughter Nancy ("Nannie") are sick as they begin their trip to Hot Springs; the 17 September and 1 October 1895 entries, speaking of the family's malarial chills and fevers during the summer months; and the 1 September 1898 entry, which notes again that family members have been sick during the hot months. On the pronounced concern of nineteenth-century settlers considering Arkansas as a new homeplace about the endemic malaria, chills, fever, and agues of the summer months, see Conevery Bolton Valen ius, "The Geography of Health and the Making of the American West: Arkansas and Missouri, 1800–1860," in *Medical Geography in Historical Perspective*, ed. Nicolaas A. Rupke (London: Wellcome Trust Centre for the History of Medicine at UCL, 2000), 121–45, esp. 126.

55.   As noted previously, this is their son Vick, their next-to-last child. Pauline will be born in 1874. The choice of the name Victor Hugo for this son is interesting. *Les misérables* had been published in 1862, and appeared in an English translation (by Charles E. Wilbour, with Carleton in New York as the publisher) only months after the French edition was published. Hugo's critique of the corruption of the church and the ruling class and his sympathy for workers may have appealed to Bachelor if he was already trending to freethought by this date. He would also have been drawn to Hugo's rationalistic deism akin to that of Voltaire. By the early 1870s, Hugo began to identify

himself as a freethinker, and this may have made Bachelor sympathetic to him (see Alfred Barbou, *Victor Hugo and His Times*, trans. Ellen E. Frewer [Oxford: Oxford UP, 1882], 44).

56. It's not surprising that Bachelor would have visited Fort Smith soon after the family's relocation to Franklin County, though it is perhaps surprising that he expected it to be something other than what it was, and that he expected people in his vicinity to be interested in the things that interested him and to provide "intellectual Recreation." At a distance of forty miles from Ozark (a fact he notes in this entry), Fort Smith, which was incorporated in 1842, was the only town of any noteworthy size close to Bachelor's new home-place. The city had 2,032 citizens in 1870, per the federal census (see Benjamin Boulden, "Fort Smith [Sebastian County]," *Encyclopedia of Arkansas History and Culture*, online at http://encyclopediaofarkansas.net/encyclopedia/entry-detail.aspx?entryID=988 [accessed February 2012]). It would have been the market center in his vicinity most likely to have such goods as he could not easily get in his area, including medical supplies, books, music, and musical instruments. His note that he sees much business and trade being conducted there and wagons moving about reflects his probable interest in the town as a nearby market (and cultural) center, Fort Smith's situation as the gateway to Indian Territory and the West, and the town's growth immediately following the Civil War, as new settlers (including former slaves and European immigrants) have begun to flock to the rapidly developing community. The theme of disappointment with his newly chosen home will continue in subsequent entries in which he complains of the lack of intellectual companionship in his area of Arkansas, and the solace he finds in books and music—themes already apparent in this diary entry. As a frontier settlement with a reputation for row-diness and violence reflected in Charles Portis's novel *True Grit*, Fort Smith would undoubtedly have struck Bachelor as "meagre" in comparison to Savannah with its more settled ways and its academy established in 1832 and a newspaper dating from 1843 (see *Introduction to the Resources of Tennessee*, 1093). On the frontier character of Fort Smith throughout the nineteenth century, see Fletcher, *Arkansas,* 228–29. For Bachelor's reflections on the violence prevalent in northwest Arkansas in these years, see his 18 August 1874 entry, which says that in four years and six months in the state, he has heard of more deaths by violence than in all his prior life in Tennessee.

57. On the papers published in Ozark up to 1909, see the introductory essay's discussion of Bachelor's scrapbook.

58. Since he says he is instructing his "children," it appears he's educating both his sons and his daughters Nannie, Alcie, and perhaps Lula, though she is only four at the time, in all of the subjects mentioned. If so, that would have been a noteworthy decision at a time and in a place in which women's education rarely equaled that of men. But it would also have been consistent with

his commitment to women's rights expressed at various points in the diary and in occasional pieces such as his letter about societal purity to the *Zion's Ensign* paper in Independence, Missouri. Or is he the one studying these books?

59. George Bacon Wood, *A Treatise on the Practice of Medicine* (Philadelphia: Grigg, Elliott & Co., 1847).

60. C. P. Bronson, *Elocution* (Louisville: Morton & Griswold, 1845).

61. This is the first reference to a theme of great importance to Bachelor's diary and letters: music, and, in particular, his own love for the guitar. References to his guitar playing and family gatherings at which various family members play different instruments will run throughout the diary. On 11 August 1895, when son Wils has just died and Bachelor commemorates him in the diary, he will note that the family is called "the musical family," and its members play the organ, violin, banjo, and guitar.

62. The first medical case entered into this diary is dated 9 October. Following the 22 March 1871 entry, he will record a case dating from 31 December 1869 that he indicates comes from a diary he has been keeping prior to the 1870 diary. As noted in the introductory section of this book, no diary prior to 1870 appears to be extant now.

63. On the fear of southern country doctors in the latter half of the nineteenth century and early twentieth century that they would fall behind in their knowledge due to a lack of intellectual stimulation in rural settings, see Paul I. Crellin, "Country Doctor," in *Encyclopedia of Southern Culture*, ed. Charles Reagan Wilson and William Ferris (Chapel Hill: Univ. of North Carolina Press, 1989), 1366.

64. As the preceding portions of the diary suggest, the Bachelor family's new home county is along the Arkansas River in northwest Arkansas in the Arkansas River Valley, between the Ouachita Mountain chain to the south and the Ozarks to the north (see Thomas Foti and Gerald Hanson, *Arkansas and the Land* [Fayetteville: Univ. of Arkansas Press, 1992], 36, 61–69). Though the southern half of Franklin County, in which the Bachelors have settled, falls within the Arkansas River Valley region, the northern half of the county is in the Ozarks—hence the "mountains piled on mountains" that Bachelor says he and his sons can see to the north of the river when they climb promontories near their new homeplace. The land in the southern part of the county is hilly or rolling upland that also comprises deep, fertile bottomlands along the river.

65. The Boston Mountains form the southern portion of the Ozark Plateau geologic region, and are found in north-central Arkansas. They comprise the highest mountain points between the Appalachians and the Rockies (see Margaret J. Guccione, "Boston Mountains," *Encyclopedia of Arkansas History and Culture*, online at http://encyclopediaofarkansas.net/encyclopedia/entry-detail.aspx?search=1&entryID=2389 [accessed February 2012]).

66. Several locales, all in the Ozark Mountain region in northwest Arkansas, are now referred to as Bee Bluff, but none is within four miles of Ozark. The

one closest to Ozark is across the Arkansas River in Johnson County near Lamar—but since this is about thirty miles from Ozark, it seems doubtful this is the spot to which Bachelor is referring. There is a Bee Rock, a mountain pillar across the Arkansas River to the north of Ozark. It is about four miles from Ozark, and would appear to be the locale Bachelor is describing, except he says that one can see Ozark from the west at this point, whereas Bee Rock is almost directly north of Ozark.

67. As with his preceding account of the terrain as they moved toward Ozark on 20 March, in this passage, Bachelor demonstrates a strong ability to describe the natural beauty of his surroundings in prose that is both compelling and scientifically grounded. His description of the layers of sandstone, limestone, and shale is very accurate (see Foti and Hanson, *Arkansas and the Land*, 39–42), and his subsequent comments will reveal that he can also recognize both the coal and saltpeter he and his sons find in the hills—and that he has the ability to analyze the coal's carbon content. The mountains hold a particular fascination for him, it seems, perhaps because he has grown up in the Gulf Coastal Plain region of west Tennessee, so mountains are a new experience for him.

68. Coal would, in fact, begin to be mined in Franklin County in the 1870s—see Rebecca Haden, "Franklin County," *Encyclopedia of Arkansas History and Culture*, online at http://encyclopediaofarkansas.net/encyclopedia/entry-detail.aspx?search=1&entryID=768 (accessed February 2012); and John G. Ragsdale, "Coal Mining," ibid., online at http://encyclopediaofarkansas.net/encyclopedia/entry-detail.aspx?search=1&entryID=352 (accessed February 2012).

69. As this diary entry notes, he has not kept a "regular diary" in 1870 following the preceding 3 October entry, but he has clearly been keeping some other kind of medical casebook, from which he is transferring the case of a gunshot wound that he will record in the next entry. The 31 December 1869 entry that is inserted into his record of cases from the fall of 1870 specifically says that this case is being transferred from "my diary of 1869." It's also worth noting that he has begun to establish his medical practice in Arkansas by October 1870, and the hiatus in the diary between early April and early October probably has much to do with his work to build the medical practice (and settle his new homeplace).

70. From this entry until 19 March 1871, the diary shifts to medical cases, and the medical chronicle continues at various points after 19 March, too. The 19 March entry will note that the family has moved to its new house (one it had either built on the land Bachelor purchased in 1870, or a remodeled version of the already existing cottage he mentions when he buys the eighty acres). It appears that much of the time leading up to the family's move to the new house in March 1871 was taken up with beginning his medical practice. The case notes indicate that he is a fairly well-trained and knowledgeable

physician who gives solicitous and thorough care to his patients with the tools and techniques available to him as a country doctor on the edge of the frontier of a somewhat isolated and backwards state at this period.

71. As on 18 March when he mentions that he has taken laudanum for his *cholera morbus*, he prescribes an opiate—and this is consistent with medical practice of the period.

72. Since the patient has found swallowing and taking solid food difficult, the lack of bowel action may reflect his inability to eat. Opiates are, however, also constipating.

73. A simple cerate is a covering for a wound with features of both an ointment and a plaster, consisting primarily of wax—hence its name. The term is common in nineteenth-century medical literature and occasionally in the very early twentieth century, but not thereafter, when this method of dressing wounds fell into disuse.

74. The *auricularis anterior* muscle is sometimes, but rarely, identified in old medical manuals, it appears, as the *attrehens auris* muscle.

75. That is, "masseter."

76. As with the previous case of gunshot wound, he prescribes an opiate for the pain and to assure rest and uses a simple cerate to cover the wound as it heals.

77. Though the terms "midwife" and "midwifery" now have an almost exclusively female connotation (and, indeed, have always had that primary sense in English, since the word "wife" is considered a gendered term), use of the term to refer to men assisting at childbirth is found in English as early as 1577, according to the *Oxford English Dictionary*. And English medical manuals from the eighteenth century forward speak of the "art of midwifery" as the art of assisting a woman to give birth, without assigning a specific gender to the provider of the service.

78. As this and a number of subsequent cases will amply demonstrate, childbirth was a dangerous enterprise for women well into the latter part of the nineteenth century even in developed nations, and perhaps more so in frontier areas like that of northwest Arkansas. Babies were still delivered at home in rural areas and small towns throughout Arkansas up to the first half of the twentieth century, and women who experienced complications giving birth often died as a result—as did their babies, in many cases. For subsequent childbirth cases, see the ones beginning on 31 December 1869, 22 May (i.e., March?) 1871, 22 April 1871, and 22 February, 5 March, and 30 June 1873. The large majority of the medical cases Bachelor records in his diary have to do with childbirth, and as late as 15 April 1897, he will be called to walk over a mile to visit a young woman who has had a nervous attack.

79. The term "cerebral congestion" is no longer in common use. It was once used to describe conditions thought to precede an apoplectic attack. The child's illness sounds much more like a *Staphylococcus* infection. But *S. aureus*

was not recognized as a medical cause of illnesses of this sort until 1880, when Alexander Ogston identified it.

80. If the house into which they move today is the cottage mentioned on 4 April 1870, it has taken a year to prepare it for the family. The foreshortened chimney would have assured that there would not be enough draft to provide a fire that would heat well, and it would also cause smoke to blow back into the house. Descendants of the Bachelor family have a picture of the family dwelling that appears to be a photo touched up with features drawn and chalked in. The picture shows a one-story cottage style house with a porch that has columns with gingerbread fretwork around them and a hallway that seems to lead from the front porch to more than one room, with a chimney on only one side of the house. Family members are on the porch, including an elderly Wilson Bachelor sitting beside a table stacked with books. There's also an addition to the cottage built onto the back of the house. The house in the photograph appears to be built in the "hall and parlor" style that, as Clifton Coxe Ellis notes, was the predominant vernacular house style in Tennessee well into the nineteenth century and one that had roots in the English West Country and Wales, from whence the style was carried to Virginia ("Early Vernacular Plan Houses," *The Tennessee Encyclopedia of History and Culture*, online at http://tennesseeencyclopedia.net/entry.php?rec=659 [accessed February 2012]). As David Hackett Fischer notes, after it was imported into Virginia from the western part of England, the hall and parlor house style spread from the mother colony across the American South (*Albion's Seed: Four British Folkways in America* [New York: Oxford UP, 1989], 271–74). Fischer notes that houses in this style were generally a story or a story and a half, commonly with two rooms on both stories and extensions added as needed. A chimney could be at both ends of the house or only one end. The roof is typically steep. This house style was also common in the northeastern area of North Carolina from which Bachelor's parents came to Tennessee. It came to North Carolina from Virginia: see Catherine W. Bishir and Michael T. Southern, *A Guide to the Historic Architecture of Eastern North Carolina* (Chapel Hill: Univ. of North Carolina Press, 1996), 446. On hall and parlor architecture as the most distinctive folk style of the Tidewater, and from there, throughout the South, see Henry Glassie, *Pattern in the Material Folk Culture of the Eastern United States* (Philadelphia: Univ. of Pennsylvania Press, 1968), 64–67.

Bachelor's Byrd in-laws built an early example of a hall and parlor house in Hot Spring County when they arrived in Arkansas from Hardin County, Tennessee, in 1846. The house was built by Delaney Batchelor Byrd's brother-in-law Samuel Daniel Byrd about 1848, and still stands in Grant County (part of which was formed from Hot Spring County) near the community of Poyen. It is very similar in style to the Bachelor family house in Franklin County shown in the picture descendants have of the Bachelor house: a one-story house with a porch and columns on front, a hallway leading into the house from the porch, a chimney on only one side, and additions that may have been added over the years. The house is the oldest standing structure in Grant County and is now on the National Register of Historic Places (see Arkansas Historic Preservation Program, "Samuel D. Byrd, Sr., Homestead, Poyen Vic., Grant Co." online at http://www.arkansaspreservation.com/ historic-properties/_search_nomination_popup.aspx?id=2146 [accessed February 2012]). Byrd descendants say that family traditions indicate that Samuel's brother Lawrence Cherry Byrd and wife, Delaney, lived just down the road from this house, where they operated an inn. The community in which these families lived, initially known as Cross Roads and now as Poyen, stands near the intersection of several historic roads traversing the state from north to south, including the Southwest Trail: see Goolsby, *Our Timberland Home,* 165; and Hanson and Moneyhon, *Historical Atlas of Arkansas,* 33. Delaney's (and Wilson's) brother Moses Batchelor also lived in this vicinity. It seems very likely that Wilson Bachelor would have visited this Byrd house on his trips to see relatives in Hot Spring and Grant Counties.

81. As the family moves into its new house and continues to improve it, they plant a garden in the season in which rural folks across the South are planting gardens. A diary of Bachelor's distant cousin Cushing Biggs Hassell (1809–1880) of Martin County, North Carolina, provides a detailed account of items he was planting in his garden in March 1847 in the region of northeastern North Carolina in which Bachelor's parents were born. On 2 March 1847, Hassell writes that he is planting Irish potatoes, and the next day, he says he has gone again to gardening, planting turnips, radishes, beets, squash, prickly and long cucumbers, butter and white beans, watermelons, three kinds of garden peas, mustard, kale, and purple eggplant (see Cushing Biggs Hassell Papers, Southern Historical Collection, Univ. of North Carolina, #810). As was Bachelor, Hassell was a descendant of the Biggs family of Lower Norfolk County, Virginia. His mother, Martha Biggs (1784–1860), was a daughter of James Biggs and Jemima Cherry, of the same Cherry family to which Bachelor's siblings Moses and Delaney connected by marriage. It's not at all unlikely that what the Bachelors would have planted in their Arkansas garden would have been similar to what their North Carolina and Tennessee cousins planted in gardens back east. One other point is worth remarking on here: Bachelor's personal interest in his garden is unusual in southern culture, where gardening was primarily considered a woman's task: see Mary Thomas, "Gardening," in *Foxfire 4,* ed. Eliot Wigginton (Garden City, NY: Anchor/Doubleday, 1977), 150. Bachelor will note on 11 May and 2 June 1895 that he is still cultivating his garden into his old age, and it is a place of refuge for him, in which he has built a vine-covered arbor where he sits to read.

82. Bachelor will note at several points in his diary that his medical cases sometimes require him to stay up all night with patients—always at their homes, as was the common practice among country doctors of his era.

83. Bachelor has clearly written "May the 22nd" at the heading of this case entry, though the context (and the dating of later cases) suggest the case probably occurred on March 22, and is the case to which the March 21st entry refers. As he notes in the entry of the twenty-first, the case was difficult and kept him occupied all night, and these notes seem to fit the case of "May" 22nd.

84. That is, a *primipara*.

85. The use of venesection as a therapeutic intervention in this case is somewhat surprising, since the practice of bleeding had already begun to fall out of fashion in American medicine by this point (see Gerry Greenstone, "The History of Bloodletting," *BC Medical Journal* 52, no. 1 [January–February 2010]: 12–14). Perhaps Bachelor tries the intervention because the case seems extreme and he fears that the young woman will die.

86. As with the use of bleeding (discussed in the previous note), the use of blisters was somewhat old-fashioned at this point in the history of American medicine, and may well be a vestige of older medical practices in an out-of-the-way part of the country. However (and this is noted in the previous note about venesection), it's possible that Bachelor considers the case so extreme and the possibility of the young mother's death so imminent that he is willing to try any and all therapeutic interventions that promise to save her life. The range of remedies he tries in this case is interesting to note: they include chloroform, bleeding, anesthetics, a massage with brandy infused with capsicum and turpentine, morphine, oil of turpentine, a cathartic dose of mercury, emollient poultices, and, finally, when the anxiety and hysteria continue, tonics and recommendation of a change of scenery—which seem to help.

87. Ergot is a fungus that grows on rye, from the genus *Claviceps*. Though the substance is poisonous, an extract of small quantities of it was often used in an infusion or tincture for medical purposes in the nineteenth century (note that the case of difficult labor recorded on 25 March 1871 also says that Bachelor administered "a scruple" of ergot in that case). As the entry indicates, a primary use was to induce or enhance labor. Certain extracts of ergot are still so used, in fact. Bachelor may have chosen to record this unhappy case from 1869 (before the family moved to Arkansas), in which a mother carrying twins gives birth to one child and then dies after the other presents as a breech birth and dies *in utero*, because it reminded him of the happier case of the young *primipara* he recounts twice in entries between which the 1869 case is sandwiched.

88. Crotchet: a curved, hooked instrument used for various medical purposes including child delivery. The term (and instrument) are no longer in use.

89. Fillet: a loop-shaped instrument used in childbirth to assist in pulling a breech-birth baby from the uterus. A fillet was often made of chord: note that the entry says Bachelor had an assistant who drew on the chord as they tried to remove the body of the twin that had died *in utero*.

90. The reference to hysteria is interesting. As a pseudo-medical term, the term "hysteria" was still relatively new in English usage, with a nineteenth-

century provenance, so its use by a country doctor in frontier Arkansas in the latter part of the nineteenth century is worth remarking on.

91. The recommendation of a change of scene and associations indicates psychological acuity on the part of Bachelor as a doctor, and an awareness that illness has both physical and psychological components.

92. A third case of complicated childbirth, following immediately on two others: has he grouped these three cases together deliberately because they have similar themes? If nothing else, the gathering of these cases side by side demonstrates how common these complicated childbirths were in the nineteenth century, and how large they could loom in the practice of a country doctor of the latter half of the century. In this case, it appears the birth is premature, and that the child does not survive because it is born too early in the gestational course.

93. Note that, with the exception of the 19 March 1871 entry noting the family's move to their new home, there are no diary entries from 3 October 1870 until today that are not accounts of medical cases. At the end of the 3 October 1870 entry that begins the series of medical cases, Bachelor notes, in fact, that he has not been keeping a regular diary and is "passing on" to 1871, though he intends to record first the medical case beginning on 9 October 1870. It seems evident that he begins to use his diary from the time of the family's move to their new house primarily as a medical casebook, as he gets his new medical practice in Franklin County underway. As this entry notes, he is writing on 1 March 1873 to commemorate the family's move to Arkansas in 1870, which began on 1 March, and to offer a "retrospective view." The use of a title for this entry is consistent with his practice in the medical cases preceding it, which also have titles.

94. Mill Creek Township is about twelve miles south and west of and across the Arkansas River from Ozark. The river forms the northern boundary of the township. In 1870, 152 people lived in the township, per the federal census for that year. By 1884, Bachelor will be postmaster of the small community within the township in which he lives, which he will name Pauline after his daughter born in 1874. R. L. Polk's *Arkansas State Gazetteer of Business Directories* (St. Louis: R. L. Polk Co., 1884) shows Pauline with a population of 35 families in 1884, and, in addition to listing Wilson R. Bachelor as postmaster, it lists his son Jim as constable, and his son Monroe as a blacksmith in the community (440). Wilson R. Bachelor is also listed as a druggist. Another small community several miles east of Pauline, Cecil, was also named by its postmaster Thomas McClain for one of his children, and by the early 1900s, as Pauline dwindled, its name disappeared and the name Cecil became the name for both small communities.

95. "The bourn, from whence no traveler returns" is from *Hamlet* (act 3, scene 1), and was repeated numerous times in nineteenth-century literature and epitaphs. Dickens cites the phrase in *Nicholas Nickleby* as a common

byword. Bachelor's next entry on 2 March 1873 will note that he has been reading Dickens. Note, too, the 29 May 1873 entry that says he never tires of reading Shakespeare; and the next day, he will note again that *Richard III* (which he has read that day again) and *Romeo and Juliet* are among his favorites.

96. The pecuniary embarrassments to which Bachelor refers are never elucidated. Setting up a new homeplace, farm, and medical practice would have been expensive. If his medical practice failed to take off quickly, that might have added to his financial difficulties. Did these financial problems account, in part, for the lacuna in the diary between 1871 and 1873?

97. This is a theme that will recur repeatedly in the diary: the observation that he is sitting in his office alone writing, often late at night. Many of his entries written under these conditions note his loneliness and disappointment that he has not found many intellectual companions in Arkansas and that he takes solace in reading and music. Many of the subsequent diary entries will also refer to his office as his "studio" or "library."

98. That is, an expectorant.

99. Again, "my wife," who is never mentioned by name.

100. Professor Paul Graham will be mentioned a number of times after this in the diary—on 21 March 1871, 7 June 1873, and 28 October 1874 (recounting activities of the 24th–25th). The 1870 federal census shows him to be twenty-six years old, English-born, and living in Ozark. In 1880, he is again listed on the census as a teacher in Ozark and born in England, now aged forty-five and divorced. The age in 1870 appears to be a mistake, since he is listed in 1860 in Osage, Benton County, Arkansas, aged twenty-five, where he is teaching school. He was also naturalized in April 1859 in Benton County. He was county examiner for the Franklin County schools in 1884, per *Biennial Report of the State Superintendent of Public Instruction* (Little Rock: Joseph Griffith, 1884), 84. A diary of Mrs. T. Moore of Franklin County notes on 3 May 1882 that Professor Graham had organized a choir called the Murphys for the temperance meetings, and on 27 October 1887, the diary states that he had died that day in Alma, Arkansas (see "Diary of Mrs. T. Moore," transcribed by Mrs. W. W. Moore, *Franklin County Historical Association Observer* 1, no. 1 [1976–1977]: 9). Paul Graham is buried in the Alma city cemetery with a tombstone giving his birthdate as 27 February 1835 and the date of death given in the Moore diary. It appears Bachelor named his daughter Pauline Graham Bachelor, born 6 May 1874, after Professor Graham. Bachelor's friendship with Paul Graham is noteworthy against the backdrop of his observation on 3 October 1870 that he has found little intellectual recreation after moving to northwest Arkansas. Graham evidently shares his interest in both science and music.

101. On 21 March, Bachelor will again note that he and Graham have spent the evening reading from *Harper's Magazine*. It appears the friends passed their time reading aloud to each other, since on 28 October 1874 when he,

Graham, and several other friends take a trip to Fort Smith and bring along Twain's *Innocents Abroad* to read, he notes that Graham amuses them by reading aloud from the book in the evening.

102. Again, as on 3 October 1870 (and at many points later in the diary), he mentions his love of the guitar. The sole picture of Bachelor's brother Moses that has survived—a much-faded tintype—shows Moses holding a guitar.

103. Catarrhal infection: an upper respiratory infection. The term has gone out of use.

104. "The people": conventional nineteenth-century usage in both Britain and America, when professional or educated (or socially elite) classes speak of or write about "the common people." And so this is to say that "ebizootie" (i.e., "epizootie") is folk speech, and Bachelor wants to underscore this point.

105. Erysipelas: a streptococcal infection of the skin.

106. Another of the many rather plaintive entries in the diary in which he mentions sitting alone in his office writing at night, practicing his guitar, and reviewing the diary and remembering where he and his family were on this date as they made the journey to Arkansas.

107. Lacinating: that is, lancinating, a sensation of cutting or tearing.

108. An anodyne diaphoretic: a medicine that both diminishes pain and increases sweating.

109. Since he has mentioned the possibility of erysipelas in another patient three days earlier, he may have concern about the possibility of an outbreak of infectious disease. He will note again on the fourteenth that there is an epidemic of the catarrhal problem from which he has found patients suffering on the second, and which he attributes to erysipelas.

110. Gathering at the county seat for the periodic court sessions throughout the year was an important custom in the American South well into the first part of the twentieth century. People from all over a county would come to town for the court gathering to transact business, swap gossip, catch up on local news, and enjoy the theater of the court sessions themselves (on the roots of these customs in colonial Virginia, see Fischer, *Albion's Seed*, 361, 407; see also Richard Pillsbury and Suzanne Andres, "Courthouse Square," in *Encyclopedia of Southern Culture*, 569–70). This court session begins on Monday, since the diary mentions that Sunday is the sixteenth.

111. Samuel Rutherford, who is listed on the 1870 federal census as a physician living in Ozark.

112. Note that this entry suggests Bachelor has stayed in Ozark two nights. He is obviously there primarily for the court session, as his 10 March entry indicates, but also secondarily to assist Dr. Rutherford with the case he describes on the eleventh. He may be staying at the Forest Hotel, which he mentions on his return to Ozark on the seventeenth. As his entry of the fifteenth notes, the trip is some 12 miles—a distance not easily traveled on Arkansas roads of the period—so that he cannot go to Ozark and back home

each day without difficulty. As his July 1891 travelogue of his and Monroe's and Nannie's trip to Hot Springs will indicate, it will take them six days to travel 135 miles.

113. Bachelor's medical practice is clearly growing, and the trip to Ozark during court session may also have been to drum up business for the practice. The sick lady he visits today is evidently the one about whom he has written on the fifth and sixth. He's visiting her to do follow-up.

114. Encient: that is, *enceinte*, pregnant.

115. St. Vitus's dance: Sydenham's chorea. Iron carbonate was used as a cure. Bromide of potassium was an anticonvulsant used in the nineteenth and early twentieth century. It had been introduced in 1857, and was the drug of choice for epilepsy until phenobarbital came along in 1912.

116. Bachelor will note on 1 September 1874 that he has just treated the first case of syphilis he has encountered in Arkansas.

117. Note that this entry confirms something Bachelor suspects when he first encounters the catarrhal illness several days earlier and thinks it has a connection to erysipelas: namely, the illness was threatening to become epidemic in the community.

118. This is the juror taken violently ill in court on the eleventh. He has died on the fifth day from the beginning of his grave illness. Bachelor has returned to Ozark perhaps because court session has continued, but also, perhaps, to do follow-up for this case on which he has been consulting.

119. Note that the statement about prescribing and issuing medicine confirms something indicated earlier on 1 March—that is, that people are now coming to his home medical office for diagnosis and medicine, as his reputation as a local doctor is established. He'll repeat on the twentieth that after he and his wife have been away from home for the day and returned home, he finds men waiting for him, wanting medicine.

120. Another indicator that he's now increasingly practicing medicine from his home office, where people may be coming for consultation on this particular day since it's Sunday and they're not working at their weekday farm work or jobs. He has also followed up on the case of the woman with St. Vitus dance whom he began treating on the thirteenth.

121. Once again, Bachelor has gone to Ozark on Monday and is staying overnight—very likely because court remains in session. The 1870 federal census shows James Lotspeich and Johnson Reynolds as druggists living in Ozark. They are, in fact, living at the same Forest Hotel that Bachelor mentions in this entry, noting that he himself has stayed there on the trip to Ozark.

122. This entry adds to the impression that Bachelor is visiting Ozark during court weeks because, in part, he is seeking to build his medical practice.

123. It seems likely that the old friends from Tennessee are visiting the Chesley Mack Gammill family, discussed in the introductory section of this book. The Gammills lived about five miles south of the Bachelors in the

community of Sub Rosa, and he and Gammill, who was born in 1832, are roughly contemporaries. At least one of Gammill's sons, Sterling, was to become a doctor in Franklin County.

124. The term "Faderland" may be a jocular reference to how Anglo settlers of Franklin County imagine they hear German immigrants, who are then moving in large numbers to the area, speaking of their homeland. He is writing this diary entry in a period in which the German and Swiss immigration to the area around what would become the town of Altus has begun to pick up. For instance, the Post family, who came to Franklin County from the vicinity of Baden-Baden in Germany and whose descendants still operate a winery in the county, arrived in 1872: see Lola Shropshire, "Altus (Franklin Co.)," *Encyclopedia of Arkansas History and Culture*, online at http://encyclopediaofarkansas.net/ encyclopedia/entry-detail.aspx?search=1&entryID=5599 (accessed February 2012). In his 1868 inaugural address, Governor Powell Clayton had encouraged the active recruitment of European immigrants to the state, and the extension of the railroad up the Arkansas River Valley in these years was increasing the arrival of German immigrants: see Shirley Sticht Schuette, "Germans," ibid., online at http://encyclopediaofarkansas.net/ encyclopedia/entry-detail.aspx?entryID=2731 (accessed February 2012). Throughout the diary, Tennessee will be a kind of lodestar for Bachelor—the original homeland to which everything else is compared. He repeatedly mulls over the fateful decision to come to Arkansas, the journey to Arkansas, and his ambivalence about what he finds after moving to Arkansas. On the trip he and his family make to Hot Springs in 1891, when he finds springs in the Ouachitas on 6 July 1891, he compares them to "oldfashioned Tennessee springs."

125. This case involving uterine tumors and inflammation is yet another reminder of how many of Bachelor's cases involve women's health issues and childbirth.

126. This calls to mind the 2 March 1873 entry that first introduces Graham and speaks of him as "my honored and Scientific friend."

127. *Harper's* is the second oldest continuously published monthly in the United States and over the course of its publication history has been generally considered as offering a progressive political and cultural perspective. The issue he and Graham are reading (evidently out loud to each other) is the March 1873 edition (vol. 46, #274) of *Harper's New Monthly*, which contained both an installment of Wilkie Collins's novel *New Magdalen* (597–607) as *Harper's* published the novel in serial form, and "Earth and Air" by S. S. Conant (545–62), the latter a scientific article about the lunar landscape and the earth's atmosphere.

128. As noted previously, at this time, *Harper's* was publishing Wilkie Collins's novel *New Magdalen* in serial installments. The plot involves a twist in which a German brain surgeon saves a woman's life, which would probably

have appealed to Graham and Bachelor. When we first meet Graham in the 2 March 1873 entry, he and Bachelor are reading Dickens together, and their interest in Collins may reflect their shared interest in Dickens, who was Collins's lifelong friend.

129. Another entry in which he has spent much of his time in his study reading, practicing guitar, and dispensing medicine as people come to him for assistance. Bachelor will quote Byron (though not "Childe Harold's Pilgrimage") on 15 March 1874. Note that following this entry and up to 9 May, it appears he is copying into the diary accounts of medical cases that have taken place earlier. The section of his scrapbook that contains pictures of freethinkers has a picture of Byron.

130. Note that this entry is one of several places in the diary in which the chronology of entries appears to be out of order.

131. Hour-glass contraction of the uterus following labor, with the mother's inability to expel the placenta and afterbirth, is a problem much discussed in nineteenth-century medical literature. The danger this medical phenomenon posed to the mother's life was, of course, serious—hence Bachelor's concern to try in any way possible to relieve the contraction and/or remove the placenta manually. At this period, there were not medicines readily available to relieve the contraction, though the usefulness of amyl nitrite for this purpose was soon to be discovered.

132. In various cases recorded in the diary, he will use toddies to help soothe a patient. A toddy is, of course, a mix of liquor (in these cases, very likely bourbon whiskey) and water, often with some sugar and/or lemon juice, and frequently served warm.

133. Puerperal fever following childbirth was a leading cause of female mortality through the late nineteenth century. It was often caused, in fact, by the doctors assisting with the delivery, who had very limited understanding of the connection between hygiene and uterine infections that were frequently introduced unwittingly by the doctors themselves. The recommendation of use of a female syringe does indicate some knowledge on Bachelor's part that treatment of the infection by solutions to wash the infected area was indicated.

134. Because of the corruption of the text, it's difficult to make complete sense of this entry. It appears Bachelor has gone to a school examination at Lowe's Creek some ten miles south of Ozark. The school year would have been ending in May so that pupils could assist with the spring chores as crops got underway. As a school year ended and a class graduated, it was customary to invite the surrounding community to hear the scholars recite, debate, compete in spelling bees, and, in general, display their academic accomplishments— on this practice in Grant County, see Goolsby, *Our Timberland Home*, 257–58. See also the 18 May diary entry, noting that Bachelor has attended a similar event at a local Sunday School to hear the pupils sing—evidently as this school, too, ended its school year before the spring farm chores picked up.

Exams were also administered at these events, and he may have gone to the examination either as a member of the public listening to the students' recitals or as an examiner. In either case, his attendance demonstrates his interest in local education, already in evidence through his friendship with Paul Graham. The next diary entry will note that he has stayed the following day with P. F. Webb, whose daughter Julia married Richard F. Hooper, another local professor.

135. Clarksville is the county seat of Johnson County, and is some twenty-two miles east of Ozark, along the Arkansas River. As the 19 and 20 May entries will indicate, his probable reason for making this journey is to obtain information about new tracts of land for sale along the railroad, which is then reaching his area. The railroad line from Little Rock to Clarksville was just being completed in 1873, and was to reach Ozark late in 1875, with train service beginning in January 1876. Clarksville had a branch of the federal land office whose primary location was at Dardanelle. In fact, when Bachelor enters the eighty acres he buys on his arrival in Franklin County in 1870, he does so at the Clarksville branch of the Dardanelle federal land office. Bachelor will note on 1 March 1874 that he has become discontent with his life in Arkansas, and his reference to pecuniary embarrassments on 1 March 1873 suggests that he may have financial struggles, and may be looking at land along the railroad for speculation, to assist him with his monetary problems. The friend with whom Bachelor is traveling to Clarksville is evidently Oscar Jackson, who is mentioned in his 14 May entry. The 1870 federal census indicates he was a son of Mark Jackson of Mulberry in Franklin County, aged twenty-one in 1870.

136. *History of . . . Franklin and Sebastian Counties, Arkansas* (619) has information about Perry F. Webb in its biography of Richard Franklin Hooper of Ozark. This source notes that Webb was a pioneer merchant of Ozark whose daughter Julia married Hooper, a teacher at Ozark College and representative from Franklin County to the Arkansas legislature 1886–1888 and 1892–1894. The 1870 federal census shows Webb born in 1823 and living in Ozark, where he has a dry-goods business. In 1880, Bachelor's friend Paul Graham will be enumerated on the federal census just a few houses from Webb in Ozark. Like the Webbs and Bachelors, the Hoopers also came to Arkansas from Tennessee.

137. The mention of the railroad survey lines here, and his note on the nineteenth that he has been riding over the land adjacent to the railroad survey and has consulted records about the locality of the railroad survey and also where the depot (in Ozark) would be situated, further suggest that his primary interest in going to Clarksville is to obtain information about land for sale. There was considerable speculation in land along the railroad lines in this period in which the lines were being laid, since the land's value would increase because of its proximity to the railroads. Farmers also often sought land near railroads so that they could ship their crops directly to market via the railroad: the husband of Bachelor's niece Minerva Louisa Batchelor—Seaborn Walters—to

whom Bachelor will write a letter on 20 December 1898, had a large farm operation in Hot Spring County, and shipped much of his produce directly to market via the railroad, using a nearby depot as the shipping point.

138. It appears he has attended the Sunday School singing primarily to hear the recital. W. W. Jennings is listed on the 1880 federal census living in Ozark and conducting a dry-goods business. He is English born (in 1843) and lives only a few houses away from Bachelor's friends Paul Graham (also English born) and Perry F. Webb, another dry-goods merchant.

139. Judge Sutherland is George Washington Sutherland. The 1870 federal census shows him living in White Oak Township near Ozark, and born in 1816 in North Carolina. *History of . . . Franklin and Sebastian Counties, Arkansas* shows him as a county judge from 1868 to 1872 (620). Sutherland was a charter member of the Ozark Masonic Lodge No. 79, which Bachelor joined when he originally became a Mason about 1873, according to his Masonic eulogy (see also ibid., 650).

140. And so he purchases the land that has attracted his attention and is adjacent to where the railroad will come through in the next two years. A horse ferryboat: a ferry drawn back and forth by a horse or horses on the riverbank.

141. Note that as the dates of the two entries for this hydrocephalus case indicate, this is a case that Bachelor has inserted at a later date into this part of his diary; both entries postdate the entries preceding and following the two case entries. In addition, it should be noted that Bachelor appends the date 18 June 1873 to the entry rather than using it as a header.

142. As the case notes indicate, he is recording this case in his diary *post factum*—hence the shift in chronology here to June 1873, then to April 1874 as he continues follow-up, then back to the proper chronological sequence of May 1873. His notes indicate that the case had actually begun prior to June 1873 when he began recording it.

143. A standard treatment for hydrocephalus because of its diuretic effects.

144. As with preceding entries written on days when he spends the day mostly at home, he mentions reading—this time, *Romeo and Juliet*. He'll mention Shakespeare, of whom he never tires (as this entry declares) again the following day, when he again spends the day at home and reads *Richard III*.

145. The preference for *Richard III* and *Romeo and Juliet* had long been established in the American South: on both as favorite plays of the southern stage in the eighteenth century, see Richard Beale Davis, *A Colonial Southern Bookshelf: Reading in the Eighteenth Century* (Athens: Univ. of Georgia Press, 1979), 95. In his occasional pieces "Don't Let the Senate See God's Denuded Arm" and "Correspondence," about Reverend Sam Jones's 1892 revival, Bachelor quotes *Richard III*.

146. This case brings to mind the previous case of the man shot with buckshot from October 1870, and his note on 18 August 1874 that in four years and six months in Arkansas, he has heard of more people dying by violence

than in all his years growing up in Tennessee. At the time he writes this entry, he is treating another victim of violence, a young man whose brother has fractured his skull in an act of rage. On 27 August 1873, he'll once again treat a case of gunshot wound.

147. That is, the *teres major* muscle.

148. The "cised" is legible here.

149. Bachelor chooses a spring wagon—a wagon whose box was mounted on springs, as opposed to one without any springs—to spare the patient pain and further injury, but as he notes, he is nonetheless concerned about permitting him to be transported at all in his condition.

150. That is, the *pectoralis major* muscle.

151. The castor oil is to move the bowels.

152. That is, he is to have a nourishing diet, but not one that will place strain on his digestive system.

153. See the 14 October 1870 entry.

154. A solution containing alkaline salts obtained from leaching wood ash with water.

155. That is, the discharge has bloody fluids in it.

156. The prescription of tonics, barks, stimulants, good diet, and good hygiene suggest that Bachelor considers the slow recuperation and emaciation to be due, in part, to the weakness of the patient's constitution and lack of good circulation.

157. There is no date heading. The date is embedded in the text.

158. That is, a case of spontaneous abortion resulting in a premature stillborn child.

159. The *semispinalis capitis* muscle. The man has been shot in the back.

160. A surgical instrument with a slender curved blade.

161. The entry is undated, but the date is inserted into the text.

162. And so, having recorded four medical cases, the diary shifts again to a retrospective, meditative account of Bachelor's experiences since he has moved to Arkansas, circling back—as it repeatedly does—to the events of the journey from Tennessee to Arkansas. In this instance, he is also reviewing the diary entry for a year ago, when he was, he notes, sitting up at 4 A.M. writing in the diary. This year, he's up at midnight writing in his slippers and cloak, observing the sky and listening to the creek.

163. The Pleiades, the Seven Sisters constellation, are prominent in the winter sky in the northern hemisphere. The 31 December entry for this year will also have him watching the Pleiades as the year ends, as will the entry on New Year's Eve 1894 and 1895.

164. The Greek goddess of the moon Artemis is sometimes called Cynthia because of her birthplace, Mount Cynthus on Delos. The New Year's Eve entry in 1895 will also mention that he is watching the Pleiades and pale Cynthia as 1896 arrives. To speak of the moon as pale Cynthia and Queen Cynthia is a

common rhetorical device in English literature as far back as Spenser. The observation here that pale Cynthia is shedding her mild radiance over rocks and mountains echoes Johnson, "Irene": "See how the moon, through all th' unclouded sky, / Spreads her mild radiance . . . ."

165. "All nature seems lulled to repose": Charlotte Turner Smith, *The Young Philosopher* (1782). It appears Bachelor has intended to write the word "nothing" between "and" and "is."

166. A promontory of some 860 feet about 2.4 miles southwest of Bachelor's homeplace. It's the mountain that he will mention climbing with two of his young sons in the next entry on 15 March 1874.

167. "Its" lacks the final "s" here, but to note that with square brackets would be confusing, when other letters in the same word are bracketed because they are obscured by the diary's margins.

168. This retrospective entry again notes his "toils and care" and his evident discontent with his new home. This brings to mind his observation on 1 March 1873 that instances of a pecuniary nature have operated against him. The search for new land earlier this year has suggested he is trying to deal with the financial challenges, as have his evident attempts to expand his medical practice. He also notes here that he has found a "few select friends only who like myself love meditation, and Books"—a rather plaintive observation that echoes his statement early in the diary, on 3 October 1870, that he had been disappointed in the lack of intellectual companionship he has found in Arkansas. And as he also adds, his mind has been so constituted that he is restless, constantly seeking new knowledge, and unable to settle for what might please someone whose mind is not so arranged.

169. The lines are a slightly erroneous citation from Pope, "Essay on Man, Epistle II," who writes, "on his peculiar spot," not "one peculiar spot."

170. The little sons are evidently Wils and Vick, though the latter is not yet quite four years old.

171. Again, a meditative and somewhat plaintive entry written at night after a disagreeable wet day in the dreary season between winter and full spring, as he looks back at his previous diary entries, reflects on the journey to Arkansas, and—significantly—cites Byron's "I Would I Were a Careless Child."

172. Sarah ("my wife," again) has given birth to their last child, Pauline, a "fine daughter" whom Bachelor names Pauline Graham Bachelor for his friend Paul Graham. The birth was at 9 A.M., and it's now 8 P.M., and he has spent the day at home since Sarah has been "feeble" during this pregnancy, though she is doing as well as may be expected after childbirth.

173. Another indicator of the wide-ranging scope of his mind: he has added ornithology and taxidermy to the range of his interests (and is still collecting geological specimens from the nearby mountains).

174. He has, indeed, spotted a comet. He will note another sighting of it on the fifth, in the next entry, remarking that its tail is now visible. This is Coggia's

comet, about which the news media will report frequently in this month. The *New York Times* will have reports of the comet on 4 and 8 July ("Coggia's Comet," *New York Times* 23, no. 7113 [4 July 1874], 5, col. 3; and "The Comet: No Danger of a Collision with the Earth," ibid., 23, no. 7116 [8 July 1874], 2, col. 7). In an article entitled "The Comet: It Is Rapidly Disappearing," the *Omaha Daily Bee* (4, no. 24 [17 July 1874], 4, col. 4) will write that the comet "has almost every evening been plainly visible to the naked eye, and of all the heavenly bodies has been 'the observed of all observers.' . . . It has gathered strength in the northern heavens for the past three months, and will be intrinsically brighter than now a few days hence, but will shine to us only in competition with the sunlight. After to-night, as we learn from a gentleman well versed in the interesting science of astronomy, it will set before the expiration of twilight, and not rise to us still [until] after the morning twilight has begun. . . ."

175. Bachelor will note on the eighteenth that the young man's skull was fractured by his brother at their father's house, in the midst of the family.

176. That is, morphine.

177. Since he's prescribing this as a dose, he's likely administering it as a laxative.

178. It appears that the extent (and location) of the fracture, combined with his observation that the man is slightly comatose when he arrives and is having neurological symptoms, account for Bachelor's concern that there is damage of the meninges.

179. The paralysis confirms, of course, Bachelor's initial suspicion that there is some brain damage in the case.

180. The recognition that chlorinated washes are indicated here is an interesting note. It suggests a more than usual awareness on the part of Bachelor that careful hygiene, abetted by medications, is an essential element of healing in such cases. Bachelor is recommending the chlorine wash (just as he had recommended an application of lixivium on 11 June 1873) at a point before the germ theory is well developed, and not too many years down the road from Ignaz Semmelweis's breakthrough discovery of the effectiveness of chlorine washes in preventing infections in Austrian hospitals.

181. The detail with which this case is observed, the solicitude he shows for his patient on repeated visits, the effective treatment, and the generally favorable outcome of a case involving a dire injury all suggest that Bachelor is a doctor of no little skill, with a good working knowledge of the latest treatments indicated for many of the cases he treats.

182. This entry follows the preceding one in October 1874, but clearly pertains to the trip that Bachelor and his son Monroe and daughter Nannie will take to Hot Springs in 1891. This piece of that travel narrative is written on the bottom of a page that appears to have been left blank following the final entry about the man with the fractured skull. For the rest of the account of the Hot Springs trip in 1891, see the entries from 2 July to 28 August that year.

Since that narrative says that the travelers reached Hot Springs on 7 July, and this one says that they left there after a week, I am assuming that this entry is to be dated 14 July. At Malvern, they are only a few miles from the families of Bachelor's sister Delaney Bachelor Byrd and brother Moses B. Batchelor, whom they will visit on this trip, according to a 22 September 1891 thank-you letter he writes to Delaney's daughter Melissa Byrd Robinson after his return home in August. Bachelor writes Melissa again on 14 October telling her that other relatives he has written following the trip, "several of them in your country," have never answered his letters. The subsequent 1891 travelogue suggests, however, that after having gone from Hot Springs north to see relatives in Hot Spring and Grant Counties on 14 July, the Bachelor family then returns to Hot Springs for a period of time and leaves the city again on 25 August for its final journey home.

183. Since the account of the case of the man with the fractured cranium runs from 7 August to 19 October 1874, the note that he has not been keeping a diary for some time appears to indicate that he has recorded this medical case *post factum* in the diary, at some point after it had occurred.

184. As the entry will make clear, what preoccupies him now is the extent of the violence he is observing in Arkansas. He's writing this entry as he's treating the case of the young man whose skull has been fractured by his brother in an incident at the family's home. As he notes, two young men have also shot each other to death in Charleston (in Franklin County) about eight to ten weeks previous; there has been a lynching in Roseville (Logan County); and a shooting of a school pupil at or near a schoolhouse in an unnamed community has recently occurred.

185. Violence had long been endemic in Arkansas and may have been even more pronounced in the northwest frontier region in which Bachelor had settled. As Charles Bolton notes (*Arkansas, 1800–1860*), Arkansas's political life was already marked by violence in the territorial period (33–35), and the political violence continued after statehood (177–78)—see also McNeilly, *Old South Frontier*, 87–90, 159–60. As Bertram Wyatt-Brown has noted, southern society in general has long been prone to unusual levels of violence because of the centrality of the concept of honor among males: see *Southern Honor: Ethics and Behavior in the Old South* (New York: Oxford UP, 1982); and Edward L. Ayers, "Honor," in *Encyclopedia of Southern Culture*, 1483–84.

In Arkansas, violence due to lawlessness became particularly strong during the Civil War and the years following it, because of the state's divided loyalties, pitting neighbor against neighbor and family against family. During much of the war, bands of marauders claiming to represent one side or the other terrorized citizens of the state, pillaging and looting at will in the absence of legal authority to stop them. Stories handed down in the family of Bachelor's sister Delaney suggest that her husband, Lawrence Cherry Byrd, may, in fact, have been tortured to death by such a band in Hot Spring

County, where the lawlessness due to such marauders was especially problematic. Bachelor is writing, as well, just as the Democrats have taken control of the state legislature for the first time since Reconstruction and have produced a new state constitution at a summer constitutional meeting. As these events are taking place, political tensions rooted in the war and its aftermath are running very high in the Arkansas River Valley area in which he lives, where loyalties have been divided in the war years and afterward, and where Republicans are also strongly represented, particularly in the northwest part of the valley where he lives. The following year, on 23 January 1875, a planter living in Union County in the southern part of the state, James Russell Winn, will write his son John Milton Winn in Iowa to tell him that conditions have become so unsettled due to the political turmoil of the period and the resurgence of old animosities following the end of Reconstruction that he has thought of leaving Arkansas: see William D. Lindsey, "Brown or White Sugar: The Story of a Mixed-Race Plantation Family in Nineteenth-Century Arkansas, Part 4," *Arkansas Family Historian* 48, no. 4 (December 2010): 237–38. In the Arkansas River Valley, things will soon reach a boiling point with the murder of John Clayton, brother of Reconstruction governor Powell Clayton, in 1889 in Plumerville in Conway County about seventy-five miles downriver from Ozark—see Kenneth C. Barnes, *Who Killed John Clayton? Political Violence and the Emergence of the New South, 1861–1893* (Durham, NC: Duke UP, 1998).

186. Bachelor's observations about how the violence he is witnessing is abetted by the widespread (and unrestricted) practice of carrying firearms—even to church—have an eerily contemporary ring to them as a number of states including Arkansas have enacted laws permitting carrying guns to church. As he notes, the combination of omnipresent guns, whiskey ("busthead"), and male rivalry for the attentions of female suitors all too often resulted in tragedy in his frontier part of the state.

187. This entry is noteworthy as one of the few times when Bachelor ever mentions Native Americans in any of his writings, though he is living only forty miles from Indian Territory and his daughters Lula and Pauline will spend part of their lives in Oklahoma, and his sons Vick, Yeager, and Monroe will also spend time there. His occasional piece about the book of Job as viewed by an agnostic also mentions the native peoples.

188. There was extreme and widespread drought in the summer of 1874, commented on by news articles in many places. The U.S. Senate *Report of the National Conservation Commission*, vol. 3 (Washington, D.C.: Government Printing Office, 1909), says production of corn was down 8 bushels per acre in Arkansas in 1874 due to the drought (228). The 23 January 1875 letter of James Russell Winn of Union County to his son John in Iowa cited previously notes the agricultural difficulty and short crops produced by the weather conditions of the summer of the 1874. According to Milton D. Rafferty, the highest temperature ever recorded in the Arkansas Ozarks (as of 2001)—120°F—

was recorded at Ozark (*The Ozarks: Land and Life* [Fayetteville: Univ. of Arkansas Press, 2001], 28).

189. Another of the travelogues that appear at various points in the diary, including the account of the family's journey from Tennessee to Arkansas in 1870, and his narrative of his trip with children Monroe and Nannie to Hot Springs in July–August 1891. Though he gives the date of the twenty-eighth at the head of this entry, note that the trip actually begins on the twenty-third, per the account itself. He provides no particular reason for this trip. Unlike the journey he took in May 1873 with a young friend to Clarksville with the apparent purpose of obtaining information about land for sale along the railway as it approached Franklin County, this appears to be a pleasure excursion—hence, perhaps, the decision to take along Twain's recently published excursion-themed novel *Innocents Abroad* (1869). The only other member of the party the travelogue will name is his friend Paul Graham. Since Bachelor has also stated on 1 March this year that he's discontent with his life in Franklin County, it's also possible he is taking another look at Fort Smith as a place to which he might relocate his family and medical practice. Because the Little Rock and Fort Smith Railroad line is nearing completion in 1874, this could have made Fort Smith an increasingly attractive place to live for those thinking of a new home.

190. The pattern of camping overnight by a church house is one that will be noticeable when he, Monroe, and Nannie go to Hot Springs in 1891. For those traveling along the state's rough and often dangerous roads in the nineteenth century, church yards would have been appealing places to stop for the night because they would have been safe, would not have been in use except on Sundays, would have trees for shade, would have had roadways for wagons and horses, and would have had wells with good water for both the horses and the travelers.

191. His traveling companion is evidently reading Twain aloud for both their benefit. On the twenty-fifth, Bachelor will note that Paul Graham amuses the company by reading the novel aloud during the evening.

192. Various newspapers of the period, including the *New York Times*, carried an account of the eclipse and meteor shower. The *Times* published its article on these occurrences on the twenty-fifth ("The Eclipse of the Moon," 24, no. 7209 [25 October 1874], 7, col. 2).

193. It's interesting that, with his inclination to freethought growing in the 1870s, Bachelor has attended not one but two church services this Sunday. His observation that the music was "verry fine" suggests that the music offered by these churches is part of their appeal. If he is an avowed freethinker by this date, his freethought also seems not to have made him so much hostile to religious people as skeptical about all expressions of religion insofar as they reject scientific findings and do not recognize the cultural determination of religious faith in all religions around the world. I speak of his "inclination" to

freethought because his occasional piece entitled "Reasons for Being an Agnostic, No. 1" will suggest he actually became an avowed freethinker around 1878, and his subsequent diary entry on Christmas Day 1890 will say that this turn to outright freethinking occurred in the period from 1874 to 1890.

194. This pensive entry, in his office on the night of his forty-seventh birthday, brings to mind his similarly nostalgic reflections on 1 and 15 March the same year in which he quotes Byron's "I Would I Were a Careless Child," whose themes are similar to those found in this diary entry—the painful dissociation from childhood and its innocence, the passing of time that brings with it the loss of childhood friends, and so on. He consoles himself with the thought that he has sought not to harm but to help others, to relieve physical pain and mental anguish. The emphasis on the latter is interesting, since a leitmotiv of his practice as a physician appears to be that he seeks to deal simultaneously with the physical and psychological-emotional components of an illness.

195. And so, having just written about his commitment to relieving pain, he is called away on the evening of his forty-seventh birthday to tend to the needs of a sick woman.

196. This is the first in what becomes a recurring series of notes in the diary written on various Christmas nights, recording what has taken place in the family during the preceding year, who has been to the house for Christmas Day or where family members have spent Christmas, and where other family members not able to take part in the family celebration are living at the time.

197. The reference to a student reading medicine with him is interesting. The entry suggests that the old practice of "reading" medicine with an established doctor still obtained in this part of northwest Arkansas at this period. The state's medical school will not be established until 1879. James D. Massey was a native of Hardin County, Tennessee, son of Thomas C. and Sarah Massey. He appears on the 1860 federal census in his parents' household in Hardin County, and is listed as a physician in Sulphur Township in Sebastian County, Arkansas, in 1880, aged thirty-one. It's interesting to note that Bachelor's apprentice, Massey, shares his love of music and they play the violin and guitar together. This is, I believe, the first official mention Bachelor makes of his violin in his diary. The violin passed after his death to his son Vick, whose widow, Henrietta Dean Bachelor, gave it to her great-nephew James Paul Russell of Fort Smith, Arkansas. His widow Janelle Russell is the present owner of the violin. The violin has an inscription stamped inside its body that reads, "Jacobus Stainer ex Absam Prope Oenipontum 1735." Since many violins of the nineteenth century were made according to the fashion of the famous Austrian violin-maker Jacobus Stainer, it seems very unlikely that the violin dates from 1735, and far more likely that it was made in Germany or the United States in the nineteenth century according to the style of Stainer.

198. Again, this will be a recurring motif of his Christmas entries year after

year—hearing gunfire or the sound of anvils being fired in the surrounding area, an old southern custom to celebrate Christmas. As David Hackett Fischer notes, in contrast to the practice in Puritan New England, which outlawed the celebration of Christmas, in colonial Virginia (and, subsequently, throughout the Southeast), Christmas was a season of dances, parties, visiting, and general merriment for the entire Christmas season (*Albion's Seed*, 370). It was also tra- ditionally a season for courting in the American South and was the preferred time for couples to marry. Fischer notes that Philip Fithian mentions the firing of guns in Virginia to celebrate Christmas in the 1770s (370, citing Fithian's *Journal and Letters*, 52). The merriment (and the shooting of weapons) could spill over into dangerous rowdiness: on 16 February 1897, Bachelor's great- nephew John Richard Batchelor, son of his brother Moses's son John Wilson Batchelor, will find himself in trouble with the law in Sheridan, Arkansas, for disturbing the peace on Christmas Day 1896 with other young men "by loud and unusual noise and running about at unusual speed through the town" (see Grant County Justice of the Peace Docket Book, 1869–1917, 114–15).

  199. Hill is probably Thomas Hill, who is enumerated near the Bachelors in Mill Creek Township on the 1880 census. He was a Missouri native and roughly a contemporary of Bachelor.

  200. This entry has no date heading, but the date is embedded in the text.

  201. Bachelor doesn't explain the long hiatus in diary keeping from 1874 to 1890, though this entry notes that it was during this period that he made the momentous decision to become an avowed freethinker who rejects the doc- trine of the literal inspiration of the scriptures. As he also notes, his children have now grown up (Pauline, the youngest, is sixteen), and he would have spent the intervening years assisting with their raising—and this would have taken up much of his time, in addition to his farming and medical practice. His son Jim and his daughters Nannie, Alcie, and Lula have all married (though Nannie's husband, Frederick Eubanks, has died and she has returned home to live with her parents), and Yeager is apparently in Texas at this date. Remaining at home are sons Monroe, Wils, and Vick, along with their sisters Nannie and Pauline. Monroe and Wils will both die unmarried before the decade has ended. During the period in which he has been silent, his friend Paul Graham has also died (in 1887).

  202. S. G. Teague is Samuel Garrison Teague, a neighboring farmer.

  203. The "baby daughter" is Pauline, who will soon be studying music with Carrie White (see the 31 May 1895 entry), and then teaching the organ in the community, according to a 21 February 1899 letter Bachelor will write to his great-niece Janie Byrd. Carrie White is perhaps the friend with whom Pauline has spent this Christmas Day.

  204. This will be Bachelor's first mention of the organ, which he says in a 5 September 1899 letter to niece Melissa Byrd Robertson he has introduced to the community, so that by 1899, there will be ten organs in four square miles

in the neighborhood and his daughter Pauline will be teaching organ.

205. Gertrude (born in March 1888) is the daughter of Bachelor's daughter Nannie Eubanks.

206. Shelly is Shelley, of course. Tennyson would perhaps have appealed to Bachelor as a freethinker because of his unconventional religious views, particularly in the latter period of his work, and his famous observation in "In Memoriam" that "[t]here lives more faith in honest doubt, believe me, than in half the creeds." Shelley had published *The Necessity of Atheism* in 1811. And George Eliot had similarly repudiated conventional religious ideas and had made a careful study of such German historical-critical exegetes as David Strauss and Ludwig Feuerbach—a field of research that also seems to have had great influence on Bachelor's own religious and philosophical thought. The section of Bachelor's scrapbook that has pictures of freethinkers has pictures of Shelley (and Mary Wollestonecraft), as well as of George Eliot.

207. Unfortunately, much of this page is missing, so it is difficult to make much sense of the phrases that explain Bachelor's important transition to freethought. One can hazard a guess, from the fragments still legible, that he explains the turn to freethought as a rejection of the notion of the literal inspiration of the Jewish and Christian scriptures, as a rejection of superstition in favor of reason as a guide (a favorite theme of scientific thinkers of this period), and as a move to a socially progressive philosophy accenting the struggle for social justice and a more humane and rational society. The note that hell is a fantasy is telling, since around the period in which it appears Bachelor became a freethinker, Henry Ward Beecher and Frederic W. Farrar both preached famous series of sermons denying the existence of a physical, literal hell. Since Bachelor mentions both of these religious thinkers in his occasional piece "Leaving the Old Ruts," it seems very likely that they significantly influenced his thinking as he made the transition to freethought.

208. The 9 July entry and subsequent ones will indicate they're making this trip in a wagon drawn by mules. On mules and their longstanding association with southern agriculture, see William Ferris, "Mules," *Encyclopedia of Southern Culture*, 511–12.

209. Fevers of various etiology with nausea and vomiting were characterized as bilious fevers in the eighteenth and nineteenth century in the South. The term would very soon fall out of use. In a 5 September 1899 letter to his niece Melissa Byrd Robinson, Bachelor will mention that Nannie's health has always been feeble.

210. Chisimville is Chismville in Logan County. In his WPA oral history of life in early Franklin County, C. Frank Spillers of Charleston, whose family came to Franklin County from Pickens County, Alabama, in the same year that the Bachelor family arrived there, speaks of a road that ran from Ozark to Waldron through Chismville. Spillers says that people bringing horses and mules into Arkansas from the north would frequently stop at a tavern outside

Ozark, then would go on to a tavern at Chismville the next night, and following that, to one at Waldron (see Federal Writers' Project early Arkansas settlers'
history from the manuscript collection of the Special Collections Library of
the University of Arkansas, and online at http://ghsweb.k12.ar.us/early/
Franklin/spillers.htm [accessed February 2012]). Note that this is more or less
exactly the route the Bachelors will take as they travel to Hot Springs. This
route follows what is now state highway 23, which is known as the Pig Trail
in its Ozarks section, due to its steep inclines and hairpin turns.

211. As on the October 1874 trip to Fort Smith, they camp near a church.
This church has a school attached—a not uncommon pattern in rural Arkansas
of the period, when the church and schoolhouse together usually functioned
as the center of small rural communities. The preceding diary entry that
appears to have been written on 14 July on this same trip, and which is out of
sequence in the diary, notes that the family has camped that evening near a
black church outside Malvern.

212. Kadidids = katydids, crickets of the family *Tettigoniidae*.

213. "Rose Waltz" seems to have been used as the name of a number of different waltzes popular at the period. The "Yellow Rose Waltz" was a popular
fiddle tune in the South in the nineteenth century, often played at fiddle con-
tests. "Lost Indian" is an old-time fiddle tune popular across the mountain
South. The Digital Library of Appalachia has many examples of it collected
from various places at various times (online at http://dla.acaweb.org/cdm/
[accessed February 2012]).

214. Because the mountain with this name is well to the east of their route, I
think it's more likely Bachelor is speaking here of the Petit Jean River, which
rises in the Ouachita Mountains near Waldron.

215. The Poteau River runs through Scott County in extreme west-central
Arkansas in the Ouachita Mountains through which they are traveling. William
C. Featherston established a post office in 1838 in the Poteau (sometimes
Poton) Valley—see Wes Goodner, "Scott County," *Encyclopedia of Arkansas
History and Culture*, online at http://encyclopediaofarkansas.net/
encyclopedia/entry-detail.aspx?search=1&entryID=805 (accessed February
2012). The community of Poteau was a significant early settlement that even-
tually gave way to Waldron as the county seat.

216. He will mention the empty house again on 28 August 1891, as they
return from Hot Springs to Ozark. They stay there again that evening, and he
notes then that it's five miles north of Waldron.

217. Dog fennel is *Eupatorium capillifolium*, an invasive weed in fields and gardens left untended.

218. Various owls of the genus *Megascops* are referred to as screech owls,
because of their distinctive nocturnal cry. Bachelor is probably hearing the
Eastern screech owl, *Megascops asio*.

219. Because his father and sister are sick, the brunt of the work of driving,

caring for the mules, cooking, et cetera, falls on Monroe's shoulders for much of the trip. And then, as Bachelor notes repeatedly in the travelogue, Monroe entertains them in the evening. "Mollie Milligan" appears to be an early American fiddle tune. On the way back, on 27 August, the diary will note that Monroe will play "Mollie Milligan" again, and he will play "Lost Indian" again on 25–26 and 28 August.

220. "Katy Hill" is a reel; Digital Library of Appalachia has many examples of the tune online at http://dla.acaweb.org/cdm/ [accessed February 2012]).

221. He means the Fourche La Fave River, which rises in the Ouachitas and empties into the Arkansas near the town of Fourche in Perry County. But by various indicators in the trip narrative, they are probably camping south of the Fourche La Fave quite a bit west of Fourche and heading into what is today the Ouachita National Forest. It has taken them three days to traverse about ninety miles. The 27 August entry as they return will specify it was the Fourche La Fave they had crossed. Friedrich Gerstäcker's *Streif- und Jagdzüge durch die Vereinigten Staaten Nord-Amerikas* (Dresden: Arnoldischen, 1844) and *Die Regulatoren in Arkansas* (Dresden: Otto Wigand, 1846) are set in this area and based on his experiences hunting along the Fourche La Fave in 1841–1842. It was then and remains a remote and wild and thinly settled area of the state.

222. As noted previously, they have now entered mountainous, rough, and uninhabited terrain that is in the Ouachita National Forest today.

223. Arkansas roads have long been famously bad and remain bad even in the first part of the twenty-first century, particularly in the mountainous areas of the state, where county-maintained roads can be nothing but rocky, badly maintained dirt trails. In his *Excursion through the Slave States* (London: John Murray, 1844), George W. Featherstonhaugh comments on the bad repair of Arkansas roads and the miles they could add to any journey in or through the state.

224. It seems that by sheer accident this evening, they've camped yet again near a church in this wild and almost uninhabited region. This one is off in the pine woods near their camping place. He draws a freethinker's lesson about superstition when he hears shouting and singing from the church.

225. There were a number of places named Sulphur Springs in nineteenth-century Arkansas, including one in Montgomery County about ten miles northwest of what is today called Black Springs. This is the most likely candidate for the Sulphur Springs at which they've camped this evening.

226. They're now out of the pine woods and in a more inhabited area with better roads, about twenty-one miles from Hot Springs, as the final statement in this entry will observe.

227. Tellingly, the springs in Arkansas remind him of ones in his home state of Tennessee. The Bluff Springs he mentions in the next sentence may have been in Hardin County. There is a Bluff Spring Branch on maps of the county just southwest of Counce, which is in the area in which Bachelor grew up.

228. The Washita is, of course, the Ouachita River.

229. Bear Mountain is south of Lake Ouachita today, in the Ouachita National Forest. The lake has been formed by damming the river, and if I'm not mistaken, much of the area they've crossed today may now be under the manmade lake. They're now in Garland County, of which Hot Springs is the county seat.

230. As this entry notes, it has taken them six days to travel 135 miles to Hot Springs.

231. It's unclear why the statement about their lodging arrangements does not mention Monroe. Perhaps he has other friends in Hot Springs with whom he is staying? It appears that William Wells is a former neighbor of the Bachelors in Franklin County who moved south after 1890, since he appears on the 1900 federal census in Prairie Bayou in Hot Spring County not far from Hot Springs. On the 1880 census, William Wells is living near the Bachelors in Franklin County. He was a Tennessee native, born about 1845.

232. As noted previously, following his diary entry dated 19 October 1874, Bachelor inserts into the diary an entry that appears to have been written on 14 July 1891 as the family leaves Hot Springs after having spent a week there. For the next installment in the travelogue, see that entry. The current entry (7 July) appears to imply that they arrive at and then leave Hot Springs the same day, or the day after their arrival. It seems very unlikely they'd go to the trouble of traveling there for many days over rough mountain roads, only to spend the night and turn around. As noted in my comments about the entry that seems to date from 14 July 1891, it appears the family spends a week in Hot Springs and then travels north to visit relatives in Hot Spring and Grant Counties, returning after that visit to Hot Springs and leaving the city again on 25 August for their final journey home.

233. Since they're staying at the same house on Walnut Fork at which they stayed as they came to Hot Springs, this must be at Bear Mountain, since the 6 July entry says they camped twenty-one miles outside Hot Springs at Bear Mountain, and the current entry says they're now twenty-two miles outside Hot Springs at Walnut Fork.

234. After Bachelor plays "Arkansas Traveler" on the fiddle before they retire in the evening, Monroe plays "Lost Indian" again, and Bachelor notes that it's "in order" for them to play the former tune as they make their journey. On the "Arkansas Traveler," see William B. Worthen, "Arkansas Traveler" at *Encyclopedia of Arkansas History and Culture*, online at http://encyclopediaofarkansas.net/encyclopedia/entry-detail.aspx?search=1&entryID=505 (accessed February 2012). As Worthen notes, the phrase refers to a song, a painting, and a dialogue, and has become a catch-all phrase for almost anything Arkansan. Worthen notes that the tune was first published in Cincinnati in 1847. See also Fletcher, *Arkansas*, 19–22.

235. It's not entirely clear what Bachelor means when he speaks of the Dallas road here. It's possible he means what is now Arkansas highway 88, which runs east-west through the Ouachita National Forest, before intersecting with Highway 71 at Mena near the Oklahoma border.

236. They seem to be in the vicinity of where they stopped on 4 July on their trip down to Hot Springs, near the Fourche La Fave River.

237. Campbell's Back may be the stretch of some thirteen miles without many inhabitants they encountered on their way down, mentioned on 5 July.

238. Once again, they're in what is today the Ouachita National Forest, a region still very sparsely inhabited, south of the river and near what is today the tiny community of Parks in Scott County—an area that has never had many inhabitants, due to its mountainous terrain and poor land. Waldron is the county seat, and the whole county in 2010 had 11,233 inhabitants.

239. They are camping at the empty house near Waldron where they camped on 3 July coming down.

240. It appears they have stopped at a barbershop in Waldron for a shave for the men.

241. They are now back at the place where they stopped near Chismville on 2 July.

242. He has mentioned their buying a chicken and frying it for supper two evenings prior to this, as well. Restaurants and even inns or taverns were almost nonexistent in many parts of Arkansas in this period. An old saying in some parts of the state for people who travel says, "They've been places and et in hotels."

243. The weary travelers apparently return home sometime after the twenty-ninth. On 21 September, Bachelor will write a letter to his niece Melissa Byrd Robinson (and evidently ones to other family members they saw on the trip), thanking her for the hospitality she and her husband, Joshua, showed him, Nannie, and Monroe on their visit.

244. Another in the series that recur from 1874 forward, in which he writes on Christmas Eve or Christmas night, recounting the whereabouts of family members as the year nears its end.

245. Alcie and her six children have now returned to live near her parents.

246. This is the first mention Bachelor makes of his sister Sarah, who has lived with his family for many years. In the following year's Christmas night entry, he will mention that she has died in the preceding year. His scrapbook contains a copy of a eulogy he wrote at the time of Sarah's death on 19 January 1892.

247. Son Jim has married Allie Vilola Rogers on 5 February 1888, and by 5 September 1899, Bachelor will tell his niece Melissa in a letter that "Dr. Jim Bachelor lives near Fort Smith," where he would practice medicine for a number of years at the communities of Sulphur and Central City. Yeager, Wils, Vick, and Pauline are all living at home in 1891, as is Nannie with her

daughter Gertrude following the death of Nannie's husband. The 5 September 1899 letter of Bachelor to Melissa will note that Yeager is in Texas at that point.

248. The daughter in Texas is Lula.

249. Monroe did not remain permanently in Indian Territory. In his Christmas entry in 1896, Bachelor will speak of Monroe as one of the family members at home who has gone to a dance that day. In fact, already by Christmas 1892, Bachelor will speak of Monroe being with the family, though this may have been on a visit back from Indian Territory, since the Christmas 1894 entry will again speak of him as being in Indian Territory. Oklahoma will become a state in 1907, and in the 1890s, there is strong interest in its lands. Monroe will be back in Arkansas at the time of his death: he will die in Fort Smith on 22 October 1897, and his father's eulogy for him is in the scrapbook, along with a notice of the death on 29 October 1897.

250. The custom of setting up Christmas trees came from Germany to English-speaking countries in the nineteenth century and had begun to be popularized by the Victorians, but was still a novelty for many people. This may have been a party to decorate a tree or even to see a decorated tree.

251. Members of the Burcham family are near-neighbors whom Bachelor will mention frequently in the diary from this point forward. Like the Bachelors and most of their associates, they have Tennessee roots.

252. No festive celebration can be complete without music—in particular, his beloved guitar and violin.

253. And so his commitment to freethought does not prevent Bachelor from enjoying the annual family Christmas celebration, with its gatherings of young and old, parties, and celebration of good will toward all. In fact, he notes as he ends this piece that he does so with "a feeling of brotherhood for all humanity," and he cites Thomas Paine, *Rights of Man* (London: J. S. Jordan, 1791). Paine actually wrote, "My country is the world, and my religion is to do good." Tellingly, Bachelor cites the well-circulated version of the quotation provided by Ingersoll, in his 1880 lecture, "On Thomas Paine." Bachelor will quote Ingersoll again in his Christmas entry the following year. On Paine, see Jacoby, *Freethinkers*, 31–65.

254. The entry has no date heading, but the text gives the date.

255. The Fulks are Joseph Benjamin Fulks and his wife, Emma Jane Bumpers, neighbors of the Bachelors (and through the wife, ancestral connections of Arkansas senator Dale Bumpers, who was born in Franklin County).

256. On 31 May 1895, Bachelor will note that Carrie White is Pauline's music teacher. The 1880 federal census shows Joseph White and his family living in Hurricane Township in Franklin County. He's roughly a contemporary of Bachelor's, having been born in Ohio in 1824. Carrie is seventeen years old in 1880. I can't decipher the meaning of the word "Solia." Is Bachelor referring to the fact that Joseph White is a widower? The 1880 federal census for Franklin County shows him with wife, Eliza, but by 1900, she had died. But if

the reference is to White's marital status, wouldn't "solus" be the correct word? Or is this perhaps a Masonic term?

257. Ingersoll, *The Limitations of Toleration: A Discussion between Robert G. Ingersoll, Frederic R. Coudert, Stewart L. Woodford, before the Nineteenth Century Club, of New York, at the Metropolitan Opera House* (New York: Truth Seeker, 1889), 43.

258. The entry has no date heading, but the text gives the date.

259. Central City is a community in Sebastian County near Fort Smith about twenty-five miles west of Pauline. This diary entry suggests that the move of Jim and his family to Sebastian County may have taken place sometime in 1894.

260. This is the first mention of Wils's poor health due to tuberculosis, from which he'll die on 7 August the following year.

261. The summer of 1894 was one of severe drought, particularly in the Midwest, with a resulting loss of crops and severe economic misery for many citizens (both of these noted in Bachelor's previous sentence). It's possible that the reference to revivals has quite specifically to do with the formation of the Holiness Church of Christ (later the Church of the Nazarene) by Methodist revivalist Robert Lee Harris in Tennessee in 1894. In the following year, after Harris died, his widow, Mary Lee Harris, had considerable success in spreading the new church's message in Arkansas through revivals—see Stan Ingersoll, "Church of the Nazarenes," *Encyclopedia of Arkansas History and Culture*, online at http://encyclopediaofarkansas.net/encyclopedia/entry-detail.aspx?entryID= 4330 (accessed February 2012). The revivals preceding the formation of the church in 1894 were especially strong in west Tennessee not far from where Bachelor grew up, and would no doubt have attracted his attention for that reason, as well as because of their proximity to Arkansas.

262. The nation was in a state of economic depression at the time, creating widespread misery, particularly in the South and Midwest. The cycle of misery had actually begun in the 1880s in the South and Midwest and had deepened with the beginning of the depression in 1893. In political response, many farmers in the southern states were seeking to create populist-agrarian movements. The Arkansas agrarian party, the Agricultural Wheel, had joined with the Knights of Labor in 1888 to create a party called the Union Labor party of Arkansas—though this movement had begun to wane by 1894.

263. The concern that "the people evolute slow," as religious revivals distract them and keep superstition alive, reflects his commitment as a freethinker to the progressive movements of the period, which envisaged the gradual death of religion as reason and science begin to carry the day in the political and cultural realms. This belief in progress and the eventual triumph of reason and science will be put to a severe test with World War I. This and the subsequent New Year's Eve entry demonstrate Bachelor's growing interest in politics, and, in particular, in the interface between his philosophy of freethinking progres-

sivism and American politics of the period. These preoccupations are evident in the scrapbook that he compiled during this decade, and in these diary entries that, for the first time, exhibit a strong concern for political matters that has not been so apparent in previous entries.

264. The fact that Bachelor gives this entry a title and then signs it, also including its place of composition (Pauline, Arkansas), suggests that he is writing it for publication. And, in fact, the piece evidently *was* published, since a version of it appears, with the same title, among the occasional pieces clipped and saved in his scrapbook (he actually wrote two separate New Year's pieces with this title—one in 1890, the other in 1894). If the published piece indicates that he has taken a diary entry and then copied and sent it to a newspaper for publication, this suggests that he is writing some of the material in the diary with an eye to publication. It's also possible that he has written this piece separately, intending to publish it, and has then copied the original draft into the diary.

265. Bachelor appears to have a particular fascination for end-of-year reviews that enumerate various disasters that have occurred during a particular year. His scrapbook contains such a document from 1893, evidently clipped from a newspaper or magazine, which lists the year's notable natural and other disasters, month by month.

266. He's apparently referring to the Sino-Japanese war of this year.

267. See the preceding Christmas night entry.

268. There were noteworthy floods during this year in Oregon, Wisconsin, and Minnesota.

269. The severe drought of the summer of 1894 resulted in a number of serious fires, the most noteworthy of which occurred in Hinckley, Minnesota, on 1 September, resulting in deaths that historians place anywhere from 400 to 800.

270. On 9 August, a Chicago, Rock Island, and Pacific train plunged from a railroad bridge near Lincoln, Nebraska, resulting in the deaths of eleven passengers and crew members.

271. The widespread economic misery caused by the Depression of 1893–1894 resulted in numerous suicides, about which there were reports on an ongoing basis in newspapers across the United States.

272. On 25 June, Cesare Santo, an Italian anarchist, assassinated French president Marie François Sadi Carnot—and so the heightened fear of socialism and anarchy as old parties dissolve and new ones form in the United States, often mentioned in papers of the time and alluded to in this diary entry.

273. At least thirteen black men are known to have been lynched in Arkansas in 1894. The 1890s were a period of horrific violence directed against black citizens of Arkansas by their white neighbors, in an attempt to push African Americans back into quasi-servitude following the end of Reconstruction. A 24 March 1892 report of Reverend E. Malcolm Argyle entitled "Report from

Arkansas" in the *Christian Recorder* (Philadelphia) documents stomach-turning racial violence in Arkansas in that month, with no less than eight African American citizens "strung up to telegraph poles, . . . burnt at the stake and . . . shot like dogs." Argyle states that five hundred black citizens had gathered in Pine Bluff as he was writing, awaiting passage on steamboats to Oklahoma to escape the reign of terror (as cited and transcribed in *A Documentary History of the Negro People in the United States*, vol. 2, ed. Herbert Aptheker [New York: Citadel, 1970], 793–94). As Grif Stockley notes in *Ruled by Race* (Fayetteville: Univ. of Arkansas Press, 1999), the violence against Arkansas freedpersons following the war was "numbing" (66). Stockley notes a "dramatic increase" in lynchings in Arkansas in the 1890s as Jim Crow legislation was enacted and black citizens were disenfranchised (126).

274.   There was a coal miners' strike this year affecting many parts of the country, and in Colorado, the Cripple Creek miners' strike with silver and gold miners involved. The Pullman strikes involving railroad workers also occurred in this year. Eugene Debs, who will found the Social Democratic party a year or so later, was involved—and so Bachelor's allusion to the formation of political parties anticipates this development, which could already be seen in the rise of new political coalitions. And his comment about tramps and economic distress reflects the widespread economic troubles and loss of jobs at this period. Debs was tried and imprisoned for his role in the strikes, with Clarence Darrow, the railroad company's lawyer, switching sides to represent him. All of this gained national attention, with the *New York Times* editorializing about Debs as a lawbreaker and agitator. In all of the strikes, there were state or federal troops involved, trying to break the back of labor.

275.   In Arkansas, there was political and economic turmoil at this time over the issue of railroad bonds. Governor Fishback had introduced a bill to amend the state constitution to prevent the state paying Holford railroad and levee bonds, producing economic crisis in the state for some years to come.

276.   Bachelor appears to be referring here in part to the growing influence of the German historical school of economic thinking in the United States. The influence of this school of thought among socialists, in particular, was eliciting great fear in many sectors of American culture at the time.

277.   "Darkling" is a self-consciously literary term, a word hardly used in American English, but found frequently in English literature.

278.   "Endless chain of eternal cycles" echoes the phrase "vast cosmic repose" in the diary's opening entry, along with many analogues for that phrase that recur throughout the diary and his occasional pieces, as he looks at the flux of time and the ceaseless operations of nature to produce both death and new life on a recurring basis.

279.   As in the 1 March 1874 entry and again on New Year's Eve that year, he mentions that he's watching the Pleiades—a reminder that he's writing all of this in the middle of the night as the old year ends and the new one begins.

280. And so the meditation on the changing of the year ends with a rousing appeal to do good (indicating that his religious skepticism is clearly not about rejecting a moral code or moral impulse). The reference to "the grand deeds of virtuous womanhood" is also noteworthy, echoing the preceding entry's statement about "the tendency of the masses is towards better and grander manhood and womanhood." It appears to have been around this time that Bachelor wrote his occasional piece defending women's rights and the equality of women with men—strong themes in the thinking of many American freethinkers and progressive thinkers of the period.

281. Hog butchering is usually done in the colder months of the year because the lower temperatures help to preserve the meat and keep it from spoiling quickly.

282. Snow is by no means unheard of in Arkansas in winter, particularly in the north part of the state in which he lives; but as he notes, eight inches is a good-sized snow for Arkansas.

283. That is, Fahrenheit.

284. In the 1890s, it becomes usual for Bachelor to refer to what he has previously called his office or studio as his library.

285. Another reference indicating his concern about the poor health of son Wils. He has mentioned Wils's feeble health on Christmas 1894.

286. Maud is Alcie's oldest daughter—Clara Maude Russell, born 16 October 1880.

287. The observation, "Reading—writing—compareing, investigating," followed by the observation that he's more than ever a freethinker, is noteworthy. The implication of the two sets of phrases juxtaposed is that he is inclined to freethought because what he observes as a scientific observer (confirmed by what he learns through reading) inclines him in that direction. And he caps the thought with the observation that he has never seen anything above nature. The 17 September entry the same year will explicitly connect his freethought and "naturalism." All of this, of course, against the backdrop of watching a son who has just turned thirty dying slowly and painfully of tuberculosis.

288. As noted previously (see the entry for Christmas Day 1890), by 1899, Pauline will be teaching music in the community—the organ, in particular, an instrument he tells his niece Melissa Byrd Robinson he has introduced to the area. In a 21 February 1899 letter to his great-niece Janie Byrd, Bachelor will note, "Pauline is at home, she is teaching music (organ) visits her pupils once a week."

289. Again, concern for Wils's health, which elicits thoughts of how quickly time passes and seasons change—and people come and go. This recalls his entry of 29 November 1874 speaking of the friends of the past who are no longer with him.

290. The book Bachelor is reading under his vine "harbour" is either Simon Greenleaf's *Treatise on the Law of Evidence,* 3 vols. (Boston: C. C. Little and J.

Brown, 1842–1853), a classic work of American jurisprudence, or his *The Testimony of the Evangelists, Examined by the Rules of Evidence Administered in Courts of Justice* (New York: J. Cockcroft and Co., 1846). As his negative comment about Greenleaf's special pleading for his "client," the church, suggests, Greenleaf was a member of a school of thought called legal or juridical apologetics, which sought to apply the principles of legal cross-examination to the Christian gospels to prove their validity. *Testimony of the Evangelists* was very influential in that respect.

291. As noted previously, Bachelor brought the silver poplars, which are a European tree, not an American one (*Populus albus*), with him from Tennessee, and his descendants indicate that the trees still grow around the site of what was his family's homeplace in Franklin County.

292. Chuck-will's-widow is *Caprimulgus carolinensis*, a bird of the nightjar family that often calls at night. Mockingbirds are, of course, a well-known songbird of the southern states.

293. Note that he combines gardening with scientific experimentation and new agricultural techniques—in this case, feeding some vines and potatoes with "fluid manure" (i.e., manure dissolved in water).

294. Political matters continue to occupy Bachelor's attention at this time, in part, because his own Republican party is in disarray, but (as he also notes), because the other major political party, the Democrats, are, as he observes, "hopelessly divided" over the free coinage versus sound money problem. And this is leading to the rise of third-party movements that concern him and other political thinkers who regard these movements as signs of instability threatening the nation's future. The intra-party debate among the Democrats has pitted the pro-gold financial establishment of the Northeast against the free-silver farmers of the Midwest and South, along with western miners, all of whom want free coinage of silver rather than the gold standard defended by the financial establishment. Free silver will be the central issue for Democrats in the presidential election of 1896 and again in 1900, under the leadership of William Jennings Bryan. His famous "cross of gold" speech was about this issue. The Populists were also for free silver, and the Republicans, of course, stoutly resisted it. Bachelor will mention the silver-gold controversy again in his Christmas entry in 1896.

295. Wils is approaching death and will die on 7 August.

296. As many previous entries suggest, Bachelor likes to use his diary to reminisce about scenes and events from the past—in this case, the start of his trip with Monroe and Nannie to Hot Springs on this day in 1891.

297. For the published eulogy that Bachelor delivered at the burial of his son, see his scrapbook essays. This notes that Wils was buried in the family cemetery above the homeplace. The obituary notes that Wils met death with calmness and without fear, and describes him as a filial son, a loving brother, and a true friend. The eulogy was evidently published as an obituary in the

Ozark paper, and contains a note asking the newspapers in Van Buren and Fort Smith to pick up the obituary.

298. Note how Bachelor's commemoration of Wils focuses on the loss of his talents to "the musical family." Though as a freethinker (like his son who has just died) Bachelor does not believe in a life beyond the natural one, he notes that his son will continue to be alive through the memory of his actions and deeds, and, in particular, when music is played at the homeplace.

299. Family traditions among Bachelor's descendants indicate that he frequently offered to debate issues of religion, science, and the Bible with local ministers. This entry suggests he is preparing for such a debate the coming Sunday, and states that his motive for engaging in such debates is to be "up and doing" as a freethinker, claiming the world from ignorance and "sowing the healthy seed of naturalism." Bachelor's occasional pieces on his reasons for becoming an agnostic note that he had read the various scriptures of world religions and had a strong interest in comparing them with one another.

300. It appears that rather than having shaken his commitment to freethought, his son's early death—as an avowed freethinker—has only made Bachelor more resolute about promoting freethought as a kind of mission to eradicate superstition and ignorance.

301. Again, the theme always in his thoughts: the passing of time and changing of seasons, as the summer of 1895 comes to an end, an ending made more poignant because of his son Wils's recent death. As always, when he writes about the natural scenes around him, Bachelor writes strong and rather beautiful prose.

302. Bachelor has mentioned on 17 September that family members have been having chills and fevers. As noted previously (see the entry for 3 October 1870), malaria with accompanying chills and fevers was prevalent in the South during the hot months of the year, particularly in areas near waterways best suited for agriculture.

303. Another of several diary entries written on his birthday—in this case, the sixty-eighth.

304. This is one of several entries of the 1890s and early 1900s that indicate that he is growing cotton as a cash crop during this period.

305. Ben White was farming with his father in Weaver Township, Franklin County, per the 1900 federal census.

306. Whereas previous entries are signed by hand, this one is stamped with the signature, his M.D. title, and the place.

307. One of his trademark New Year's Eve reflections, this one noting that, as is his custom, he is up and writing in the night as Cynthia pours her mellow light on the earth and the Pleiades hold their course. And, of course, as the year comes to a close, he remembers the son he has lost in 1895.

308. Elbert Wright Bachelor (1869–1935) is a great-nephew, a son of Bachelor's nephew John Wilson Batchelor, his brother Moses's oldest son,

whose family lives at Poyen in Grant County. John has died in 1894, but his widow, Talitha Emeline Robinson Batchelor, is still living in 1896. Elbert had gone to California and then came back to live some years in Arkansas, returning to California by 1910, where the 1910 federal census shows him living at Cedarville in Modoc County and working as a farm laborer. The census lists his wife, Sylvia, as a cook at a ranch. Elbert would later return to Arkansas where he would die on 3 February 1935 in Madison County.

309. The three sons making a crop at the homeplace are evidently Monroe, Vick, and Yeager. Yeager will soon leave Arkansas for Texas and then Colorado.

310. The mention of the silver poplars again and Pauline playing the organ in the parlor while others play the violin as he writes in his study give the entire entry a plaintive note—a word he himself uses to describe the sound of the whippoorwill this evening. He is no doubt thinking of how in June and July the preceding year, he had been commenting on Wils's approaching death.

311. Another reference to the free coinage-sound money debate he has mentioned previously on 12 June 1895. He now notes that McKinley has been elected president over William Jennings Bryan and that the election has been exciting. It appears Bachelor's sympathies lie with McKinley the Republican, and his disdainful attitude to the Spanish-American and Philippine-American Wars (see the entry for 31 December 1899) reflects his support for McKinley, who initially opposed the war and was then pushed into it by the Democrats. As a Republican, Bachelor would have welcomed this election because it was seen as a resurgence for the Republican party. Several of the occasional pieces in the scrapbook indicate Bachelor's intense interest in the 1896 election, including the undated letter to the editor speaking of the "theocratic prohibition party" and attempts to revive Puritanism, and the piece entitled "A Democratic Wall."

312. Another entry mostly related to farming news and observation of nature, with a reminder that one of the first things he does when he obtains his Arkansas land in March 1870 is to plant apple and peach orchards on it; see the entry for 3 April 1870.

313. This is the first entry in many years that has mentioned his medical practice. Is he now keeping a separate diary of his medical cases, or has his practice begun to wind down in these final years of his life? It's interesting that Bachelor mentions that the one and a half mile walk to see a sick patient is "quite a walk": he'll turn seventy in about six months.

314. Here and in the preceding entry, appealing descriptions of the May weather he loves so dearly—bees, hummingbirds, honeysuckle overhanging the verandah, and the perfume of flowers. The word "veranda(h)" applied to what is now more commonly called a porch has sometimes been considered a shibboleth word that divides British and Canadian from American English, and yet in the American South prior to the twentieth century, what are now called porches were almost always called veranda(h)s, galleries, or piazzas: see Virginia

and Lee McAlester, *A Field Guide to American Houses* (New York: Knopf, 1989), 52. As the McAlesters note, from the colonial period forward, southerners of both Anglo and French backgrounds highly prized verandahs on their houses, because they allowed families to sit outside in the cool of evening and morning, to take advantage of breezes in sultry seasons.

315. There is no date heading for this entry; the date is embedded in the text.

316. The final exhortation in this paean to the natural beauty of the summer of 1897 is noteworthy: "O, let us appreciate it." The exhortation calls to mind the aphorism from Ingersoll in the Christmas 1893 entry: "The time to be happy is now, The place to be happy is here, And the way to be happy is to make others happy."

317. There is no date heading; the date is embedded in the text.

318. The reference to the day as midsummer is telling: as with previous entries, these markers of seasons passing have an exceptionally strong significance for him. He's clearly not using the term in its technical sense to refer to the summer solstice, since that would have been in June. It appears he's marking midsummer by the appearance of Sirius in the evening sky.

319. A precise and well-crafted description of how the dog days of summer affected families (and their farm animals) in the American South during the pre-electricity period: both livestock and people alike spent the hot days seeking shelter from the sun insofar as they could, sleep was difficult, et cetera. And through it all, "we have picnics, protracted meeting, political conventions, while some are courting, some trying to get religion, and some electioneering for office. " "Protracted meeting" was the usual term among Baptists in the South for what is now called a revival. Methodists tended, by contrast, to speak of their summer revivals as campground meetings. As Bachelor suggests here, these summertime religious meetings were entertainment in the hot months after crops had been "laid by" (i.e., after they were no longer cultivated and were allowed to mature on their own), and often involved socializing and courting. There was, in other words, a strong element of entertainment in these revival meetings for people living in rural areas and small communities. A letter of Bachelor's great-niece Janie Byrd on 13 August 1911 to her aunt Melissa Byrd Robinson speaks of the Baptist protracted meeting and the Methodist campground meeting that had just taken place at Redfield in Jefferson County, both of which she'd attended—clearly, in part because of their entertainment value and the chance to catch up on community and family gossip, some of which her letter communicates to Melissa about their Batchelor relatives living near and in Redfield.

320. There is no date header; the date is embedded in the text.

321. Another of those change-of-season entries that characterize the latter part of Bachelor's journal—in this case, one noting the transition from a very hot summer to fall, or, as he writes, "autumn," which begins that day.

322. And so another entry in which Bachelor sadly recounts the death of another family member: as he notes, his oldest son, Monroe, has died on the twenty-second at the city hospital in Fort Smith. The entry notes that the family had thought Monroe was convalescing, and so he was alone when he died. The entry also notes that Bachelor had his son brought back to Pauline to be buried beside his brother Wils in the family cemetery. As in the case of Wils, the scrapbook contains a eulogy written by Bachelor, which he delivered at his son's graveside, and which was published as an obituary in the local paper. It notes that Monroe was a freethinker who had died of a painful illness and whose life had been marked by a desire to assist others, reflections that bring to mind the solicitude he showed his father and sister Nannie as they traveled to Hot Springs in 1891.

323. The statement that death is Mother Nature taking her children back into her arms, since all who live must die and death feeds on life, is echoed in the eulogy Bachelor gave at Monroe's funeral, which states, "Friends, we should not fear death. It is only Nature taking back what she gave. For the fountain of life is fed by death."

324. Bachelor and his wife, Sarah Tankersley ("my wife" again), married in Savannah, Tennessee, around this date fifty years before. One of the items pasted into his scrapbook is a newspaper notice of the golden wedding celebration submitted by an "attendant" and published on 4 December 1897. The article notes that "the Doctor had some mottoes—'This World is What You Make it;' 'The Way to be Happy is to Make Others Happy,' etc." The article also says that "there was music and festivity through the day," and in the evening, "the Doctor played the violin while his children and grand-children danced." See Appendix III for a full transcript of the golden wedding notice.

325. It is remarkable that Bachelor's critique of religion does not lead him to be inhospitable to missionaries in need of hospitality who are traveling in his region—in this case, Mormon missionaries. It is entirely possible that these missionaries may even have come to Pauline for the golden wedding celebration, and that they had some connection to Bachelor's Mormon brother William, who had died the year before.

326. James Nolen is a James M. Nolen who is found on the 1900 federal census in Mill Creek Township in Franklin County, along with his family. Nolen was born in 1853 in Tennessee, according to the census.

327. The daughter visiting from Texas is Lula Harris, who lives with her family in Atlas, near Paris, Texas.

328. Another of his Christmas remembrance pieces that ends on a plaintive note—in this case, as he recalls the death of his eldest son, Monroe, earlier in the year. Note that the reference to "in the dwelling," as contrasted to "my library," implies that his library or office studio is somehow detached from the family house proper.

329. Another time-is-passing meditation, this one written on the "last day of beautiful May of 1898."

330. There is a Virgilian quality to the gorgeous prose here, with its description of the "tired farmer" seeking rest on a "grand, glorious June" evening as bees drone, birds call, the odor of flowers wafts into the study, and a guitar sounds in the adjoining room. The passage calls to mind the *Georgics*.

331. June now becomes "glorious mature womanhood." The phrase echoes the statement on 31 December 1894 about the grand deeds of virtuous womanhood. Bachelor will write again on 17 June 1899, "June makes me think of the glorious Female loveliness of perfect womanhood."

332. What Bachelor makes of the phrase "plenary indulgence" is interesting. The term's technical meaning refers to a religious privilege granted by Catholic authorities to Catholics seeking forgiveness of their sins. But he uses the phrase, with its specifically religious overtones, to refer, instead, to nature, which surfeits us with its plenary indulgences. Nature contains all that it needs in itself: his constant rejoinder to the claims of all religious groups.

333. Again, a note about family sickness during the hot months of the year, echoing many previous entries, most recently the statements on 17 September and 1 October 1895 that the family (Bachelor included) has been sick with malarial chills and fevers.

334. This entry continues the nature-dominated, idyllic prose of the previous postings this year, which move as in a three-act play from spring to summer to fall—again, with that wistful tone he always employs as transition occurs, and the katydids' call diminishes as cold weather begins to set in.

335. As always, Christmas is marked by remembrance—of family members distant from the family circle this year and of those no longer living. This particular reflection is stamped by the observation "the Old Homestead is not what it used to be" following the deaths of two sons and the moving away of other children. But as he observes, there's still music—violin and organ—and as he has stated on 11 August 1895 after Wils dies, music is what keeps alive the memory of the loved ones now gone.

336. The god of Bacchus: a reference to the custom of drinking (sometimes, to great excess) that has historically marked the observance of Christmas in the southern states—something he mentions frequently in his Christmas reveries.

337. As always, with almost everything Bachelor writes in his diary—and notably in the final decade of his life—there is that sense of swiftly passing time, which has a cosmic significance for him as a freethinker, since all is flux in the natural world (hence the title of his monograph *Fiat Flux*): "It Seems Short since last Christmans [*sic*]: thus Speeds time, while the whirling Sp[h]eres move and wheel in their circuits."

338. Pauline has now begun her music teaching—on this, see the 31 May 1895 entry. Alcie has gone back to Texas, something Bachelor also mentions in

a 5 September 1899 letter to his niece Melissa Byrd Robinson, but by 8 June 1900, she will be enumerated on the federal census next to her parents in Franklin County, having taken her maiden name back. As this entry itself indicates, she and her family have been living next door to her parents.

339.   On a bitterly cold evening, the entry ends with a typical expression of his concern for those who are down and out, on a cold night when people without shelter may freeze.

340.   The entry has no date heading. The date is embedded in the text.

341.   This was the winter of the "great blizzard of 1899," when it snowed in Florida and iced over in New Orleans on 12 and 13 February.

342.   Bachelor continues the female metaphor of his May–June entries of the year before: May is now "a beautiful maiden fresh & fas[c]inating," and June is "the glorious Female loveliness of perfect womanhood," "a well-sexed woman." This is the only point in the diary at which he ever overtly broaches matters of sexuality. Even when he notes the case of gonorrhea (13 March 1873) and of syphilis (September 1874) that he is treating, there is no mention of the sexual matters that preoccupied many American moralists of the period as they dealt with these issues.

343.   Nannie's daughter Gertrude Eubanks is now eleven years old and, with none of the sons left at home but Vick, is assisting her uncle in making the crops.

344.   A brush "harbour" is a brush arbor. In the period called "laying-by time" after crops had begun to grow and no longer required cultivating, it was common for churches to hold revivals in the rural South of this period—as the notes for the entry of 25 July 1897 indicate. These were often held outside and under arbors constructed of saplings cut down and formed into a canopy to shade worshipers: see Orville W. Taylor, "Arkansas," in *Encyclopedia of Religion in the South*, ed. Samuel S. Hill (Macon: Mercer UP, 1984), 53. The comments about the barking dogs and the price of liberty—eternal vigilance—are, of course, Bachelor the freethinker speaking about many of the local religious practices as vehicles for ignorance and superstition.

345.   This is the same Burcham family Bachelor mentions as neighbors and friends in his Christmas Eve entry of 1891. The 1900 federal census shows them as near-neighbors of the Bachelors, with a Felix L. Burcham heading the family and his mother, Barbara, aged sixty-three and born in Tennessee, in the household. She is the Mrs. Burcham whom Bachelor has visited this Christmas Day. "Neighbor Burcham" was with the Bachelors for Christmas dinner in 1892, and Bachelor also mentions visiting Mrs. Burcham on Christmas Day in 1900.

346.   The "sanguinary strife of nations" to which the entry refers is probably the Philippines-American War of 1899. The year before, in a 20 December 1898 letter to Seaborn Walters, husband of his niece Minerva Louisa Batchelor, Bachelor had written dismissively about this war's precursor, the Spanish-

American War: "Well <u>Uncle Sam</u> and Spain had a war, I recon you have no notion of moving to Cuba." Bachelor's sympathies appear to have been with President McKinley, who was pushed into these conflicts—see notes for the diary entry for Christmas Day 1896.

347. Another celebration of the beauty of May, with a note that he has been a-fishing during the day on Mill Creek below Mrs. Burcham's.

348. The diary's penultimate Christmas reflection, with themes familiar from previous Christmas entries.

349. It's possible that the phrase "throbbing humanity" originates with Thomas Hardy's short story "On the Western Circuit," which was published in 1891 in *Harper's Weekly* 35, no. 1823 (26 November 1891). The story contains the line (946): "Throbbing humanity in full light was, on second thoughts, better than ecclesiology in the dark"—a thought that would definitely have appealed to Bachelor the freethinker. The phrase runs through a great deal of popular literature after that.

350. "Ceaseless tide of universal life" echoes the notion of the endless chain of eternal cycles mentioned on 31 December 1894, an idea that seems to have fascinated Bachelor—the *fiat flux* of a nature that remains constant but ever changing, constantly ebbing and flowing.

351. Another New Year's Eve reflection, this one noting his optimism about the future and his belief in the coming of the "glorious brotherhood of humanity"—a progressivist optimism shared by many American thinkers up to the World War I period, when it became critically apparent that scientific "progress" and the application of reason to social institutions do not automatically result in a new age of glorious brotherhood for humanity.

352. That is, orchards.

353. "As a man thinketh, so is he": Proverbs 23:7. This is one of the few instances in which Bachelor quotes scripture approvingly in any of his works, and not with the intent of refuting a biblical passage.

354. The concluding statement in the diary. Wilson R. Bachelor would die on 5 May 1903, at his home in the community he named Pauline, and in which he had settled in March 1870.

Occasional Pieces from the Scrapbook of Wilson R. Bachelor (1890s)

1.None of the three essays on Bachelor's reasons for becoming an agnostic suggests why or where they were published. The essays concisely show his transition from believer to freethinker. Possibly Bachelor drafted them for the debates he had about science and religion with local ministers. It's also possible he wrote these essays as a vindication when his Masonic lodge expelled him after he published *Fiat Flux* in 1884. Bachelor mentions in his diary on 17 September 1895, "Freethinkers must be up and doing—Sowing the healthy

Seed of naturalism." Perhaps he considered this a mandate to publish his freethought views in local newspapers.

2. This essay frames Bachelor's transition to freethought in an interesting way: as a young person, he read the Genesis account of creation, with its statement that God formed Adam from dust. And then twelve years later, he read the Hindu creation narrative, which says Brahma formed man and woman from himself, and he came to the conclusion that both are representing the story of creation mythically and not scientifically. If this essay were written around 1890 (and all the occasional pieces in the scrapbook do definitely seem to date from the 1890s), then it suggests that Bachelor's transition to freethought occurred in the 1870s—perhaps around 1878. This dating synchronizes with his statement in his diary on Christmas Day 1890 that he has become "a confirmed Freethinker or Agnostic" in the period between 1874 and 1890. Note that this occasional piece also confirms that he did receive religious instruction as a boy ("fifty years ago I read in the Bible") and had a religious upbringing—most likely as a Methodist, since his autobiography in *History of . . . Franklin and Sebastian Counties, Arkansas* states that his mother belonged to the Methodist Episcopal Church, though, as noted in the introductory section of this book, she apparently converted to Mormonism in the late 1830s, but it seems open to question whether she remained Mormon to the end of her life. His statement in the next sentence, "Had I adhered to the teachings of my youth," also confirms his religious upbringing. Note, too, his fundamental rationale for adopting a freethinker's perspective: he takes reason as his "compass and guiding star."

3. And so he sketches the process that led him to freethought as follows: comparing the scriptures of the world religions insofar as they treat the same themes (e.g., the origin of the world and of human beings) led him to research ("reading and reflection"), which convinced him that "all ancient nations trace their origin to mystery and myth." This is an insight that Christian theologians and biblical scholars, except those of a strongly conservative bent, would come to take for granted in the twentieth century. Note that these statements imply that he has deliberately been reading about and studying these issues in order to come to some conclusions of his own—Bachelor has made himself a scholar of world religions and their scriptures because these issues matter to him personally. The myth of Brahma dividing his body into male and female is in the *Brahma Purana*, and was circulating among scholars of religion in the nineteenth century in English translation—for example, see John Muir, *Original Sanskrit Texts on the Origin and History of the People of India, Their Religion and Institutions*, vol. 1 (London: Trübner, 1868), 36.

4. Max Müller and other scholars were doing pioneering work in the field of comparative religion and the history of religion in the nineteenth century, and Müller had a particular interest in Sanskrit thought and literature. In 1868,

Oxford created a chair of comparative religion for him, and he and a society of Oriental scholars he founded began publishing translations of Sanskrit texts. In 1873, he published his classic *Introduction to the Science of Religion* (London: Longmans, Green & Co., 1873).

5. The "origin and groundwork" of Bachelor's freethought arises from the recognition that if many peoples of the world have employed creation myths to talk about their origins, then it is not possible for any of them to claim that theirs is the true account, to the exclusion of all others.

6. Again, following on the hints given in the first essay in this series on his reasons for becoming an agnostic, Bachelor indicates he embarked on a serious study of world religions at some point in the past—probably in the latter half of the 1870s, according to clues in the first essay. Here, he says his research led him to study comparative chronology and hieroglyphics—that is, Bachelor read not only translations of the Sanskrit texts to which he alludes in the first part, but also literature about the origin of religious ideas in Egypt and the Near East.

7. "Bishop Usher" is James Ussher (1581–1656), the Church of Ireland prelate famous for his *Annales Veteris Testamenti* (1650), which maintained the world was created in 4,004 B.C. Ussher is the usual spelling, though Usher also appears. Bachelor cannot accept this claim since geology shows that humans antedate the last glacial period, which was more than twenty million years ago. When Bachelor speaks of Ussher's proposal that the earth became "hard" 6,000 years ago, he is evidently referring to the same phenomenon he describes in his 1892 New Year's Eve reflection "Midnight," which speaks of nebular matter cohering into an orb in the primeval state of the world. In Bachelor's view, of course, science places this nebular cohering far back in primeval time, in comparison to Ussher's chronology. The type used to print the word "hard" is imperfect here. The top bar of the letter "r" is missing, and thus gives the impression that the word is "haid" in the original.

8. The consensus is that the mythic sagas of Assyria, Phoenicia, and Egypt are older than the Hebrew scriptures. Thus, the claim of the latter to some primacy based on their age is insubstantial.

9. Note again the reference to the "parallel myths" about creation in the Hebrew and Sanskrit texts, as Bachelor stresses in his previous essay, which is why he chose agnosticism. The existence of such parallel myths in the scriptures of the world religions leads him to the conclusion (using reason as his guiding star) that the only *accurate* account of how the world came into being is the evolutionary one. As Kenneth W. Bailey notes, most mainline Protestant churches of the American South were resolutely opposed to the notion of evolution in the latter part of the nineteenth century and the early part of the twentieth, precisely because it appeared to contradict biblical inerrancy: *Southern White Protestantism in the Twentieth Century* (New York: Harper & Row, 1964), 73–74.

10. Bunsen is Christian J. B. Bunsen, author of *Outlines of the Philosophy of Universal History as Applied to Language and Religion* (London: Longmans, Green & Co., 1854).

11. The argument is building to a refutation of the account of the origin of multiple languages in the Babel story, which presupposes the primacy of Hebrew, while, as Bachelor notes, his study of comparative linguistics and philology points to the conclusion that other languages of the ancient Near East—for example, Coptic or Assyrian—are older.

12. The argument of the essay moves, as well, to a conclusion that science trumps religion as a guide to explaining the origin of the universe and how the universe functions: "The world do move"—Galileo's famous statement, *Eppur si muove!*

13. Genesis 6:6–7.

14. Genesis 18:25. Note that in this essay, Bachelor is moving through the Genesis narratives of the creation of the world and the stories of the fall and the deluge, to subject these foundational narratives of Judaeo-Christian belief to a freethinker's analysis.

15. This third essay in the series rehearses traditional arguments against venerable theodicies that view God as omnipotent and omniscient: for example, Bachelor asks how an omniscient and omnipotent God could have created a universe whose inhabitants were capable of wrongdoing, only to punish those inhabitants for doing deeds that an omniscient God could have foreseen and an omnipotent God could have prevented. And he asks whether it is merciful or just to condemn children for the wrongdoings of their parents.

16. His freethinker's perspective on the Genesis account of the deluge: how does one fit these stories into a scientific framework that makes sense to modern thinkers? He notes that even religious authorities tacitly admit that many details of miraculous events in the scriptures smack of thaumaturgy, a tacit admission suggested by the fact that the clergy no longer preach about these matters.

17. Genesis 7:11. Where Bachelor writes "foundations," the original (KJV translation) reads, "fountains."

18. The word "far" is interjected in the original; it is unclear what Bachelor intends with the series of statements. Possibly a portion of the original manuscript was inadvertently omitted by the typesetter at this point.

19. This statement suggests that as he dealt with the questions his freethinking religious skepticism raised about the inspiration of the Jewish and Christian scriptures, Bachelor read contemporary work on the historical-critical method and the topic of biblical inspiration. This is suggested as well by his occasional piece entitled "Leaving the Old Ruts" later in the scrapbook.

20. He appears to be referring here to several of the most important *codices* on which the published canonical versions of the Bible are based, including the *codex Vaticanus*, the *codex Alexandrinus*, and the *codex Siniaticus*. His knowledge of these technical terms further underscores his apparent more than passing

acquaintance with historical-critical literature of the latter part of the nineteenth century.

21. Again, these are biblical passages that suggest to Bachelor moral imperfection in the deity, if the passages are read literally. To ascribe to God the drowning or slaughter of thousands of human beings is to make God the author of evil—the primary philosophical problem with which theodicy struggles. Bachelor finds it impossible to accept the notion of the existence of a deity worthy of worship, if that deity is implicitly the author of evil.

22. The references in this letter to the editor regarding the influence of third parties and of prohibitionists suggest that the letter was commenting on the 1896 national elections, when Eugene Debs's Socialist Labor party played a strong role in the elections with the support of many prohibitionists who identified themselves as Christian Socialists. Bachelor is skeptical about the motives and role of these third-party movements, in part, because the prohibitionists have strong ties to the churches. As he notes at the conclusion of the letter, he thinks these movements exert undue pressure on citizens who are not permitted to think for themselves about political matters, but are swayed by the influence of third-party groups. Bachelor also opposed the influence of these third-party movements because, as his diary entries dated 25 December 1896 and 31 December 1899 suggest, he was strongly pro-McKinley and saw the third-party movements threatening the Republican candidate's chances of winning the election.

23. This occasional piece parallels similar New Year's Eve meditations in the diary, as well as the 1894 New Year's Eve piece with the same title later in the scrapbook. Note that the scrapbook also contains a New Year's piece written on 31 December 1899. There is a parallel piece in the diary for the published "Come and Gone" piece written on New Year's Eve in 1894, but no parallel in the diary for this published meditation written on New Year's Eve 1889 that welcomed 1890. In fact, the diary has no entries at all from Christmas Eve 1874 to Christmas Day 1890.

24. The phrase, "factory girl with hands hardened with toil," is interesting, since Bachelor did not live in an area with extensive industry and appears to have been using the phrase as a literary device rather than one reflecting his life experience. The phrase has a literary ring, as if he has read stories or novels focusing on the plight of working women—a theme beginning to be significant in American literature of the period as advocates for the rights of women, including Lucretia Mott and Jane Addams, began to write about women's lives and work. Dreiser would publish *Sister Carrie* at the end of the decade in which Bachelor is writing this meditation. See Amal Amireh, *The Factory Girl and the Seamstress: Imagining Gender and Class in Nineteenth-Century American Fiction* (London: Routledge, 2000).

25. The phrase "Niagara of humanity" crops up occasionally in nineteenth-century literature (and also later)—see, for example, Andrew John Ramsay,

"French Chaos," in *One Quiet Day* (Hamilton, Ontario: Lancefield, 1873), 46.

26. The "vast concourse" moving to the "silent Ocean of the future" echoes the observation in the opening entry of the diary about the vast cosmic repose on which he and his family find themselves as they journey to a new life in Arkansas. These water metaphors with their suggestions of constant flux and the ceaseless passage of time evidently fascinated Bachelor and have overtones of Eastern religious thought—with which he was apparently familiar, since he refers here to Buddhism, and also his first essay on his reasons for becoming an agnostic refers to his reading of Sanskrit religious literature. Here, he draws a moral lesson from the recognition that all human beings are moving as a vast concourse to the ocean of eternity by noting that, whether one accepts the Buddhist, Christian, or agnostic account of the destiny of our lives, we nonetheless have an overriding obligation to live our lives with justice, kindness, and mercy.

27. Bachelor's willingness here to make common cause with anyone seeking a more humane society brings to mind statements made in the Masonic lodge's eulogy of him. This states that after the lodge expelled him following the publication of *Fiat Flux* in 1884, he petitioned for readmission and was reinstated on 11 April 1903, but never attended a lodge meeting from the time of his expulsion until his death. The eulogy implies that Bachelor wanted to recant his freethinking views at the end of his life, but did not have the opportunity to do so before he died. It notes, however, that even as a freethinker, he adhered to the following philosophy: "Be just and kind to all men, do right because it is right, without the recognition of or the intervention of a higher power and without the fear of future punishment, or the hope of a blissful immortality beyond the grave."

28. This is possibly another of those occasional pieces that Bachelor wrote to use as he debated biblical themes and subjects with local pastors, though the essay notes that he is responding to a J. E. J., who is not otherwise identified. Debates between representatives of various religious groups (and, in the latter part of the nineteenth century, between pastors and freethinkers) were an important part of cultural life in the pre-twentieth-century South. These religious debates could focus on what might now be regarded as minute differences of doctrine or practice—for example, the difference between Arminian and Calvinist understandings of salvation; the form of baptism (immersion or sprinkling); the nature of the church (the exclusivism of some traditions versus the inclusivism of others). Not only were such public debates a way to hash out religious ideas considered important in local communities, but they were also entertainment and theater for people living in rural areas prior to the twentieth century. The text itself will note that it was composed in 1892. It contains conventional arguments against traditional theodicies that envision God controlling natural events and the fates of human beings, supported with examples drawn both from Bachelor's medical practice and contemporary

political life. He suggests that the rational approach to illness and suffering is to seek to alleviate it, not to attribute it to divine or satanic intervention. Bradford Torrey refers to Bildad as "that ancient agnostic" in a July 1888 article entitled "A Green Mountain Cornfield" in *Atlantic Monthly* (vol. 62,369, p. 48); though this is obviously not the J. E. J. to whom Bachelor is writing here, the reference demonstrates that the notion of Bildad as the forerunner of freethinkers was "in the air" at this period.

29. Samples of Bachelor's handwriting (e.g., his diary) show that he made the letter "u" in a distinctive way that is easily misread as "w." In his occasional pieces, typesetters persistently misread the "u" of his handwritten manuscripts for "w," as they've done here, changing Job's homeland from Uz to "W z."

30. Note that, since this occasional piece states it was written in 1892, the statement "I have been a practitioner of medicine for nearly 40 years" places the date when Bachelor became a doctor sometime not long after 1852, though his autobiography in *History of . . . Franklin and Sebastian Counties, Arkansas* states that he began the "active practice of the medical profession" in 1859. As noted in the introductory section of this present work, perhaps the 1852 date refers to the date at which Bachelor began to "read medicine" with a local doctor.

31. It seems apparent that Bachelor has chosen this particular biblical book to demonstrate the significance of the claims of freethinkers that science offers necessary explanatory perspectives about how the world operates, because the book's mythology is, as he notes, not believable from a scientific standpoint. God permits the devil to torment Job, causing all sorts of calamities that we'd attribute today—as Bachelor observes—to sources other than the diabolical. Bachelor's argument that exegesis challenges literal readings of this book shows his awareness of contemporary biblical exegesis, which viewed Job as a work of fiction and allegory, as he concludes.

32. "Wrticarie" is, again, the typesetter's misreading of a word that begins with "u": "urticaria" (i.e., hives). Antikamnia tablets were a remedy of the period to relieve aches, pains, and fevers. The Antikamnia Company began in St. Louis in 1890. The tablet was of dubious composition, and is thought to have contained a coal-tar derivative mixed with acetanilide, a habit-forming compound. The company also offered the solution mixed with codeine. The Pure Food and Drugs bill of 1906 led to the drug's demise.

33. As with his three essays on why he became an agnostic, this piece demonstrates Bachelor's familiarity with major themes being discussed in his period, re: the history of religion and religious philosophy. For instance, he attributes the dualistic worldview of Job to Zorastrian influence, and he notes that the fascination with the demonic in some brands of contemporary American religion had to do with the influence of Teutonic mythology. This shows a more than passing acquaintance with scholarship about the history of world religions being produced in his day. A number of scholars of this period,

including Thomas K. Cheyne, were writing about the possibility of influence of Zoroastrian dualism on Jewish thinking—see *Origin and Religious Concepts of the Psalter* (London: Kegan, Paul, Trench, Trübner, & Co., 1891). The recognition of Zoroastrian strands in Job's dualistic thought actually has an ancient lineage in Jewish literature, and the Spanish rabbi Abraham ibn Ezra was writing about these themes as early as the eleventh century.

34. This conclusion—that the book of Job is allegory and myth, and not history—reflects the findings of biblical historical-critical research, which were just coming upon the scene in the years in which Bachelor was writing.

35. On Bachelor's sister Sarah, see the 1891 Christmas Eve and 1892 Christmas Day entries in his diary. As the eulogy states, it was written by her brother and is clearly part of the collection of eulogies he wrote to be delivered at the burials of relatives. The eulogy was read "by request" by a Rev. J. T. Evans at her funeral. Evans was pastor of Oak Grove Missionary Baptist Church in Franklin County in the early 1890s. The eulogy provides yet another example of Bachelor's habit of referring to his sister affectionately as "Blind Sally." La grippe is, of course, influenza.

36. The eulogy continues a theme apparent in many reflections Bachelor wrote about death in both his diary and occasional pieces—namely, that in death, everyone is equal, a theme he found especially pertinent in the case of his sister, who had been both blind and deaf.

37. As with the rest of the occasional pieces in the scrapbook, this eulogy for Bachelor's granddaughter Rubie appears to have been written in the 1890s. Following their marriage in Franklin County on 5 February 1888, Jim Bachelor and his wife, Allie Vilola Rogers, had a son Clint W. born in November of that year, a daughter Pauline Zella born 24 November 1892, and a daughter Henrietta born 14 August 1896. It appears that Rubie was born between either Clint and Pauline or Pauline and Henrietta.

38. Again, as in other Bachelor meditations on the theme of death, there is the assertion that there is nothing above nature, and that death is the building of "new organizations" in the natural cycle, with the interesting observation that human beings are arrows "shot from the darkness into darkness across a ray of light." In his eulogy for his son Wilson in 1895, he will write, "Death is the inexorable law of nature. . . . All in nature—all in the Universe."

39. Thomas F. Boles (1837–1905) was a Dardanelle lawyer who became a judge in Fort Smith and then a U.S. representative from Arkansas and U.S. marshal for the western district of Arkansas (see his biographical notice in *Biographical Directory of the United States Congress*, maintained by the Office of History and Preservation of the U.S. Senate and online at http://bioguide. congress.gov/scripts/biodisplay.pl?index=B000603 [accessed February 2012]). As a well-known Republican in northwest Arkansas, Bachelor would have known (and, this letter suggests, admired) Boles.

40.   This statement seems to imply that Bachelor is responding to a letter that Boles has sent to him personally. His reply to the letter was, however, published, and it is possible the letter to Bachelor was, as well.

41.   Draper, *History of the Conflict between Religion and Science*, 265 (but where Draper writes "wattled stakes," Bachelor has copied "vaulted stakes"). Bachelor's reply to Boles relies on Draper's "conflict thesis," which maintained, "The history of Science is not a mere record of isolated discoveries; it is a narrative of the conflict of two contending powers, the expansive force of the human intellect on one side, and the compression arising from traditionary faith and human interests on the other" (vi).

42.   These are significant statements, since they strongly confirm Bachelor's sympathy for the Union side during the Civil War, and indicate that one reason that he favored the Union side was that he opposed slavery. For more information about Bachelor's moderate racial views, see his diary entry for 3 March 1870.

43.   Due to the defective type used by the typesetter, the final "l" in this word is very faint, almost missing. It appears the word Bachelor intends is "level."

44.   This essay reflects a belief in progress and the eventual triumph of science and reason that characterized late-nineteenth and early-twentieth-century thought in enlightened circles, and which was very seriously challenged by World War I.

45.   It seems clear from Bachelor's response that Boles had taken a reactionary stance to the political and social unrest in the country in the early 1890s, where Bachelor saw such unrest as part of the gradual unfolding of reason and individual liberty in the "transitional age" through which they were living. The phrase "transitional age" will be echoed in his essay against the death penalty.

46.   The fact that this was written to respond to questions about the world's fair allows us to date it sometime before the fair's dedication ceremonies on 1 October 1892 and the opening of the fair on 1 May 1893. It is likely the piece was composed before the October 1892 dedication, during the planning stages of the fair when the question of Sabbath opening had become a major national political issue.

47.   One of the main reasons Bachelor opposes Sabbath closing of the fair is that this represents, in his view, an unwarranted intrusion of "ecclesiasticism" in secular law. He also argues that the burden of this Sabbath enforcement falls unfairly on the backs of the working poor, who have no other day off to attend the fair. The essay also flatly argues that the United States was not founded to be a theocracy, and cites George Washington on this point: "The government of the United States is not a Christian government."

48.   Bachelor is echoing here the views of his freethought hero Ingersoll: in an 1876 statement commemorating the signing of the Declaration of

Independence, Ingersoll states, "We the People did away forever with the theological idea of government" (as cited, Jacoby, *Freethinkers*, 1, citing *The Works of Robert Ingersoll,* vol. 9 [New York: Dresden, 1900], 74, 76).

49.   Federal courts upheld the appeal of churches to shut the fair down on Sunday: see Gaines M. Foster, *Moral Reconstruction: Christian Lobbyists and the Federal Legislation of Morality, 1865–1920* (Chapel Hill: Univ. of North Carolina Press, 2002), 101f. Sabbath reformers organized a nationwide campaign to pressure Congress to assure that the fair would be closed on Sunday and to make federal appropriations for it contingent on this. As Foster notes, Josephine C. Bateham of the Women's Christian Temperance Union declared the crusade "a turning point in our nation's career. If the Christianity of the nation can control this question, they can control the career of this country."

50.   This occasional piece has the appearance of an item written as a letter to a newspaper editor. Possibly Bachelor is commenting on something local that happened in northwest Arkansas in the 1890s. If so, nothing in the piece gives a clear indication of what occasions the commentary. For Bachelor's concern with lynchings in the 1890s, see his diary entry dated 31 December 1894.

51.   This commentary is responding to the claims of those who argue that mobs have the right or obligation to supersede courts in cases in which they imagine justice has miscarried in a court. This was one of the common justifications provided for lynchings by those who took part in them in the South of the nineteenth and early twentieth centuries.

52.   In his occasional piece opposing the death penalty, Bachelor will speak of "mobomania" and will equate it with other "epidemics" like "demonomania" and "theomania," as well as the period of public self-flagellants and the witch craze.

53.   According to Leon Litwack, "Hellhounds," in *Without Sanctuary: Lynching Photography in America,* ed. James Allen, Hilton Als, John Lewis, and Leon F. Litwack (Santa Fe: Twin Palms, 2000), in the late nineteenth and early twentieth century, two or three black southerners were hanged, burned at the stake, or quietly murdered every week (12). In the 1890s, an average of 139 lives were claimed each year by lynching, a majority of these black men (ibid.). Few who engaged in these activities were ever brought to trial (20). Juries routinely concluded that those lynched had met their deaths at the hands of unknown parties even when an entire community knew who had perpetrated the lynching (ibid.).

54.   This piece is responding to some of the same political happenings as those mentioned in the item on a freethinker's view of politics in Franklin County on the eve of the 1892 elections. Both pieces refer to political events in Alabama at this time in which there was contention among factions in the Democratic party.

55.   John Enos appears to be a fictional character. Bachelor makes him to be

a Jones advocate, and the story thus becomes an allegory about the kind of corruption that Thomas Goode Jones represented in the Democratic party in one-party states like Alabama. Perhaps Bachelor also links the story to national politics by connecting Jones's corrupt victory over Kolb to the anti-Harrison politics of the Democratic party. Enos is "mortal" in Hebrew.

56. The 1892 gubernatorial election in Alabama was notoriously corrupt, with Reuben F. Kolb, a Jeffersonian Democrat, allying with the People's party and some Republicans against Jones, the incumbent Democrat. Jones won the election by stealing votes in the Black Belt. Whiskey was used to buy votes, hence Bachelor's reference to it.

57. This essay is followed by yet another about the Cleveland-Harrison election and how it affected local politics in Franklin County, and by another ("Democratic Wall") that is also about allegations of political corruption at a national level—a theme obviously preoccupying Bachelor's attention at this point in time.

58. A gallinipper is a southern and midwestern dialect term used to describe any of several varieties of large mosquitoes.

59. This is probably a letter addressed to the editor of the local paper in Ozark. The references to Cleveland and Harrison tell us that the letter is commenting on the 1892 presidential election. Bachelor will state in this piece that he is not an ardent partisan as the election nears: his criterion for political judgment is, "I . . . hold liberty of thought above all political organizations." He finds the campaign "apathetic," and says, "I see the signs of the times point to the future when politics will determine everything"—to be specific, he points to the use of various litmus tests to determine who will or won't be elected, and he thinks this will foster corruption and hypocrisy.

60. David B. Hill and Horace Boies were contenders for the president's and vice president's positions on the Democratic ticket in 1892, and James G. Blaine and Thomas B. Reed competed for the Republican ticket. Blaine would no doubt have been on Bachelor's radar screen because Robert G. Ingersoll had nominated him for the presidency at the Republican national convention in 1876 (Jacoby, *Freethinkers*, 166), and Blaine was a strong advocate of separation of church and state—though Blaine repudiated Ingersoll in 1884 to obtain the nomination (ibid., 167).

61. Bachelor's conclusion reflects the growing political confusion of the early 1890s, confusion that made hidebound partisanship difficult, as the major parties veered in one direction or another and power passed back and forth between them at the federal level. As Samuel Eliot Morison notes, "In 1890 American politics lost their equilibrium and began to pitch and toss in an effort to reach stability among wild currents of protest that issued from the caverns of discontent" (*The Oxford History of the American People* [New York: Oxford UP, 1965], 789). The essay also suggests that, though he had identified himself in his 1889 autobiographical essay as a Republican, by the 1890s, the

corruption of both parties and his commitment to freethought had caused Bachelor to adopt a political stance that today might be called independent.

62. Again, this piece has the appearance of an item written as a letter to an editor of a newspaper. The specific references to Cleveland and Tammany Hall suggest that the piece is commenting on events that occurred during the presidential election of 1892.

63. "Tell it not in Gath, publish it not in the streets of Askelon; lest the daughters of the Philistines rejoice, lest the daughters of the uncircumcised triumph": 1 Samuel 2:20. The verse was frequently used as a proverb in English and American literature—see Bartlett Jere Whiting, *Early American Proverbs and Proverbial Phrases* (Cambridge: Harvard UP, 1977), 173. When David killed Goliath of Gath and the Israelites pursued the Philistines, they fled back to Gath. The verse occurs in David's lament for Saul and Jonathan, when he hears news of their deaths. And so it is an injunction not to give aid and comfort to one's enemy by sharing news of one's losses.

64. The Democrats had tagged the high tariff of Benjamin Harrison's administration (1888–1892) as the "robber tariff," and Cleveland was campaigning against it in 1892. The tariff act was introduced by Republican representative William McKinley and became law in 1890. It raised the average duty on imports to almost 50 percent, an act designed to protect domestic industries from foreign competition. Cleveland made the tariff the subject of his state of the union address in 1887, and the issue then became a highly partisan one, remaining thus when Harrison was elected in 1888. A large percentage of the population resented the tariff, since it made goods expensive, and this contributed to the Republican rout in 1892. The Force Bill had existed since 1833 when Congress gave Andrew Jackson the power to use any force necessary to enforce federal tariffs.

65. David B. Hill, Cleveland's primary Democratic opponent during the campaign, and governor of New York.

66. "Gray Buzzards": Cleveland was spending the summer up to the time of the nominating convention at his summer retreat at Gray Gables in Buzzards Bay, Massachusetts—hence also the reference to seagulls. So the silence of Gray Buzzards is the silence of Cleveland himself.

67. Cleveland sought to show his independence from the political machine of Tammany Hall in New York, but it appears Bachelor is suggesting there were intimations during the 1892 campaign that Cleveland was willing to court the Tammany folks in order to gain their support. There were rumors going around that, prior to his nomination, Cleveland cut a deal with Tammany to obtain the nominating vote of New York. Bachelor is responding to these reports of behind-the-scenes deal-cutting involving Cleveland, Hill, and Tammany Hall. *American Magazine* 66, no. 6 (October 1908), 618–19, "The Pilgrim's Scrip," has a letter by a Charles Dillon, who was a telegraph operator

in Chicago and who received communications of the Democrats during the convention, who denies that Cleveland ever cut any such deals, however.

68. The "hippodroming of the occupant of Gray Buzzards" appears to be a reference to a meeting supposed to have taken place between Cleveland and the Tammany leaders at the Hippodrome theater in New York.

69. The quotation is, of course, Shakespeare, *Richard III* (act 1, scene 1)— a play Bachelor notes in his 30 May 1873 entry that he particularly admires.

70. Bourke Cockran, U.S. representative from New York, was a Tammany man and a Democrat, but in the 1896 election would cross over to the Republican side to support McKinley and oppose William Jennings Bryan and free silver. As a result of his political maneuvering, he had the reputation of being less than scrupulous and an opportunistic political kingmaker.

71. Reverend Thomas De Witt Talmage was an influential religious leader and revivalist of the period. The sermon to which Bachelor is responding was entitled "The Bare Arm of God." Talmage gave it at Central Presbyterian Church (Brooklyn Tabernacle) in Brooklyn on 21 January 1894, and in the sermon, he announced his intent to resign from his pastoral position at the church to do evangelizing ministry. Talmage's "Bare Arm" sermon was carried by many local papers of the day.

72. In his "Bare Arm" sermon, Talmage enumerates the "enthroned difficulties" that require the bared arm of God to remove or overthrow them, and in the list is Mohammedanism with its "one hundred and seventy-six million victims." Bachelor is mocking the assertion of evangelists of his period including Talmage who imagined that political leaders should answer to religious leaders as they governed.

73. Corbett: James J. ("Gentleman Jim") Corbett, the famous American pugilist.

74. Onan married Er's wife, Tamar, after God struck Er down due to the wickedness of his son Judah, and was then himself struck down when he spilled his seed on the ground rather than impregnate Tamar: see Genesis 38. On Nabal, see 1 Samuel 25.

75. This historical commentary on how the feast of Christmas developed in Christian areas of the world, on its non-Christian roots and biblical themes, reads as if were written as lecture notes for the debates Bachelor is known to have had with local ministers. He provides a variety of reasons for concluding that the date of Christmas was chosen to coincide with pre-Christian winter solstice festivals, and that the biblical accounts of the birth of Jesus couldn't have pointed to winter as the season for the birth and cannot be historically accurate. As numerous passages in his diary illustrate, however, even as a freethinker, Bachelor relished the family holiday and celebrated it with delight.

76. It is possible Bachelor wrote this Christmas piece after Ingersoll gave his famous Christmas sermon in 1891, which was printed in the *New York Evening*

Telegram 24,8059 (19 December 1891), 5, col. 1–2, eliciting much controversy nationwide. The sermon makes points similar to those Bachelor makes here about the non-Christian roots of the Christmas celebration.

77. Genesis 18:18.

78. Genesis 19:3.

79. Judges 13:16.

80. Bachelor is referring here to the Annunciation passage in Luke 1.

81. Revelation 10:5.

82. These observations—there is no longer a place in the world for angels when we now have steam engines, the telegraph, and the press—refer to the meaning of the Greek word αγγελος, "messenger," and to the role of angels in the scriptures as divine messengers.

83. The phrase "manhood and womanhood" here echoes the same parallel structure (manhood: womanhood) in the 1894 New Year's Eve meditation entitled "Come and Gone," which is repeated in the diary on the same date. It also demonstrates Bachelor's commitment to equal rights for women and his sensitivity to the needs of women as evinced in his essay on social purity for women.

84. Another of Bachelor's several New Year's Eve meditations in both the diary and the scrapbook with its occasional pieces. There is no 1892 New Year's Eve commentary in his diary. The 1892 Christmas entry, which is the last entry in the diary in 1892, ends with a remark about his sister Blind Sally's death earlier in the year (19 January), and the note that he is retiring that evening with "a feeling of brotherhood for all humanity," and that he cheerfully agrees with Thomas Paine, "The world is my country[,] to do good my religion." These are sentiments echoed in the 1892 New Year's Eve commentary of the scrapbook, as well.

85. Bachelor's political commentaries throughout this year (see, e.g., "A Dream," "A Freethinker's View of Franklin, on the Presidential Election," and "A Democratic Wall") are marked by dismay at what was happening to the political process, and the mood induced by the political disarray is reflected in this New Year's Eve commentary—"high throbbing hopes and abject despair" have gone into the "maelstrom of nature's laboratory." The latter phrase is a new formulation for what he calls in other places the "silent ocean of the future," the "vast cosmic repose," and the "ocean of Eternity"—see "Come and Gone," the New Year's Eve reflection in 1890.

86. A number of ships sank in 1892, but perhaps most notably the SS *Bokhara*, a steamship that sank in a typhoon on 20 October off the coast of Sand Island in the Pescadores, resulting in 125 deaths. It was bound from Shanghai to Colombo and Bombay with 148 people aboard.

87. On 27 May 1892, a cyclone devastated Wellington, Kansas, killing seventeen people and destroying much of the town. The same night, a cyclone in Harper, Kansas, killed five people. On 17 May, a cyclone in Greer County,

Oklahoma, took a number of lives and destroyed much property. On 15 June, tornadoes in southwestern Minnesota killed twelve people. On 5 January, a tornado struck in eastern Alabama, causing a number of fatalities. Illinois had several devastating tornadoes in 1892, and the town of Washington, Arkansas, was destroyed by a tornado the same year. On 27 June, the "great cyclone of 1892" tore through Williamsport, Pennsylvania, with destruction ranging from the Jersey Shore to Eagles Mere.

88. There was a cholera epidemic in September 1892 in Hamburg, Germany, that caused some 8,600 deaths, and this caused an outbreak of cholera at New York Harbor in August and September, with ships arriving from Hamburg.

89. "Nebular coheared" = "nebular cohered." Bachelor is actually quoting Walt Whitman here (but slightly erroneously). His scrapbook contains an excerpt from Whitman's "Song of Myself," with its lines "Before I was born out of my mother generations guided me, / My embryo has never been torpid, nothing could overlay it. / For it the nebula cohered to an orb . . . ." As noted in the introductory survey of his life and work, Bachelor appears to have had a particular interest in Whitman.

90. The wide range of references here—the primeval cohering of nebular matter, the millions of solar systems, primeval oceans, mastodons, cave bears, the Incas of Peru and Negritos of India: these seem to have an educational intent. In this essay, Bachelor appears to be in educational mode, teaching people in his community about the vast scope of time both prehistoric and historic, and the vast range of world history.

91. Bachelor (or perhaps a member of his family) has marked this sentence and the one preceding it in the scrapbook copy of this occasional piece by putting the two sentences in large parentheses. The theme developed in the two sentences seems to summarize his philosophy of *fiat flux*.

92. Balbec = Baalbek, Lebanon, the site of the ruined city of Heliopolis.

93. Cholua: the site of the largest pyramid structure of the Americas, where Cortéz massacred many inhabitants in 1519, partly burning down the city.

94. Many of the themes about which Bachelor is writing here were "in the air" at this period because of the upcoming Chicago world's fair, which had sites devoted to some of these themes: see Julian Ralph, "Our Exposition at Chicago," *Harper's Monthly* 84,500 (January 1892), 212. The world's fair was to feature Aztec ruins and an Aztec temple, for instance. See also Mauricio Tenorio-Trillo, *Mexico at the World's Fairs: Crafting a Modern Nation* (Berkeley and Los Angeles: Univ. of California Press, 1996), 185: "Mexico's presence in Chicago was especially notable for its ethnographic views. In the department of ethnology, numerous Mexican antiquities were exhibited, both by the Mexican government and by American anthropologists and ethnographers, together with pictures of ruins and models of *tipos populares*, Indian cloth, and Indian skulls." The fair also included replicas of Mayan ruins (186).

95. "Human life is an electric sunbeam": a new, "scientific" way of formu-
lating the significance of human life in a world always in flux, in which nothing is above nature. This goes hand-in-hand with the formula "maelstrom of
nature's laboratory" earlier in this piece. The "electric sunbeam" formulation
will be repeated in Bachelor's review of Bourland's *Entolai*.

96.   A response to recent developments in biblical and religious commentary—in particular, citing the work of Charles Augustus Briggs, whom
Bachelor claims as a freethinker. Bachelor appears to be writing this in 1892,
since he mentions that Farrar and Beecher had announced their disbelief in a
literal hell some fifteen years before, and is apparently referring to Farrar's
1877 series of sermons that had to do with this theme. He is also writing after
Briggs's trial for heresy in 1892. The essay demonstrates Bachelor's interest in
and familiarity with current historical-critical study of the Bible—an area about
which laymen then were not usually well informed (as they are not now).

97.   Canon Farrar is Frederic W. Farrar, canon of Westminster who became
dean of Canterbury. In a series of sermons in 1877 he advanced the idea of
universal salvation. He followed these with books *Eternal Hope* (New York: E. P.
Dutton, 1878) and *Mercy and Judgment* (New York: Macmillan, 1881) developing the theme and challenging the notion of a literal hell.

98.   Henry Ward Beecher, influential pastor of Plymouth Congregational
Church in New York. He repeatedly preached sermons denying the literal
existence of hell. Ingersoll mentions Beecher as an admirer of his in *Hell, Warm
Words on the Doctrine of Eternal Salvation* (London: Watts & Co., 1882), 2.

99.   As Bachelor notes, the ideas of various critical religious thinkers had
begun to influence the thinking of many churches in the latter part of the
nineteenth century, though there would be considerable backlash against the
historical-critical method and the kind of theology for which Beecher and
Farrar stood as the fundamentalist movement came on the scene in the early
twentieth century.

100.   The Westminster Confession of Faith is the Reformed tradition's classic
credal statement.

101.   Charles Augustus Briggs was an American Presbyterian theologian. In
1892, he was tried for heresy by the Presbytery of New York and acquitted.
The charges against him were based on the inaugural address he gave in 1891
when he became professor of biblical theology at Union Theological Semi-
nary. They included that he held that errors may have existed in the original
text of the Bible, that many of the predictions of the Old Testament had been
reversed by history, that the great body of Messianic prediction has not and
cannot be fulfilled, and that Moses was not the author of the Pentateuch. It is
to the Briggs controversy that Bachelor is referring when he mentions the
Westminster Confession and Presbyterians.

102.   Midnight, 1893–1894: that is, he is writing this piece on New Year's
Eve. The diary contains no New Year's Eve statement for 1893. This essay sug-

gests that the ones he entered into his diary on New Year's Eve for a number of years may have been written separately (perhaps as pieces he hoped a newspaper would publish) and then transcribed into the diary.

103. James Croll was a mathematician who developed a theory of climate change based on changes in the earth's orbit. He developed his views that the earth moves through glacial epochs due to climate change in *Climate and Time* (New York: Appleton, 1875) and *Climate and Cosmology* (New York: Appleton, 1886).

104. He is citing Ingersoll here, and he does so as well, using the same quotation, on Christmas Day 1893 in his diary.

105. This article appears to be addressing a debate occurring in this period due to the rise of the Adventists, who had a theory (the doctrine of "soul sleep") that the soul ceases to exist in a conscious state after death. Many other Christian groups saw this theology as heretical and classified it as a kind of materialism: see, for example, Herbert McLellan Riggle, *Man: His Present and Future* (Anderson, IN: Gospel Trumpet Company, 1904). Bachelor asserts that, though freethinkers are materialists, they believe in the soul, regarding it as the "consensus of all the faculties of the human organism"—and so the soul does not continue existing once a human being dies. The reference to Cleveland's election near the end of the article suggests it was written sometime after 1892, the second election of Cleveland.

106. The questions show Bachelor far ahead of his time and anticipating questions philosophers and medical ethicists continue to debate, including how to define the "moment" of death, and whether the definition of death depends on the status of the brain stem.

107. Thomas Henry Huxley, "Darwin's bulldog," coined the term "agnostic"—"Agnosticism: A Rejoinder," in *Collected Essays*, vol. 5: *Science and Christian Tradition* (London: Macmillan, 1889), 209–63. The classic source for Huxley on cerebration is Huxley and William Jay Youmans, *The Elements of Physiology and Hygiene: A Text-Book for Educational Institutions* (New York: Appleton, 1868). Huxley may be the source for Bachelor's assertion that "[t]hey [i.e., materialists] hold that every function of the living organism— will, observation, reflections and memory, are the results of molecular changes in the cerebrum." On Huxley as the most effective popularizer of Darwin's theory of evolution in American society, especially in his 1876 lectures, see Jacoby, *Freethinkers*, 134f. As testimony to how challenging Huxley's popularization of Darwin's theory of evolution was to American religious thinkers of the latter part of the nineteenth century, note what prominent social gospel leader Shailer Mathews says about his first encounter with Huxley in his autobiography *New Faith for Old* (New York: Macmillan, 1936): Mathews says that when he first read Huxley on evolution as a student at Colby College in the 1880s, he asked his teacher to recommend a book that would demonstrate the errors of evolutionary thought. His teacher responded that insofar as science

proves Christian tenets untrue, the latter must be reconsidered—an insight that Mathews credits with shifting his entire theological universe (18).

108. Because this piece is entitled "correspondence," it may have been written as a letter to the editor or to be published as an op-ed piece. Since it is side-by-side in the scrapbook with the next essay on providence commenting on Harrison's defeat by Cleveland in 1892, it appears to be further reflection on Harrison's claim that he was elected in 1888 by providence—a claim problematized by his defeat in 1892, as Bachelor notes.

109. Luke 12:7 and Matthew 10:30.

110. The essay rehearses reasons traditionally advanced by those discussing the topic of theodicy and the problem of evil to question God's direct control of the minute details unfolding in the world—a world in which horrific natural disasters take countless human lives. Bachelor's description of some of the scenarios that call into question the notion of God's direct providential control of the world's affairs is a good example of his novelistic style that owes much to writers like Dickens.

111. "Him who tempers the wind to the shorn lamb": Jennifer Speake, ed., *Oxford Dictionary of Proverbs* (New York: Oxford UP, 1998), says that the proverb has longstanding provenance—for example, Speake cites H. Estienne, *Prémices* (1594): "*Dieu mesure le froid à la brebis tondue.*" The formulation, "God tempers the wind to the shorn lamb" is from Sterne, *Sentimental Journey* (1768), but William Alexander Clouston, *Wine and Walnuts* (London: Ward, Lock & Tyler, 1876), 235, suggests Sterne got the proverb from George Herbert, *Jacula Prudentum* (1640), "To the shorn sheep God gives wind by measure." And Clouston thinks Herbert is citing Estienne's 1594 formulation.

112. The concept of intelligent design is articulated by William Paley in his *Natural Theology* (London: J. Faulder, 1802), and was one of the problems with which Darwin struggled in his theory of evolution, which stems from Darwin's recognition that any accurate perception of nature recognizes that much in nature seems poorly designed—but Darwin did not want to give up belief in an intelligent Designer. The concept of intelligent design was soon to become a major talking point of fundamentalist Christians in reaction to Darwinian theories of evolution and modern historical-critical study of the Bible.

113. So the theme of providence as applied to politics deserves further consideration, Bachelor suggests. The tragic events he recounts, which problematize easy notions of God's providential control of the world, provide an opening for Bachelor the freethinker to comment on the fatuity of the claim that God directs the political life of nations and selects a nation's leaders, that the United States is a "Christian nation" under God's direct providential control, and so on.

114. Bachelor's counsel here—learn to trust with humility when disastrous events challenge our faith in a providential and loving God—might well be

drawn from Job. But it is clear he means this counsel in an ironic sense, since his preceding comment about intelligent design is juxtaposed against the litany of things that go horrifically wrong in the world, leading him to be radically skeptical about the proposal that God is in charge of all of this, numbering the hairs of our heads.

115. The essay appears to reflect the kinds of questions about theodicy and providence with which Bachelor wrestled both as a freethinker and as a doctor committed to relieving suffering. As he notes in the diary on 29 November 1874, "[W]hen I think I have not been the cause of pain to any person, but have Sympathized with the Suffering, and endeavoured to relieve corporeal pain, and mental anguish; the reflection is pleasant." These themes are obviously of personal significance to Bachelor, since he keeps writing about them.

116. The typesetter has actually misspelled the name here as "Bacheror."

117. This statement suggests Bachelor is writing after Benjamin Harrison's defeat in the 1892 presidential election, as power passed back to the Democrats and Cleveland. He's lampooning the idea—held on all sides and by many different governments, as he notes—that God governs political affairs by providence.

118. Harrison had attributed his victory over Cleveland in 1888 to providence, making it easy for Bachelor to ridicule the appeal to providence in 1892 when the reverse happened.

119. In the original, the typesetter has run the words "to show" together as one word.

120. Royal Commission on Capital Punishment, *Report of the Capital Punishment Commission* (London: Eyre & Spottiswoode, 1866): "The shadow of the gallows frightens men from those serious contemplations which ought to occupy the mind in the presence of a great crime" (316).

121. The phrase "the salt of civilization" may be from Walter Scott, *The Fortunes of Nigel* (1822). In 1894, which seems to be around the time in which Bachelor wrote this piece, *The Altruistic Review* 3, no. 1 (July 1894): 1–4, published an editorial entitled "The Salt of Civilization" calling for progressive reform of social institutions (though the essay does not mention the death penalty).

122. In arguing against capital punishment in this essay, Bachelor is arguing against what has been the prevailing opinion of a majority of the citizens of his state throughout its history. As David Richard points out, the death penalty was practiced in Arkansas even before it became a state, and continues to be provided for in the state's criminal code—see "Capital Punishment," *Encyclopedia of Arkansas History and Culture*, online at http://encyclopediaofarkansas.net/encyclopedia/entry-detail.aspx?search=1&entryID=4160 (accessed March 2012).

123. Tuberculous infection of the lymph nodes.

124. Alcoholism.

125. The argument Bachelor develops in this essay has a curiously contemporary ring to it, and in this sense is prescient (since the points he makes here are still being pressed by those advocating for abolition of the death penalty). He notes that when the death penalty has been abolished in various nations and states, crime has not increased. And so he concludes that capital punishment does not deter crime, but hardens the sensibilities of everyone in a society that employs it and, ironically, increases the likelihood of violent crimes. He also observes that "sometimes innocent people are executed," and notes that the legal system is set up to serve the needs of the ruling class, and the use of the death penalty is therefore radically skewed against those on the bottom of society—making its use even more barbaric and unacceptable in civilized societies.

126. For further reflections illustrating Bachelor's concern with the topic of lynching, see "Mob Law."

127. "Mobomania" appears to be a neologism that provides a scientific (or pseudo-scientific) gloss to the notion that mob rule produces a mob psychology permitting those acting as a mob to do things they wouldn't do as individuals.

128. These terms refer to periods of history in Christian cultures in which people seemed to go on hysterical binges, flagellating themselves to obtain divine mercy, hunting and killing witches, believing demons were everywhere—as in the period of the Black Death or in the early modern period, when a witch craze swept through both parts of Europe and some of the American colonies.

129. On the phrase "transitional age," see "Unrest and Tendencies of Organization."

130. "Sheet-iron thunder": in the stage effects of theater of the period, thunder was simulated by beating on sheet iron.

131. He borrows here from notions of social evolution that were "in the air" among progressives of the period: the presupposition is that by improving social conditions for everyone, we diminish the probability that people will be brought up in conditions that foster crime. That is, people will "evolve" to a less barbaric and primitive state of behavior if we spur social evolution along by ameliorating their social and economic circumstances. Jacoby, *Freethinkers* (154), notes that opposition to capital punishment was a central tenet of the freethought movement in the latter part of the nineteenth century.

132. The conclusion suggests that Bachelor's interest is not merely with the question of punishing crime, but also with reforming those with criminal tendencies.

133. Henderson Rice appears to be the brother of Benjamin Franklin Rice, who moved from Champaign County, Illinois, to Mill Creek Township in Franklin County between 1870 and 1880. It seems his brother Henderson made the move from Christian County, Illinois, where he appears on the 1880

federal census, to Arkansas to join his brother Franklin sometime after 1880, dying in Franklin County in 1888. In addition to the misspelling of the given name of the deceased, the piece contains several other typesetter's errors, including "ane free invertigation," when "and free investigation" is meant; and "sear and yellow lief" for "sere and yellow leaf." The right margin of the clipping is also somewhat frayed, making some words difficult to decipher. The fact that the piece is signed "Observer" also suggests someone at the funeral recorded Bachelor's eulogy as he delivered it and submitted the text to the newspaper.

134. As with the other eulogies authored by Bachelor and preserved in the scrapbook, this contains themes typical of his thought regarding death: there is nothing above nature; heaven and hell are myths; one is obliged to live kindly; and death is a release, a journey into the "cool shade"—which echoes themes of Greek and Roman thought, Stoic philosophy in particular, about death.

135. As the reference to "Editor Ensign" indicates, Bachelor is writing to the Mormon newspaper in Independence, Missouri, that published a letter of his on 3 February 1893 about his family's religious history, and would publish the obituary of his brother William in June 1896. As noted in the introductory essay for this volume, in this occasional piece, Bachelor is responding to an article the *Ensign* published in January 1893 entitled "Social Purity." The next issue of the *Ensign* contains Bachelor's letter about his family's religious history—see Appendix IV. The printed letter saved in the scrapbook, which responds to the "Social Purity" article, was evidently submitted to the *Ensign* sometime after the January 1893 article appeared. But it has the appearance of the other published documents saved in the scrapbook, and was no doubt published in Bachelor's local paper, even though the original was sent to the *Ensign*.

136. The social purity movement was a proto-feminist movement of the latter part of the nineteenth and early twentieth centuries, which sought to ameliorate the conditions of women, prevent exploitation of prostitutes, and provide "rational" and scientific improvements for women's lives that eventually included reproductive rights and technology (see John D'Emilio and Estelle B. Freedman, *Intimate Matters: A History of Sexuality in America* [New York: Harper & Row, 1988]), 150–56; and Linda Gordon, *Woman's Body, Woman's Rights: A Social History of Birth Control in America* [New York: Penguin, 1977], 95–115). The movement coalesced with other progressive movements of social reform of the period, and espoused equality between men and women.

137. Genesis 3:16.

138. 1 Peter 3:1.

139. This is another instance of Bachelor's commitment to a progressivist philosophy common among freethinkers of his period, which assumed that social institutions were evolving away from primitive and barbaric conditions to more enlightened ones. Here, he argues that since women are no longer regarded as property, servants, and beasts of burden, the full humanity of

women and their full range of human rights need to be respected by societies of his day. See also Bachelor's response to Addison M. Bourland's *Entolai* for a further statement of his commitment to women's emancipation. Jacoby, *Freethinkers*, 154, notes that a central tenet linking freethinkers of diverse political and ideological stripes together in the latter part of the nineteenth century was a commitment to "expanded legal and economic rights for women that went well beyond the narrow political goal of suffrage." Ingersoll defended equal rights for women in his essay "The Liberty of Man, Woman, and Child"—see Jacoby, *Freethinkers,* 168.

140. John Chrysostom (ca. 347–407), early Christian theologian and bishop of Constantinople. The authenticity of the Chrysostom quote has been challenged, but it was being circulated by freethinkers as Chrysostom's aphorism in this period; see, for example, C. Cohen, "Christianity and Women—II," *The Freethinker* 27, no. 12 (24 March 1907), 180.

141. Gregory Thaumaturgus (ca. 213–ca. 270) was an early bishop in Asia Minor. Ingersoll uses the Thaumaturgus quote in a work he wrote with Henry Morehouse Taber: *Faith or Fact* (New York: Peter Eckler, 1897), 11.

142. *Paradise Lost*, book X, ll. 888–992.

143. According to Michael Dougan, Arkansas was in advance of other southern states when it came to recognizing women's rights: see "Arkansas Married Woman's Property Law," *Encyclopedia of Arkansas History and Culture*, online at http://encyclopediaofarkansas.net/encyclopedia/entry-detail.aspx?search= 1&entryID=4745 (accessed March 2012). On the women's suffrage movement in Arkansas, see Paula Kyzer Taylor, "Woman's Suffrage Movement," ibid., online at http://encyclopediaofarkansas.net/encyclopedia/entry-detail. aspx?search=1&entryID=4252 (accessed March 2012).

144. Sections of this particular scrapbook piece have been corrupted or have faded, such that portions of the text are now almost illegible. This is particularly true of the last two sentences. The typesetting itself is imperfect—for example, rendering the word "drifting" as "difting."

145. Samuel Porter Jones, a celebrated evangelist of the latter part of the nineteenth century who was Methodist until 1893, when Methodist leaders raised questions about his flamboyant style and he then became an unaffiliated evangelist. He preached a revival in Memphis in 1884. Bachelor is writing this piece after a crusade by Jones in Memphis in 1892 resulted in mass conversions. Jones had strong political views—for example, he took sides in the controversy over gold and free silver, attacking the adherents of the latter.

146. The concern with mob law is reflected in other occasional pieces Bachelor published—for example, in the essay with that title, in the piece on the death penalty, and in the 1894 piece entitled "From Pauline" mentioning Eugene Debs and third parties.

147. On 2 February 1893, President Benjamin Harrison nominated Howell E. Jackson for the Supreme Court.

148. On 7 March 1893, Grover Cleveland made Walter Q. Gresham his secretary of state.

149. Bachelor appears to have approved of the nominations of both Jackson and Gresham, since a Republican president, Harrison, had nominated a Democrat and former Confederate, Jackson, to the Supreme Court, and a Democratic president, Cleveland, had appointed a Republican and former Union officer, Gresham, secretary of state. Hence the reference to the dawning of the millennium—an unexpected bipartisan outcome of the political turbulence of the 1892 election that so dismayed Bachelor, and which he considered Jones to be threatening now by his incitement of the mob.

150. Had Jones restricted his sermon to themes like Isaiah's prophecy of the lamb and lion lying down together (Isaiah 11:6) or Jesus's admonition to resist no evil (Matthew 5:39), Bachelor would have been convinced the millennium had arrived (hence the reference to Gabriel sounding his trumpet).

151. This is another quotation from the Shakespeare play that Bachelor tells us in his diary entry of 30 May 1873 he particularly likes: the line is from *Richard III*, act 3, scene 1.

152. These are among Bachelor's clearest formulations of what it was that particularly concerned him about mob rule: it is "the ebullition of the worst passions of a lawless majority," and it permits a majority to trample the rights of a minority. If one places these statements against the racial context in which they are being written, when Jim Crow laws and widespread white racial violence against African Americans in the South often ignored the dictates of law, the statements appear to have a racial application.

153. For Bachelor as a freethinker, irrational religion often appeals to the "worst passions of human nature," especially in the hands of religious leaders inciting mobs and appealing to their passions, as he judges Jones to be doing. As he will note in the conclusion of the essay, he recommends, instead, reason, freedom, and intelligence coupled with individualism as the foundation of a humane society. Jones was notorious for his declaration "rape means rope," which defended lynch mobs that executed black men accused of raping white women: on this, see Kelly Miller, *Race Adjustment: Essays on the Negro in America* (New York: Neale, 1909), 69, 83; and Darren E. Grem, "Sam Jones, Sam Hose, and the Theology of Racial Violence," *Georgia Historical Quarterly* 90 (Spring 2006): 35–61. As W. Scott Poole notes, Jones bragged openly about his role in the violence that ended Reconstruction, and his ministry openly linked "work for the Kingdom" with "ghastly violence" in the 1890s ("Confederate Apocalypse: Theology and Violence in the White Reconstruction South," in *Vale of Tears: New Essays on Religion and Reconstruction,* ed. Edward J. Blum and W. Scott Poole [Macon: Mercer UP, 2005], 49–50). In 1906, Jones issued a justification for a race riot in Atlanta in which 25 African Americans were killed, over 150 wounded, and over 1,000 fled the city in fear for their lives ("Confederate Apocalypse," 50).

154. Bachelor was writing soon after the horrific lynching of Henry Smith on 1 February 1893 in Paris, Texas. Smith was a mentally retarded black man accused of the murder of a little girl, Myrtle Vance, whose father, a policeman, had beaten Smith. When Smith was accused of the crime, he fled to Hope, Arkansas, where he was apprehended and brought to Paris. At Paris, he was ritually tortured with hot irons in front of a crowd of 10,000. He was then burned to death in front of the crowd. Methodist bishop Atticus Haygood spurred the violence on through injudicious (and erroneous) remarks about the murder, and Sam Jones would later claim to convert Henry Ward, one of the instigators of the violence who participated in the torture, in 1895 (see Poole, "Confederate Apocalypse," 50). This story from Paris would perhaps have been in Bachelor's mind as he wrote this piece because his daughter Lula and her family lived five miles from Paris at Atlas, Texas.

155. The stress on individualism here echoes what he says in his essay about Franklin County on the eve of the 1892 elections: he is distrustful of all political parties and holds "liberty of thoughts above all political organizations."

156. The text contains a number of typesetter's errors—for example, "rut" when "but" is clearly meant; and "unfathomably" when "unfathomable" is meant.

157. Addison McArthur Bourland was a physician who practiced in Van Buren, Arkansas, at the time he wrote his book *Entolai, or This Letter to Those I Love about Science and the Ideal* (Van Buren, AR: Lloyd Garrison, 1893). He had been a Confederate army surgeon and had also served in the war with Mexico. He graduated from the University of Nashville Medical School in 1857 and lived in Franklin County until 1864, when he moved to Van Buren. A literary notice about *Entolai* in *Popular Science Monthly* 15 (October 1894): 852, describes it as "a philosophical romance," or a "life history, with a religious element." The notice also states, "Its purport may be conceived from the dedication: 'To those whose love of Nature has so thoroughly possessed them that they have been able to escape from every vestige of superstition, and as a consequence of which have embraced an unfaltering faith in the loving confidence in righteousness, that sustains all things, and rejoices in all truth.'" The word *entolai* means "commandments" in Greek. Bourland also wrote (with J. E. Godbey), *Religion Philosophically Discussed in a Correspondence between A. M. Bourland and J. E. Godbey* (Van Buren, AR: Argus Job Printery, 1900).

158. Bachelor's response to the book develops themes common to his thought as a freethinker: that there is nothing above nature, and nature therefore demands respect; that religion distracts from respect for nature by creating strife and irrationality; that death represents the dissolution of our individual atoms by which we join the universal whole—the latter reflecting those passages in his diary in which he seems to be echoing themes of Eastern religion that appear to have attracted him (see his essay, "Reasons for Being an Agnostic

[No. 1],'' the 1889 New Year's Eve reflection "Come and Gone," and his diary entries of 1 March 1870 and 31 December 1894).

159. Note again the affirmation of women's rights, which he also makes in his letter to *Zion's Ensign* on social purity for women.

160. The recognition of his own impending demise gives a pensive and melancholy cast to his reflections in this piece.

161. *Sic.* The typesetter has used a capital "R" in place of a capital "B."

162. Bachelor's reflections might have been penned by the early American Quaker naturalist William Bartram, who wrote in his commonplace book in 1783 that he would not leave his garden because, "I love to recall to my mind the cool and silent scenes of Solitude; to oppose them to the heat and bustle of the world; to meditate on those advantages which the great and good of every age have acknowledged they possess . . . when the number of our years bends us to the ground; to contemplate, in short, the benign influence of Solitude upon all the troubles of the heart" (as cited in Thomas P. Slaughter, *The Natures of John and William Bartram* [New York: Random House, 1996], 228).

163. The obituary parallels the diary entry for 11 August 1895, noting Wils's death. The obituary adds details not found in the diary's account of Wils's death. The closing line of the obituary, asking that Fort Smith and Van Buren papers pick it up and copy it, suggests that this obituary was published in a local paper, probably in the county seat of Ozark. It appears that as with the obituary of Henderson Rice, which is signed "Observer" but which notes that Bachelor gave the eulogy at Rice's funeral, the spoken eulogy for Wils was recorded by an observer at the funeral, who has heard the word "supplications" as "supprications."

164. "What shall I say of death? It is birth. It is Life"—this succinctly defines Bachelor's freethinking philosophy of death and the reasons that, in his view, one should face death with stoic resolution, as he maintains his son did.

165. The diary entry for 29 October 1897 recounts the circumstances of Monroe's death on the twenty-second, noting that Monroe had been in the City Hospital in Fort Smith and had died alone, since the family thought he was convalescing. The diary entry ends by noting that "Mother Nature is gathering back her children in her arms. All that live must die—for death feeds on life." The obituary reiterates these themes in almost the same language.

166. As in the obituaries of Rubie Bachelor, Henderson Rice, and W. R. Bachelor Jr., Bachelor takes a "long farewell" of his son Monroe. The phrase is, of course, conventional and has a long history in British and American culture, but it may have appealed to Bachelor as well because of its use by Shakespeare in *Henry VIII* (act 3, scene 2).

167. The references to Monroe's kind-heartedness and willingness to help others bring to mind the diary's account of the 1891 trip to Hot Springs from 2 July to 29 August, when Bachelor and his daughter Nannie are sick for much

of the trip and Monroe nurses them while cooking, tending to the mules, and so forth.

168. "He has joined that innumerable caravan" echoes the 1889 New Year's Eve reflection "Come and Gone," in which Bachelor sees a "passing caravan" all headed in one direction—toward the Ocean of eternity. Monroe has joined the innumerable caravan to the "great universal life," which echoes the "silent Ocean of the future" and "Ocean of eternity" in the "Come and Gone" pieces, and the "vast cosmic repose" of the 1 March 1870 diary entry.

169. Josiah Gilbert Holland, *Bitter-Sweet* (New York: Scribner, 1858), 74.

170. The obituary ends with Bachelor's reflection on the freethinker's asser-tion that there is nothing above nature—a thought he finds consoling here, since death is an aspect of natural life, and Mother Nature takes her children back to her bosom in death. For formulations similar to those with which this eulogy ends, see the eulogies for Sarah Bachelor and Wilson Bachelor Jr.

171. Bachelor is writing after a national meeting of various third-party polit-ical groups in July 1894 to form a coalition. He is fearful of such a coalition, which, in his view, will tend to anarchy, though he grants that the two prevail-ing parties have, by their failure to meet the challenges of the period, helped to create the conditions for these movements to succeed. The 31 December 1894 diary entry talks about the political turmoil of the nation in that year as well, making points similar to those made in this piece. As John Gould Fletcher indicates, the third-party Populist movement, which drew on the Granger, Agricultural Wheel, and Farmers' Alliance movements, was "sweeping the West like wildfire" following the depression of 1893, and had very strong support at this time in some parts of the state: *Arkansas*, 233–34.

172. Bachelor is referring here to the Pullman railroad strike that Eugene Debs had helped to effect as leader of the American Railway Union. Because of Debs's role in the strike, Bachelor regards him as an agitator and distrusts him. As an illustration of how widespread the hysteria about Debs's influence was at this period, and how high the hysteria reached in American academic and journalistic circles, see the anti-Debs cartoon that *Harper's Weekly*—gener-ally considered a moderate-to-left-leaning publication—ran on the cover of its 12 September 1896 edition ("On a Populistic Basis," *Harper's Weekly* 40, no. 2073 [12 September 1896], 889).

173. Here, and with the preceding reference to "dangerous liberty," we dis-cover that Bachelor's constant appeal for liberty and his sympathy for the working classes have political limits, particularly when it comes to the aspira-tions of workers expressed through political parties. "Dangerous liberty" leads the masses in the direction of anarchy, even as they clamor for "governmental pap," he believes.

174. Governor John Peter Altgeld of Illinois, a progressive Democrat, freed the prisoners Oscar Neebe and Michael Schwab in 1893. They had been con-victed for their alleged participation in the Haymarket bombing incident in

May 1886 in Chicago and charged with killing police officer Matthias Degan. There were serious questions about the guilt of those charged with the crime and given capital sentences for it, but also much outrage among social conservatives when Altgeld pardoned Neebe and Schwab. Altgeld was also pilloried for refusing to break the Pullman strike. The typesetter has given Schwab's name as Schuab. This is another of the points at which typesetters have confused Bachelor's "u" and "w," as in the piece "Job and His Book as Viewed in the 19th Century by an Agnostic," where "Uz" is rendered as "W z," and "urticaria" as "wrticarie."

175. This is essentially the same as the diary entry for 31 December 1894. The fact that this New Year's meditation appears in both the diary and in print suggests that Bachelor may either sometimes have written entries in his diary with an eye to publication, or copied material from the diary and sent it to the local newspaper for publication.

176. The word is partly obliterated in the original, and may well be "economics" instead of "economists."

177. The diary entry reads "darklin" at this point, and as my notes for this diary passage suggest, it appears Bachelor intended the word "darkling," spelling it phonetically. Because the word "darkling" is an unfamiliar word in American English, I think the typesetter has changed the word "darklin" to "dark in" for the published piece.

178. This appears to be a companion piece to the "From Pauline" item, which demonstrates the limits of Bachelor's sympathy for workers and workers' rights. This letter is evidently being written after the 1896 Democratic National Convention took place, since it refers to the Pullman strike, Debs and Altgeld and Cleveland, as well as to the convention itself. After the Pullman strike, civil and criminal charges had been brought against the organizers and Debs in particular, and the Supreme Court issued a unanimous decision, *In re Debs,* upholding President Cleveland's decision to send federal troops to break the strike. Altgeld was furious at Cleveland for putting the federal government at the service of the employers, and for rejecting Altgeld's plan to use the state militia to keep order. As the leader of the Illinois delegation to the Democratic Party National Convention in 1896, Altgeld used his influence and blocked Cleveland's bid for renomination at the convention. As in the "From Pauline" piece, Bachelor fears the influence of the third-party socialist and labor movements of the period and the anarchy he believes they're promoting, and he castigates Debs and Altgeld for their involvement in these movements. The heading for this letter spells Bachelor's name as Batchelor, by the way, as does the signature.

179. John McBride had served as a Democratic representative in the Ohio legislature from 1884–1888, and then founded the Ohio People's party in 1891 and was elected president of the United Mine Workers in 1892.

180. This echoes the "Come and Gone" piece written on New Year's Eve

1889, which similarly notes the negative influence of the "wild theories of economists." For American political thinkers fearful of socialism in the latter part of the nineteenth century, this phrase was a code phrase for socialism, which many commentators believed the German historical school of economics to be promoting.

181. This statement draws what is for Bachelor the bottom line in the labor disputes of the 1890s: law and order and the individual liberty of owners trump the liberty and rights of workers when the latter threaten to disrupt civil order and to create anarchy.

Letters of Wilson R. Bachelor (1890s)

1. The original of this letter was in possession of Elsie Hodges and now belongs to her son Norman; the transcript is from a photocopy of the original given by Elsie Hodges to William D. Lindsey. The letter is on Bachelor's letterhead, which identifies him as a dealer in drugs, paints, and oils of Pauline, Arkansas.

2. Melissa Ann Byrd (1849–1936) is the daughter of Bachelor's sister Hannah Delaney Batchelor and her husband, Lawrence Cherry Byrd. Melissa married Joshua Marion Robinson (1853–1925), a son of Washington Robertson and Louisa Waters. Following the death of his first wife, Minerva Monk, in 1860, Bachelor's brother Moses B. Batchelor married Washington Robertson's widow, Louisa Waters Robertson. Washington Robertson had died in 1855. To add to the intricacy of family connections here: as noted in the introductory overview of the life and work of Wilson Bachelor, Lawrence Cherry Byrd was a first cousin of Moses Batchelor's wife, Minerva Monk. Their mothers were sisters—Lovie Cherry Byrd and Talitha Cherry Monk, daughters of Jesse Cherry and Elizabeth Gainer of Martin County, North Carolina. Moses's oldest son, John Wilson Batchelor (1840–1904), would also marry Washington and Louisa Waters Robertson's oldest daughter, Talitha Emeline (1841–1909). In the generation following Washington Robertson and Louisa Waters, the spelling of the surname tended to become Robinson, and may well have been pronounced Robinson even when spelled Robertson. Bachelor will spell it both ways in his letters to his niece Melissa.

3. Ops was a small community in Big Creek Township about nine miles southeast of Malvern, the county seat of Hot Spring County. See "Trails Grow Dim," *The Heritage* [Hot Spring County Historical Society Quarterly] 9 (1982): 81, citing Polk's *Arkansas State Gazetteer and Business Directory* (1892–1893). The community no longer exists.

4. He is referring here to the trip to Hot Springs described in his diary in entries from 2 July to 29 August 1891. It appears that at some point on the trip, perhaps around 14 July, Bachelor, his daughter Nannie, and his son Monroe left Hot Springs to go north to Hot Spring County and visit relatives

there. As the letter suggests, at some point in that portion of the journey the Bachelors stayed with Melissa and her husband, Joshua, and Bachelor is writing to thank them for their hospitality.

5. This is his daughter Alcie Russell—see the diary entry for 24 December 1891.

6. This letter, too, was in possession of Elsie Hodges, who provided William D. Lindsey a photocopy from which this transcript has been made. As with the other letters of Bachelor to his niece Melissa published here, the original now belongs to Elsie Hodges's son Norman. And this letter, as well, is on Bachelor's letterhead.

7. After Bachelor wrote his niece on 21 September, it appears she responded to his letter, and he is now responding to her letter answering his.

8. This suggests that he, Nannie, and Monroe visited other relatives in Hot Spring and Grant Counties on their trip in July and August. Melissa's brothers William Edward, Samuel Delaney, John Lawrence, and Henry C. Byrd were all living near her, and, though Bachelor's brother Moses and his (second) wife, Louisa, had both died, Moses's oldest son, John Wilson Batchelor, and wife, Talitha Emeline Robinson, were living at Poyen in Grant County near the Byrds, and Moses's sons George Richard and Edward Eli Batchelor were living on the eastern side of Grant County near Redfield. Wilson, George, and Edward's half-sister Minerva Louisa Batchelor and her husband, Seaborn Walters, were also living near the Byrds in Hot Spring County at Gifford, and on 20 September 1898, Bachelor would write them.

9. Melissa's resemblance to her mother, Delaney, is a theme Bachelor will repeat in his 6 February 1899 letter to her.

10. See the diary entry for 28 November 1895.

11. The diary has no entries at all for the period from Christmas 1891 to Christmas 1892, so it's difficult to ascertain whether he made this subsequent trip.

12. This is the only instance I've found in which Wilson Bachelor signed his name as "Batchelor." Perhaps he does so in addressing Melissa because his siblings who had settled in Hot Spring and Grant Counties used the latter spelling.

13. The original of this letter was in possession of Flora Rondeau of Malvern, Arkansas, who provided William D. Lindsey with a photocopy from which the transcript has been made.

14. Samuel Walters is Seaborn Walters (1843–1900), husband of Bachelor's niece Minerva Louisa Batchelor (1862–1938), a daughter of Moses B. Batchelor. Seaborn Walters was a native of Wilkinson County, Georgia, son of William B. Walters and Louisa Fountain—see his biography in *Biographical and Historical Memoirs of Central Arkansas* (Chicago: Goodspeed, 1890), 357–58; and Flora Lou Walters Rondeau, "Waters/Walters Family," *The Heritage* [Hot Spring County Historical Society Quarterly] 21 (1994): 143–47. Seaborn

Walters owned a substantial farm of about 500 acres at Wyandotte in Gifford Township about six or seven miles northeast of Malvern. It's not clear to me why Bachelor addresses him as Samuel in this letter. Perhaps this was his middle name. As Frances House-Greiss notes, Wyandotte is now a "ghost town"— see "Ghost Towns of Hot Spring County," *The Heritage* [Hot Spring County Historical Society Quarterly] 7 (1980): 115.

15. The sickness Bachelor mentions here, the malarial fever, is also mentioned in his diary on 1 September 1898, when he says the whole family had been sick.

16. As does the 14 October 1891 letter to Melissa Robertson, this letter indicates that one of the money crops Bachelor was growing was cotton. Cotton was normally picked before December and before snow had fallen. The letter suggests that the reason the picking is delayed is that he did not have the "force" to get the picking done in a timely way—that is, the work force. As the letter notes, Bachelor's only son remaining at home is Vick.

17. The dismissive attitude to the Spanish-American War reflects the diary entry of 31 December 1899. It appears that as a Republican (though one tending to independence in the 1890s), Bachelor was sympathetic to President McKinley, who tended to isolationism but declared the war under pressure, while he was ambivalent about doing so.

18. Bachelor's sons mentioned here are Victor Hugo, John Yeager Lynn, and James Hugo.

19. Evidently Seaborn and Minerva's daughter Roenia/Rosie (1884–1908).

20. Seaborn and Minerva had seven sons, of whom the "wild boy" appears to be one.

21. Bachelor is speaking of his nephew John Lawrence Byrd (1859–1946), a son of Delaney Batchelor and Lawrence Cherry Byrd. Byrd practiced medicine at Gifford and Poyen, and was also a Baptist minister for some years, pastoring the Poyen Missionary Baptist Church. He attended premedical school at Ouachita College and then obtained a medical degree from the University of Arkansas Medical School. For biographical information, see "Dr. Byrd of Big Creek Recalls Early Experiences," *The Heritage* [Hot Spring County Historical Society Quarterly] 2 (1971): 96–98, citing a 7 October 1941 article in the *Malvern Daily Record* by Ernestine Cunningham. The minutes of Poyen Missionary Baptist Church state that John L. Byrd was its third pastor. A constituting member of this church was Samuel Daniel Byrd, uncle of John Lawrence Byrd and a brother of John's father, Lawrence Cherry Byrd. As a freethinker, Bachelor is skeptical about the religious dimensions of his nephew's career, while he's evidently interested in his practice of medicine.

22. As with the previous letters to Melissa Robinson, the original of this letter was in possession of Elsie Hodges, who provided the photocopy from which the transcript has been made.

23. This letter provides further details about Bachelor's sympathy for his niece Melissa. In addition to looking and behaving like his sister Delaney, she had raised her brothers and sisters when their parents both died tragically young during the Civil War. Melissa was the only daughter, and had six brothers, one of whom, Wilson Batchelor Byrd, had predeceased his parents. The youngest two children, Henry and John Lawrence, were only infants when their parents died. The oldest son, Pleasant A., married in 1864 and moved to Texas after 1870, taking the two young boys to Texas with him for some years.

24. This letter provides information about the death of Bachelor's sister Delaney found in no other sources: that she "succombed to disease and mental hallucination" in the "wilds of Arkansas." As Bachelor notes, he never saw his sister again after she and husband, Lawrence C. Byrd, moved to Arkansas in 1846 when he was nineteen years old. The date and circumstances of the deaths of Lawrence and Delaney Byrd are unclear. The biography of their son John Lawrence, "Dr. Byrd of Big Creek," states that his father died fighting in the Civil War, but there is no service record for him as either a Union or a Confederate soldier. In a 22 April 1997 letter to William D. Lindsey, Lucille Goodman Mason of Malvern, Arkansas, a descendant of Lawrence Cherry Byrd's sister Mary C. Byrd, says that family stories shared with her by descendants of John Lawrence Byrd state that Union soldiers or marauders hanged Lawrence C. Byrd during the Civil War in an attempt to force him to disclose the whereabouts of money they thought he had buried. These family stories also state that those who perpetrated this act then burned down his family's house and Delaney died of exposure following this. It appears these events would have occurred sometime before 1863 and during the war. *Biographical and Historical Memoirs of Central Arkansas* notes that though initially, most of the men from Hot Spring County who served in the war were CSA soldiers, as the war drew to a close, a number of these then joined Union regiments. These included George Anderson Robinson, a brother of Melissa's husband, Joshua, who was first a CSA soldier and then became a Union officer after having been captured by Union troops in Kentucky. The county was torn by strife in the latter years of the war, with lawless bands of marauders claiming to represent either side roaming the area and terrorizing citizens (see Goolsby, *Our Timberland Home*, 93–94).

According to Sue Bricelin Fletcher, *Reminiscences of Arkansas Pioneer* (Little Rock: Arkansas Pioneer Association, 1912), John Young Lindsey, a pioneer Baptist minister of Saline County, was also hanged by bushwhackers or soldiers during the war in an attempt to force him to disclose where he had hidden money (14). Descendants of Lindsey pastored the Baptist church in Poyen later pastored by John Lawrence Byrd. Moses Batchelor and his second wife, Louisa Waters, are buried in Lindsey Cemetery in Poyen, named for this Lindsey family.

25. The widow Elliott is likely John Lawrence Byrd's mother-in-law, Maranda Jane Smith Elliott (1831–1909), widow of Hardy Elliott. Their daughter Susan Catherine married John Lawrence Byrd on 27 October 1881 in Hot Spring County.

26. Bachelor is referring to Elijah Warrington, a contemporary of his (b. 1834 in Alabama), who lives near Melissa and Joshua in Big Creek Township.

27. John W. Bachelor is John Wilson Batchelor, oldest son of Moses Batchelor by his wife, Minerva Monk, who married the oldest daughter of Moses's second wife, Louisa Waters (Robertson), Talitha Emeline (who was also a sister of Melissa's husband, Joshua). John W. Batchelor had died in 1894, hence his uncle's question in 1899 about who was living at his nephew's old place, which had previously been Moses's farm.

28. "The children" to whom Dr. Bachelor sends love are Melissa and Joshua's two daughters and five sons.

29. The original of this letter was also in possession of Elsie Hodges of Pine Bluff, who provided the photocopy from which this transcript has been made. The letter has a note penned at the top, which reads, "Tell Melissa I will write her soon." The letter to Melissa dated 5 September 1899 is evidently the one Bachelor is promising to send with this note.

30. Jane is Janice Delaney Byrd (1879–1963), a daughter of Samuel Delaney Byrd (1852–1890), a son of Lawrence Cherry Byrd and Hannah Delaney Batchelor, who was a teacher prior to her marriage to Madison Levi McBurnett in Jefferson County in 1907. It appears from Bachelor's letter that she and her aunt Melissa had written him at the same time, perhaps sending both letters together.

31. Jane's mother, Polly Ann Thrower Byrd, had died in 1883, and her father in 1890. It appears she is keeping house for an uncle, possibly a maternal uncle in Jefferson County.

32. The word is difficult to read, in part, because the ink on the downstroke of what appears to be an initial "p" is very faint. I think "protect" is correct, but am not absolutely certain.

33. Bachelor's remarks about the treatment of women are consistent with his occasional piece published in *Zion's Ensign* supporting women's equality with men and women's rights. See also his diary entries for 31 December 1894, 2 January 1895, and Christmas Day 1897.

34. The picture that Bachelor sends his great-niece with this letter passed from Jane to her daughter Elsie McBurnett Hodges and from Elsie to her son Norman Hodges of Little Rock.

35. This is another letter that belonged to Elsie Hodges, who provided the photocopy from which the letter has been transcribed.

36. The two families to which Bachelor refers, which Melissa had raised, are, of course, her five brothers (following their parents' deaths), and then her own family of seven children.

37. Bachelor's diary entry for 4 August 1899 says that August had begun with temperatures above 100°F.

38. The July–August 1891 account of the trip of Bachelor, Nannie, and Monroe to Hot Springs notes that Nannie was sick for much of the trip.

39. A nephew of Bachelor, Moses's son Daniel Tucker Batchelor, was crippled by rheumatoid arthritis throughout much of his life. The illness has recurred in subsequent generations of families descending from Moses. For instance, a son of Moses's son George Richard—his son George Hugh Batchelor—also suffered from crippling arthritis.

40. The account of the whereabouts of his children Bachelor provides here echoes the recurrent pattern in his diary, particularly at Christmastime and New Year's, when he frequently notes where each family member is living or happens to be as that particular holiday arrives. Alcie has just gone back to Texas on 30 January according to his diary entry of 11 February 1899.

41. This is a detail not mentioned in Bachelor's diary. Though he frequently mentions that the family played the organ at their musical gatherings, and that his daughter Pauline taught organ in the local community after having studied music with Carrie White, he doesn't mention in the diary that it was he himself who introduced the organ to his community.

Appendices

1. The bottom portion of the eulogy is, unfortunately, torn away and missing.

2. From this point, the text is torn and missing. The word "third"—for the third resolution—can be made out, but nothing below it.

Works Cited

Books

Allen, James, Hilton Als, John Lewis, and Leon F. Litwack, ed. *Without Sanctuary: Lynching Photography in America*. Santa Fe: Twin Palms, 2000.

Amireh, Amal. *The Factory Girl and the Seamstress: Imagining Gender and Class in Nineteenth-Century American Fiction*. London: Routledge, 2000.

Aptheker, Herbert, ed. *A Documentary History of the Negro People in the United States*. Vol. 2. New York: Citadel, 1970.

Arkansas State Superintendent of Public Instruction. *Biennial Report of the State Superintendent of Public Instruction*. Little Rock: Joseph Griffith, 1884.

Ashe, Samuel A. *History of North Carolina*. Greensboro, NC: Charles L. Van Noppen, 1908.

Ashe, Samuel A., et al. *Biographical History of North Carolina from Colonial Times to the Present*. Greensboro, NC: Charles L. Van Noppen, 1905.

Audubon, John James. *Birds of America* (1840). Vol. 5. Ed. J. W. Audubon. Repr. New York: Roe Lockwood & Son, 1861.

Bailey, Kenneth W. *Southern White Protestantism in the Twentieth Century*. New York: Harper & Row, 1964.

Baird, W. David. *Medical Education in Arkansas, 1879–1978*. Memphis: Memphis State UP, 1979.

Barbou, Alfred. *Victor Hugo and His Times*. Trans. Ellen E. Frewer. Oxford: Oxford UP, 1882.

Barnes, Kenneth C. *Journey of Hope: The Back-to-Africa Movement in Arkansas in the Late 1800s*. Chapel Hill: Univ. of North Carolina Press, 2004.

————. *Who Killed John Clayton? Political Violence and the Emergence of the New South, 1861–1893*. Durham, NC: Duke UP, 1998.

Barnes, Robert W. *Colonial Families of Anne Arundel County, Maryland*. Westminster, MD: Family Line Publications, 1996.

Bartram, William. *Travels*. Philadelphia: James & Johnson, 1791. Ed. Mark Van Doren. New York: Dover, 1928.

Battle, Kemp Plummer. *Memories of an Old-Time Tar Heel*. Ed. William James Battle. Chapel Hill: Univ. of North Carolina Press, 1945.

Beecher, Henry Ward. *Hell, Warm Words on the Doctrine of Eternal Salvation*. London: Watts & Co., 1882.

Biggs, Rayma, and Mary Louise Biggs. *The Jesse Tree: History of Biggs-Dexter Families in America*. Iuka, MS, 1980.

Billingsley, Carolyn Earle. *Communities of Kinship: Antebellum Families and the Settlement of the Cotton Frontier.* Athens: Univ. of Georgia Press, 2004.

Bishir, Catherine W., and Michael T. Southern. *A Guide to the Historic Architecture of Eastern North Carolina.* Chapel Hill: Univ. of North Carolina Press, 1996.

Black, Susan Easton. *Early Members of the Reorganized Church of Jesus Christ of Latter Day Saints.* Vol. 1. Salt Lake City: Brigham Young Univ., 1993.

Blair, Diane D., and Jay Barth. *Arkansas Politics and Government.* 2nd ed. Lincoln: Univ. of Nebraska Press, 2005.

Blevins, Brooks. *Hill Folks: A History of Arkansas Ozarkers & Their Image.* Chapel Hill: Univ. of North Carolina Press, 2002.

Blum, Edward J., and W. Scott Poole. *Vale of Tears: New Essays on Religion and Reconstruction.* Macon: Mercer UP, 2005.

Boddie, John Bennett. *Historical Southern Families.* Vol. 8 (1964). Repr. Baltimore: Geneal. Publ. Co., 1970.

———. *Seventeenth-Century Isle of Wight County, Virginia.* Chicago: Chicago Law Printing Co., 1938.

Bolsterli, Margaret Jones, ed. *A Remembrance of Eden: Harriet Bailey Bullock Daniel's Memories of a Frontier Plantation in Arkansas, 1849–1872.* Fayetteville: Univ. of Arkansas Press, 1993.

Bolton, S. Charles. *Arkansas, 1800–1860: Remote and Restless.* Fayetteville: Univ. of Arkansas Press, 1999.

Bourland, Addison McArthur. *Entolai, or This Letter to Those I Love about Science and the Ideal.* Van Buren, AR: Lloyd Garrison, 1893.

Brazelton, B. G. (Benjamin G.). *History of Hardin County, Tennessee.* Nashville: Cumberland Presbyterian, 1885.

Bridenbaugh, Carl. *Jamestown, 1544–1699.* New York: Oxford UP, 1980.

Bronson, C. P. *Elocution.* Louisville: Morton & Griswold, 1845.

Bruce, Philip A. *Institutional History of Virginia in the Seventeenth Century.* Vol. 1. New York: G. P. Putnam's Sons, 1910.

Bryan, Lettice. *The Kentucky Housewife* (1839). Ed. Bill Neal. Columbia: Univ. of South Carolina Press, 1991.

Bunsen, Christian J. B. *Outlines of the Philosophy of Universal History as Applied to Language and Religion.* London: Longmans, Green & Co., 1854.

Catton, Bruce. *Grant Moves South.* Boston: Little, Brown, 1960.

Cheyne, Thomas K. *Origin and Religious Concepts of the Psalter.* London: Kegan, Paul, Trench, Trübner, & Co., 1891.

Clayton, Powell. *The Aftermath of the Civil War, in Arkansas.* New York: Neale, 1915.

Coldham, Peter Wilson. *The Bristol Registers of Servants Sent to Foreign Plantations, 1654–1686.* Baltimore: Geneal. Publ. Co., 1988.

———. *English Adventurers and Emigrants, 1609–1660: Abstracts of Examinations in the High Court of Admiralty With Reference to Colonial America.* Baltimore: Geneal. Publ. Co., 1984.

Croll, James. *Climate and Cosmology*. New York: Appleton, 1886.

————. *Climate and Time*. New York: Appleton, 1875.

Dabney, Joseph E. *Smokehouse Ham, Spoon Bread, & Scuppernong Wine*. Nashville: Cumberland House, 1989.

Daniels, Larry. *Shiloh: The Battle That Changed the Civil War*. New York: Simon & Schuster, 1997.

Davidson, Alan. *The Oxford Companion to Food*. Oxford: Oxford UP, 1999.

Davidson, Donald. *The Tennessee*. Vol. 1: *The Old River: Frontier to Secession*. Nashville: J. S. Sanders, 1946.

Davis, David E. *History of Tyrrell County, North Carolina*. Norfolk: Joseph Christopher, 1963.

Davis, Richard Beale. *A Colonial Southern Bookshelf: Reading in the Eighteenth Century*. Athens: Univ. of Georgia Press, 1979.

D'Emilio, John, and Estelle B. Freedman. *Intimate Matters: A History of Sexuality in America*. New York: Harper & Row, 1988.

Dobson, David. *Scottish Emigration to Colonial America*. Athens: Univ. of Georgia Press, 1994.

Dougan, Michael B. *Arkansas Odyssey: The Saga of Arkansas from Prehistoric Times to Present*. Little Rock: Rose, 1995.

Dozier, Rebecca L. *Twelve Northampton County, North Carolina, Families*. Baltimore: Gateway Press, 2004.

Draper, John William. *History of the Conflict between Religion and Science*. New York: Appleton, 1874.

Egerton, John. *Southern Food*. New York: Alfred A. Knopf, 1987.

Farrar, Frederic W. *Eternal Hope*. New York: E. P. Dutton, 1878.

————. *Mercy and Judgment*. New York: Macmillan, 1881.

Featherstonhaugh, George W. *Excursion through the Slave States*. London: John Murray, 1844.

Finger, John R. *Tennessee Frontiers: Three Regions in Transition*. Bloomington: Indiana UP, 2001.

Fischer, David Hackett. *Albion's Seed: Four British Folkways in America*. New York: Oxford UP, 1989.

Fletcher, John Gould. *Arkansas*. Chapel Hill: Univ. of North Carolina Press, 1947. Repr. Fayetteville: Univ. of Arkansas Press, 1989.

Fletcher, Sue Bricelin. *Reminiscences of Arkansas Pioneer*. Little Rock: Arkansas Pioneer Association, 1912.

Foster, Gaines M. *Moral Reconstruction: Christian Lobbyists and the Federal Legislation of Morality, 1865–1920*. Chapel Hill: Univ. of North Carolina Press, 2002.

Gerstäcker, Friedrich. *Die Regulatoren in Arkansas*. Dresden: Otto Wigand, 1846.

————. *Streif- und Jagdzüge durch die Vereinigten Staaten Nord-Amerikas*. Dresden: Arnold, 1844.

Glassie, Henry. *Pattern in the Material Folk Culture of the Eastern United States.* Philadelphia: Univ. of Pennsylvania Press, 1968.

Gordon, Linda. *Woman's Body, Woman's Rights: A Social History of Birth Control in America.* New York: Penguin, 1977.

Goodspeed Publishing Company. *Biographical and Historical Memoirs of Central Arkansas.* Chicago: Goodspeed, 1890.

———. *History of Benton, Washington, Carroll, Madison, Crawford, Franklin, and Sebastian Counties, Arkansas.* Chicago: Goodspeed, 1889.

———. *History of Tennessee, from the Earliest Time to the Present, Together with an Historical and a Biographical Sketch of Henderson, Chester, McNairy, Decatur, and Hardin Counties.* Chicago: Goodspeed, 1886.

Goolsby, Elwin L. *Our Timberland Home: A History of Grant County, Arkansas.* Little Rock: Rose, 1984.

Greenleaf, Simon. *The Testimony of the Evangelists, Examined by the Rules of Evidence Administered in Courts of Justice.* New York: J. Cockcroft and Co., 1846.

———. *Treatise on the Law of Evidence.* 3 vols. Boston: C. C. Little and J. Brown, 1842–1853.

Haley, Alex, and David Stevens. *Queen.* New York: Avon, 1994.

Hanson, Gerald T., and Carl H. Moneyhon. *Historical Atlas of Arkansas.* Norman: Univ. of Oklahoma Press, 1989.

Harbury, Katherine E. *Colonial Virginia's Cooking Dynasty.* Columbia: Univ. of South Carolina Press, 2004.

Harriot, Thomas. *Briefe and True Report of the New Found Land of Virginia.* London, 1588.

Hatfield, April Lee. *Atlantic Virginia: Intercolonial Relations in the Seventeenth Century.* Philadelphia: Univ. of Pennsylvania Press, 2004.

Hays, Tony. *No Man's Land: The Civil War and Reconstruction in Hardin County, Tennessee.* Savannah: Tennessee River Press, 2001.

———. *On the Banks of the River: A History of Hardin County, Tennessee.* Savannah: Tennessee River Museum, 1996.

Heiskell, Joseph Brown. *Reports of Cases Argued and Determined in the Supreme Court of Tennessee.* Vol. 3. Nashville: Jones, Purvis, 1872.

Herman, Arthur. *How the Scots Invented the Modern World.* New York: Three Rivers, 2001.

Hill, Samuel S., ed. *Encyclopedia of Religion in the South.* Macon: Mercer UP, 1984.

———. *Religion in the Southern States: A Historical Study.* Macon: Mercer UP, 1983.

Hinshaw, William Wade, and Thomas Worth Marshall. *Encyclopedia of American Quaker Genealogy.* Vol. 6: *Virginia.* Ann Arbor: Edwards Bros., 1950.

Hitt, Andrew P. *Short Life Sketches of Some Prominent Hardin Countians.* Savannah: Fundco, 1980.

Holland, Josiah Gilbert. *Bitter-Sweet*. New York: Scribner, 1858.

Horn, James. *Adapting to a New World: English Society in the Seventeenth-Century Chesapeake*. Chapel Hill: Univ. of North Carolina Press, 1994.

Huddleston, Duane, Sammie Rose, and Pat Wood. *Steamboats and Ferries on the White River: A Heritage Revisited*. Fayetteville: Univ. of Arkansas Press, 1999.

Huxley, Thomas Henry. *Collected Essays*. Vol. 5: *Science and Christian Tradition*. London: Macmillan, 1889.

Huxley, Thomas Henry, and William Jay Youmans. *The Elements of Physiology and Hygiene: A Text-Book for Educational Institutions*. New York: Appleton, 1868.

Ingersoll, Robert Green. *Ingersollia: Gems of Thought from the Lectures and Speeches of Col. Robert G. Ingersoll*. Chicago: Belford Clarke & Co., 1882.

———. *The Limitations of Toleration: A Discussion between Robert G. Ingersoll, Frederic R. Coudert, Stewart L. Woodford, before the Nineteenth Century Club, of New York, at the Metropolitan Opera House*. New York: Truth Seeker, 1889.

Ingersoll, Robert Green, and Henry Morehouse Taber. *Faith or Fact*. New York: Peter Eckler, 1897.

Ingersoll, Robert Green, and Herman E. Kittredge. *The Works of Robert G. Ingersoll*. Vol. 4: *Lectures*. New York: Dresden, C. P. Farrell, 1909.

Jacoby, Susan. *Freethinkers: A History of American Secularism*. New York: Henry Holt, 2004.

James, Thomas. *Three Years among the Indians and Mexicans*. Waterloo, IL: War Eagle, 1846.

Johnson, Ben F. III. *Arkansas in Modern America*. Fayetteville: Univ. of Arkansas Press, 2000.

Johnson, Edward. *Wonder-Working Providence of Sion's Saviour in New England*. London: Nathaniel Brooke, 1653.

Jones, Rufus. *The Quakers in the American Colonies*. New York: Russell & Russell, 1962.

Kay, L. Michael, and Lorin Lee Cary. *Slavery in North Carolina*. Chapel Hill: Univ. of North Carolina Press, 1995.

Killebrew, J. B. *Introduction to the Resources of Tennessee*. Vol. 2. Nashville: Tavel, Eastman & Harrell, 1874.

Lackey, Martha Ann Williams, and Mary Lou Clayton Williams. *The Descendants of John Williams and Martha Biggs of Williamston, Martin County, North Carolina*. Savannah, 1997.

Lambeth, Mary Weeks. *Memories and Records of Eastern North Carolina*. Nashville: Curley, 1957.

Langford, Ella Molloy. *Johnson County, Arkansas, the First Hundred Years*. Clarksville, AR: Sallis, Threadgill & Sallis, 1921.

Lefler, H. T., and A. R. Newsome. *The History of a Southern State: North Carolina*. 3rd ed. Chapel Hill: Univ. of North Carolina Press, 1973.

Manning, Francis M., and W. H. Booker. *Martin County [North Carolina] History*, vol. 1. Williamston, NC: Enterprise, 1977.

Mathews, Shailer. *New Faith For Old*. New York: Macmillan, 1936.

McAlester, Virginia and Lee. *A Field Guide to American Houses*. New York: Knopf, 1989.

McCrady, Edward, and Samuel A. Ashe. *Cyclopedia of Eminent and Representative Men of the Carolinas of the Nineteenth Century*. Vol. 2. Madison, WI: Brant & Fuller, 1892.

McIntosh, Charles F. *Abstracts of Norfolk County Wills*. Richmond: Colonial Dames of America in the State of Virginia, 1914.

McNeilly, Donald P. *The Old South Frontier: Cotton Plantations and the Formation of Arkansas Society, 1819–1861*. Fayetteville: Univ. of Arkansas Press, 2000.

Miller, Kelly. *Race Adjustment: Essays on the Negro in America*. New York: Neale, 1909.

Moneyhon, Carl H. *The Impact of the Civil War and Reconstruction on Arkansas: Persistence in the Midst of Ruin*. Fayetteville: Univ. of Arkansas Press, 2002.

Monks, William. *A History of Southern Missouri and Northern Arkansas: Being an Account of the Early Settlements, the Civil War, the Ku-Klux, and Times of Peace*. West Plains, MO: West Plains Journal Co., 1907.

Morison, Samuel Eliot. *The Oxford History of the American People*. New York: Oxford UP, 1965.

Muir, John. *Original Sanskrit Texts on the Origin and History of the People of India, Their Religion and Institutions*. Vol. 1. London: Trübner, 1868.

Müller, Max. *Introduction to the Science of Religion*. London: Longmans, Green & Co., 1873.

North Carolina General Assembly. *Muster Rolls of the Soldiers of the War of 1812: Detached from the Militia of North Carolina, in 1812 and 1814*. Raleigh: Charles C. Raboteau, 1851.

Nugent, Nell Marion. *Cavaliers and Pioneers: Abstracts of Virginia Land Patents and Grants, 1623–1666*. Vol. 1. Baltimore: Geneal. Publ. Co., 1963.

Nuttall, Thomas. *Journal of Travels into the Arkansas Territory*. Philadelphia: Palmer, 1821.

Paine, Thomas. *Rights of Man*. London: J. S. Jordan, 1791.

Paley, William. *Natural Theology*. London: J. Faulder, 1802.

Palmer, William P., ed. *Calendar of Virginia State Papers*. Richmond: R. F. Walker, 1875.

Polk, R. L. *Arkansas State Gazetteer of Business Directories*. St. Louis: R. L. Polk Co., 1884.

Powell, William S., ed. *Encyclopedia of North Carolina*. Chapel Hill: Univ. of North Carolina Press, 2006.

Pruitt, Wade. *Bugger Saga*. Columbia, TN: P-Vine Press, 1977.

Rafferty, Milton D. *The Ozarks: Land and Life*. Fayetteville: Univ. of Arkansas Press, 2001.

Ragsdale, William Oates. *They Sought a Land: A Settlement in the Arkansas River Valley*. Fayetteville: Univ. of Arkansas Press, 1997.

Randolph, Mary. *Virginia House-Wife* (1824). Ed. Karen Hess. Columbia: Univ. of South Carolina Press, 1984.

Rieser, Andrew. *The Chautauqua Moment: Protestants, Progressives, and the Culture of Modern Liberalism*. New York: Columbia UP, 2003.

Riggle, Herbert McLellan. *Man: His Present and Future*. Anderson, IN: Gospel Trumpet Company, 1904.

Rohrbough, Malcolm J. *The Trans-Appalachian Frontier*. New York: Oxford UP, 1978.

Root, Waverly. *Eating in America*. New York: William Morrow, 1976.

Royal Commission on Capital Punishment. *Report of the Capital Punishment Commission*. London: Eyre & Spottiswoode, 1866.

Rupke, Nicolaas A., ed. *Medical Geography in Historical Perspective*. London: Wellcome Trust Centre for the History of Medicine at UCL, 2000.

Scharf, Thomas J. *History of Saint Louis City and County, From the Earliest Periods to the Present Day: Including Biographical Sketches of Representative Men*. Vol. 2. Philadelphia: Louis H. Everts & Co., 1883.

Sevier, Cora Bales, and Nancy S. Madden. *Sevier Family History*. Washington, DC: Kaufmann, 1961.

Slaughter, Thomas P. *The Natures of John and William Bartram*. New York: Random House, 1996.

Smallwood, Marilu Burch. *Some Colonial and Revolutionary Families of North Carolina*. Vol. 3. Gainesville, FL: Storter, 1976.

Smith, Timothy B. *The Untold Story of Shiloh: The Battle and the Battlefield*. Knoxville: Univ. of Tennessee Press, 2006.

———. *This Great Battlefield of Shiloh: History, Memory, and the Establishment of a Civil War National Military Park*. Knoxville: Univ. of Tennessee Press, 2004.

Speake, Jennifer, ed. *Oxford Dictionary of Proverbs*. New York: Oxford UP, 1998.

Stockley, Grif. *Ruled by Race*. Fayetteville: Univ. of Arkansas Press, 1999.

Stricklin, Mary Elizabeth. *History of Cherry's Chapel United Methodist Church*. Savannah: Savannah Publ. Co., 1983.

Sutherland, Donald E., ed. *Guerillas, Unionists, and Violence on the Confederate Home Front*. Fayetteville: Univ. of Arkansas Press, 1999.

Taylor, Joe Gray. *Eating, Drinking, and Visiting in the South*. Baton Rouge: Louisiana State UP, 1982.

Tenorio-Trillo, Mauricio. *Mexico at the World's Fairs: Crafting a Modern Nation*. Berkeley and Los Angeles: Univ. of California Press, 1996.

Thompson, George H. *Arkansas and Reconstruction: The Influence of Geography, Economics, and Personality*. Port Washington, NY: Kennikat Press, 1976.

Threlfall, John Brooks. *Fifty Great Migration Colonists to New England and Their Origins*. Madison, WI, 1990.

Tucker, David M. *Arkansas: A People and Their Reputation*. Memphis: Memphis State Univ. Press, 1985.

Twain, Mark. *Life on the Mississippi*. Boston: James R. Osgood, 1883.

Tyree, Marion Cabell. *Housekeeping in Old Virginia*. Louisville: John P. Morton, 1879.

U.S. Senate. *Report of the National Conservation Commission.* Vol. 3. Washington, DC: Govt. Printing Office, 1909.

Ussher, James. *Annales Veteris Testamenti*. London: Crook & Baker, 1650.

Vest, Mayme. *Remembering the Small Communities of South Franklin County, Arkansas.* Branch, AR, 1993.

Warren, Sidney. *American Freethought 1860–1914*. New York: Columbia UP, 1943.

Watkins, James L. *Production and Price of Cotton for One Hundred Years.* Washington, DC: Govt. Printing Office, 1895.

Watson, A. A. *A History of Hardin County, Tennessee: "Bits of Hardin County History."* Ed. Ronney Brewington. Savannah: Hardin County Hist. Soc., 2004.

Way, Frederick. *Way's Packet Directory: Passenger Steamboats of the Mississippi River System Since the Advent of Photography in Mid-Continent America.* Athens: Ohio UP, 1999.

Weeks, Stephen B. *Southern Quakers and Slavery*. New York: Bergman, 1968.

Whayne, Jeannie M. *A New Plantation South: Land, Labor, and Federal Favor in Twentieth-Century Arkansas.* Charlottesville: Univ. of Virginia Press, 1996.

White, Lonnie J. *Politics on the Southwestern Frontier: Arkansas Territory, 1819–1836.* Memphis: Memphis State UP, 1964.

Whitehead, Fred, and Verle Muhrer, ed. *Freethought on the American Frontier.* Buffalo: Prometheus, 1992.

Whiting, Bartlett Jere. *Early American Proverbs and Proverbial Phrases*. Cambridge: Harvard UP, 1977.

Wigginton, Eliot, ed. *Foxfire 4*. Garden City, NY: Anchor/Doubleday, 1977.

Wilcox, Pearl. *Saints of the Reorganization in Missouri*. Independence, 1974.

Williams, Ruth Smith, and Margaret Glenn Griffin. *Bible Records of Early Edgecombe.* Rocky Mount: Dixie Letter Service, 1958.

Wilson, Charles Reagan, and William Ferris, ed. *Encyclopedia of Southern Culture.* Chapel Hill: Univ. of North Carolina Press, 1989.

Wolcott, Imogene. *The New England Yankee Cookbook*. New York: Coward-McCann, 1939.

Wood, George Bacon. *A Treatise on the Practice of Medicine*. Philadelphia: Grigg, Elliott & Co., 1847.

Woodruff, Wilford. *Wilford Woodruff's Journal, 1833–1898: Typescript*. Ed. Scott G. Kenney. Vol. 1: *29 Dec. 1833–1893*. Midvale, UT: Signature, 1983.

Works Project Administration. *Arkansas: A Guide to the State* (1941). Repr. as *WPA Guide to 1930s Arkansas.* Lawrence: Univ. Press of Kansas, 1987.

Worrall, Jay. *The Friendly Virginians*. Athens, GA: Iberian, 1994.

Wyatt-Brown, Bertram. *Southern Honor: Ethics and Behavior in the Old South.* New York: Oxford UP, 1982.

Articles and Essays

Argyle, E. Malcolm. "Report from Arkansas." *Christian Recorder* (24 March 1892). Transcribed in *A Documentary History of the Negro People in the United States*. Vol. 2. 793–94.

Ashe, Samuel A. "John Porter." *Biographical History of North Carolina from Colonial Times to the Present*. 369–73.

Ayers, Edward L. "Honor." *Encyclopedia of Southern Culture*. 1483–84.

Bolsterli, Margaret Jones. "Introduction." *A Remembrance of Eden: Harriet Bailey Bullock Daniel's Memories of a Frontier Plantation in Arkansas, 1849–1872*. 1–23.

Brown, Douglas Summers. "Virginia Yearly Meeting." *Encyclopedia of American Quaker Genealogy*. Vol. 6: *Virginia*. 5–13.

"Coggia's Comet." *New York Times* 23, no. 7113 (4 July 1874), 5, col. 3.

Cohen, C. "Christianity and Women—II." *The Freethinker* 27, no. 12 (24 March 1907), 179–80.

Collins, Wilkie. "The New Magdalen." *Harper's New Monthly* 46, no. 274 (March 1873), 597–607.

Conant, S. S. "Earth and Air." *Harper's New Monthly* 46, no. 274 (March 1873), 545–62.

Conference of Elders and Members, LDS Church. "Report, Lincoln, Vermont." *Times and Seasons* 2, no. 9 (1 March 1841), 338–39.

Crellin, Paul I. "Country Doctor." *Encyclopedia of Southern Culture*. 1366.

Cunningham, Ernestine. "Dr. Byrd of Big Creek Recalls Early Experiences." *The Heritage* [Hot Spring County Hist. Soc.] 2 (1971): 96–98.

"Death of W. H. Cherry." *Courier* [Savannah] 1, no. 1 (15 September 1885), 2.

Dillon, Charles. "The Pilgrim's Scrip: Grover Cleveland—As Seen by a Telegraph Operator Who Handled His Political Secrets." *American Magazine* 66, no. 6 (October 1908), 618–19.

"Disaster on the Missouri: Sinking of the Steamboat *St. Luke*—Ten or Eleven Lives Believed to Have Been Lost." *New York Times* 24, no. 7373 (4 May 1875), 1, col. 4.

Eleanor. "Social Purity." *Zion's Ensign* 4, no. 5 (28 January 1893), 6.

Ferris, William. "Mules." *Encyclopedia of Southern Culture*. 511–12.

French, Elizabeth. "Bigge Wills and Records." *New England Historical and Genealogical Register* 56 (1912): 54–61.

"From the Tennessee River: A Battle Impending between the Forces under Generals Grant and Beauregard." *Chicago Times* 7, no. 191 (31 March 1862), 2, col. 8.

"From the Tennessee River: A Steamboat Trip from Fort Henry to Savannah." *Chicago Times* 8, no. 182 (19 March 1862), 1, col. 8.

"From the Tennessee River: Steamer *Empress* off for the Wars." *Daily Missouri Republican* 40, no. 71 (25 March 1862), 1, col. 7.

Greenstone, Gerry. "The History of Bloodletting." *BC Medical Journal* 52, no. 1 (January–February 2010): 12–14.

Grem, Darren E. "Sam Jones, Sam Hose, and the Theology of Racial Violence." *Georgia Historical Quarterly* 90 (Spring 2006): 35–61.

Harbert, P. M. "Early History of Hardin County." *West Tennessee Historical Society Papers* 1 (1947): 38–67.

Hardy, Thomas. "On the Western Circuit." *Harper's Weekly* 35, no. 1823 (26 November 1891), 946–49.

Hathaway, J. R. B. "Abstract of Conveyances [From Register's Office of Chowan County, Book C, No. 1]." *North Carolina Historical and Genealogical Register* 2, no. 2 (April 1901): 283–96.

Hays, Tony. "Savannah Male Academy." *Courier* [Savannah] 102, no. 23 (5 June 1986), 17, col. 1–4.

House-Greiss, Frances. "Ghost Towns of Hot Spring County." *The Heritage* [Hot Spring County Hist. Soc.] 7 (1980): 115–18.

Hunter, Jesse D. ("Missionary Report.") *Times and Seasons* 1, no. 4 (February 1840), 59.

Ingersoll, Robert. "A Christmas Sermon." *Evening Telegram* [New York] 24, no. 8059 (19 December 1891), 5, col. 1–2.

James, Edward. "The Church in Lower Norfolk County." *Lower Norfolk County, Virginia, Antiquary* 2, no. 3 (1897): 83–88.

———. "The Church in Lower Norfolk County." *Norfolk County, Virginia, Antiquary* 5, no. 1 (1906): 122–23.

Ketchell, Aaron K. "Contesting Tradition and Combating Intolerance: A History of Freethought in Kansas." *Great Plains Quarterly* 20, no. 4 (2000): 281–95.

Lindsey, William D. "Brown or White Sugar: The Story of a Mixed-Race Plantation Family in Nineteenth-Century Arkansas, Part 4." *Arkansas Family Historian* 48, no. 4 (December 2010): 235–47.

Litwack, Leon. "Hellhounds." *Without Sanctuary: Lynching Photography in America.* 8–37.

Mackey, Robert B. "Bushwhackers, Provosts, and Tories: The Guerilla War in Arkansas." *Guerillas, Unionists, and Violence on the Confederate Home Front.* 171–85.

McIntosh, Charles F. "Ages of Lower Norfolk County People, Abstracted from Depositions in Book E, 1666–1675, Norfolk County Clerk's Office." *William and Mary Quarterly* 25, no. 2, series 1 (October 1916): 135–36.

McPherson, Elizabeth Gregory. "Nathaniel Batts, Landholder on Pasquotank River, 1660." *North Carolina Historical Review* 43 (1966): 66–81.

Moore, Mrs. W. W. "Diary of Mrs. T. Moore." *Franklin County Historical Association Observer* 1, no. 1 (1976–1977): 6–15.

"Notice to Strahon Monk, Estate of Nottingham Monk." *Raleigh Register* 24, no. 1324 (17 June 1825), 4, col. 4.

"Obituary of William Skidmore Batchelor." *The Saints' Herald* 43, no. 29 (15 July 1896), 480.

"Obituary of William Skidmore Batchelor." *Zion's Ensign* 7, no. 26 (1896), 8.

"On a Populistic Basis." *Harper's Weekly* 40, no. 2073 (12 September 1896), 88.

Pillsbury, Richard, and Suzanne Andres. "Courthouse Square." *Encyclopedia of Southern Culture*. 569–70.

Poole, W. Scott. "Confederate Apocalypse: Theology and Violence in the White Reconstruction South." *Vale of Tears: New Essays on Religion and Reconstruction*. 36–52.

Porter, John W. H. "Norfolk Quakers." *Richmond Dispatch* 13, no. 211 (3 December 1892), 7, col. 1–2.

Ralph, Julian. "Our Exposition at Chicago." *Harper's Monthly* 84, no. 500 (January 1892), 205–15.

Rondeau, Flora Lou Walters. "Waters/Walters Family." *The Heritage* [Hot Spring County Hist. Soc.] 21 (1994): 143–47.

Smith, Claiborne. "Porters of Lower Norfolk County, Virginia, and North Carolina." *Historical Southern Families.* Vol. 8, 138–44.

"Some Virginia Colonial Records." *Virginia Magazine of History and Biography* 10, no. 4 (1903), 371–81.

Taylor, Orville W. "Arkansas." In *Encylopedia of Religion in the South*. 50–69.

———. "Arkansas." In *Religion in the Southern States: A Historical Study*. 27–56.

"The Comet: It Is Rapidly Disappearing." *Omaha Daily Bee* 4, no. 24 (17 July 1874), 4, col. 4.

"The Comet: No Danger of a Collision with the Earth." *New York Times* 23, no. 7116 (8 July 1874), 2, col. 7.

"The Eclipse of the Moon." *New York Times* 24, no. 7209 (25 October 1874), 7, col. 2.

"The Salt of Civilization [Editorial]." *The Altruistic Review* 3, no. 1 (July 1894), 1–4.

Thomas, Mary. "Gardening." *Foxfire 4*. 150–93.

Torrey, Bradford. "A Green Mountain Corn-Field." *Atlantic Monthly* 62, no. 369 (July 1888), 47–51.

"Trails Grow Dim." *The Heritage* [Hot Spring County Historical Society Quarterly] 9 (1982): 73–81.

Valenčius, Conevery Bolton. "The Geography of Health and the Making of the American West: Arkansas and Missouri, 1800–1860." *Medical Geography in Historical Perspective*. 121–45.

Walz, Robert B. "Migration into Arkansas, 1820–1880: Incentives and Means of Travel." *Arkansas Historical Quarterly* 17 (1958): 309–24.

Watson, A. A. "Bits of Hardin County History." *Courier* [Savannah] 48, no. 30 (29 July 1932), 3, col. 1.

Watson, Monty. "Early History of Hardin County, Tennessee." *Hardin County Historical Quarterly* 10, no. 4 (1993): 1–10.

"Wedding of Edward Byrd and Elizabeth Gainer Cherry." *Raleigh Register* 23, no. 1170 (22 February 1822), 3, col. 5.

Whitehead, Fred, and Verle Muhrer. "Introduction." *Freethought on the American Frontier*. 15–36.

Whitmore, W. H. "Will of John Bigg." *New England Historical and Genealogical Register* 29 (1875): 253–60.

Whittenburg, James P. "Scotch Merchants." *Encyclopedia of North Carolina*. 1012.

Withington, Lothrop. "Virginia Gleanings in England." *Virginia Magazine of History and Biography* 14, no. 3 (January 1907), 301–8.

Woods, Fred E. "The Cemetery Records of William T. Huntington, Nauvoo Sexton." *Mormon Historical Studies* 3, no. 1 (March 2002): 131–63.

Manuscript Collections and State or County Records

Batchelor, Samuel. Estate file (1806, Nash Co., North Carolina). North Carolina State Archives.

Batchelor, Stephen. Estate file (1796, Nash Co., North Carolina). North Carolina State Archives.

Brush Creek Missionary Baptist Church Minutes. Hot Spring Co., Arkansas. Arkansas History Commission.

Edgecombe Co., North Carolina, Deed Book 6.

Federal Homestead Application (1870). Dardanelle, Arkansas Land Office (Wilson R. Bachelor homestead application #5566, certificate #1727).

Francois Missionary Baptist Church Minutes. Hot Spring Co., Arkansas. Arkansas History Commission.

Garden Study Club of Nashville. "History of Homes and Gardens of Tennessee." Ms. collection, Tennessee State Library and Archives (95–602, box 2, file 4).

Grant Co., Arkansas, Justice of the Peace Docket Book, 1869–1917.

Greene Co., Tennessee, Marriage Book 1.

Hardin Co., Tennessee, Court Minutes, Book A.

Hardin Co., Tennessee, Deed Book H.

Hassell, Cushing Biggs. "Diary." Cushing Biggs Hassell Papers. Southern Historical Collection, Univ. of North Carolina (#810).

———. "Family of John J. Williams of Savannah, Hardin County, Tennessee, Brother of C. B. Hassell of Williamston, North Carolina." Cushing Biggs Hassell Papers Southern Historical Collection, Univ. of North Carolina (#810).

Lower Norfolk Co., Virginia, Order Book 1665–1675.

Lower Norfolk Co., Virginia, Record Book 4.

Lower Norfolk Co., Virginia, Record Book D.

Lower Norfolk Co., Virginia, Record Book E, 1666–1675.

"Missionary Reports [Tennessee], 1831–1900." LDS Church History Archives, Salt Lake City. (MS-6104, folder 10).

Monk, Nottingham. Estate file (1818, Bertie Co., North Carolina). North Carolina State Archives.

Morrow, William I. I. Diary. W. I. I. Morrow Collection, Western Historical Manuscript Collection. Univ. of Missouri at Columbia (box 36, vol. 75).

Nash Co., North Carolina, Court Minutes 1804–15.

Nash Co., North Carolina, Will Book 1.

Norfolk Co., Virginia, Deed Book 6.

Norfolk Co., Virginia, Will Book 12.

North Carolina Revolutionary Army Accounts, vol. 8.

Odom, Theophilus. Estate file (1811, Nash Co., North Carolina). North Carolina State Archives.

Poyen Missionary Baptist Church Minutes. Grant Co., Arkansas. Arkansas History Commission.

Virginia Patent Book 4.

Virginia Patent Book 5.

Virginia Patent Book O.

Unpublished Scholarly Theses and Dissertations

Henry, George M. "The History of Franklin County, Arkansas." Unpubl. M.A. thesis, Univ. of Wyoming, Laramie, 1940.

Stith, Matthew. "Social War: People, Nature, and Irregular Warfare on the Trans-Mississippi Frontier, 1861–1865." Unpubl. Ph.D. thesis, Univ. of Arkansas, 2010.

Online Material

Arkansas Historic Preservation Program. "Samuel D. Byrd, Sr., Homestead, Poyen Vic., Grant Co." Online at http://www.arkansaspreservation.com/historic-properties/_search_nomination_popup.aspx?id=2146.

Boulden, Benjamin. "Fort Smith [Sebastian County]." *Encyclopedia of Arkansas History and Culture*. Online at http://encyclopediaofarkansas.net/encyclopedia/entry-detail.aspx?entryID=988.

Digital Library of Appalachia. Online at http://dla.acaweb.org/cdm/.

Dougan, Michael. "Arkansas Married Woman's Property Law." *Encyclopedia of Arkansas History and Culture*. Online at http://encyclopediaofarkansas.net/encyclopedia/entry-detail.aspx?search=1&entryID=4745.

Ellis, Clifton Coxe. "Early Vernacular Plan Houses." *The Tennessee Encyclopedia of History and Culture*. Online at http://tennesseeencyclopedia.net/entry.php?rec=659.

Gleason, Mildred Diane. "Dardanelle (Yell County)." *Encyclopedia of Arkansas History and Culture.* Online at http://encyclopediaofarkansas.net/ encyclopedia/entry-detail.aspx?search=1&entryID=1020.

Goodner, Wes. "Scott County." *Encyclopedia of Arkansas History and Culture.* Online at http://encyclopediaofarkansas.net/encyclopedia/ entry-detail.aspx?search=1&entryID=805.

Guccione, Margaret J. "Boston Mountains." *Encyclopedia of Arkansas History and Culture.* Online at http://encyclopediaofarkansas.net/encyclopedia/ entry-detail.aspx?search=1&entryID=2389.

Haden, Rebecca. "Franklin County." *Encyclopedia of Arkansas History and Culture.* Online at http://encyclopediaofarkansas.net/encyclopedia/ entry-detail.aspx?search=1&entryID=768.

Hendricks, Nancy. "*Sultana* [Steamboat]." *Encyclopedia of Arkansas History and Culture.* Online at http://encyclopediaofarkansas.net/encyclopedia/ entry-detail.aspx?search=1&entryID=2269.

Hodge, Michael. "Railroads." *Encyclopedia of Arkansas History and Culture.* Online at http://encyclopediaofarkansas.net/encyclopedia/ entry-detail.aspx?search=1&entryID=1185.

Ingersoll, Stan. "Church of the Nazarenes." *Encyclopedia of Arkansas History and Culture.* Online at http://encyclopediaofarkansas.net/encyclopedia/ entry-detail.aspx?entryID=4330.

McDaniel, Vernon. "Ozark (Franklin County)." *Encyclopedia of Arkansas History and Culture.* Online at http://encyclopediaofarkansas.net/encyclopedia/ entry-detail.aspx?search=1&entryID=884.

Office of History and Preservation, U.S. Senate. "Thomas F. Boles." *Biographical Directory of the United States Congress.* Online at http://bioguide.congress.gov/ scripts/biodisplay.pl?index=B000603.

Phillips, James B. "Hardin County." *The Tennessee Encyclopedia of History and Culture.* Online at http://tennesseeencyclopedia.net/entry.php?rec= 599.

Pierce, Hal. "A History of the Rise of the Church of Jesus Christ of Latter-Day Saints in Mississippi" (2008). Online at http://www.ldshistoryblog. com/Mississippi.pdf.

Ragsdale, John G. "Coal Mining." *Encyclopedia of Arkansas History and Culture.* Online at http://encyclopediaofarkansas.net/encyclopedia/ entry-detail.aspx?search=1&entryID=352.

Richard, David. "Capital Punishment." *Encyclopedia of Arkansas History and Culture.* Online at http://encyclopediaofarkansas.net/encyclopedia/ entry-detail.aspx?search=1&entryID=4160.

Schuette, Shirley Sticht. "Germans." *Encyclopedia of Arkansas History and Culture.* Online at http://encyclopediaofarkansas.net/encyclopedia/ entry-detail.aspx?entryID=2731.

Shropshire, Lola. "Altus (Franklin Co.)." *Encyclopedia of Arkansas History and Culture*. Online at http://encyclopediaofarkansas.net/encyclopedia/entry-detail.aspx?search=1&entryID=5599.

Spillers, C. Frank. "Early Arkansas Settlers' History." Federal Writers' Project, Special Collections Library of the Univ. of Arkansas. Online at http://ghsweb.k12.ar.us/early/Franklin/spillers.htm.

Stewart-Abernathy, Leslie C. "Steamboats." *Encyclopedia of Arkansas History and Culture*. Online at http://encyclopediaofarkansas.net/encyclopedia/entry-detail.aspx?search=1&entryID=4466.

Taylor, Paula Kyzer. "Woman's Suffrage Movement." *Encyclopedia of Arkansas History and Culture*, online at http://encyclopediaofarkansas.net/encyclopedia/entry-detail.aspx?search=1&entryID=4252.

Teske, Steven. "Napoleon." *Encyclopedia of Arkansas History and Culture*. Online at http://encyclopediaofarkansas.net/encyclopedia/entry-detail.aspx?search=1&entryID=356.

Worthen, William B. "Arkansas Traveler." *Encyclopedia of Arkansas History and Culture*. Online at http://encyclopediaofarkansas.net/encyclopedia/entry-detail.aspx?search=1&entryID=505.

Index

Page numbers in italics indicate images.

abdominal irritation, 57
abortion cases, 54, 63, 208nn157–58
Addams, Jane, 237n24
Adventists, 108–9, 249n105
African Americans, 139, 223–24n273, 242n53, 255n152. *See also* lynchings; slavery
age of world, science vs. religious claims of, 94, 235n7
Agricultural Wheel (Arkansas agrarian party), 222n262, 258n171
Alabama, 1892 gubernatorial election in, 102–3, 242n54, 243n56
alkaloids, medical uses of, 146
Allen, James, 242n53
Als, Hilton, 242n53
Altgeld, John Peter, 118, 258–59n174, 259n178
Altus, AR, German and Swiss immigrants to, 204n124
American Railway Union, 258n172
Amireh, Amal, 237n24
anarchy, 118, 119–120, 139, 260n181. *See also* disorder; mob law; violence
anatomy, medical practice and knowledge of, 144–45
Anderus, Albert, 157
Andres, Suzanne, 202n110
Andrews, Joseph Albert, 20, 21
anesthetics, for convulsions after childbirth, 51, 199n86
angels, as messengers in modern era, 106, 246n82
anodyne diaphoretic, for bronchial expectoration, 202n108
Antikamnia tablets, 98, 239n33
apoplexy, case of, 57
Aptheker, Herbert, 224n273
Argyle, E. Malcolm, 223–24n273
Arkansas: formal medical education infancy in, 142–44; foundations of healing arts in, 139–142; nineteenth century medical

practice in, 7; racial violence in, 223–24n273; roads in, 74, 75, 218n223; snow in, 78, 225n282; state highway 23 in, 217n210; unrest and dissatisfaction in, 77, 222n262; western, as frontier in 1860s, 190n48; western, post-Civil War violence in, 12, 170n39, 193n56, 207–8n146. *See also* Arkansas River Valley
Arkansas Industrial University, Medical Department of, 144
Arkansas River: aground on sandbar in, 45; dangers of travel on, 139; drought of 1874 and, 70, 212–13n188; railroad extended up, 204n124; steamboats on, 43–44, 182n1; WRB's home along, 46–47, 194n64
Arkansas River Valley: railroads and prosperity in, 139; religious affiliations in, 140; social matrix of, 146–48. *See also* Arkansas
"Arkansas Traveler," 75, 219n234
arthritis, 265n39
Ashe, Samuel A., 165n16, 175n72, 179n111, 180n119
assassinations, in 1894, 78, 223n272
Assyria, mythic sagas of, Bible compared to, 94, 235n8
attrehens auris muscle, 48, 196n74
Audubon, John Jay, 192n53
Audubon, J. W., 192n53
auricularis anterior muscle, 196n74
autopsy, introduction of, 145
Ayers, Edward L., 211n185

Bacchus, god of, Christmas and, 86, 231n336
Bachelor, Adam C., 30
Bachelor, Alcie Daisy, 30–31. *See also* Russell, Alcie D. Bachelor
Bachelor, Allie Vilola Rogers, 30, 99, 220n247, 240n37
Bachelor, Anna G. Sawyers, 30, *127*

legislature, 212n185; divisions in, 80, 226n294; election of 1892 and, 110; National Convention (1896), 259n178. *See also* Cleveland, Grover

Demonomania, 112, 252n128

dentists, professionally prepared, 141

diary: **1869**, Dec. 31 entry, 52–53; **1870**, Mar. 1 and 2 entries, *38*, 39, 182–84nn1–7; **1870**, Mar. 3 to 6 entries, 40–41, 184–85nn8–19; **1870**, Mar. 7 to 15 entries, 42–44, 185nn20–30; **1870**, Mar. 16 to 23 entries, 44–46, 187–190nn31–48; **1870**, Apr. 3 entry, 46, 190–91n49; **1870**, Oct. entries, 46–48, 191–96nn50–73; **1871**, Jan. entries, 48–49, 196nn74–76; **1871**, Mar. 19 to 21 entries, 49, 197–98n80–82; **1871**, Mar. 22 entry, 50–52, 199nn83–86; **1871**, Apr. 22 entry, 54; **1873**, Feb. 27 entry, 58–59, 205nn130–31; **1873**, Mar. 1 entry, 54, 200–201nn93–99; **1873**, Mar. 2 entry, 55, 201–2nn100–5; **1873**, Mar. 11 to 21 entries, 56, 202nn111–21; **1873**, Mar. 18 to 22 entries, 57, 203–4nn122–29; **1873**, May 9 to 14 entries, 59, 205–7nn134–37; **1873**, May 18 to 20 entries, 60, 207n138–140; **1873**, June 7 to 11 entries, 61–62, 207–8nn146–54; **1873**, June 18 entry, 62–63, 208nn155–56; **1873**, June 30 entry, 63, 208nn157–58; **1874**, Mar. 1 entry, 64, 208–9n164–69; **1874**, Mar. 15 entry, 65, 209nn170–71; **1874**, Apr. 1 entry, 61; **1874**, May 6 entry, 65, 209nn172–73; **1874**, July 1 and 5 entries, 66, 209–10n174; **1874**, Aug. to Oct. entries, 66–68, 210nn175–81; **1874**, Sept. 1 and 2 entries, 70, 212–13nn187–88; **1874**, Oct. 28 entry, 70–71, 213–14nn189–93; **1874**, Nov. 29 entry, 71–72, 214nn194–95; **1890**, Dec. 25 entry, 72, 215–16nn200–7; **1891**, July 2 to Aug. 29 entries, 73–76, 216–220nn208–43; **1891**, July 14 entry, 68–69; **1891**, Dec. 24 entry, 76, 220–21n244–251; **1892**, Dec. 25 entry, 76–77, 221nn252–53; **1893**, Dec. 25 entry, 77, 221–22nn254–57; **1894**, Dec. 25 entry, 77–78, 222nn258–63; **1895**, Jan. 2 entry, 78, 225nn281–82; **1895**, Feb. 7 entry, 79, 225n283; **1895**, May 11 and 31 entries, 79, 225nn284–89; **1895**, June

2 and 12 entries, 79–80, 225–26nn290–92; **1895**, July 2 entry, 80, 226n296; **1895**, Sept. 17 and 21 entries, 80–81, 227nn299–300; **1895**, Oct. 1 entry, 81, 227n302; **1895**, Nov. 29 entry, 81, 227n303–304; **1895**, Dec. 25 entry, 81, 227nn305–6; **1896**, Jan. 1 and 23 entries, 227–28nn307–8; **1896**, June 30 entry, 82, 228nn309–10; **1896**, Dec. 25 entry, 82–83, 228n311; **1897**, Apr. and May entries, 83, 228–29nn312–14; **1897**, June and July entries, 84, 229nn315–19; **1897**, Sept. entry, 84, 230nn320–21; **1897**, Oct. entry, 85, 230nn322–23; **1898** entries, 85–87, 231nn329–37; **1899** entries, 87–88, 231–32nn338–46; **1900** entries, 89, 233nn347–51; **1901** entries, 90; **1902** entries, 90–91; chronology out of order, 58–59, 205n130; family preservation of, 5; on formative years in Hardin Co., TN, 12, 170n39; medical cases noted in, 7–8; notes about, 32–33; on science and medical topics, 6; spelling in, 35, 170n38; transcription challenges, 35–37

Dickens, Charles, 55, 200–201n95, 202n101, 205n128

diet: for stab wound patient, 62, 208n152; for typhoid pneumonia fever patient, 63

Dillon, Charles, 244–45n67

disasters: as challenge to faith in providential God, 110, 251–52n114; notable natural and other types of, 223n265; railroads and, 78, 223n270

disorder: in Arkansas River Valley (1865–1890), 146. *See also* anarchy; mob law; violence

Dobson, David, 175n72

dog fennel (*Eupatorium capillifolium*), 74, 217n217

dogs, barking, 88, 232n344

Donning, William, 165–66n21

"Don't Let the Senate See God's Denuded Arm," 105, 245nn71–74

Dougan, Michael, 254n143

Dozier, Rebecca L., 165n18

Draper, John William, 6, 100, 240n41

"A Dream," 103–4, 242–43nn54–58

droughts: of 1874, 70, 212–13n188; of 1894, 77, 78, 222n261; of 1896, 83; on 1899, 136, 265n37; of 1901, 90

WILSON R. BACHELOR (1827–1903) was a country doctor and writer who lived in Franklin County, Arkansas.

WILLIAM D. LINDSEY has chaired theology departments and held the position of chief academic officer at a number of colleges and universities. He is the author or coauthor of several books, including *Religion and Public Life in the Southern Crossroads: Showdown States*.

TOM BRUCE is former dean and emeritus professor of medicine, University of Arkansas for Medical Sciences, and inaugural dean a nd emeritus professor of health policy and management, University of Arkansas Clinton School of Public Service.

JONATHAN WOLFE is professor of pharmacy practice, University of Arkansas for Medical Sciences College of Pharmacy.